DOWNERS GROVE PUBLIC LIBRARY

3 1191 00965 3205

S0-AXJ-136

WITHDRAWN
DOWNERS GROVE PUBLIC LIBRARY
APR 2 7 2011

Downers Grove Public Library
1050 Curtiss St.
Downers Grove, IL 60515
(630) 960-1200

GAYLORD

WOLVERINE WEAPON X

TOMORROW DIES TODAY

WOLVERINE WEAPON X VOL. 3: TOMORROW DIES TODAY. Contains material originally published in magazine form as WOLVERINE WEAPON X #11-16 and DARK REIGN: THE LIST — WOLVERINE. First printing 2010. Hardcover ISBN# 978-0-7851-4650-6. Softcover ISBN# 978-0-7851-4651-3. Published by MARVEL WORLDWIDE, INC., a subsidiary of MARVEL ENTERTAINMENT, LLC. OFFICE OF PUBLICATION: 417 5th Avenue, New York, NY 10016. Copyright © 2009, 2010 and 2011 Marvel Characters, Inc. All rights reserved. Hardcover: $24.99 per copy in the U.S. and $27.99 in Canada (GST #R127032852). Softcover: $19.99 per copy in the U.S. and $22.50 in Canada (GST #R127032852). Canadian Agreement #40668537. All characters featured in this issue and the distinctive names and likenesses thereof, and all related indicia are trademarks of Marvel Characters, Inc. No similarity between any of the names, characters, persons, and/or institutions in this magazine with those of any living or dead person or institution is intended, and any such similarity which may exist is purely coincidental. Printed in the U.S.A. ALAN FINE, EVP - Office of the President, Marvel Worldwide, Inc. and EVP & CMO Marvel Characters B.V.; DAN BUCKLEY, Chief Executive Officer and Publisher - Print, Animation & Digital Media; JIM SOKOLOWSKI, Chief Operating Officer; DAVID GABRIEL, SVP of Publishing Sales & Circulation; DAVID BOGART, SVP of Business Affairs & Talent Management; MICHAEL PASCIULLO, VP Merchandising & Communications; JIM O'KEEFE, VP of Operations & Logistics; DAN CARR, Executive Director of Publishing Technology; JUSTIN F. GABRIE, Director of Publishing & Editorial Operations; SUSAN CRESPI, Editorial Operations Manager; ALEX MORALES, Publishing Operations Manager; STAN LEE, Chairman Emeritus. For information regarding advertising in Marvel Comics or on Marvel.com, please contact Ron Stern, VP of Business Development, at rstern@marvel.com. For Marvel subscription inquiries, please call 800-217-9158. Manufactured between 8/30/10 and 9/29/10 (hardcover), and 8/30/10 and 2/23/11 (softcover), by R.R. DONNELLEY, INC., SALEM, VA, USA.

10 9 8 7 6 5 4 3 2 1

WOLVERINE
WEAPON X

TOMORROW DIES TODAY

Writer: **JASON AARON**

Artist, Issues #11-15: **RON GARNEY**

Colorist, Issues #11-15: **JASON KEITH** with **MATT MILLA** (Issues #14-15)

Artist, Issue #16: **DAVIDE GIANFELICE**

Colorist, Issue #16: **DAVE MCCAIG**

Artist, *The List*: **ESAD RIBIC**

Inker, *The List*: **TOM PALMER**

Colorist, *The List*: **MATTHEW WILSON**

Letterers, Issues #11-16: **VC'S CORY PETIT** with **CLAYTON COWLES**

Letterer, *The List*: **JARED K. FLETCHER**

Cover Art, Issues #11-15: **RON GARNEY**
with **MORRY HOLLOWELL** & **CHRIS SOTOMAYOR**

Cover Art, *The List*: **ESAD RIBIC**

Assistant Editor: **JODY LEHEUP**

Editor: **JEANINE SCHAEFER**

Executive Editor: **AXEL ALONSO**

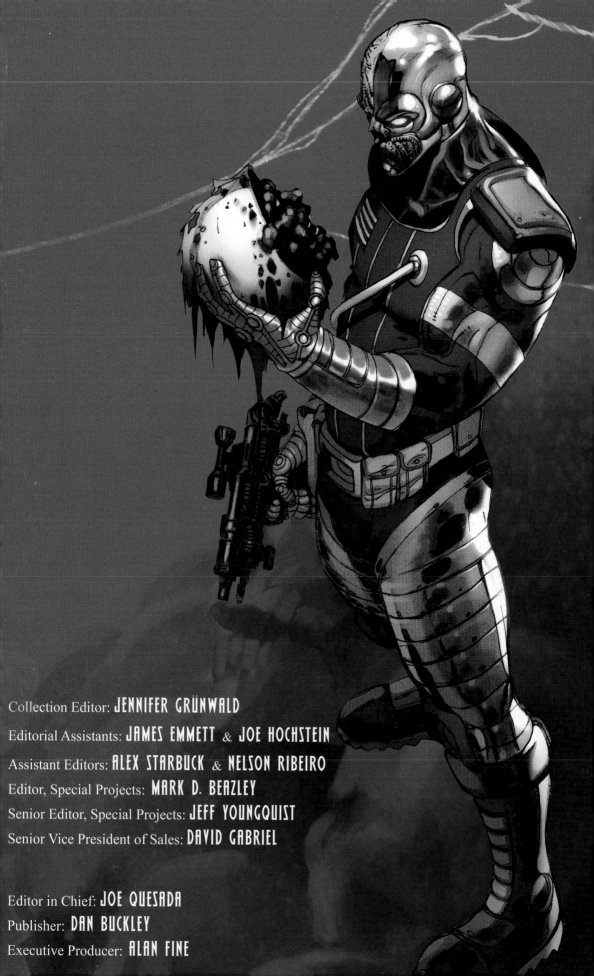

Collection Editor: JENNIFER GRÜNWALD

Editorial Assistants: JAMES EMMETT & JOE HOCHSTEIN

Assistant Editors: ALEX STARBUCK & NELSON RIBEIRO

Editor, Special Projects: MARK D. BEAZLEY

Senior Editor, Special Projects: JEFF YOUNGQUIST

Senior Vice President of Sales: DAVID GABRIEL

Editor in Chief: JOE QUESADA

Publisher: DAN BUCKLEY

Executive Producer: ALAN FINE

PREVIOUSLY

Steve Rogers, also known as Captain America, the shield-wielding World War II super-soldier and leader of the super hero group the Avengers, was recently killed in action defending his country. The loss devastated the super hero community and Logan, a fellow Avenger, took it especially hard.

Now, Steve has returned to life. But while the rest of the world celebrates his return from the grave, dark forces are mounting to send him back there. And the hero from the past may find that he has no future…

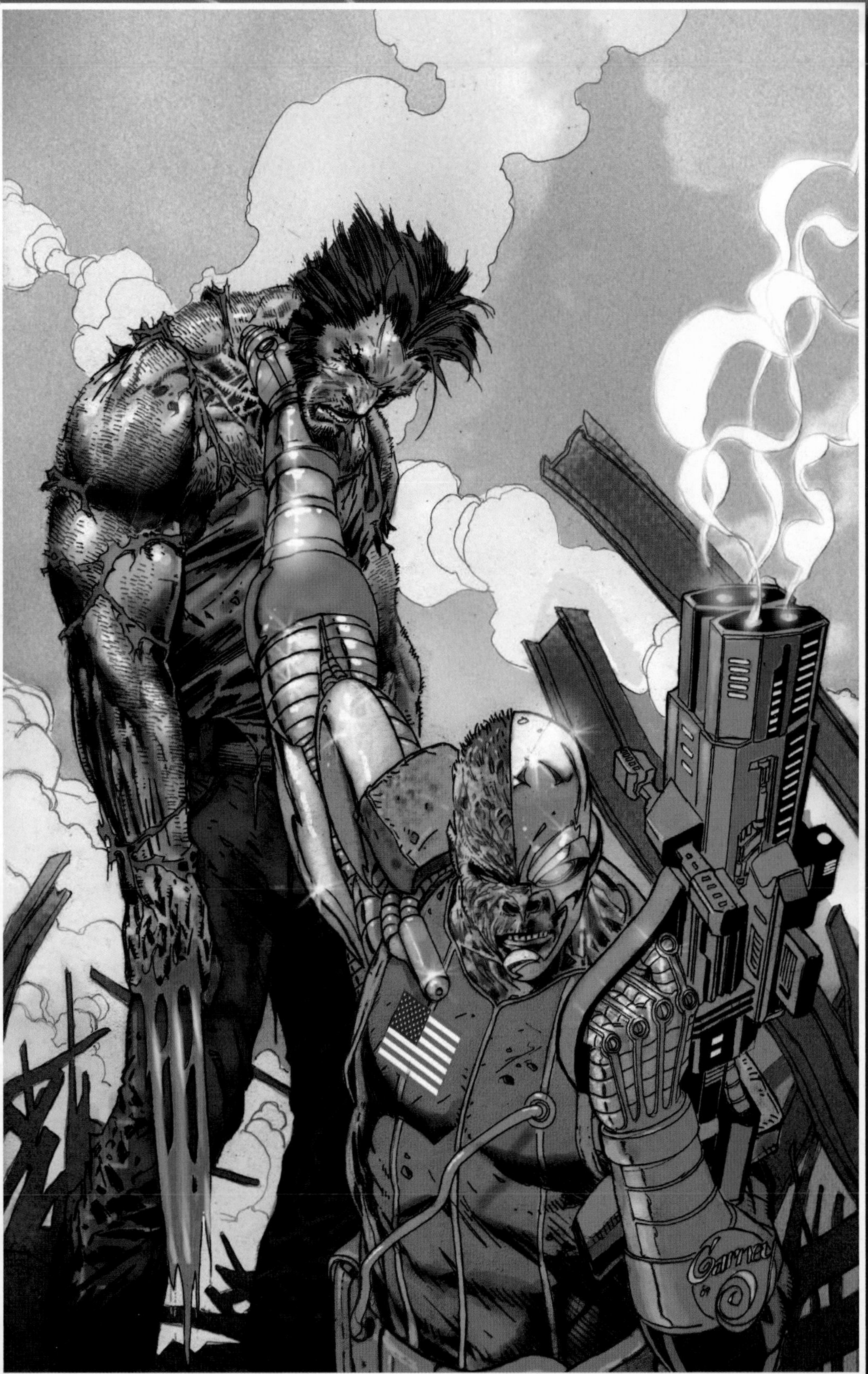

ELEVEN

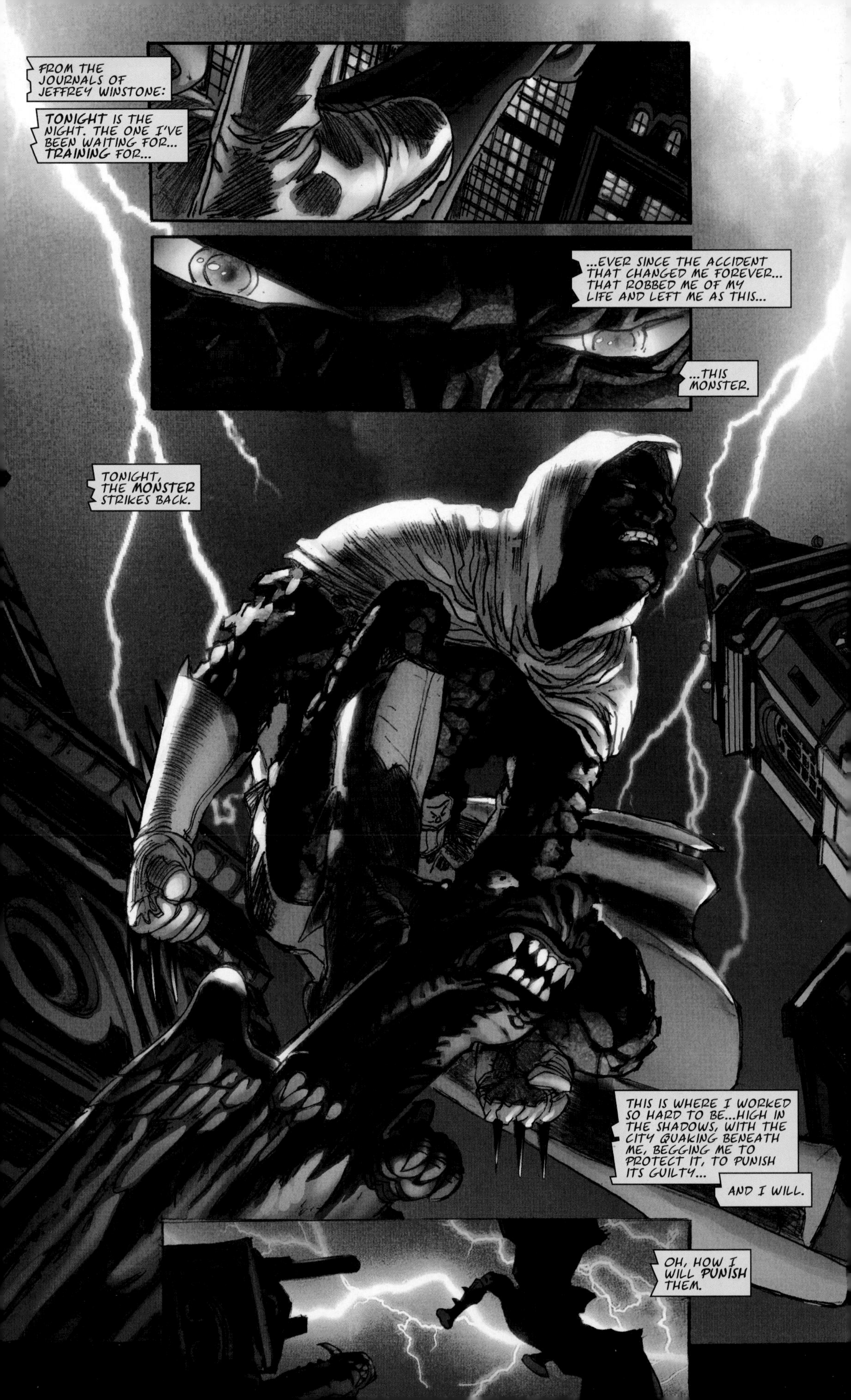
FROM THE JOURNALS OF JEFFREY WINSTONE:
TONIGHT IS THE NIGHT. THE ONE I'VE BEEN WAITING FOR... TRAINING FOR...
...EVER SINCE THE ACCIDENT THAT CHANGED ME FOREVER... THAT ROBBED ME OF MY LIFE AND LEFT ME AS THIS...
...THIS MONSTER.
TONIGHT, THE MONSTER STRIKES BACK.
THIS IS WHERE I WORKED SO HARD TO BE...HIGH IN THE SHADOWS, WITH THE CITY QUAKING BENEATH ME, BEGGING ME TO PROTECT IT, TO PUNISH ITS GUILTY...
AND I WILL.
OH, HOW I WILL PUNISH THEM.

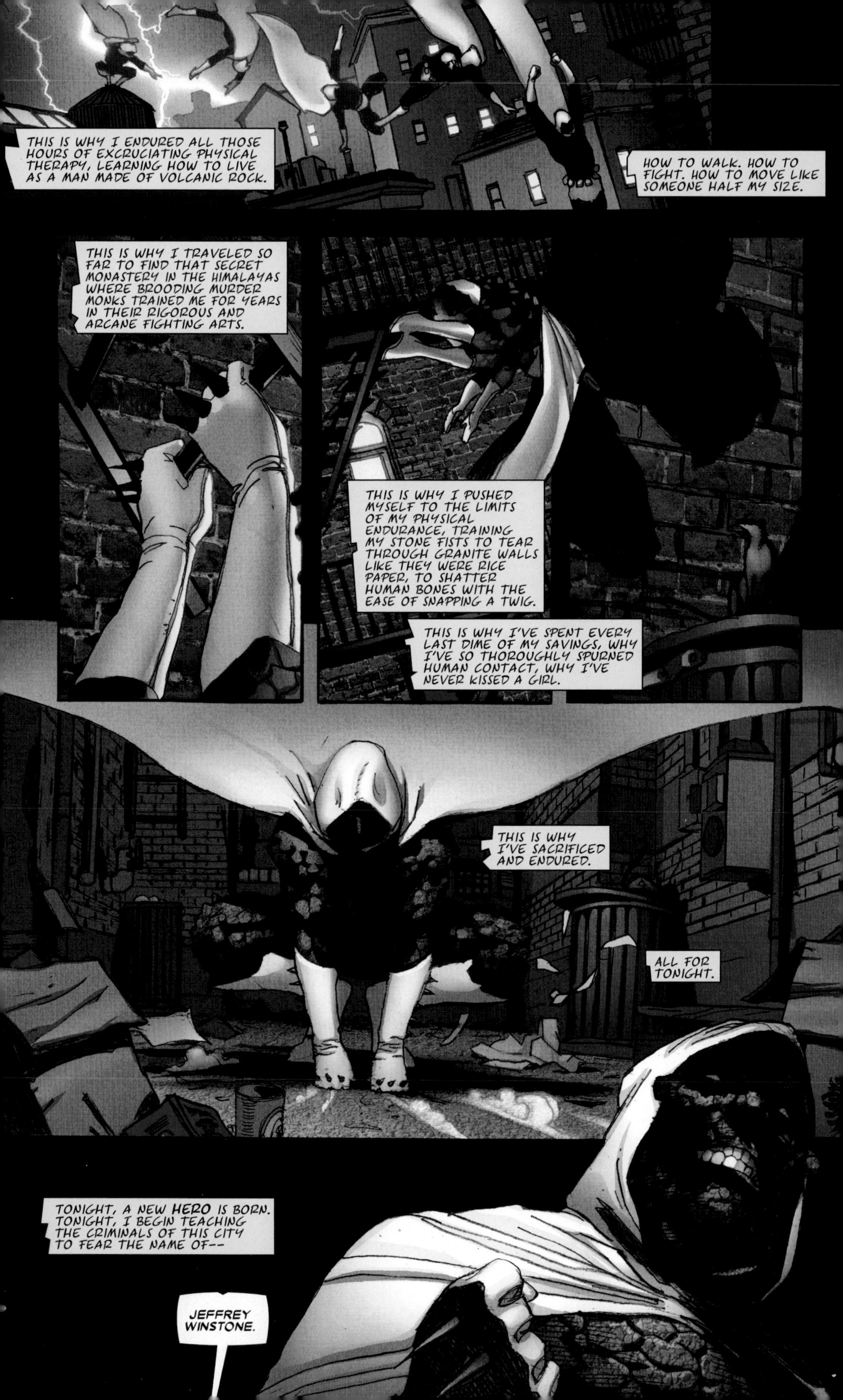
THIS IS WHY I ENDURED ALL THOSE HOURS OF EXCRUCIATING PHYSICAL THERAPY, LEARNING HOW TO LIVE AS A MAN MADE OF VOLCANIC ROCK.
HOW TO WALK. HOW TO FIGHT. HOW TO MOVE LIKE SOMEONE HALF MY SIZE.
THIS IS WHY I TRAVELED SO FAR TO FIND THAT SECRET MONASTERY IN THE HIMALAYAS WHERE BROODING MURDER MONKS TRAINED ME FOR YEARS IN THEIR RIGOROUS AND ARCANE FIGHTING ARTS.
THIS IS WHY I PUSHED MYSELF TO THE LIMITS OF MY PHYSICAL ENDURANCE, TRAINING MY STONE FISTS TO TEAR THROUGH GRANITE WALLS LIKE THEY WERE RICE PAPER, TO SHATTER HUMAN BONES WITH THE EASE OF SNAPPING A TWIG.
THIS IS WHY I'VE SPENT EVERY LAST DIME OF MY SAVINGS, WHY I'VE SO THOROUGHLY SPURNED HUMAN CONTACT, WHY I'VE NEVER KISSED A GIRL.
THIS IS WHY I'VE SACRIFICED AND ENDURED.
ALL FOR TONIGHT.
TONIGHT, A NEW HERO IS BORN. TONIGHT, I BEGIN TEACHING THE CRIMINALS OF THIS CITY TO FEAR THE NAME OF--
JEFFREY WINSTONE.

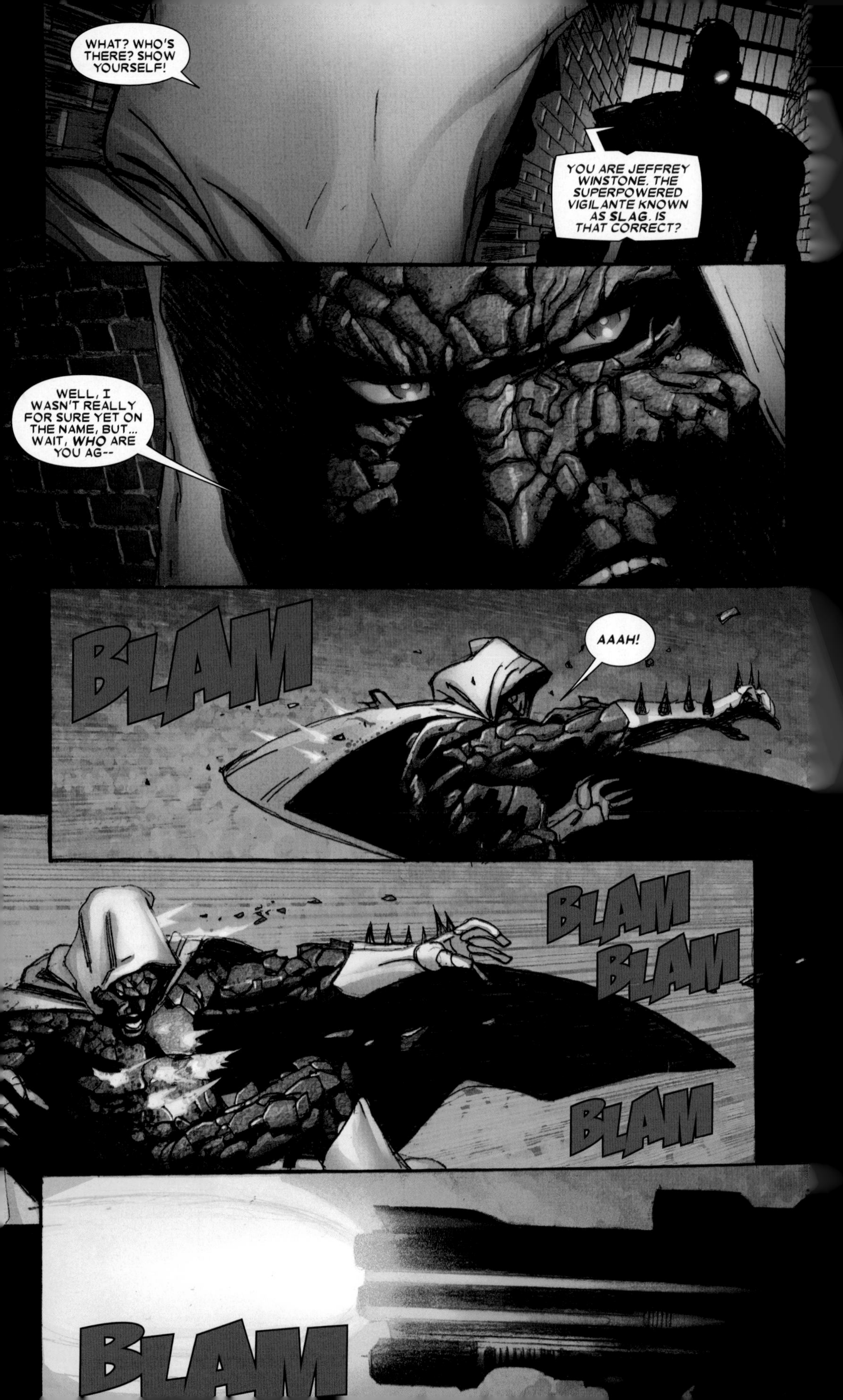

WHAT? WHO'S THERE? SHOW YOURSELF!
YOU ARE JEFFREY WINSTONE. THE SUPERPOWERED VIGILANTE KNOWN AS SLAG. IS THAT CORRECT?
WELL, I WASN'T REALLY FOR SURE YET ON THE NAME, BUT... WAIT, WHO ARE YOU AG--
BLAM
AAAH!
BLAM
BLAM
BLAM
BLAM

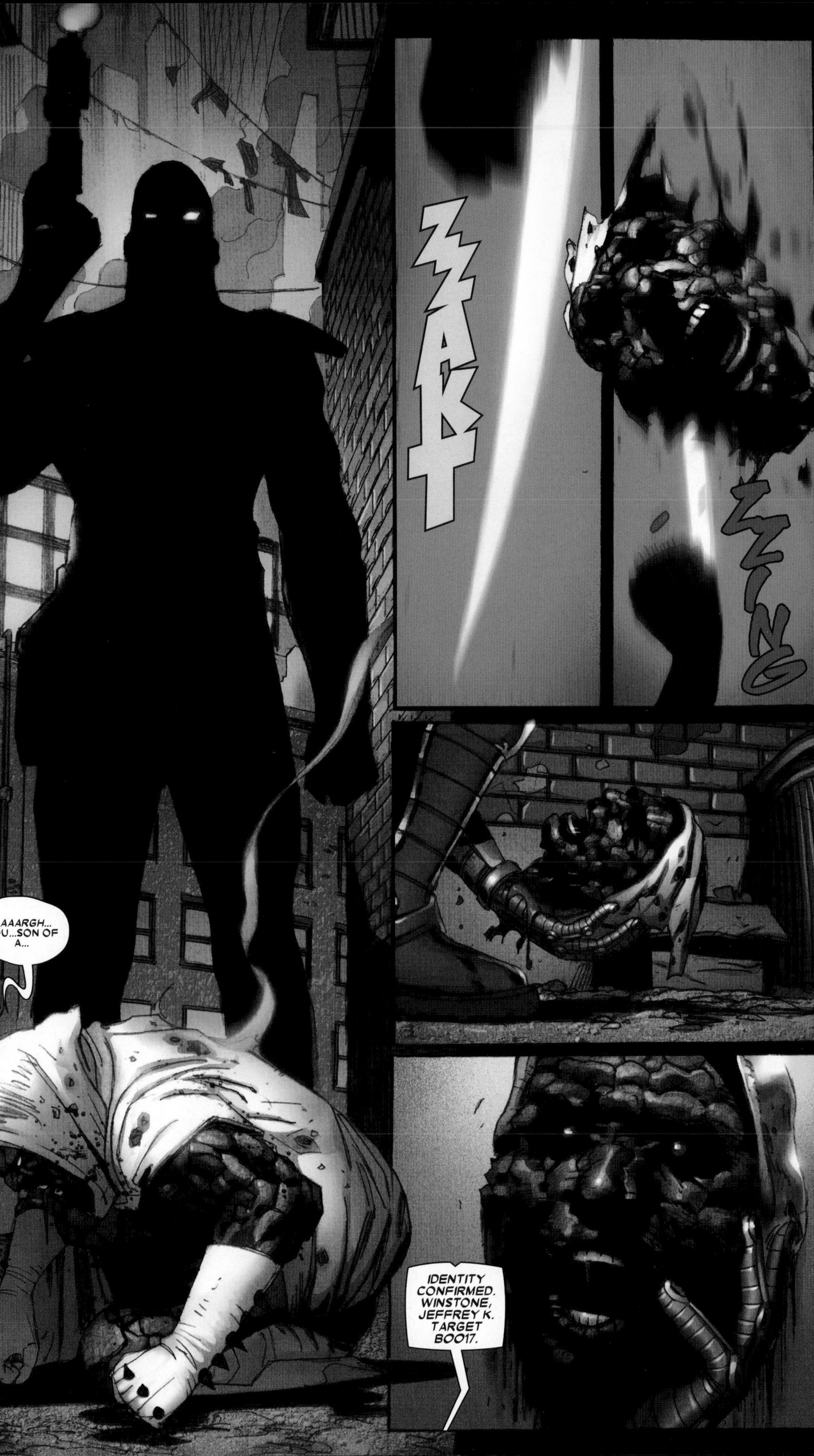
AAARGH... U...SON OF A...
ZZAKT
ZZING
IDENTITY CONFIRMED. WINSTONE, JEFFREY K. TARGET B0017.

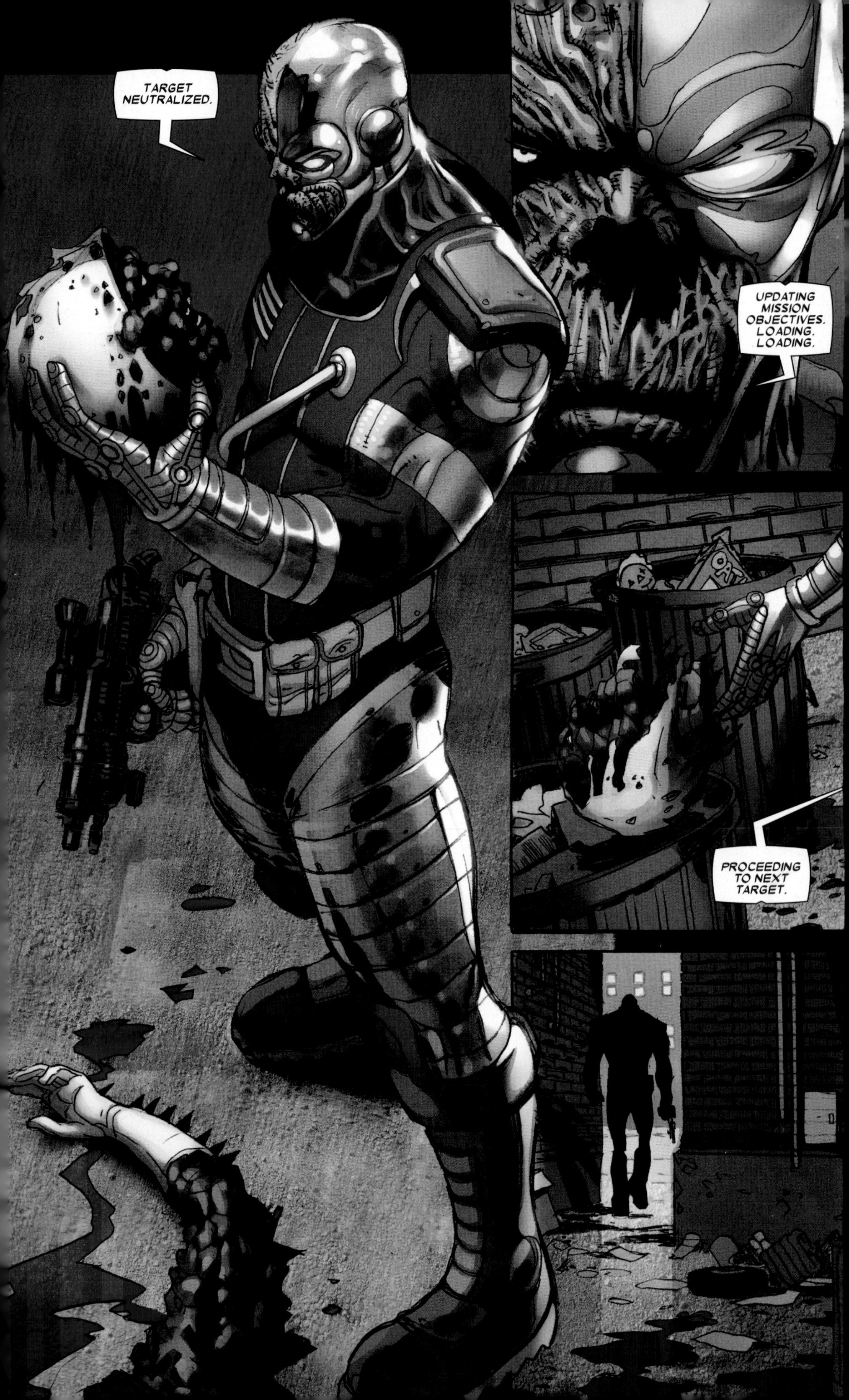
TARGET NEUTRALIZED.
UPDATING MISSION OBJECTIVES. LOADING. LOADING.
PROCEEDING TO NEXT TARGET.

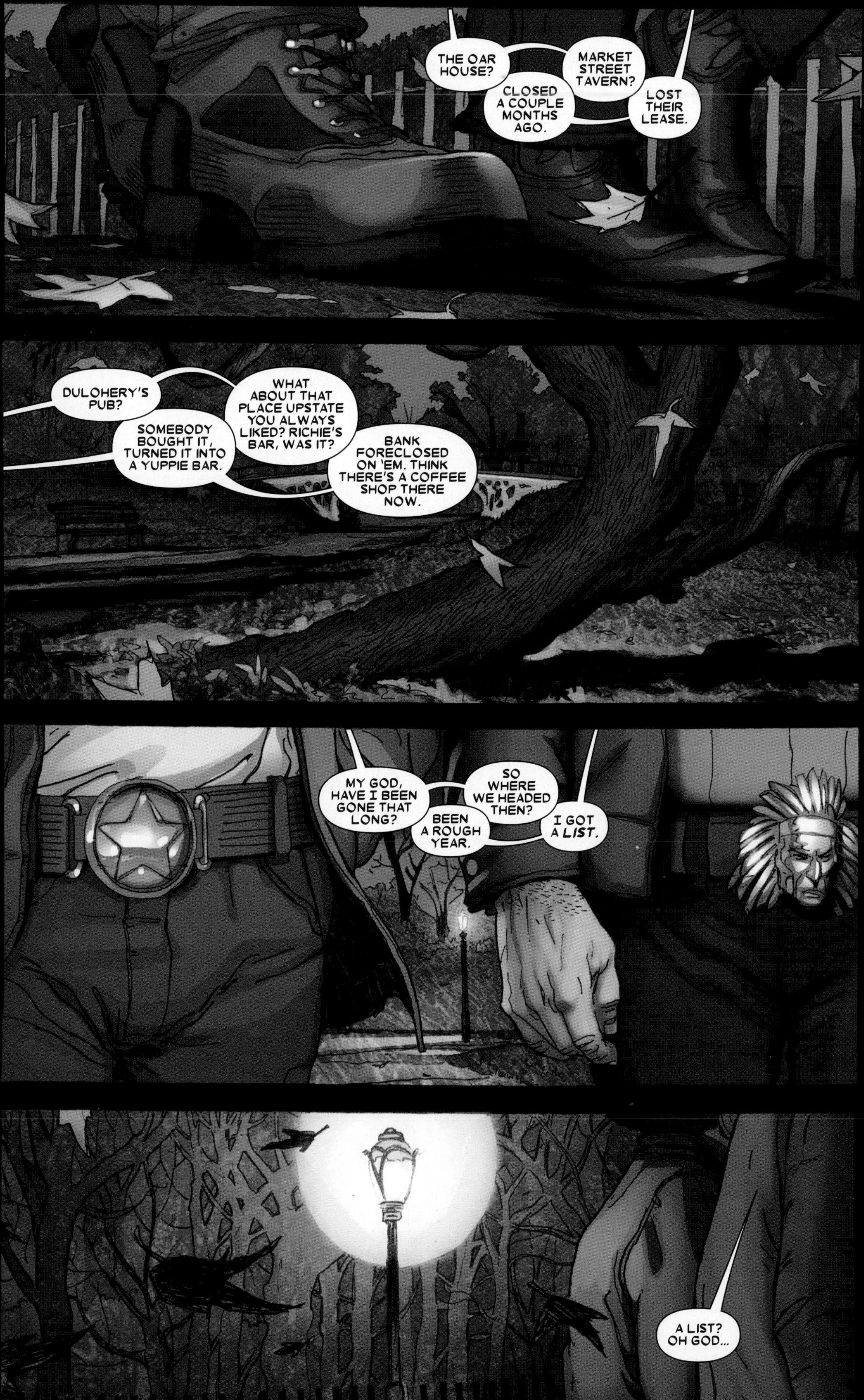
THE OAR HOUSE?
CLOSED A COUPLE MONTHS AGO.
MARKET STREET TAVERN?
LOST THEIR LEASE.
DULOHERY'S PUB?
SOMEBODY BOUGHT IT, TURNED IT INTO A YUPPIE BAR.
WHAT ABOUT THAT PLACE UPSTATE YOU ALWAYS LIKED? RICHIE'S BAR, WAS IT?
BANK FORECLOSED ON 'EM. THINK THERE'S A COFFEE SHOP THERE NOW.
MY GOD, HAVE I BEEN GONE THAT LONG?
BEEN A ROUGH YEAR.
SO WHERE WE HEADED THEN?
I GOT A *LIST.*
A LIST? OH GOD...

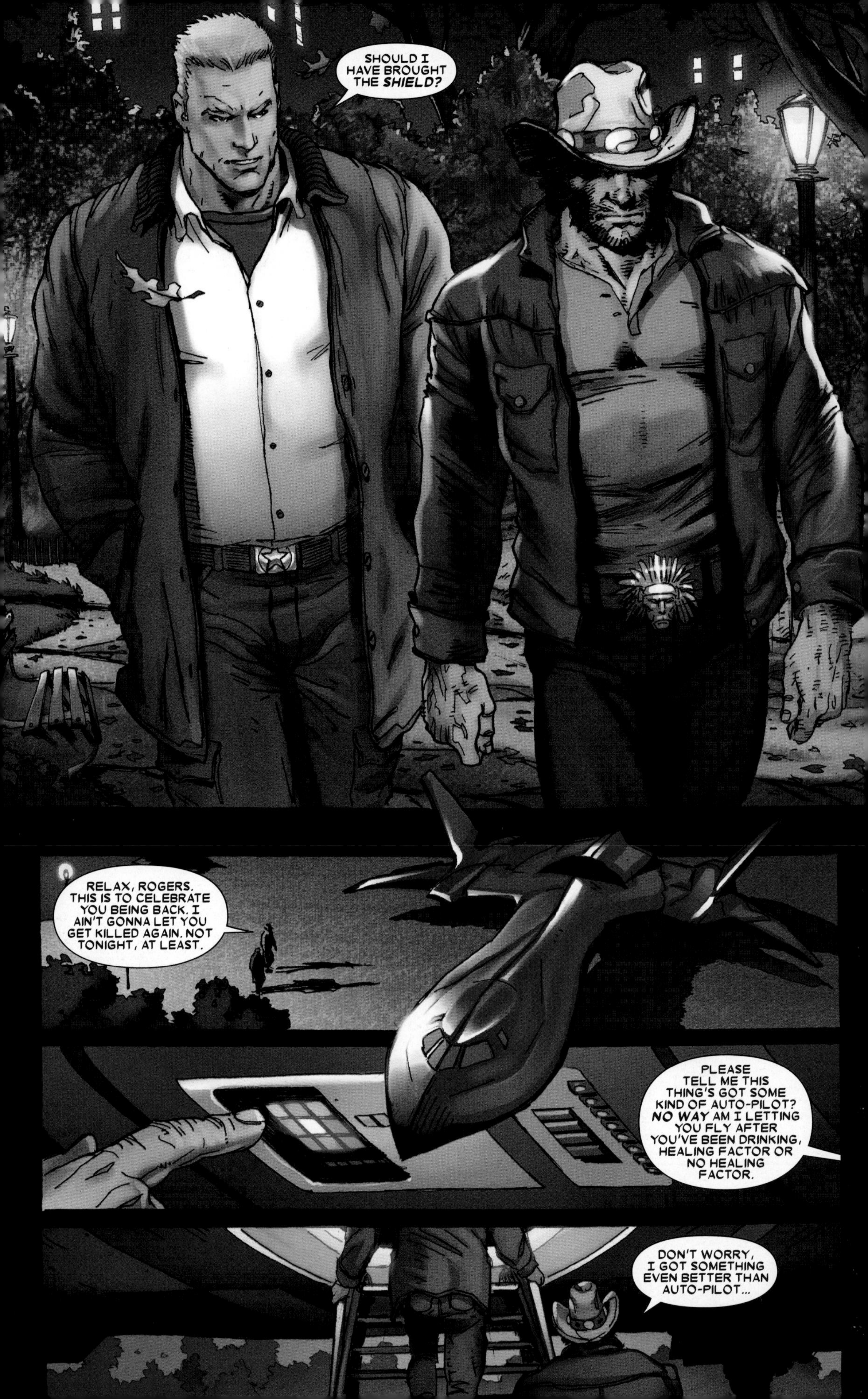
SHOULD I HAVE BROUGHT THE *SHIELD?*
RELAX, ROGERS. THIS IS TO CELEBRATE YOU BEING BACK. I AIN'T GONNA LET YOU GET KILLED AGAIN. NOT TONIGHT, AT LEAST.
PLEASE TELL ME THIS THING'S GOT SOME KIND OF AUTO-PILOT? *NO WAY* AM I LETTING YOU FLY AFTER YOU'VE BEEN DRINKING, HEALING FACTOR OR NO HEALING FACTOR.
DON'T WORRY, I GOT SOMETHING EVEN BETTER THAN AUTO-PILOT...

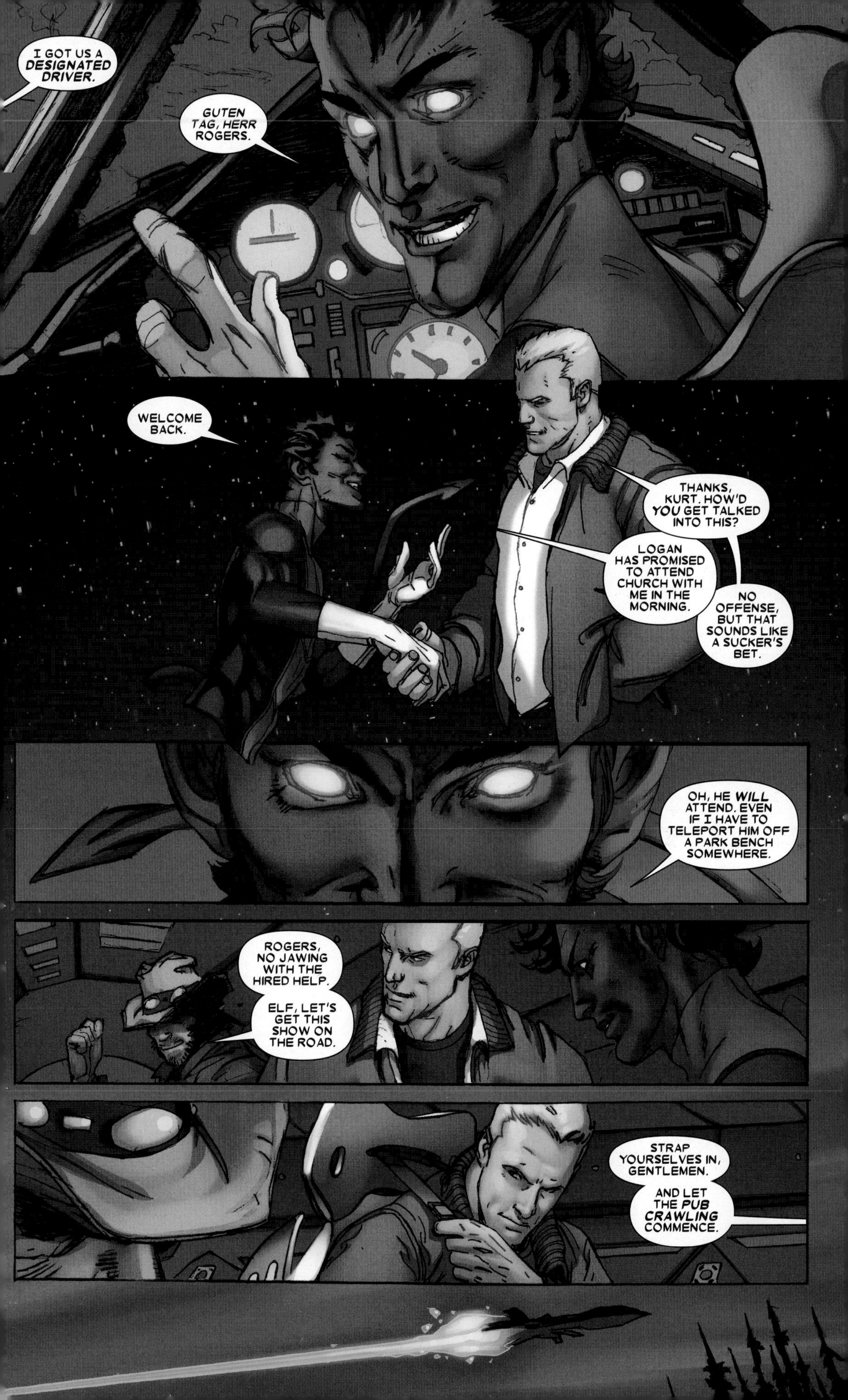
I GOT US A DESIGNATED DRIVER.
GUTEN TAG, HERR ROGERS.
WELCOME BACK.
THANKS, KURT. HOW'D YOU GET TALKED INTO THIS?
LOGAN HAS PROMISED TO ATTEND CHURCH WITH ME IN THE MORNING.
NO OFFENSE, BUT THAT SOUNDS LIKE A SUCKER'S BET.
OH, HE WILL ATTEND. EVEN IF I HAVE TO TELEPORT HIM OFF A PARK BENCH SOMEWHERE.
ROGERS, NO JAWING WITH THE HIRED HELP.
ELF, LET'S GET THIS SHOW ON THE ROAD.
STRAP YOURSELVES IN, GENTLEMEN.
AND LET THE PUB CRAWLING COMMENCE.

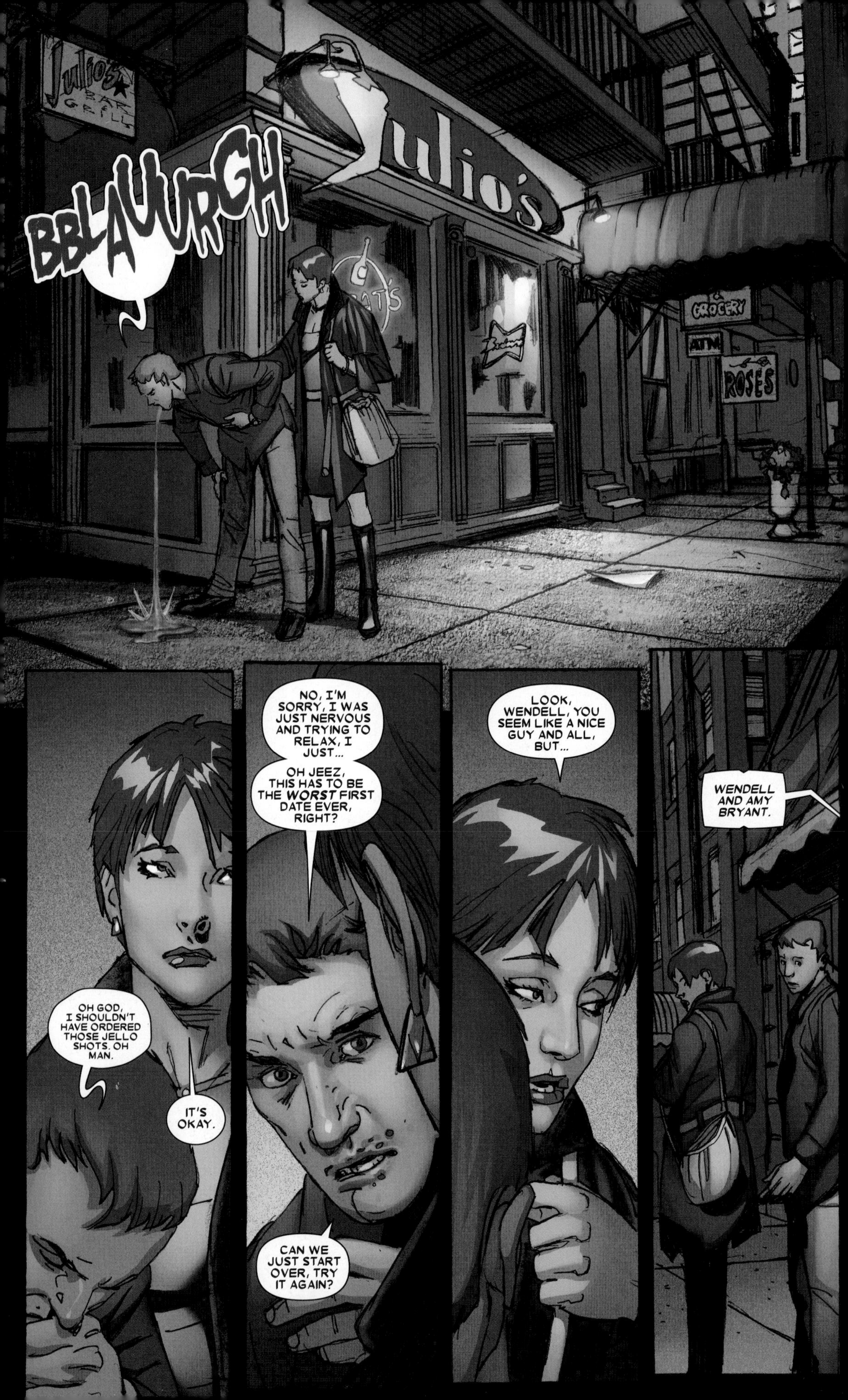
Julio's BAR ★ GRILL
Julio's
BBLAUURGH
GROCERY
ATM
ROSES
OH GOD, I SHOULDN'T HAVE ORDERED THOSE JELLO SHOTS. OH MAN.
IT'S OKAY.
NO, I'M SORRY, I WAS JUST NERVOUS AND TRYING TO RELAX, I JUST...
OH JEEZ, THIS HAS TO BE THE *WORST* FIRST DATE EVER, RIGHT?
CAN WE JUST START OVER, TRY IT AGAIN?
LOOK, WENDELL, YOU SEEM LIKE A NICE GUY AND ALL, BUT...
WENDELL AND AMY BRYANT.

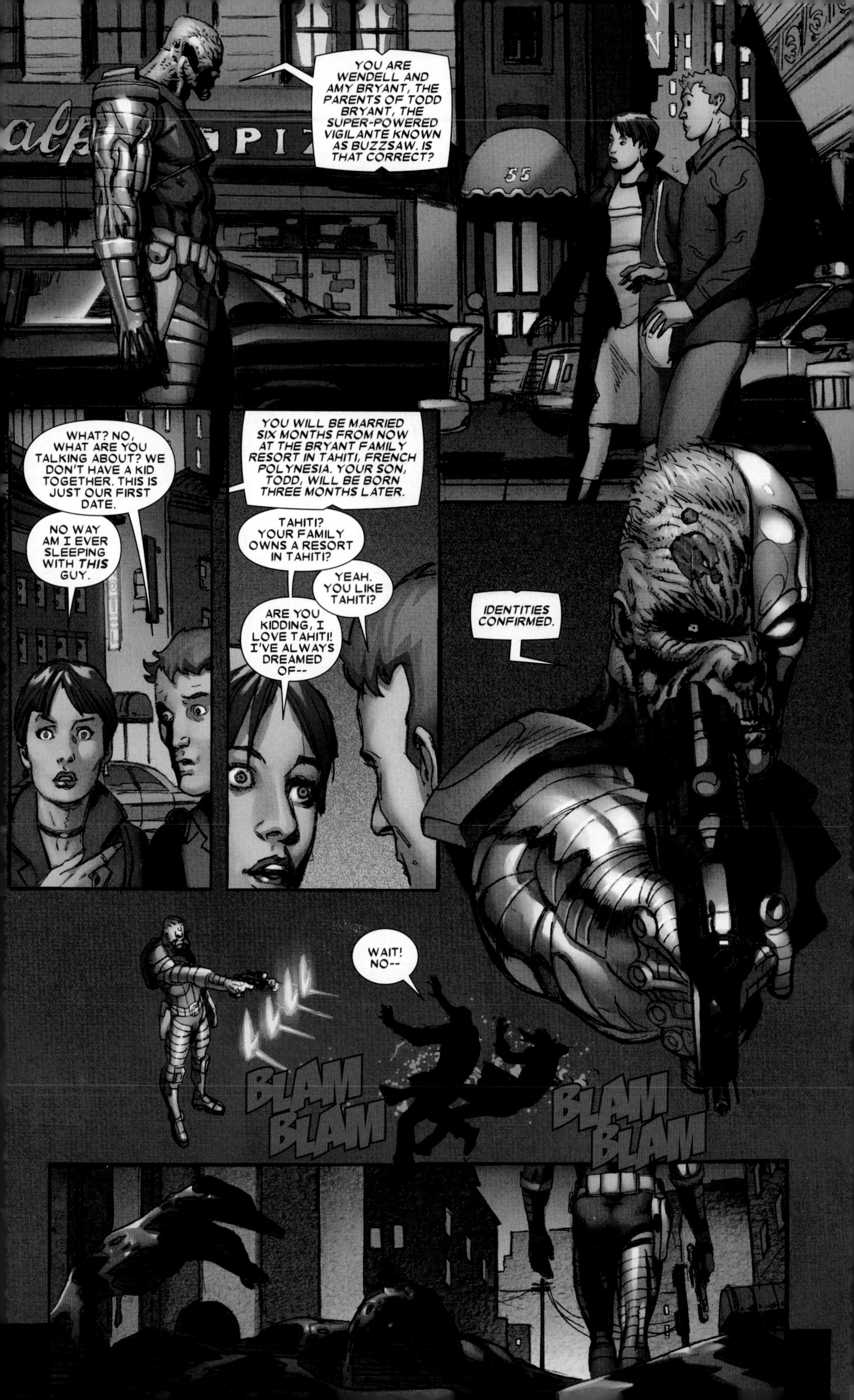

YOU ARE WENDELL AND AMY BRYANT, THE PARENTS OF TODD BRYANT, THE SUPER-POWERED VIGILANTE KNOWN AS BUZZSAW. IS THAT CORRECT?
55
WHAT? NO, WHAT ARE YOU TALKING ABOUT? WE DON'T HAVE A KID TOGETHER. THIS IS JUST OUR FIRST DATE.
NO WAY AM I EVER SLEEPING WITH *THIS* GUY.
YOU WILL BE MARRIED SIX MONTHS FROM NOW AT THE BRYANT FAMILY RESORT IN TAHITI, FRENCH POLYNESIA. YOUR SON, TODD, WILL BE BORN THREE MONTHS LATER.
TAHITI? YOUR FAMILY OWNS A RESORT IN TAHITI?
YEAH. YOU LIKE TAHITI?
ARE YOU KIDDING, I LOVE TAHITI! I'VE ALWAYS DREAMED OF--
IDENTITIES CONFIRMED.
WAIT! NO--
BLAM BLAM
BLAM BLAM

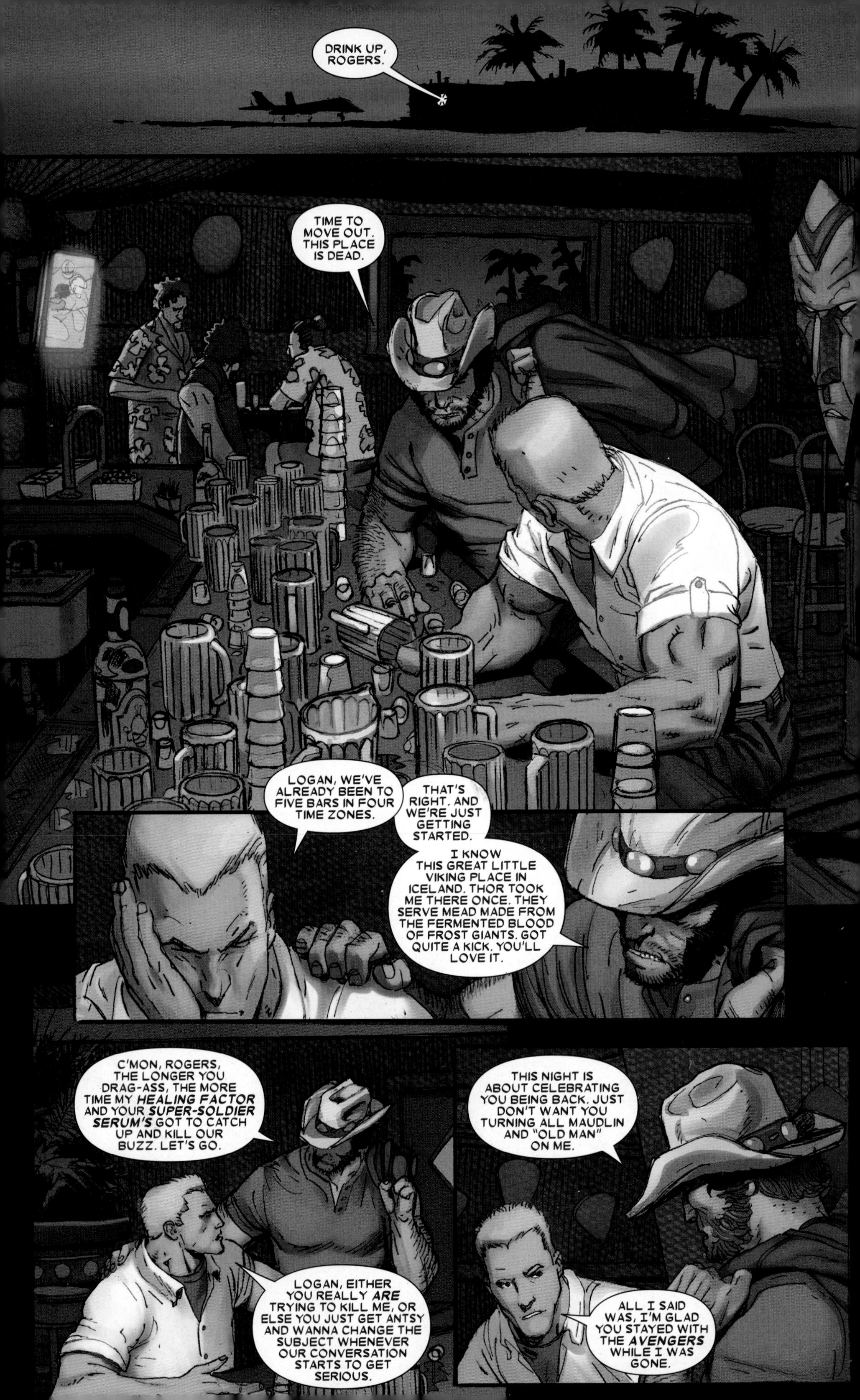
DRINK UP, ROGERS.
TIME TO MOVE OUT. THIS PLACE IS DEAD.
LOGAN, WE'VE ALREADY BEEN TO FIVE BARS IN FOUR TIME ZONES.
THAT'S RIGHT. AND WE'RE JUST GETTING STARTED.
I KNOW THIS GREAT LITTLE VIKING PLACE IN ICELAND. THOR TOOK ME THERE ONCE. THEY SERVE MEAD MADE FROM THE FERMENTED BLOOD OF FROST GIANTS. GOT QUITE A KICK. YOU'LL LOVE IT.
C'MON, ROGERS, THE LONGER YOU DRAG-ASS, THE MORE TIME MY *HEALING FACTOR* AND YOUR *SUPER-SOLDIER SERUM'S* GOT TO CATCH UP AND KILL OUR BUZZ. LET'S GO.
LOGAN, EITHER YOU REALLY *ARE* TRYING TO KILL ME, OR ELSE YOU JUST GET ANTSY AND WANNA CHANGE THE SUBJECT WHENEVER OUR CONVERSATION STARTS TO GET SERIOUS.
THIS NIGHT IS ABOUT CELEBRATING YOU BEING BACK. JUST DON'T WANT YOU TURNING ALL MAUDLIN AND "OLD MAN" ON ME.
ALL I SAID WAS, I'M GLAD YOU STAYED WITH THE *AVENGERS* WHILE I WAS GONE.

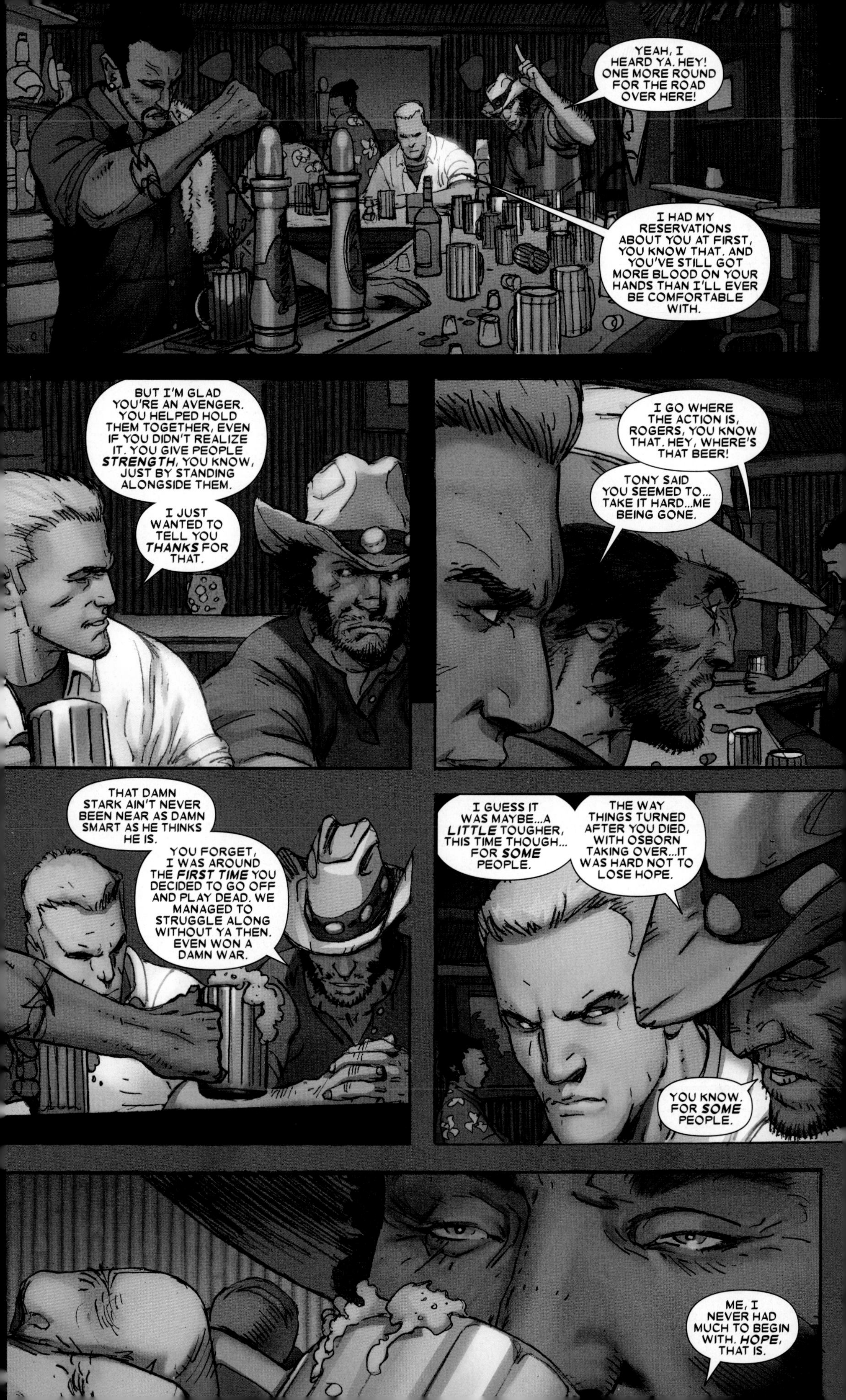

YEAH, I HEARD YA. HEY! ONE MORE ROUND FOR THE ROAD OVER HERE!
I HAD MY RESERVATIONS ABOUT YOU AT FIRST, YOU KNOW THAT. AND YOU'VE STILL GOT MORE BLOOD ON YOUR HANDS THAN I'LL EVER BE COMFORTABLE WITH.
BUT I'M GLAD YOU'RE AN AVENGER. YOU HELPED HOLD THEM TOGETHER, EVEN IF YOU DIDN'T REALIZE IT. YOU GIVE PEOPLE STRENGTH, YOU KNOW, JUST BY STANDING ALONGSIDE THEM.
I JUST WANTED TO TELL YOU THANKS FOR THAT.
I GO WHERE THE ACTION IS, ROGERS, YOU KNOW THAT. HEY, WHERE'S THAT BEER!
TONY SAID YOU SEEMED TO... TAKE IT HARD...ME BEING GONE.
THAT DAMN STARK AIN'T NEVER BEEN NEAR AS DAMN SMART AS HE THINKS HE IS.
YOU FORGET, I WAS AROUND THE FIRST TIME YOU DECIDED TO GO OFF AND PLAY DEAD. WE MANAGED TO STRUGGLE ALONG WITHOUT YA THEN. EVEN WON A DAMN WAR.
I GUESS IT WAS MAYBE...A LITTLE TOUGHER, THIS TIME THOUGH... FOR SOME PEOPLE.
THE WAY THINGS TURNED AFTER YOU DIED, WITH OSBORN TAKING OVER...IT WAS HARD NOT TO LOSE HOPE.
YOU KNOW. FOR SOME PEOPLE.
ME, I NEVER HAD MUCH TO BEGIN WITH. HOPE, THAT IS.

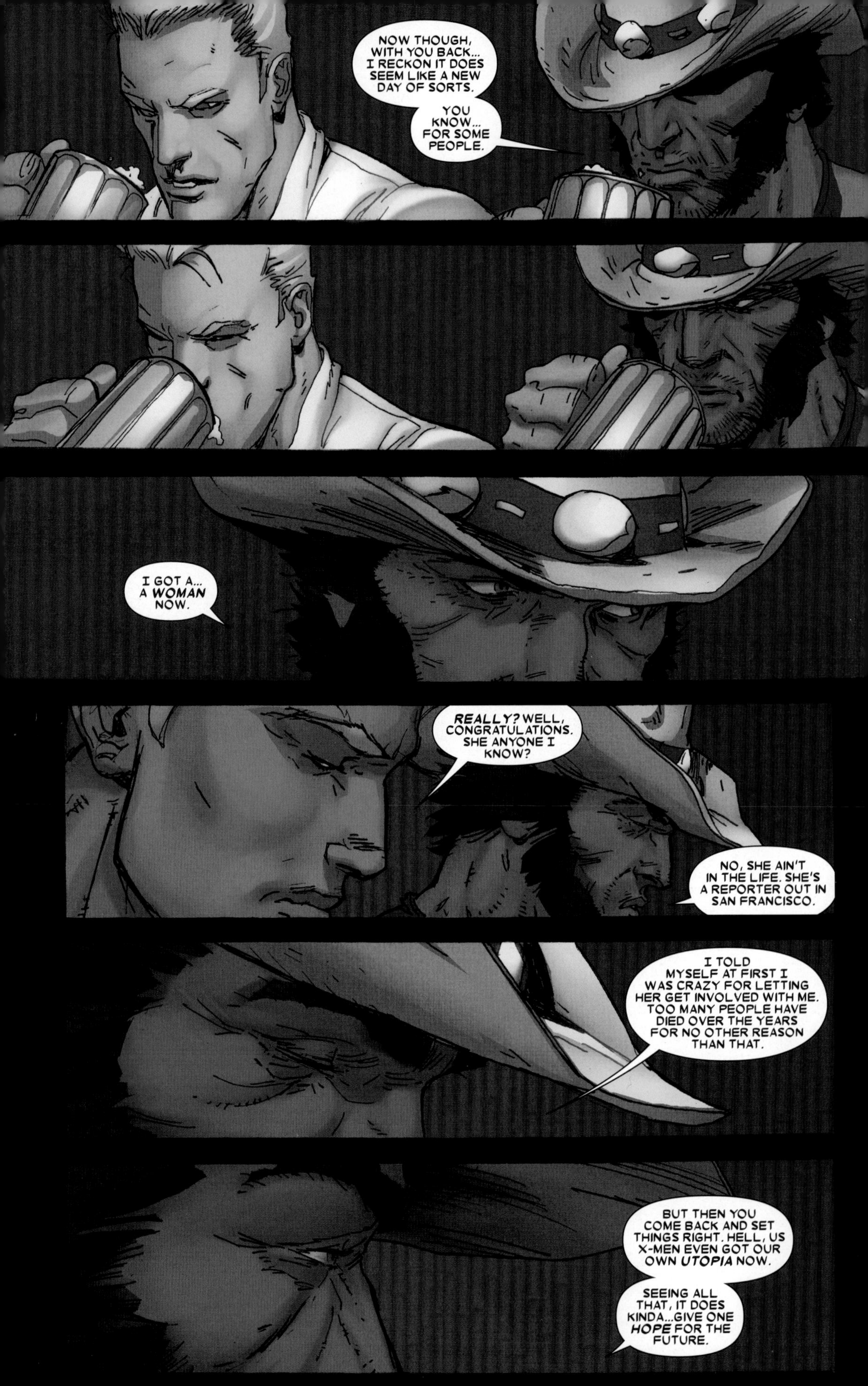
NOW THOUGH, WITH YOU BACK... I RECKON IT DOES SEEM LIKE A NEW DAY OF SORTS.
YOU KNOW... FOR SOME PEOPLE.
I GOT A... A *WOMAN* NOW.
REALLY? WELL, CONGRATULATIONS. SHE ANYONE I KNOW?
NO, SHE AIN'T IN THE LIFE. SHE'S A REPORTER OUT IN SAN FRANCISCO.
I TOLD MYSELF AT FIRST I WAS CRAZY FOR LETTING HER GET INVOLVED WITH ME. TOO MANY PEOPLE HAVE DIED OVER THE YEARS FOR NO OTHER REASON THAN THAT.
BUT THEN YOU COME BACK AND SET THINGS RIGHT. HELL, US X-MEN EVEN GOT OUR OWN *UTOPIA* NOW.
SEEING ALL THAT, IT DOES KINDA...GIVE ONE *HOPE* FOR THE FUTURE.

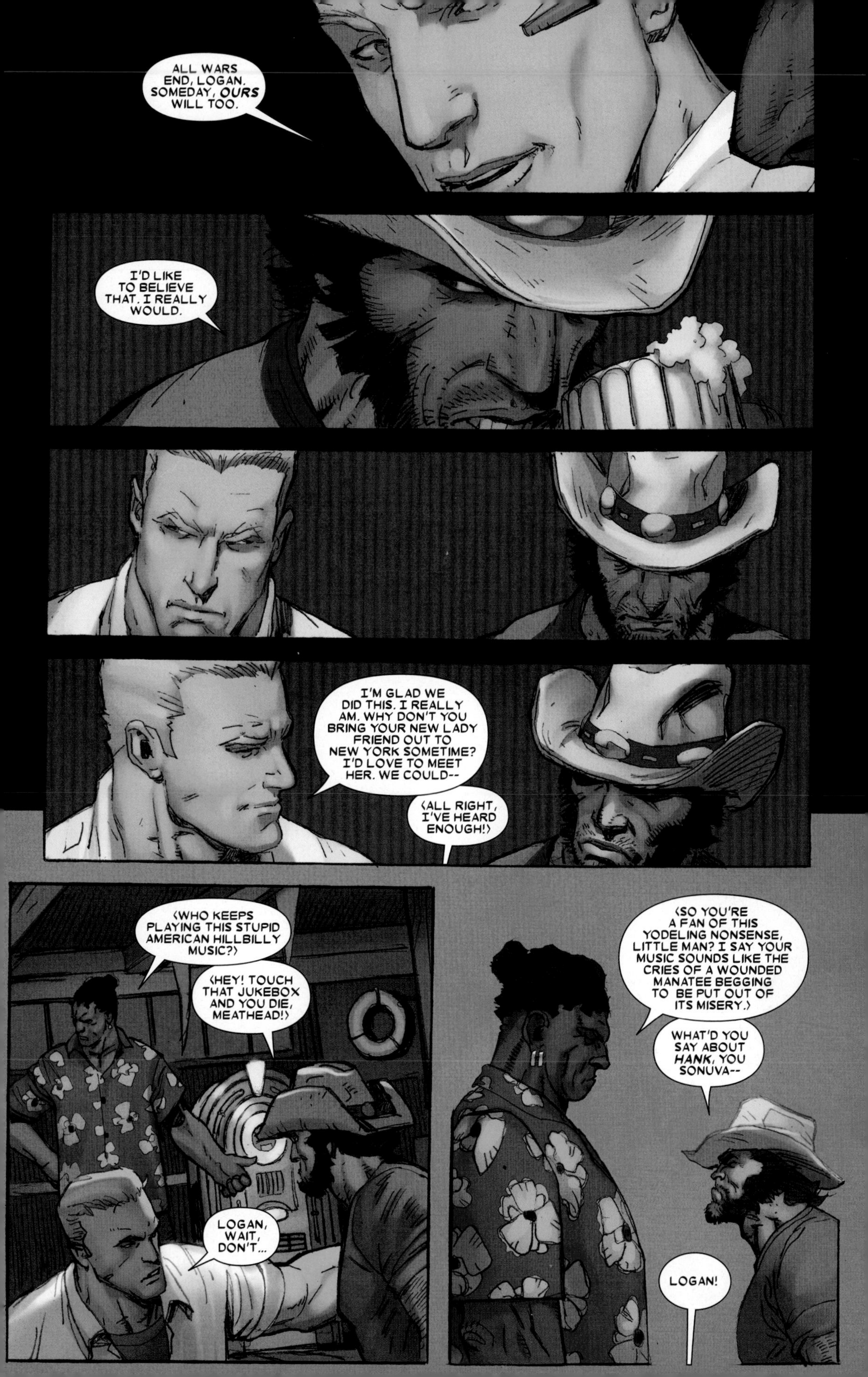
ALL WARS END, LOGAN. SOMEDAY, *OURS* WILL TOO.
I'D LIKE TO BELIEVE THAT. I REALLY WOULD.
I'M GLAD WE DID THIS. I REALLY AM. WHY DON'T YOU BRING YOUR NEW LADY FRIEND OUT TO NEW YORK SOMETIME? I'D LOVE TO MEET HER. WE COULD--
‹ALL RIGHT, I'VE HEARD ENOUGH!›
‹WHO KEEPS PLAYING THIS STUPID AMERICAN HILLBILLY MUSIC?›
‹HEY! TOUCH THAT JUKEBOX AND YOU DIE, MEATHEAD!›
LOGAN, WAIT, DON'T...
‹SO YOU'RE A FAN OF THIS YODELING NONSENSE, LITTLE MAN? I SAY YOUR MUSIC SOUNDS LIKE THE CRIES OF A WOUNDED MANATEE BEGGING TO BE PUT OUT OF ITS MISERY.›
WHAT'D YOU SAY ABOUT *HANK*, YOU SONUVA--
LOGAN!

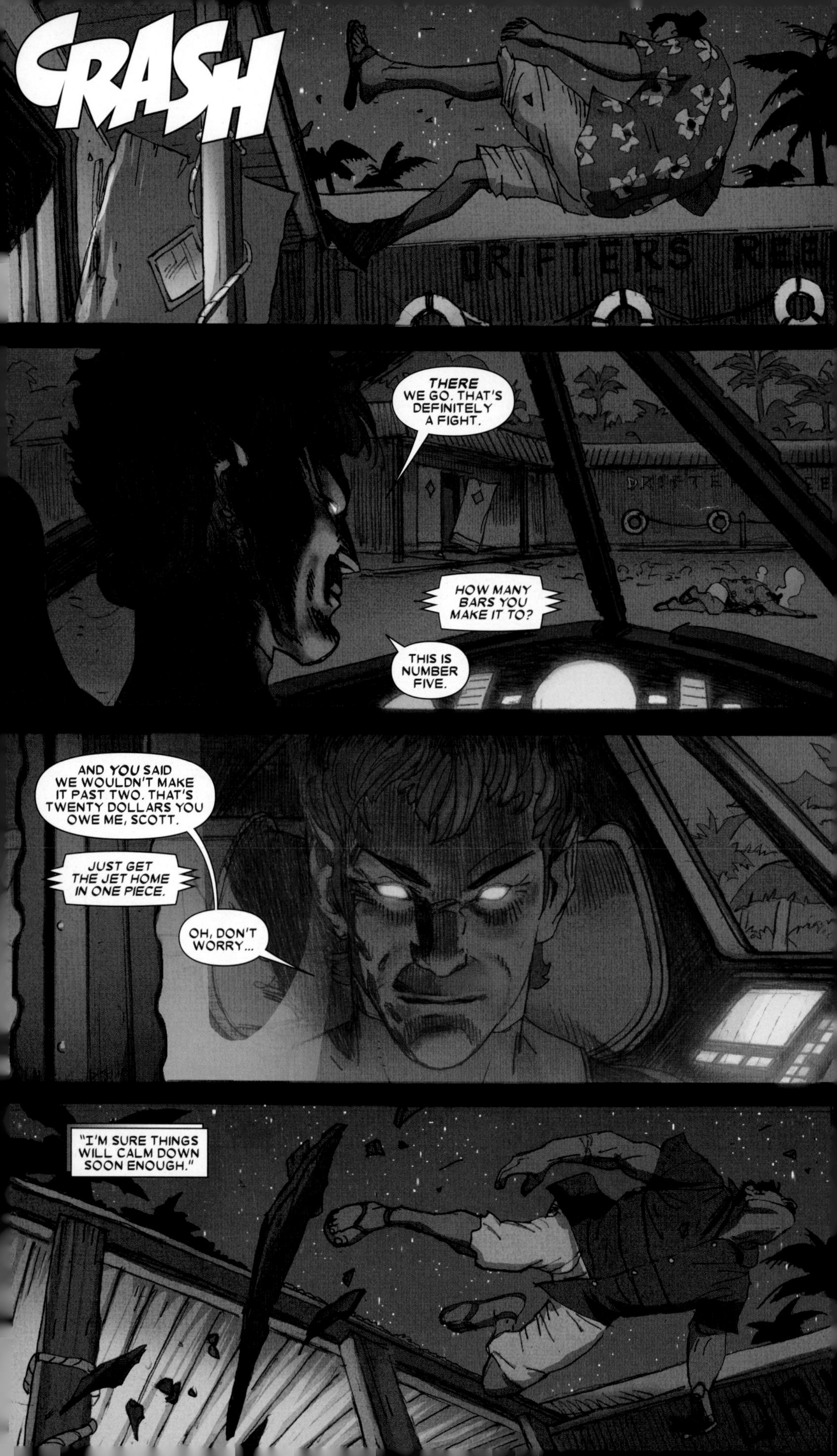
CRASH
DRIFTERS REE
THERE WE GO. THAT'S DEFINITELY A FIGHT.
HOW MANY BARS YOU MAKE IT TO?
THIS IS NUMBER FIVE.
AND YOU SAID WE WOULDN'T MAKE IT PAST TWO. THAT'S TWENTY DOLLARS YOU OWE ME, SCOTT.
JUST GET THE JET HOME IN ONE PIECE.
OH, DON'T WORRY...
"I'M SURE THINGS WILL CALM DOWN SOON ENOUGH."

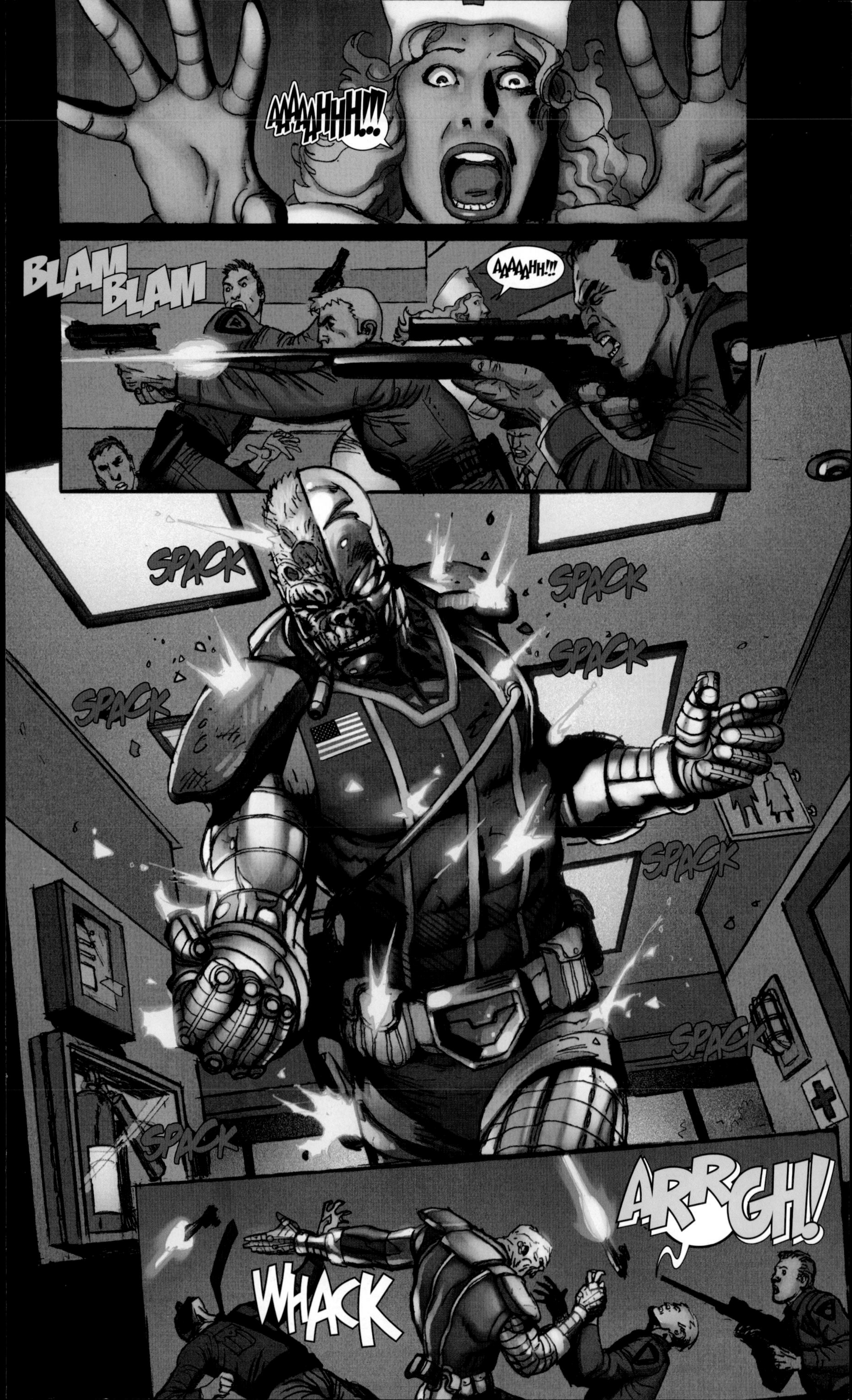

AAAAHHH!!!...
BLAM BLAM
AAAAAHH!!!
SPACK
SPACK
SPACK
SPACK
SPACK
SPACK
SPACK
ARRGH!
WHACK

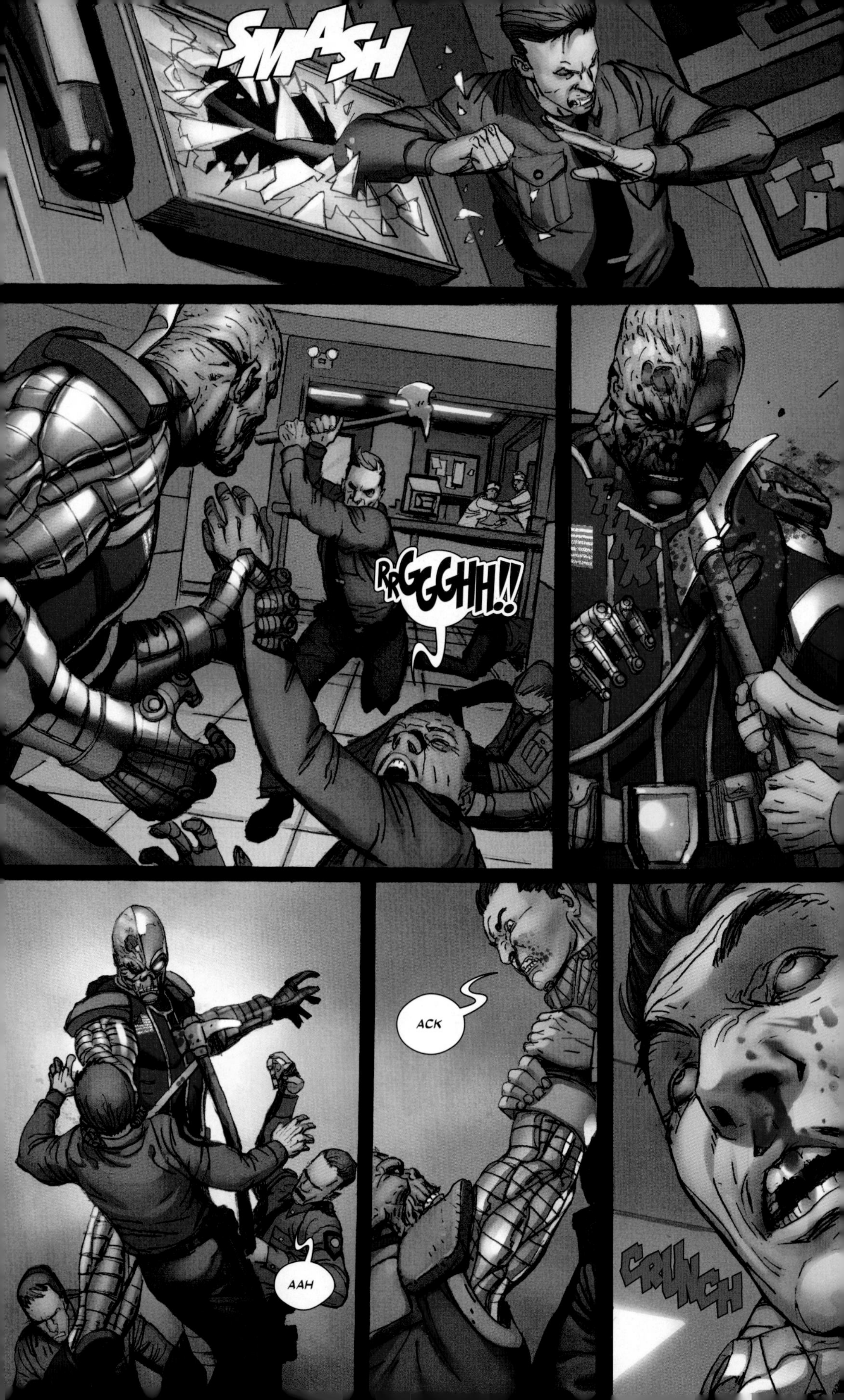
SMASH
RRGGGHH!!
FLINK
ACK
AAH
CRUNCH

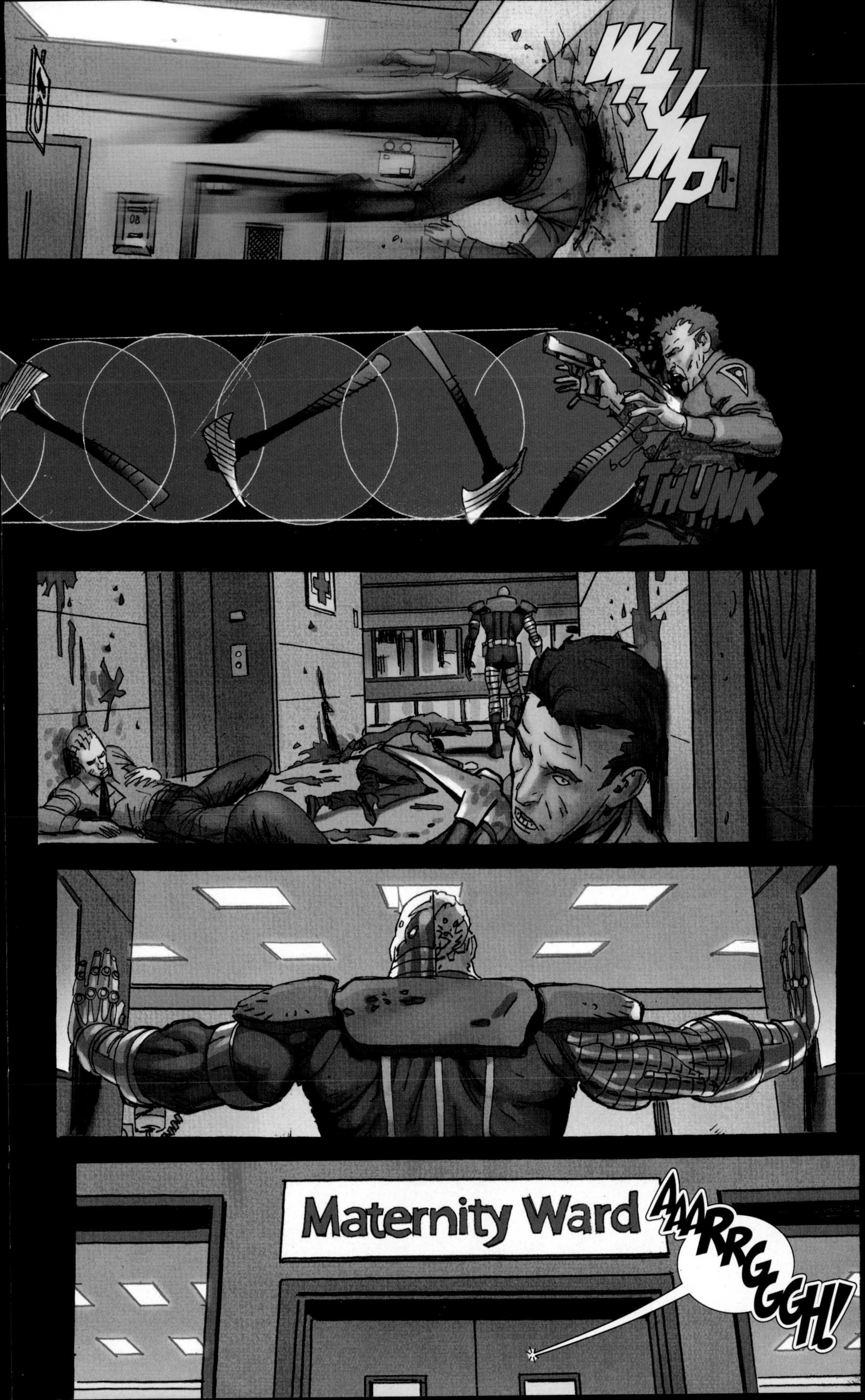
WHUMP
THUNK
Maternity Ward
AAAARRGGGH!

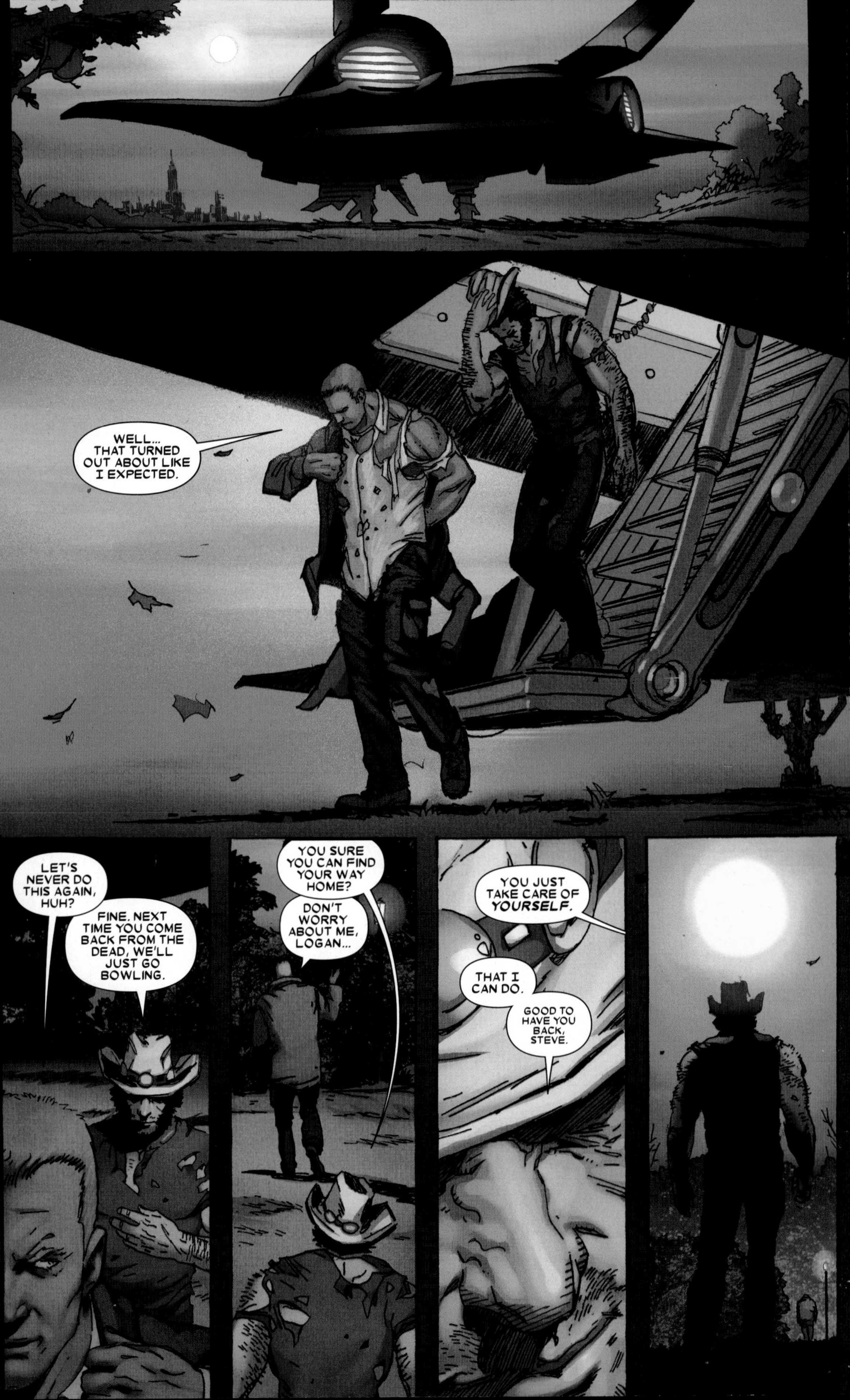
WELL... THAT TURNED OUT ABOUT LIKE I EXPECTED.
LET'S NEVER DO THIS AGAIN, HUH?
FINE. NEXT TIME YOU COME BACK FROM THE DEAD, WE'LL JUST GO BOWLING.
YOU SURE YOU CAN FIND YOUR WAY HOME?
DON'T WORRY ABOUT ME, LOGAN...
YOU JUST TAKE CARE OF YOURSELF.
THAT I CAN DO.
GOOD TO HAVE YOU BACK, STEVE.

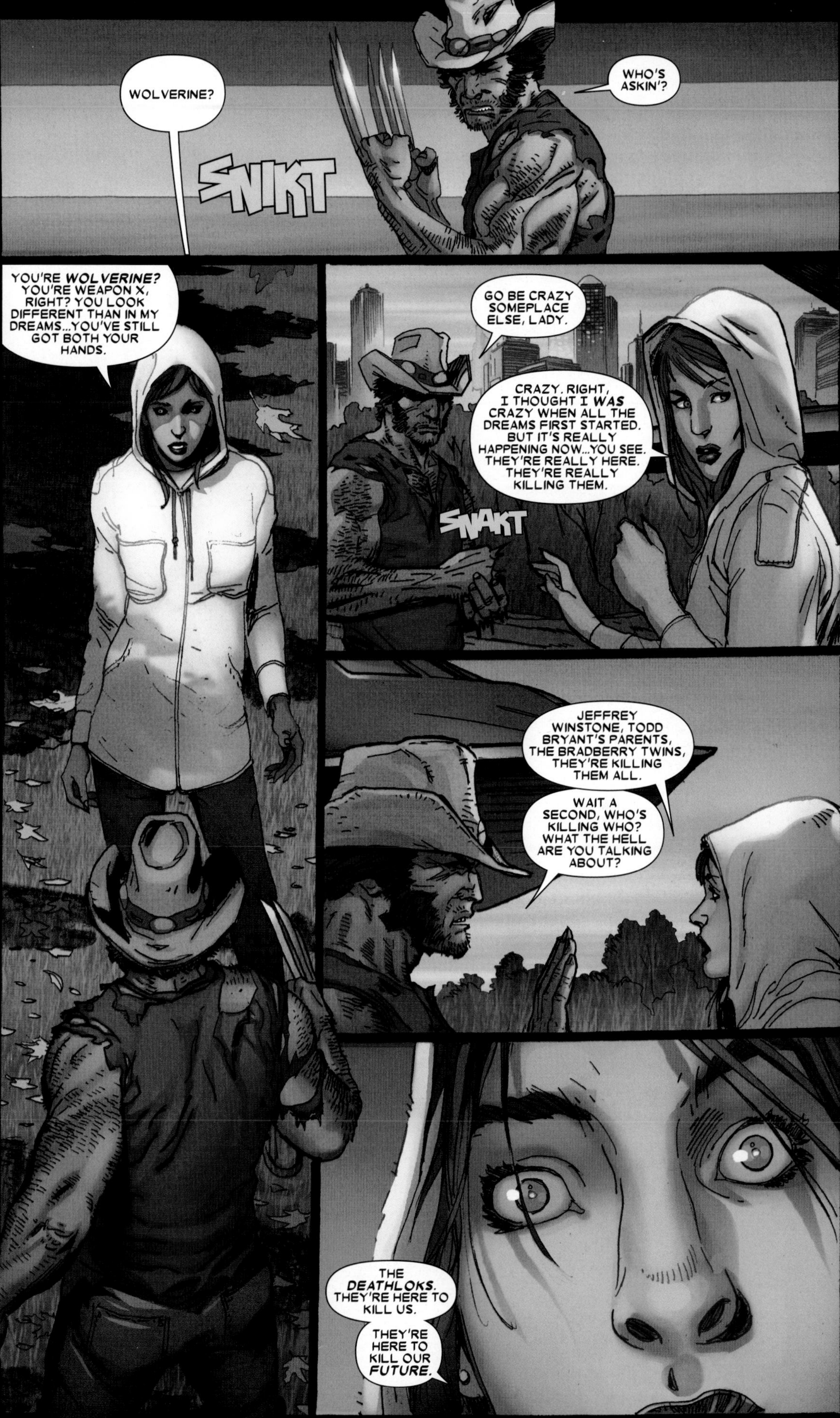

WOLVERINE?
SNIKT
WHO'S ASKIN'?
YOU'RE WOLVERINE? YOU'RE WEAPON X, RIGHT? YOU LOOK DIFFERENT THAN IN MY DREAMS...YOU'VE STILL GOT BOTH YOUR HANDS.
GO BE CRAZY SOMEPLACE ELSE, LADY.
CRAZY. RIGHT, I THOUGHT I WAS CRAZY WHEN ALL THE DREAMS FIRST STARTED. BUT IT'S REALLY HAPPENING NOW...YOU SEE. THEY'RE REALLY HERE. THEY'RE REALLY KILLING THEM.
SNAKT
JEFFREY WINSTONE, TODD BRYANT'S PARENTS, THE BRADBERRY TWINS, THEY'RE KILLING THEM ALL.
WAIT A SECOND, WHO'S KILLING WHO? WHAT THE HELL ARE YOU TALKING ABOUT?
THE DEATHLOKS. THEY'RE HERE TO KILL US.
THEY'RE HERE TO KILL OUR FUTURE.

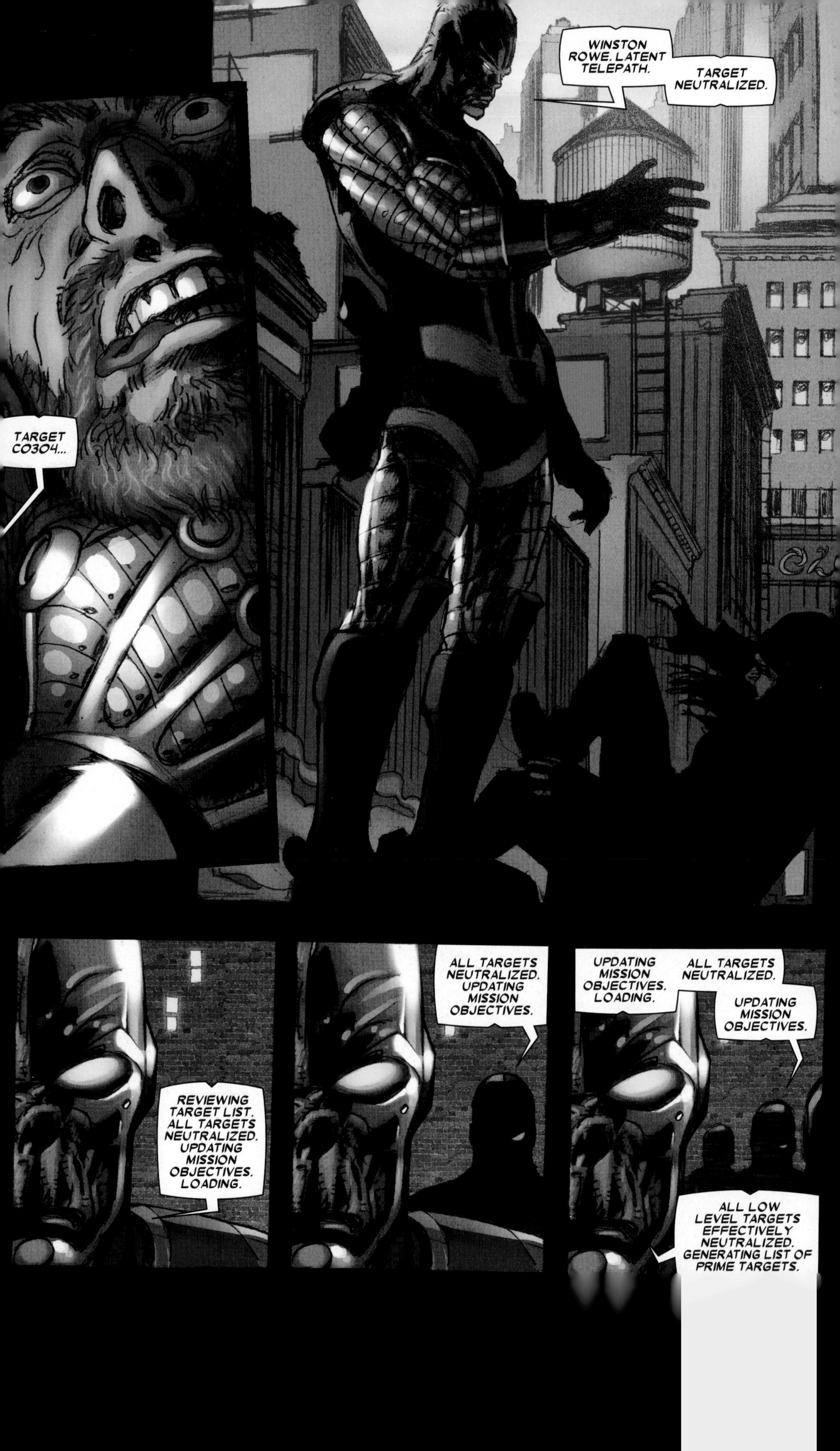
WINSTON ROWE. LATENT TELEPATH.
TARGET NEUTRALIZED.
TARGET C0304...
REVIEWING TARGET LIST. ALL TARGETS NEUTRALIZED. UPDATING MISSION OBJECTIVES. LOADING.
ALL TARGETS NEUTRALIZED. UPDATING MISSION OBJECTIVES.
UPDATING MISSION OBJECTIVES. LOADING.
ALL TARGETS NEUTRALIZED.
UPDATING MISSION OBJECTIVES.
ALL LOW LEVEL TARGETS EFFECTIVELY NEUTRALIZED. GENERATING LIST OF PRIME TARGETS.

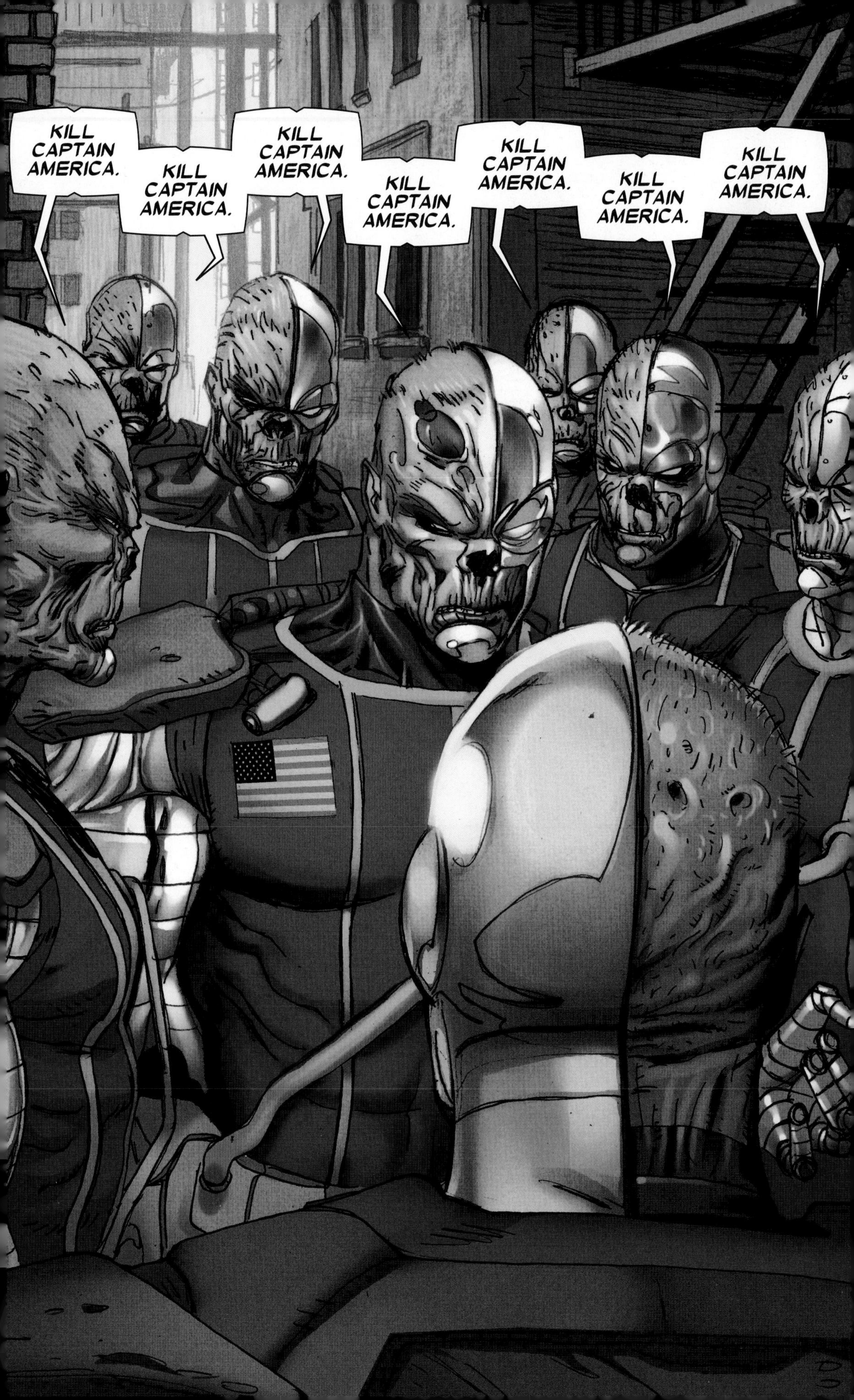
KILL CAPTAIN AMERICA.
KILL CAPTAIN AMERICA.
KILL CAPTAIN AMERICA.
KILL CAPTAIN AMERICA.
KILL CAPTAIN AMERICA.
KILL CAPTAIN AMERICA.
KILL CAPTAIN AMERICA.

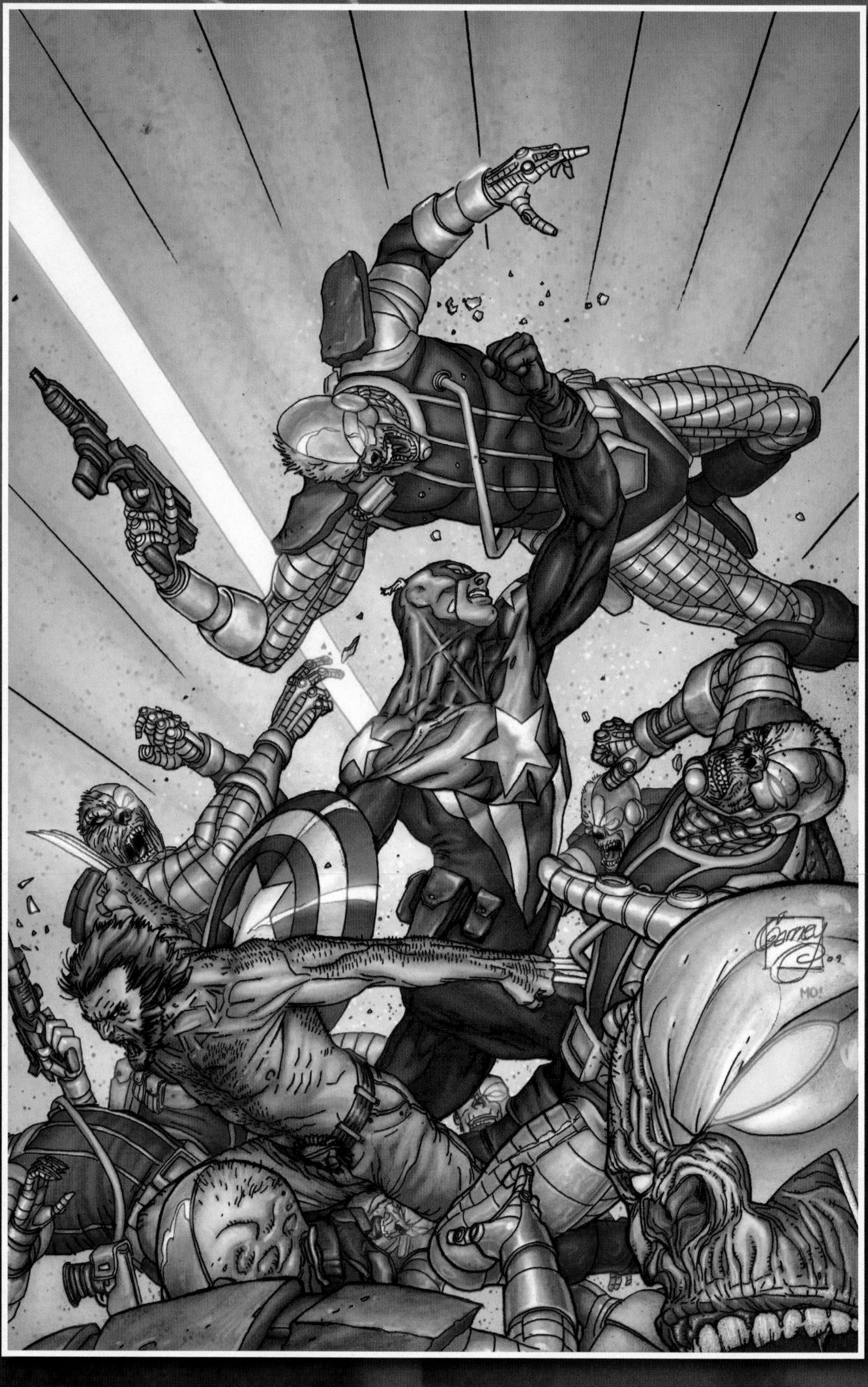

TWELVE

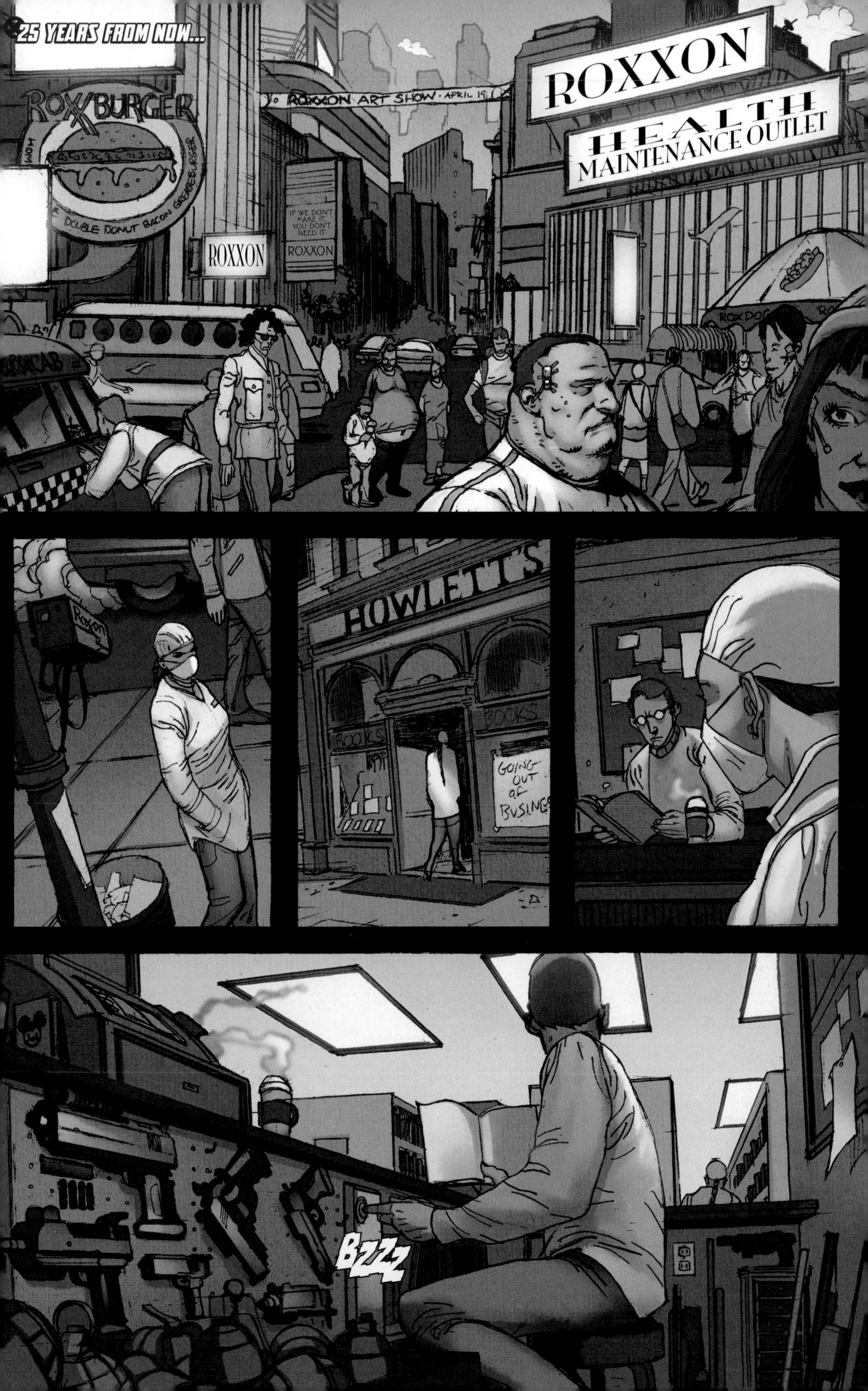
25 YEARS FROM NOW...
ROXXON
HEALTH
MAINTENANCE OUTLET
ROXXON ART SHOW · APRIL 19
ROXXBURGER
DOUBLE DONUT BACON GREASEBURGER
ROXXON
IF WE DON'T MAKE IT, YOU DON'T NEED IT
ROXXON
ROXDOG
ROXXCAB
Roxxon
HOWLETT'S
BOOKS
BOOKS
GOING OUT OF BUSINESS
BZZZ

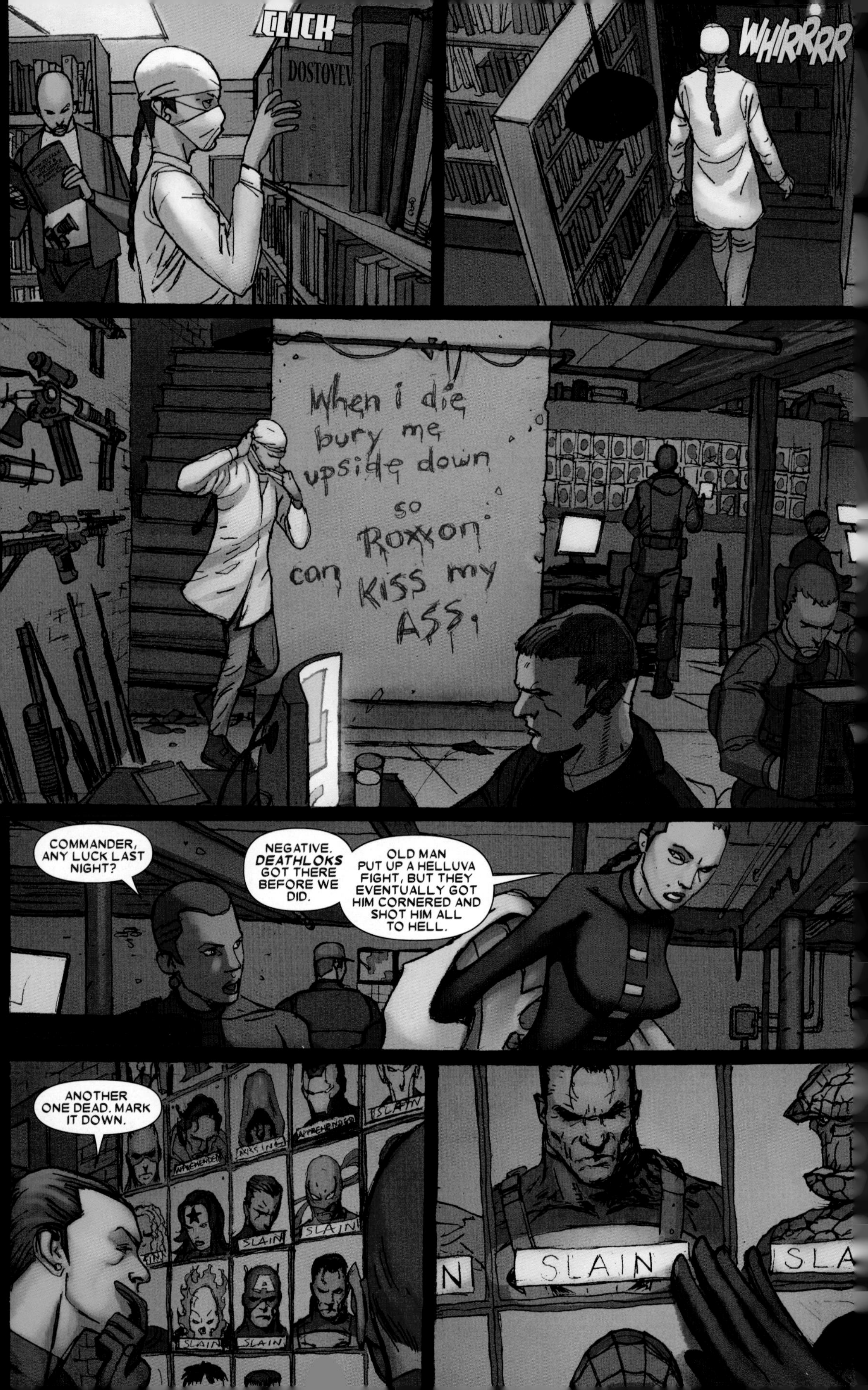
CLICK
DOSTOYEV
WHIRRRR
When i die bury me upside down so Roxxon can kiss my ASS.
COMMANDER, ANY LUCK LAST NIGHT?
NEGATIVE. DEATHLOKS GOT THERE BEFORE WE DID.
OLD MAN PUT UP A HELLUVA FIGHT, BUT THEY EVENTUALLY GOT HIM CORNERED AND SHOT HIM ALL TO HELL.
ANOTHER ONE DEAD. MARK IT DOWN.
SLAIN
SLAIN
SLAIN
SLAIN
SLAIN

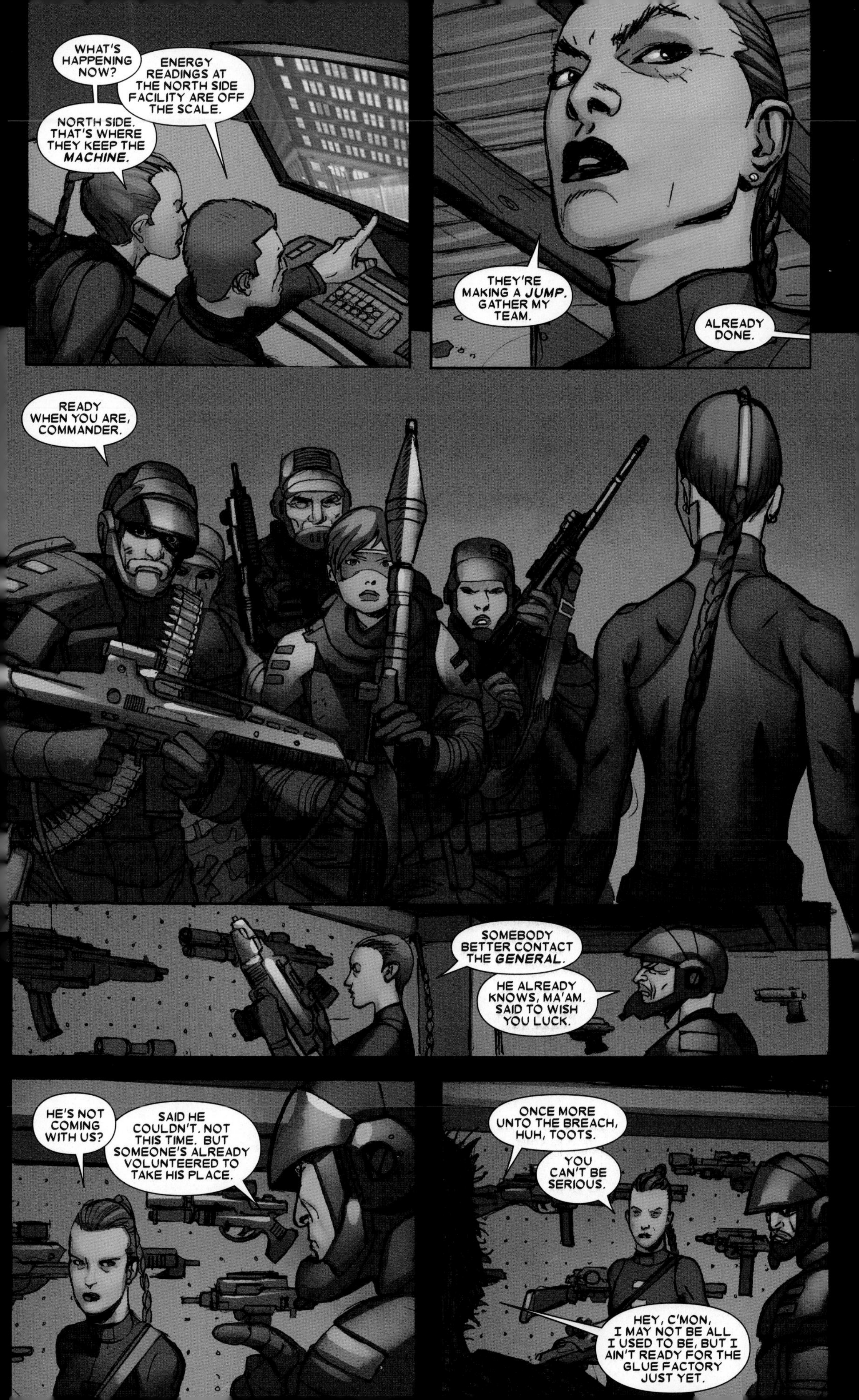
WHAT'S HAPPENING NOW?
ENERGY READINGS AT THE NORTH SIDE FACILITY ARE OFF THE SCALE.
NORTH SIDE. THAT'S WHERE THEY KEEP THE *MACHINE.*
THEY'RE MAKING A *JUMP.* GATHER MY TEAM.
ALREADY DONE.
READY WHEN YOU ARE, COMMANDER.
SOMEBODY BETTER CONTACT THE *GENERAL*.
HE ALREADY KNOWS, MA'AM. SAID TO WISH YOU LUCK.
HE'S NOT COMING WITH US?
SAID HE COULDN'T. NOT THIS TIME. BUT SOMEONE'S ALREADY VOLUNTEERED TO TAKE HIS PLACE.
ONCE MORE UNTO THE BREACH, HUH, TOOTS.
YOU CAN'T BE SERIOUS.
HEY, C'MON, I MAY NOT BE ALL I USED TO BE, BUT I AIN'T READY FOR THE GLUE FACTORY JUST YET.

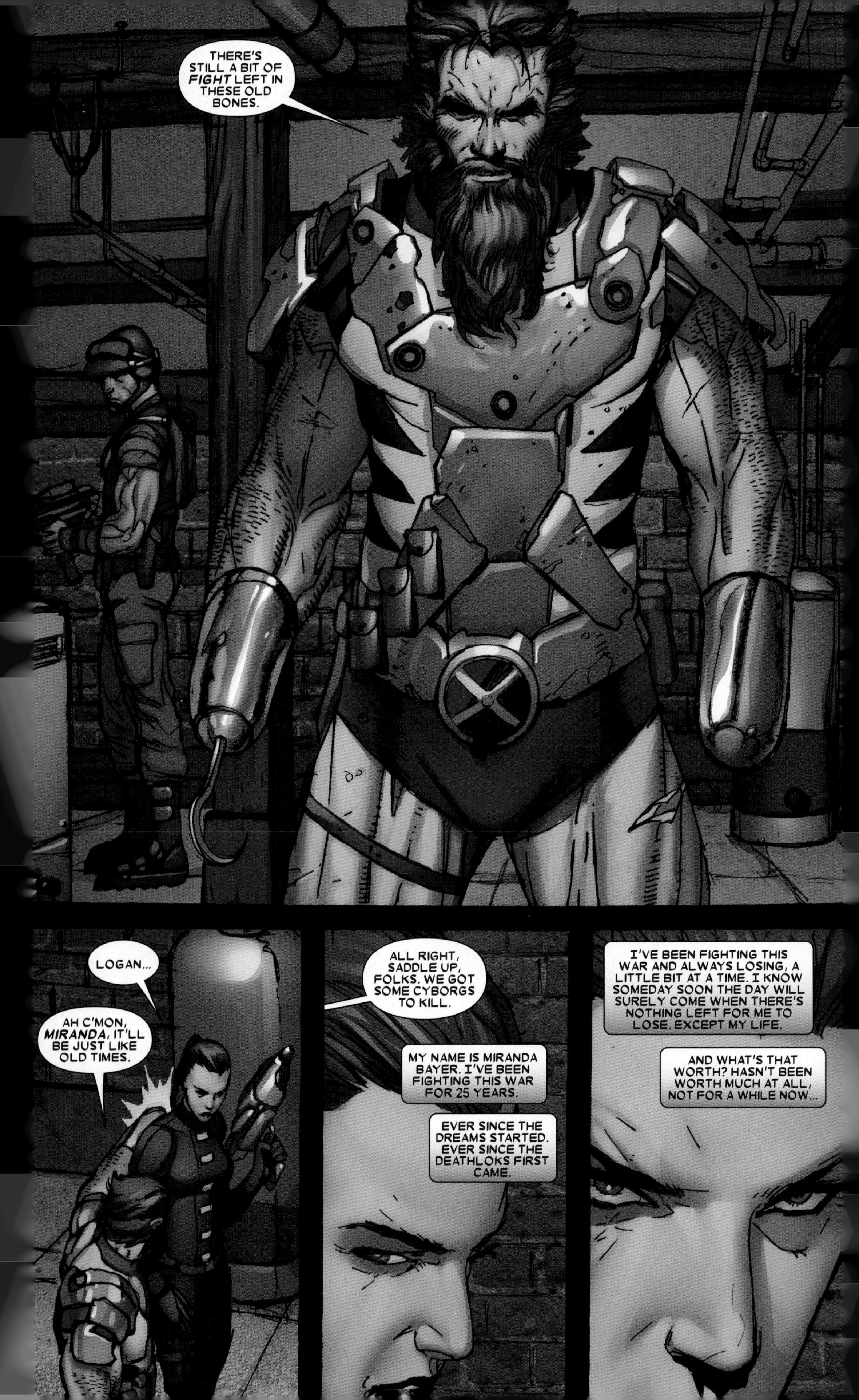
THERE'S STILL A BIT OF FIGHT LEFT IN THESE OLD BONES.
LOGAN...
AH C'MON, MIRANDA, IT'LL BE JUST LIKE OLD TIMES.
ALL RIGHT, SADDLE UP, FOLKS. WE GOT SOME CYBORGS TO KILL.
MY NAME IS MIRANDA BAYER. I'VE BEEN FIGHTING THIS WAR FOR 25 YEARS.
EVER SINCE THE DREAMS STARTED. EVER SINCE THE DEATHLOKS FIRST CAME.
I'VE BEEN FIGHTING THIS WAR AND ALWAYS LOSING, A LITTLE BIT AT A TIME. I KNOW SOMEDAY SOON THE DAY WILL SURELY COME WHEN THERE'S NOTHING LEFT FOR ME TO LOSE. EXCEPT MY LIFE.
AND WHAT'S THAT WORTH? HASN'T BEEN WORTH MUCH AT ALL, NOT FOR A WHILE NOW...

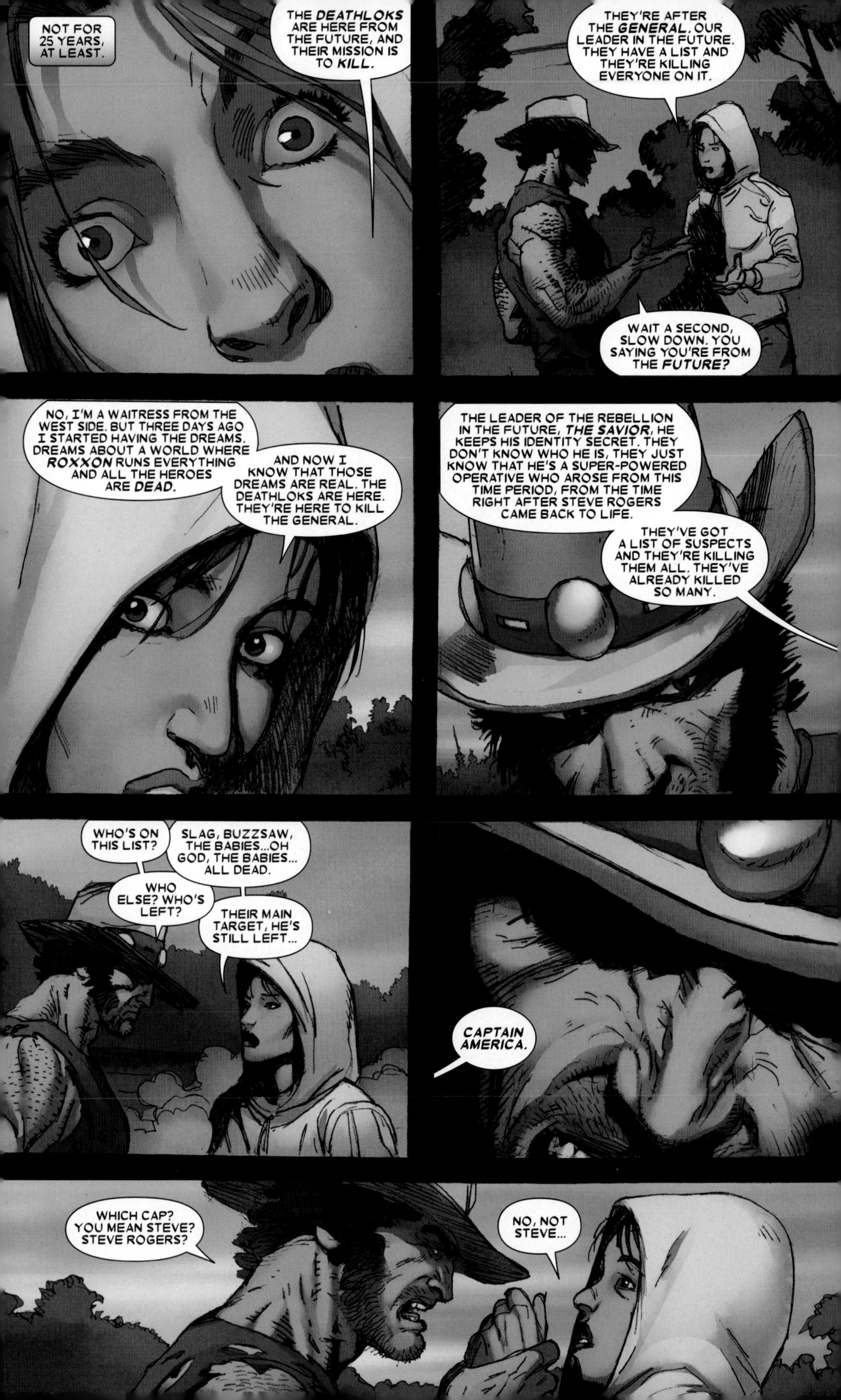
NOT FOR 25 YEARS, AT LEAST.
THE DEATHLOKS ARE HERE FROM THE FUTURE, AND THEIR MISSION IS TO KILL.
THEY'RE AFTER THE GENERAL. OUR LEADER IN THE FUTURE. THEY HAVE A LIST AND THEY'RE KILLING EVERYONE ON IT.
WAIT A SECOND, SLOW DOWN. YOU SAYING YOU'RE FROM THE FUTURE?
NO, I'M A WAITRESS FROM THE WEST SIDE. BUT THREE DAYS AGO I STARTED HAVING THE DREAMS. DREAMS ABOUT A WORLD WHERE ROXXON RUNS EVERYTHING AND ALL THE HEROES ARE DEAD.
AND NOW I KNOW THAT THOSE DREAMS ARE REAL. THE DEATHLOKS ARE HERE. THEY'RE HERE TO KILL THE GENERAL.
THE LEADER OF THE REBELLION IN THE FUTURE, THE SAVIOR, HE KEEPS HIS IDENTITY SECRET. THEY DON'T KNOW WHO HE IS, THEY JUST KNOW THAT HE'S A SUPER-POWERED OPERATIVE WHO AROSE FROM THIS TIME PERIOD, FROM THE TIME RIGHT AFTER STEVE ROGERS CAME BACK TO LIFE.
THEY'VE GOT A LIST OF SUSPECTS AND THEY'RE KILLING THEM ALL. THEY'VE ALREADY KILLED SO MANY.
WHO'S ON THIS LIST?
SLAG, BUZZSAW, THE BABIES...OH GOD, THE BABIES... ALL DEAD.
WHO ELSE? WHO'S LEFT?
THEIR MAIN TARGET, HE'S STILL LEFT...
CAPTAIN AMERICA.
WHICH CAP? YOU MEAN STEVE? STEVE ROGERS?
NO, NOT STEVE...

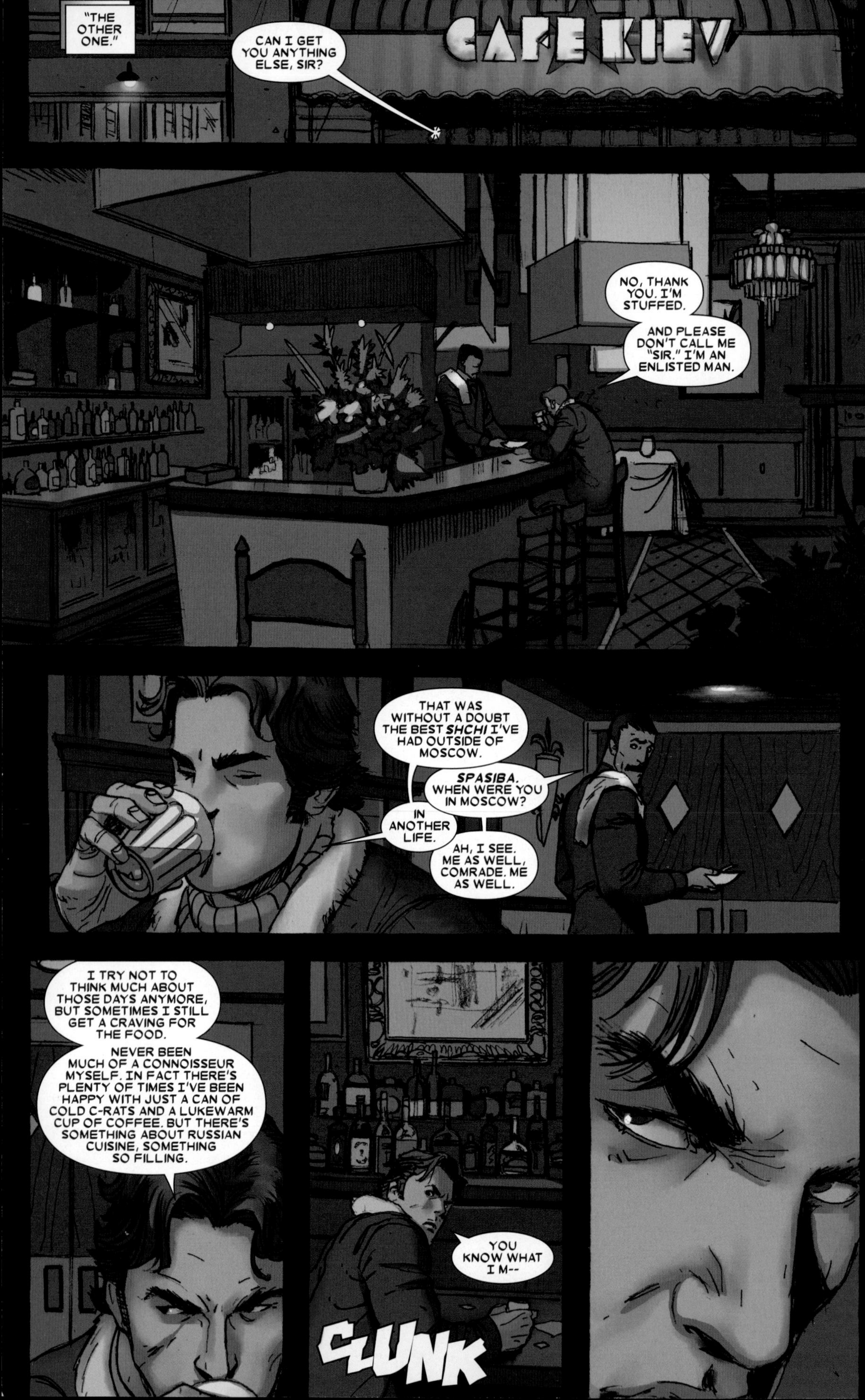
"THE OTHER ONE."
CAFE KIEV
CAN I GET YOU ANYTHING ELSE, SIR?
NO, THANK YOU. I'M STUFFED.
AND PLEASE DON'T CALL ME "SIR." I'M AN ENLISTED MAN.
THAT WAS WITHOUT A DOUBT THE BEST SHCHI I'VE HAD OUTSIDE OF MOSCOW.
SPASIBA. WHEN WERE YOU IN MOSCOW?
IN ANOTHER LIFE.
AH, I SEE. ME AS WELL, COMRADE. ME AS WELL.
I TRY NOT TO THINK MUCH ABOUT THOSE DAYS ANYMORE, BUT SOMETIMES I STILL GET A CRAVING FOR THE FOOD.
NEVER BEEN MUCH OF A CONNOISSEUR MYSELF. IN FACT THERE'S PLENTY OF TIMES I'VE BEEN HAPPY WITH JUST A CAN OF COLD C-RATS AND A LUKEWARM CUP OF COFFEE. BUT THERE'S SOMETHING ABOUT RUSSIAN CUISINE, SOMETHING SO FILLING.
YOU KNOW WHAT I M--
CLUNK

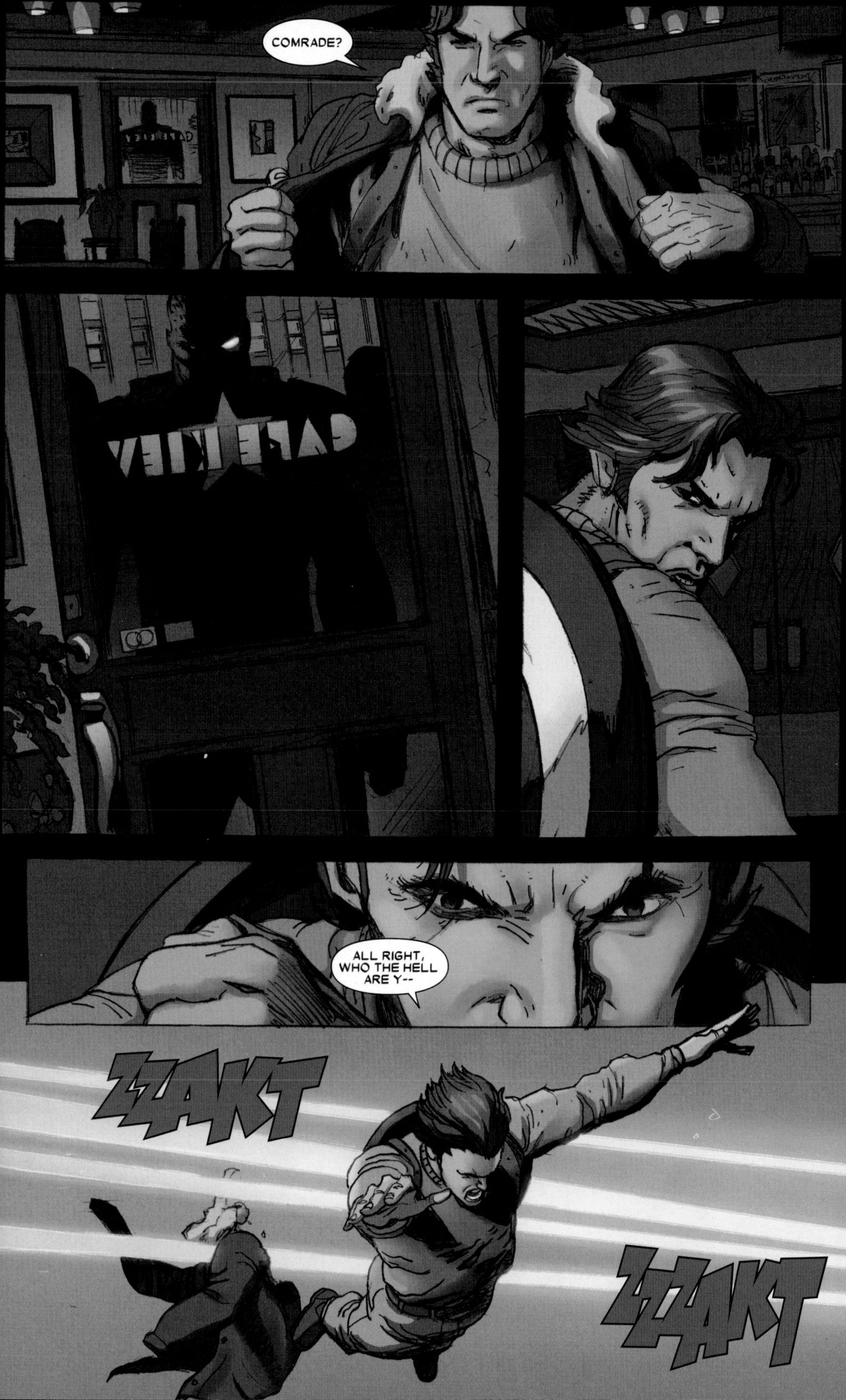
COMRADE?
ALL RIGHT, WHO THE HELL ARE Y--
ZZAKT
ZZAKT

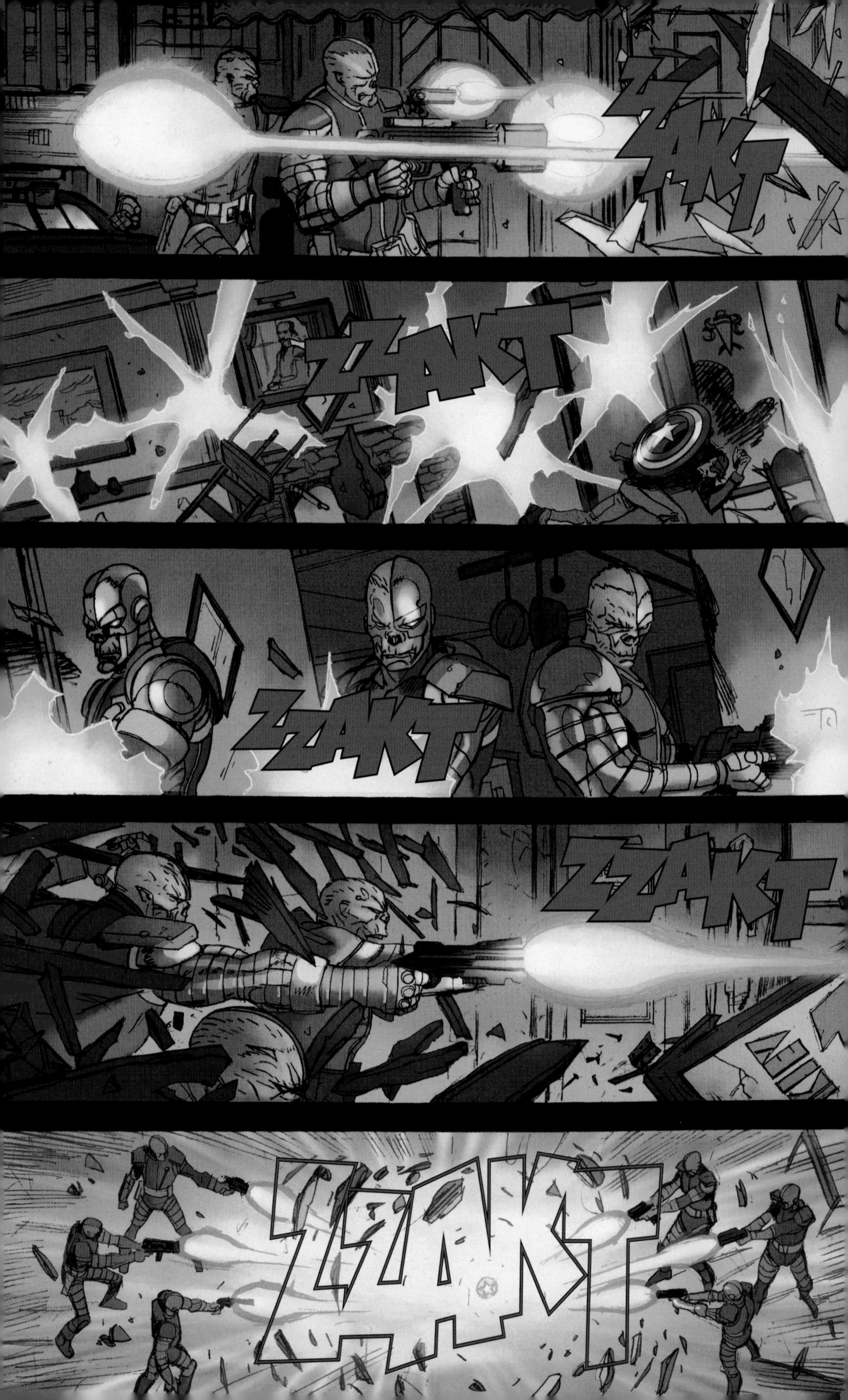
ZZAKT
ZZAKT
ZZAKT
ZZAKT
ZZAKT

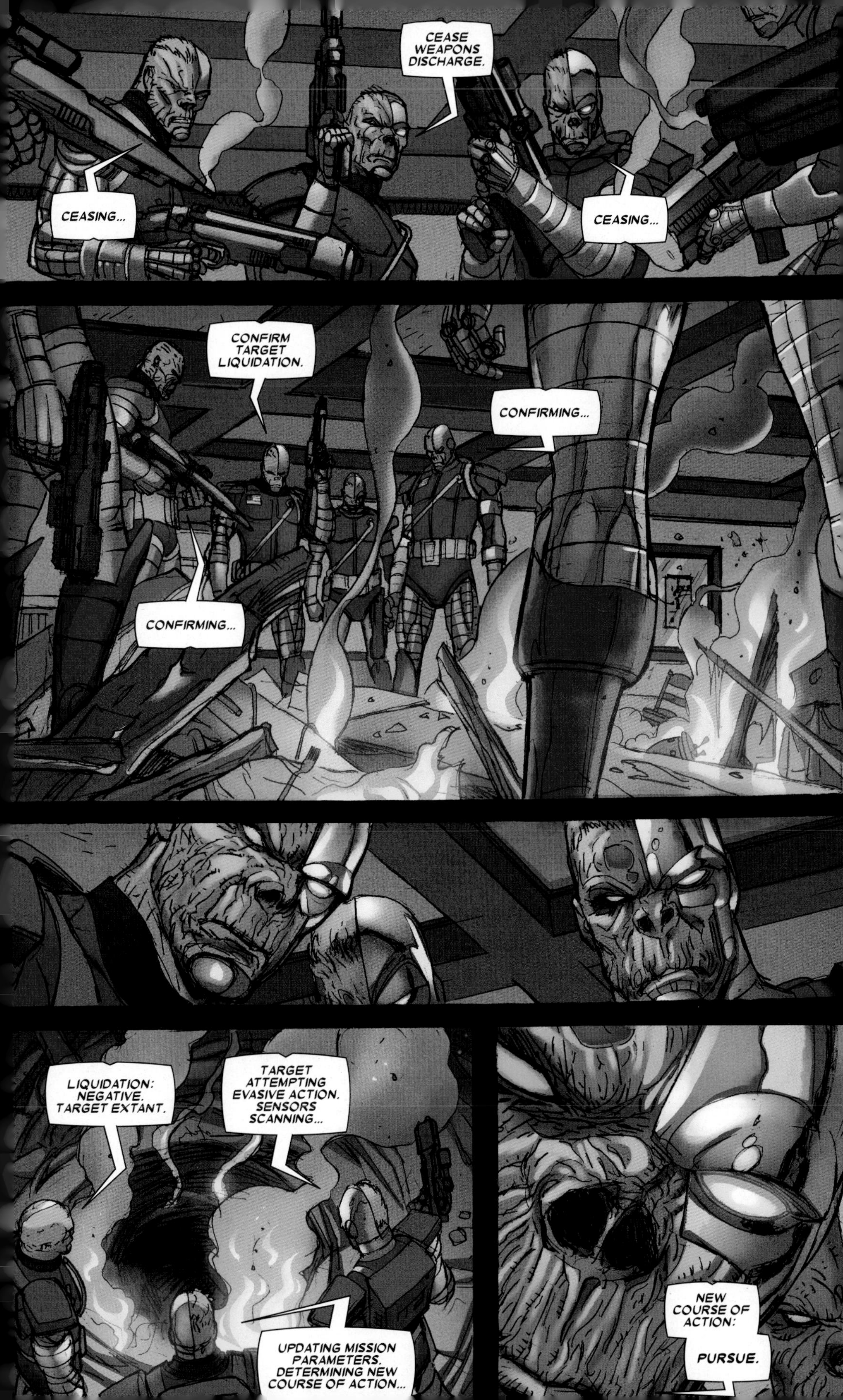
CEASE WEAPONS DISCHARGE.
CEASING...
CEASING...
CONFIRM TARGET LIQUIDATION.
CONFIRMING...
CONFIRMING...
LIQUIDATION: NEGATIVE. TARGET EXTANT.
TARGET ATTEMPTING EVASIVE ACTION. SENSORS SCANNING...
UPDATING MISSION PARAMETERS. DETERMINING NEW COURSE OF ACTION...
NEW COURSE OF ACTION:
PURSUE.

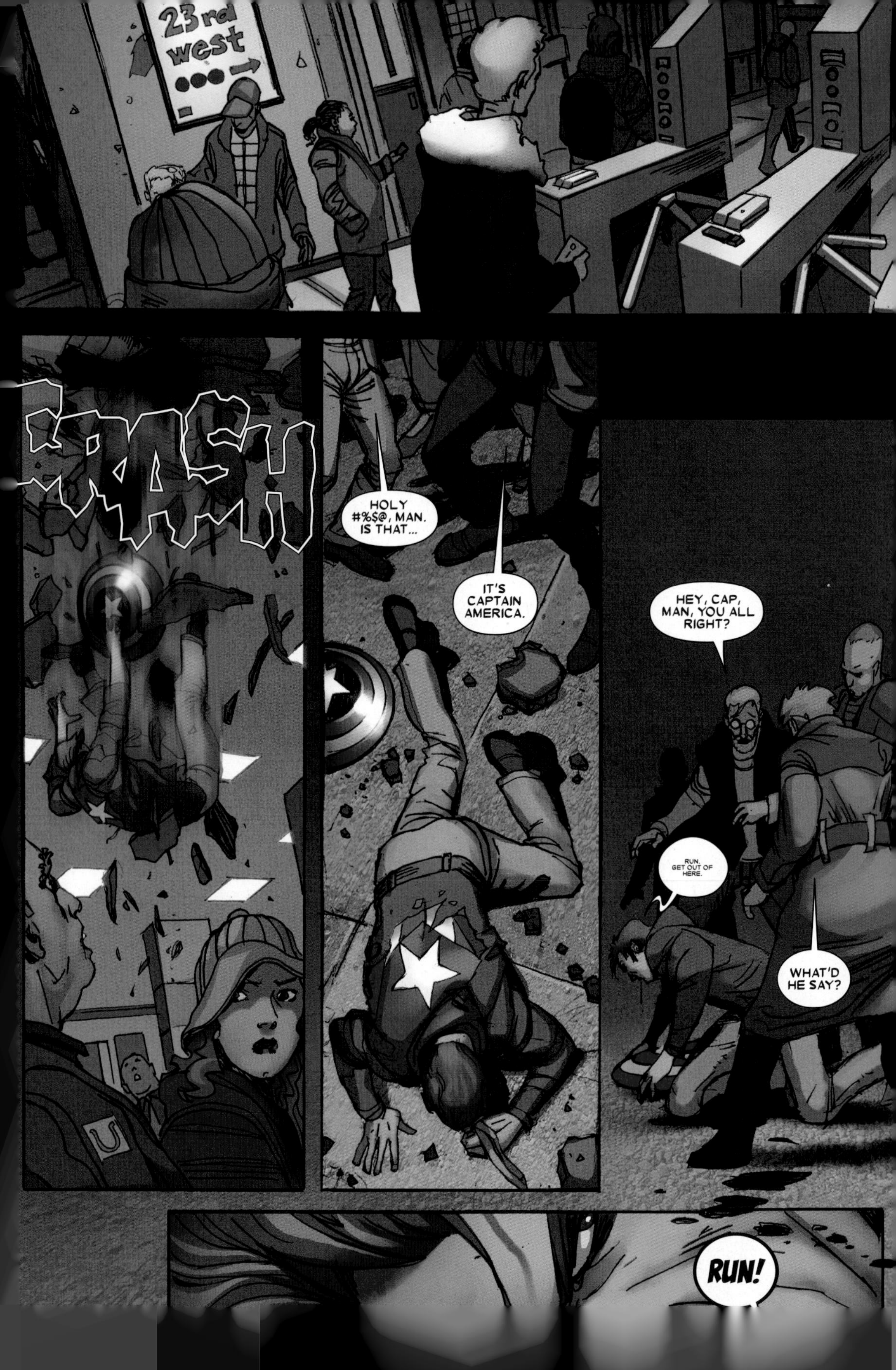
23rd
west
CRASH
HOLY #%$@, MAN. IS THAT...
IT'S CAPTAIN AMERICA.
HEY, CAP, MAN, YOU ALL RIGHT?
RUN. GET OUT OF HERE.
WHAT'D HE SAY?
RUN!

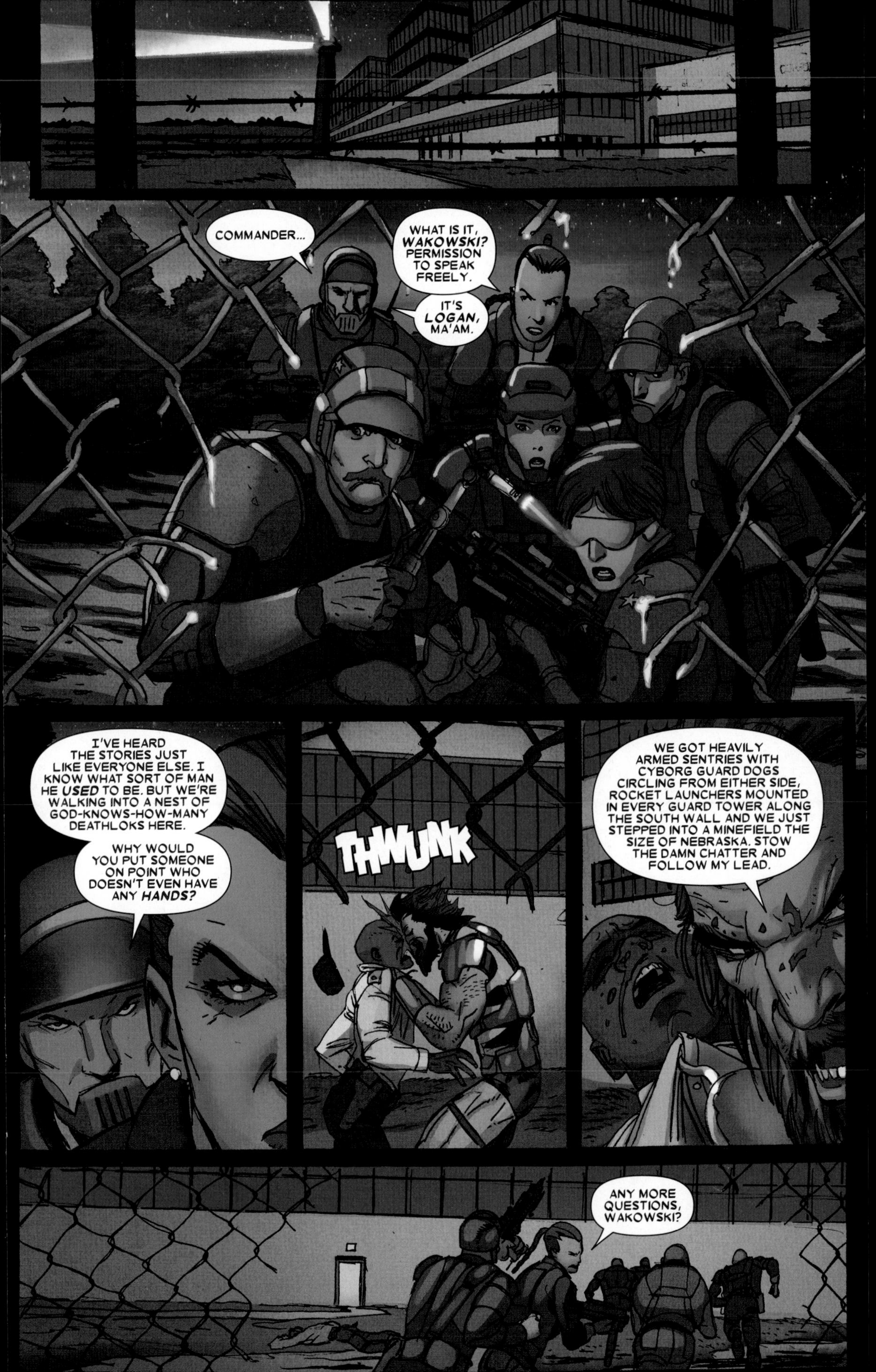
COMMANDER...
WHAT IS IT, WAKOWSKI? PERMISSION TO SPEAK FREELY.
IT'S LOGAN, MA'AM.
I'VE HEARD THE STORIES JUST LIKE EVERYONE ELSE. I KNOW WHAT SORT OF MAN HE USED TO BE. BUT WE'RE WALKING INTO A NEST OF GOD-KNOWS-HOW-MANY DEATHLOKS HERE.
WHY WOULD YOU PUT SOMEONE ON POINT WHO DOESN'T EVEN HAVE ANY HANDS?
THWUNK
WE GOT HEAVILY ARMED SENTRIES WITH CYBORG GUARD DOGS CIRCLING FROM EITHER SIDE, ROCKET LAUNCHERS MOUNTED IN EVERY GUARD TOWER ALONG THE SOUTH WALL AND WE JUST STEPPED INTO A MINEFIELD THE SIZE OF NEBRASKA. STOW THE DAMN CHATTER AND FOLLOW MY LEAD.
ANY MORE QUESTIONS, WAKOWSKI?

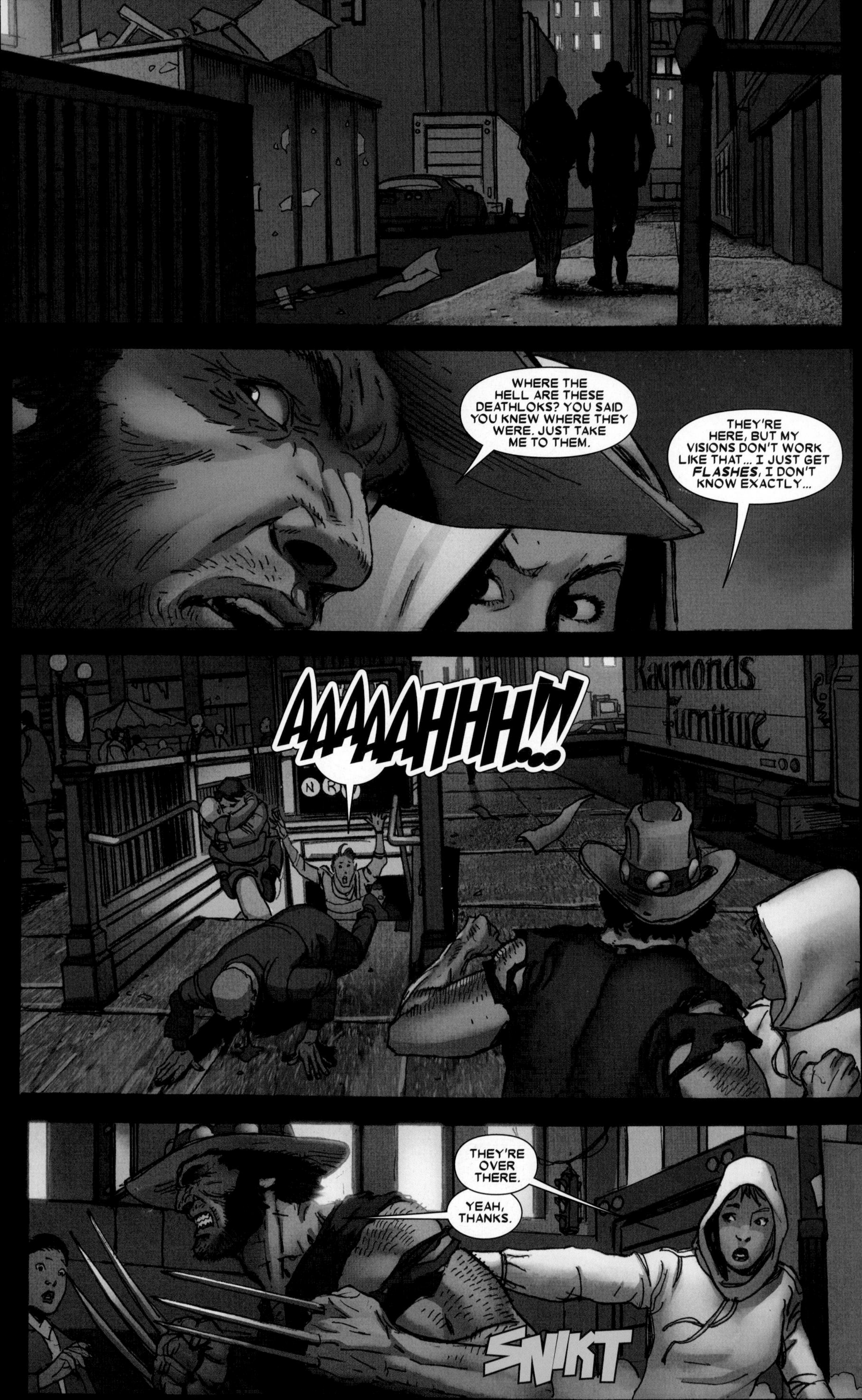
WHERE THE HELL ARE THESE DEATHLOKS? YOU SAID YOU KNEW WHERE THEY WERE. JUST TAKE ME TO THEM.
THEY'RE HERE, BUT MY VISIONS DON'T WORK LIKE THAT... I JUST GET FLASHES, I DON'T KNOW EXACTLY...
AAAAAHHH!!!...
Raymonds Furniture
THEY'RE OVER THERE.
YEAH, THANKS.
SNIKT

ZZAKT

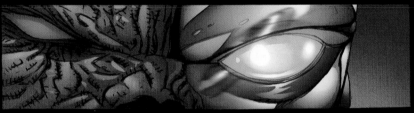

WHACK

THUNK

TARGET:
CAPTAIN AMERICA.
MISSION:
EXTERMINATE.

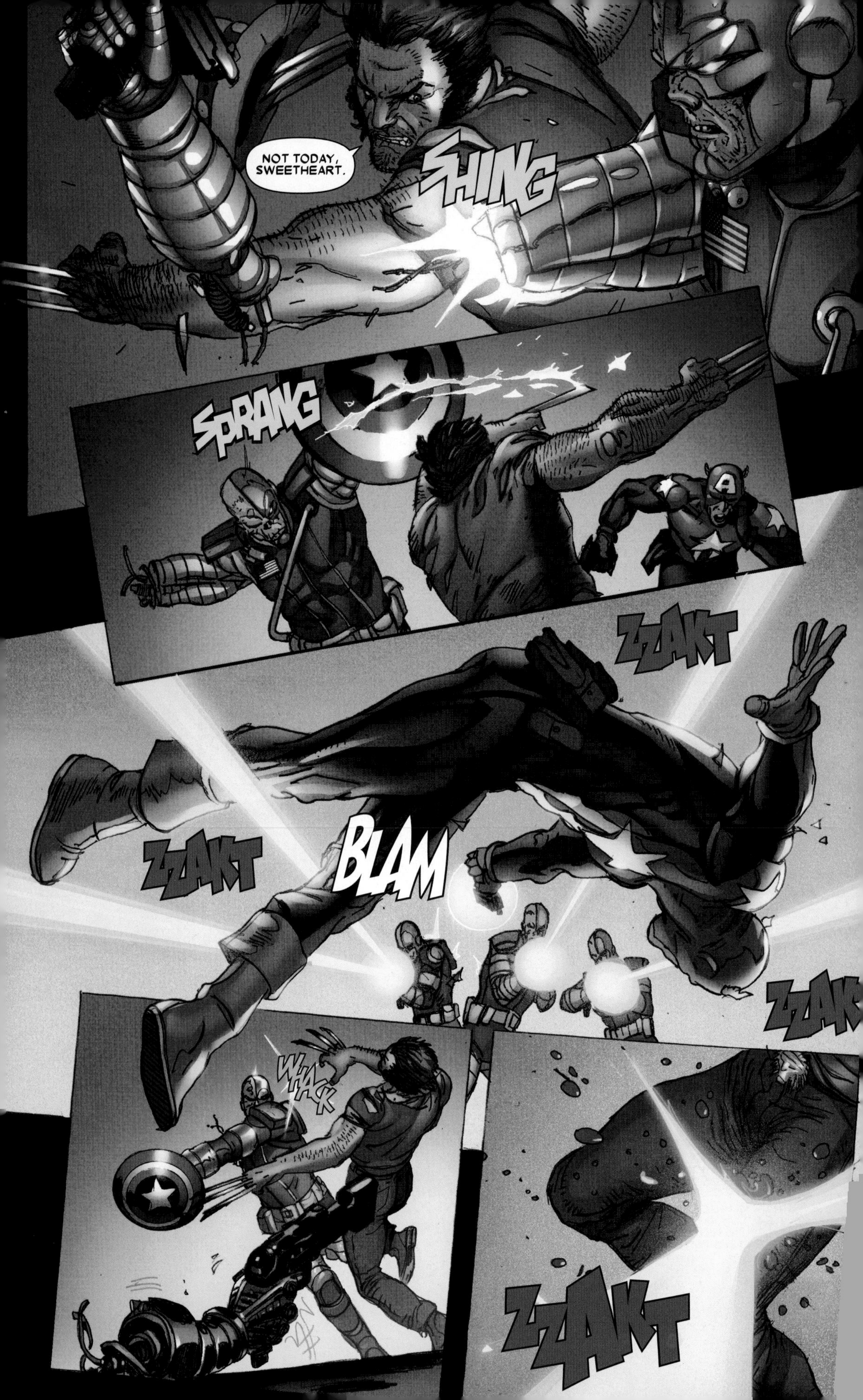
NOT TODAY, SWEETHEART.
SHING
SPRANG
ZZAKT
ZZAKT
BLAM
ZZAK
WHACK
ZZAKT

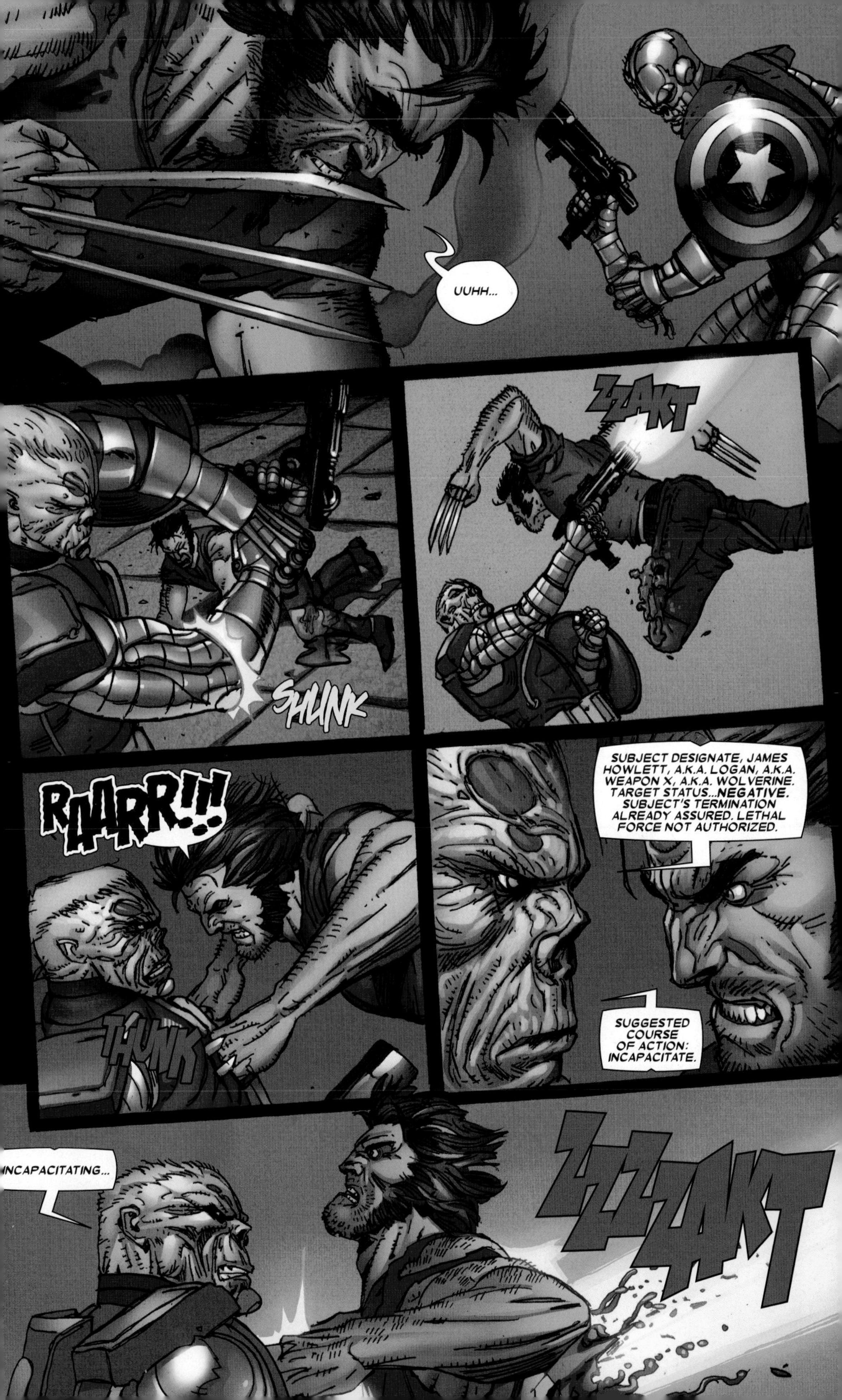
UUHH...
SHUNK
ZZAKT
RAARR!!!
THUNK
SUBJECT DESIGNATE, JAMES HOWLETT, A.K.A. LOGAN, A.K.A. WEAPON X, A.K.A. WOLVERINE. TARGET STATUS...NEGATIVE. SUBJECT'S TERMINATION ALREADY ASSURED. LETHAL FORCE NOT AUTHORIZED.
SUGGESTED COURSE OF ACTION: INCAPACITATE.
INCAPACITATING...
ZZZZAKT

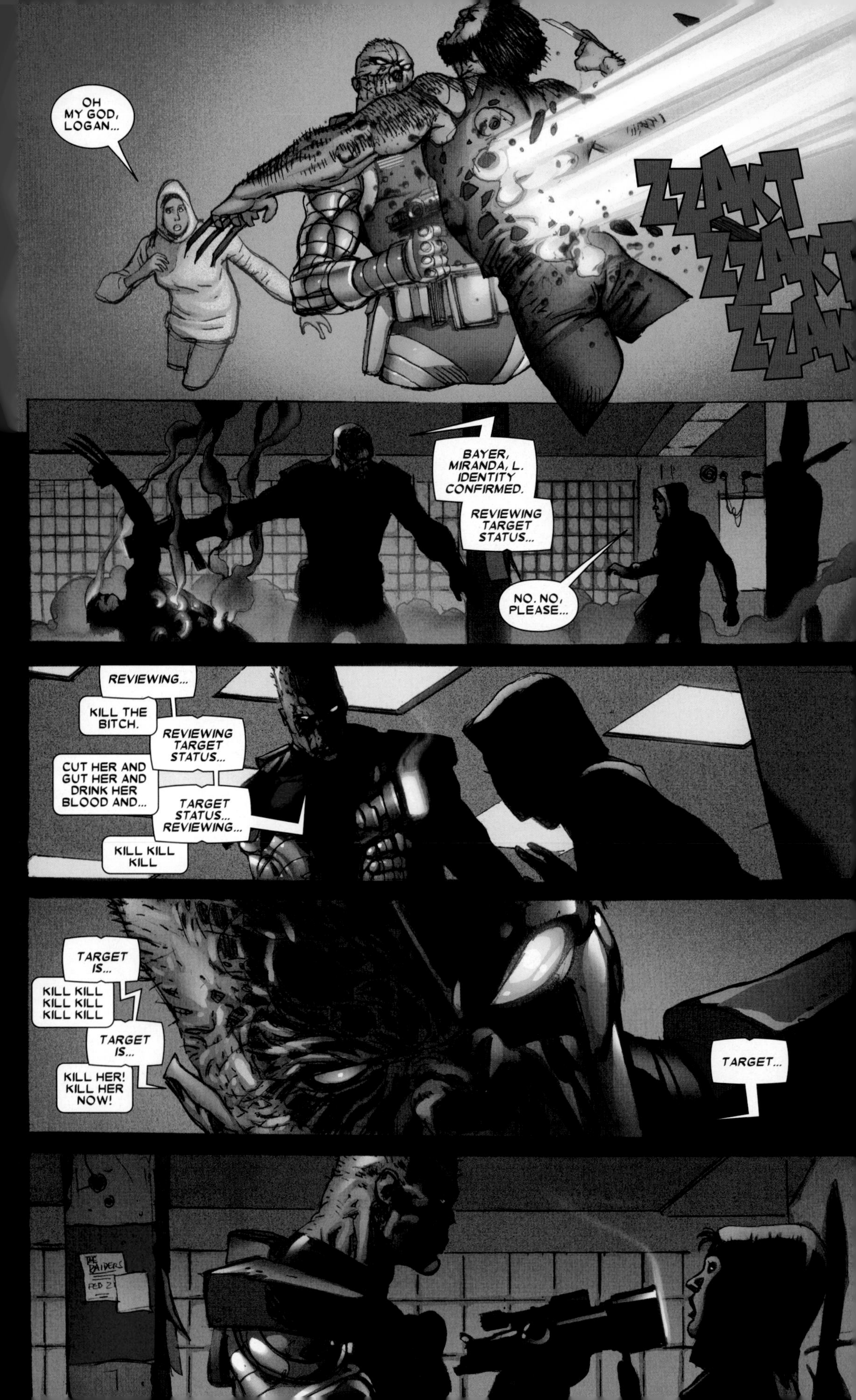
OH MY GOD, LOGAN...
ZZAKT
ZZAKT
BAYER, MIRANDA, L. IDENTITY CONFIRMED.
REVIEWING TARGET STATUS...
NO. NO, PLEASE...
REVIEWING...
KILL THE BITCH.
REVIEWING TARGET STATUS...
CUT HER AND GUT HER AND DRINK HER BLOOD AND...
TARGET STATUS... REVIEWING...
KILL KILL KILL
TARGET IS...
KILL KILL KILL KILL KILL KILL
TARGET IS...
KILL HER! KILL HER NOW!
TARGET...

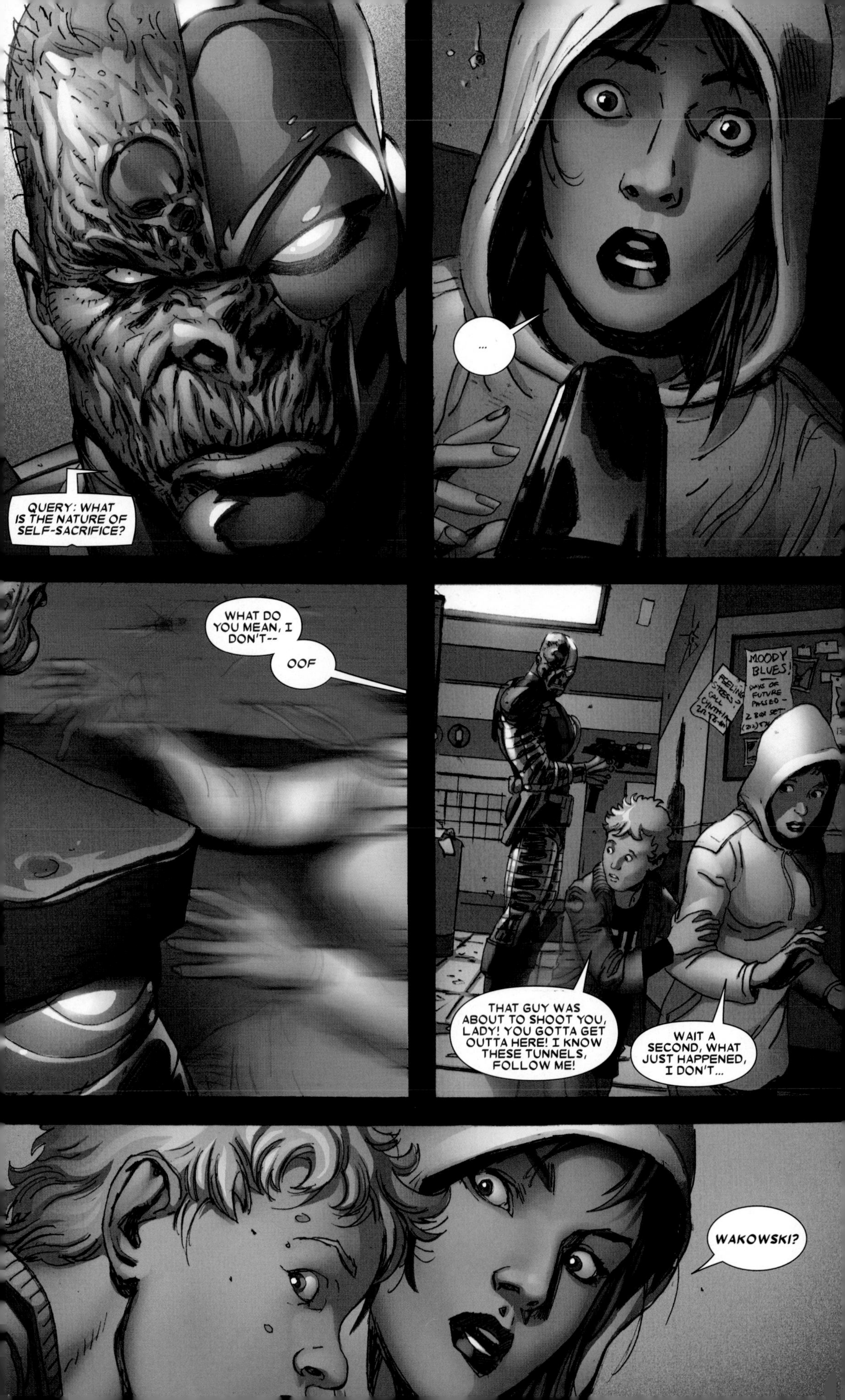
QUERY: WHAT IS THE NATURE OF SELF-SACRIFICE?
...
WHAT DO YOU MEAN, I DON'T--
OOF
MOODY BLUES!
THAT GUY WAS ABOUT TO SHOOT YOU, LADY! YOU GOTTA GET OUTTA HERE! I KNOW THESE TUNNELS, FOLLOW ME!
WAIT A SECOND, WHAT JUST HAPPENED, I DON'T...
WAKOWSKI?

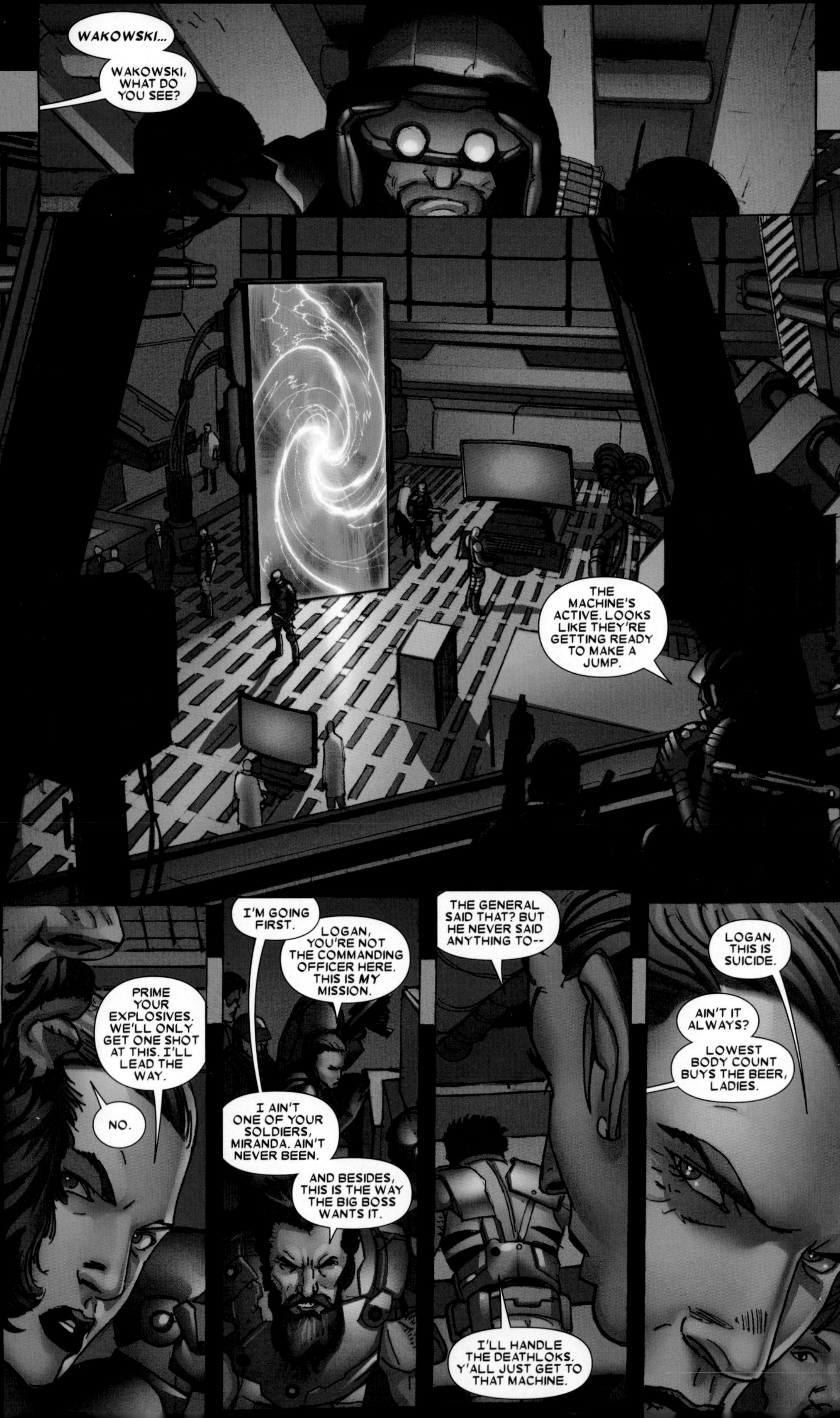
WAKOWSKI...
WAKOWSKI, WHAT DO YOU SEE?
THE MACHINE'S ACTIVE. LOOKS LIKE THEY'RE GETTING READY TO MAKE A JUMP.
PRIME YOUR EXPLOSIVES. WE'LL ONLY GET ONE SHOT AT THIS. I'LL LEAD THE WAY.
NO.
I'M GOING FIRST.
LOGAN, YOU'RE NOT THE COMMANDING OFFICER HERE. THIS IS MY MISSION.
I AIN'T ONE OF YOUR SOLDIERS, MIRANDA. AIN'T NEVER BEEN.
AND BESIDES, THIS IS THE WAY THE BIG BOSS WANTS IT.
THE GENERAL SAID THAT? BUT HE NEVER SAID ANYTHING TO--
I'LL HANDLE THE DEATHLOKS. Y'ALL JUST GET TO THAT MACHINE.
LOGAN, THIS IS SUICIDE.
AIN'T IT ALWAYS?
LOWEST BODY COUNT BUYS THE BEER, LADIES.

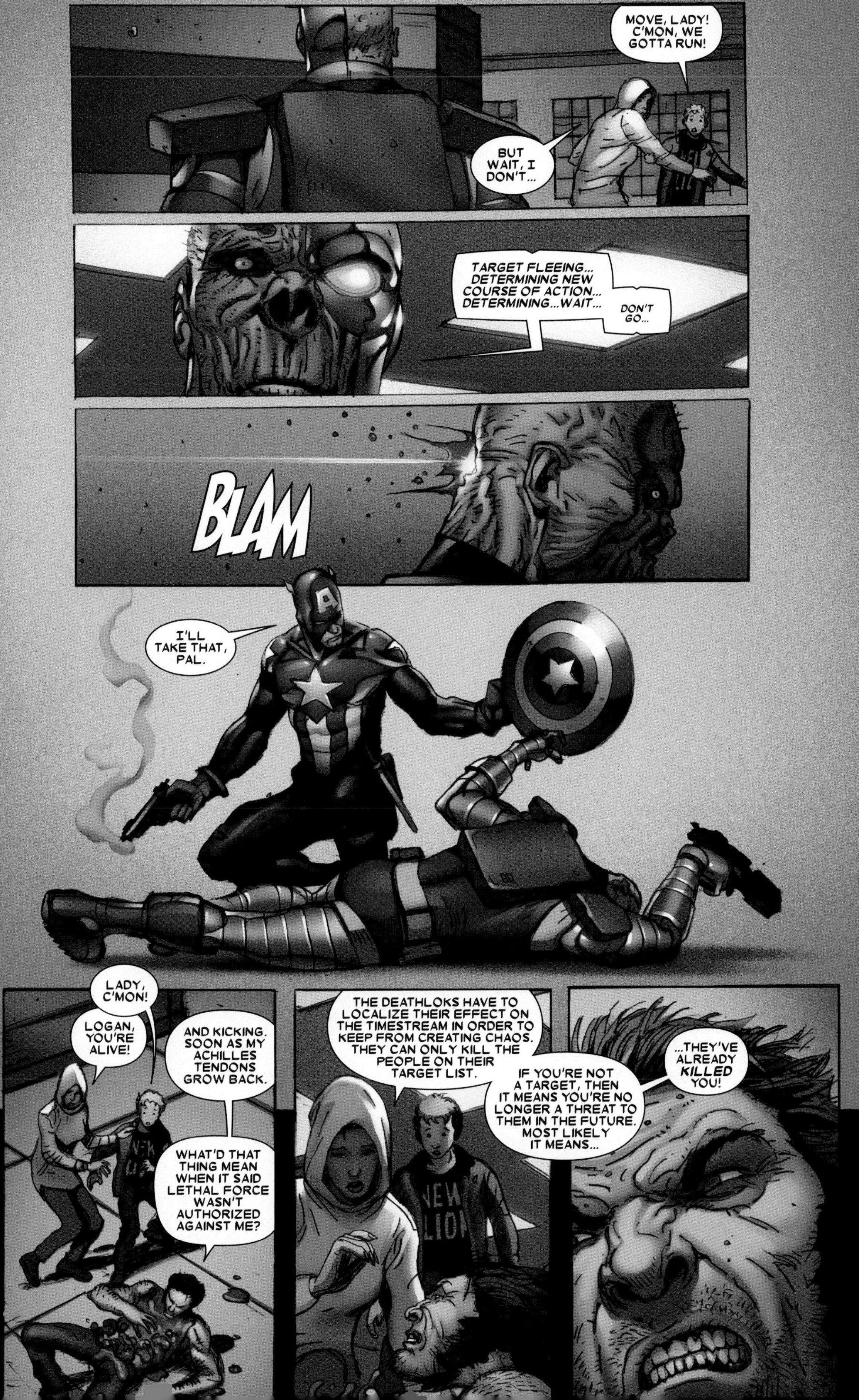
MOVE, LADY! C'MON, WE GOTTA RUN!
BUT WAIT, I DON'T...
TARGET FLEEING... DETERMINING NEW COURSE OF ACTION... DETERMINING...WAIT...
DON'T GO...
BLAM
I'LL TAKE THAT, PAL.
LADY, C'MON!
LOGAN, YOU'RE ALIVE!
AND KICKING. SOON AS MY ACHILLES TENDONS GROW BACK.
WHAT'D THAT THING MEAN WHEN IT SAID LETHAL FORCE WASN'T AUTHORIZED AGAINST ME?
THE DEATHLOKS HAVE TO LOCALIZE THEIR EFFECT ON THE TIMESTREAM IN ORDER TO KEEP FROM CREATING CHAOS. THEY CAN ONLY KILL THE PEOPLE ON THEIR TARGET LIST.
IF YOU'RE NOT A TARGET, THEN IT MEANS YOU'RE NO LONGER A THREAT TO THEM IN THE FUTURE. MOST LIKELY IT MEANS...
...THEY'VE ALREADY *KILLED* YOU!

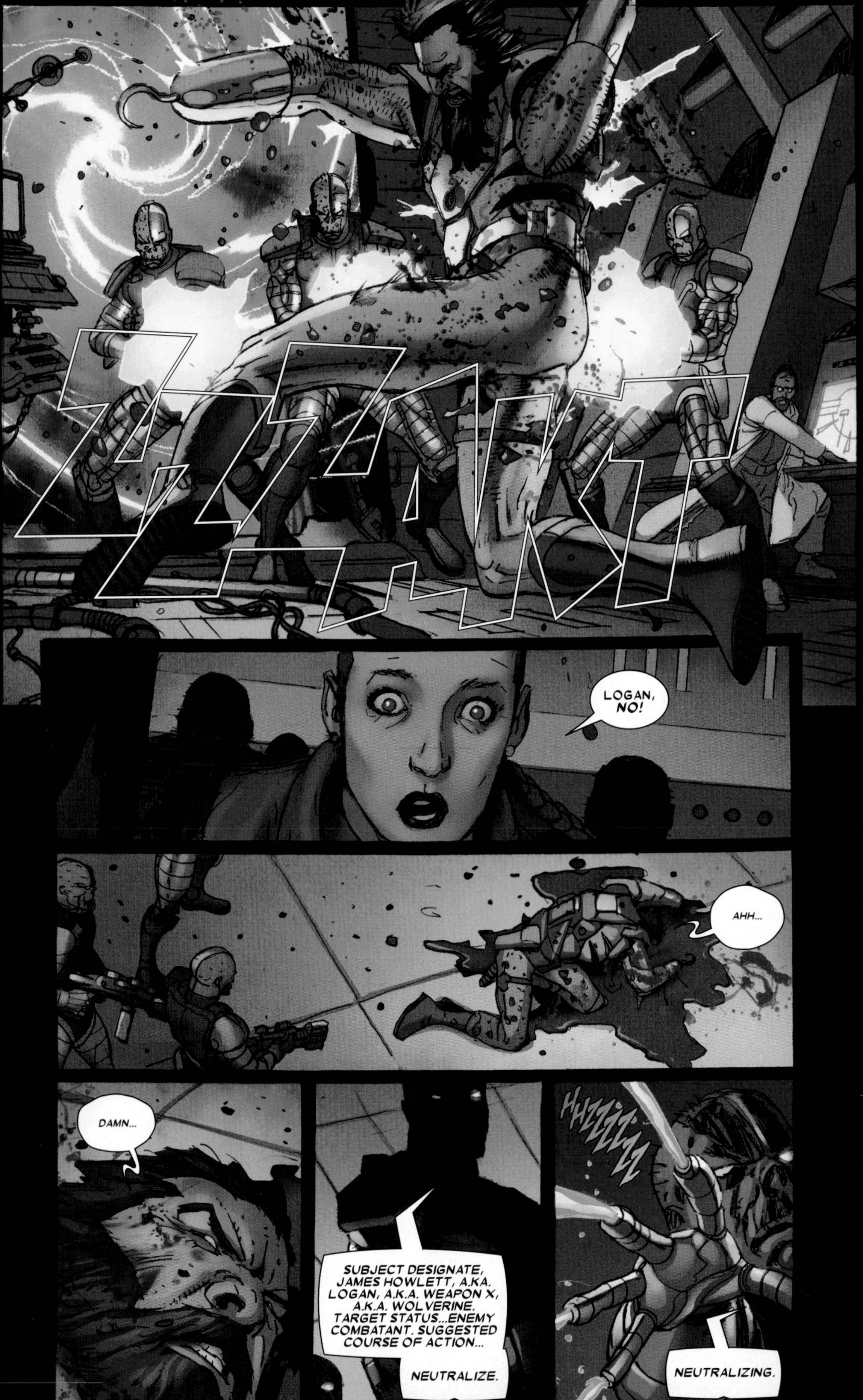
LOGAN, NO!
AHH...
DAMN...
SUBJECT DESIGNATE, JAMES HOWLETT, A.K.A. LOGAN, A.K.A. WEAPON X, A.K.A. WOLVERINE. TARGET STATUS...ENEMY COMBATANT. SUGGESTED COURSE OF ACTION...
NEUTRALIZE.
NEUTRALIZING.

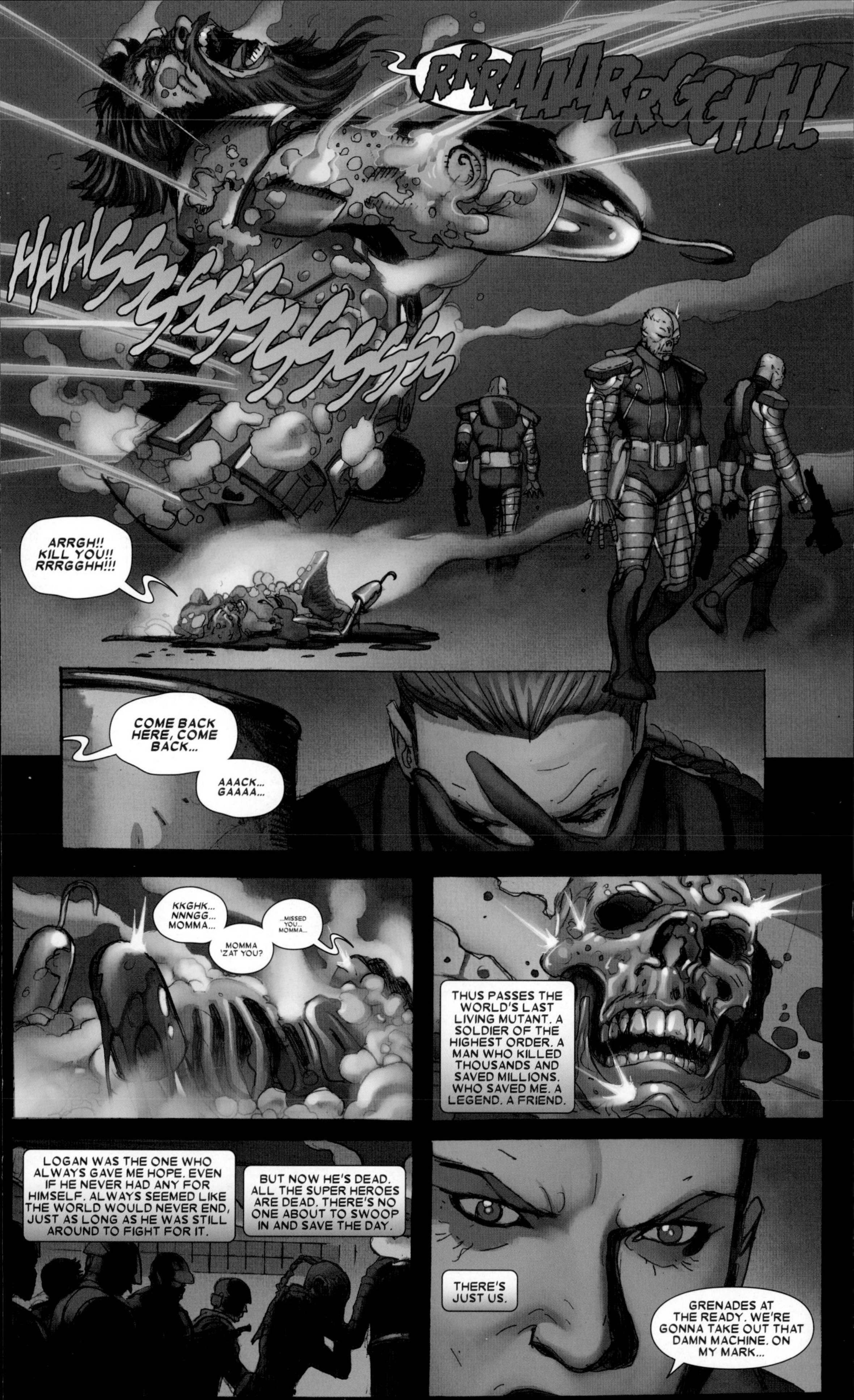

RRRAAARRGHH!
HUHSSSSSSSSSSS
ARRGH!! KILL YOU!! RRRGGHH!!!
COME BACK HERE, COME BACK...
AAACK... GAAAA...
KKGHK... NNNGG... MOMMA...
MOMMA 'ZAT YOU?
...MISSED YOU... MOMMA...
THUS PASSES THE WORLD'S LAST LIVING MUTANT. A SOLDIER OF THE HIGHEST ORDER. A MAN WHO KILLED THOUSANDS AND SAVED MILLIONS. WHO SAVED ME. A LEGEND. A FRIEND.
LOGAN WAS THE ONE WHO ALWAYS GAVE ME HOPE. EVEN IF HE NEVER HAD ANY FOR HIMSELF. ALWAYS SEEMED LIKE THE WORLD WOULD NEVER END, JUST AS LONG AS HE WAS STILL AROUND TO FIGHT FOR IT.
BUT NOW HE'S DEAD. ALL THE SUPER HEROES ARE DEAD. THERE'S NO ONE ABOUT TO SWOOP IN AND SAVE THE DAY.
THERE'S JUST US.
GRENADES AT THE READY. WE'RE GONNA TAKE OUT THAT DAMN MACHINE. ON MY MARK...

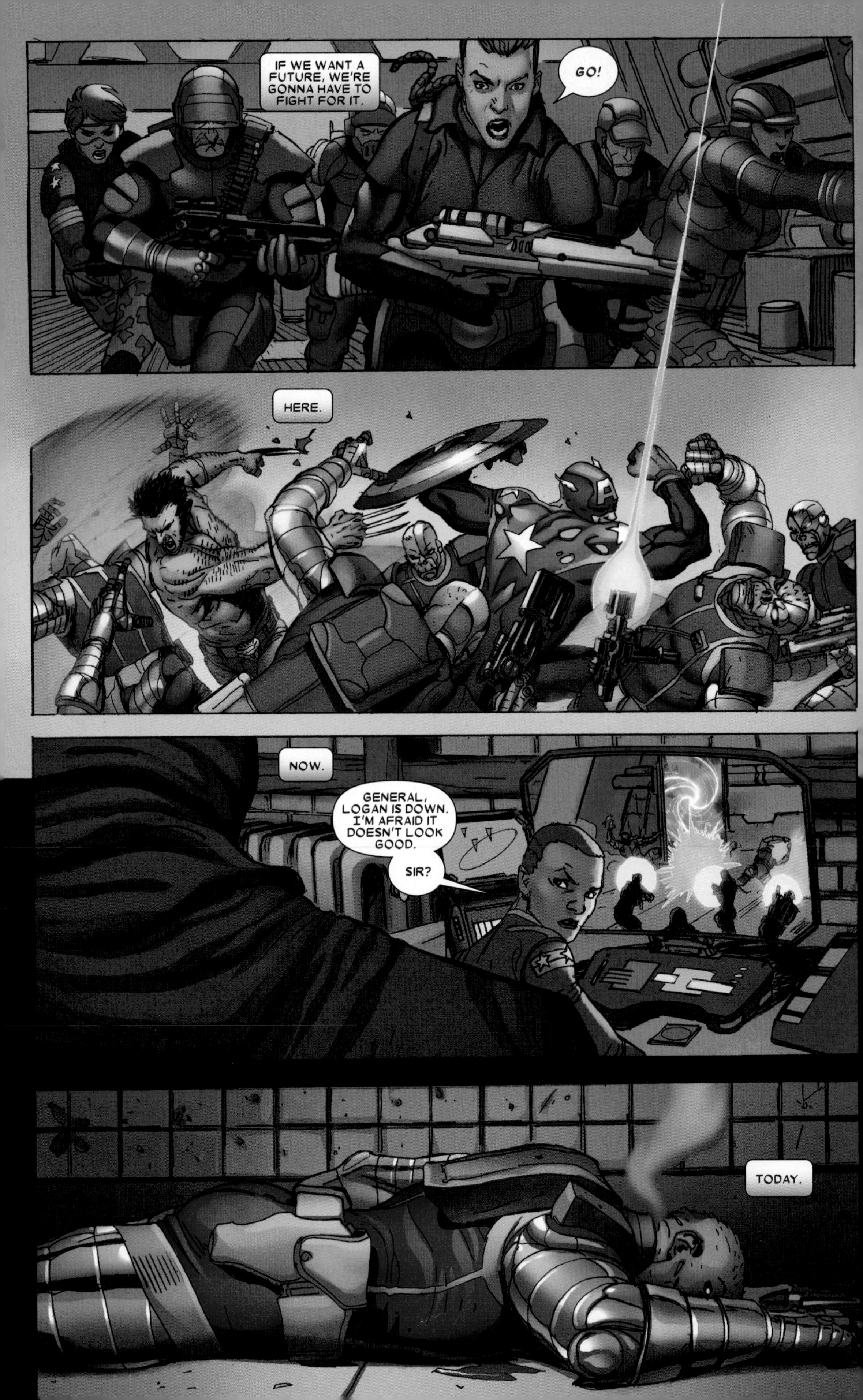
IF WE WANT A FUTURE, WE'RE GONNA HAVE TO FIGHT FOR IT.
GO!
HERE.
NOW.
GENERAL, LOGAN IS DOWN. I'M AFRAID IT DOESN'T LOOK GOOD.
SIR?
TODAY.

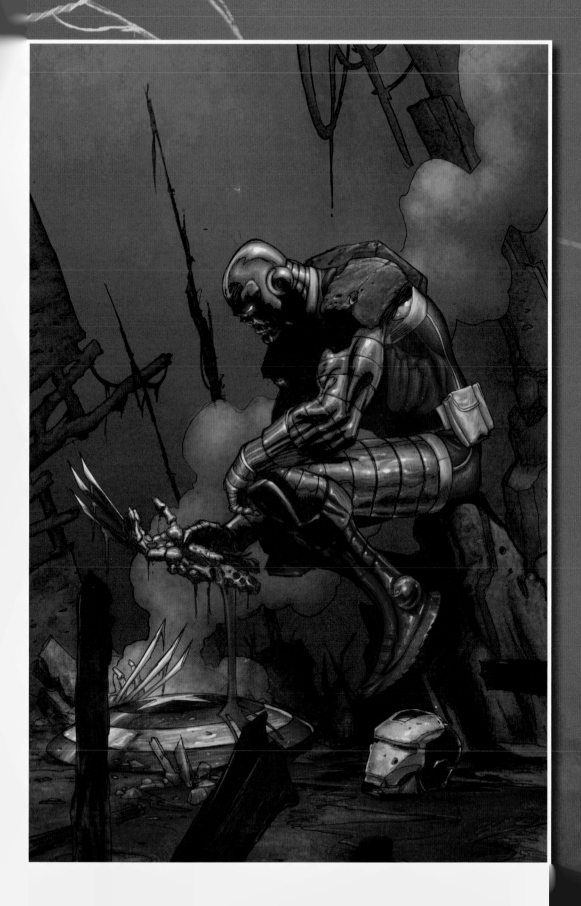

DOWN WITH THE MILITA... INDUSTRIA... COMPLE...

SAY NO TO ROXXON, YES TO FREE THOUGHT!

...XXON ...IES

WE ARE NOT YOUR DRONE...

ROXXON = MURDER

ROXXON = GREED

ROXXON = LIES

ONE TWO THREE FOUR, WE ARE NOT YOUR CORPORATE WHORE! ONE TWO THREE FOUR...

SOUTH GATE TO CONTROL. MOB REFUSES TO DISPERSE. REQUEST YOU DISPATCH *CROWD CONTROL*, OVER.

ROGER THAT. DISPATCHING.

FFRRZZZTTT

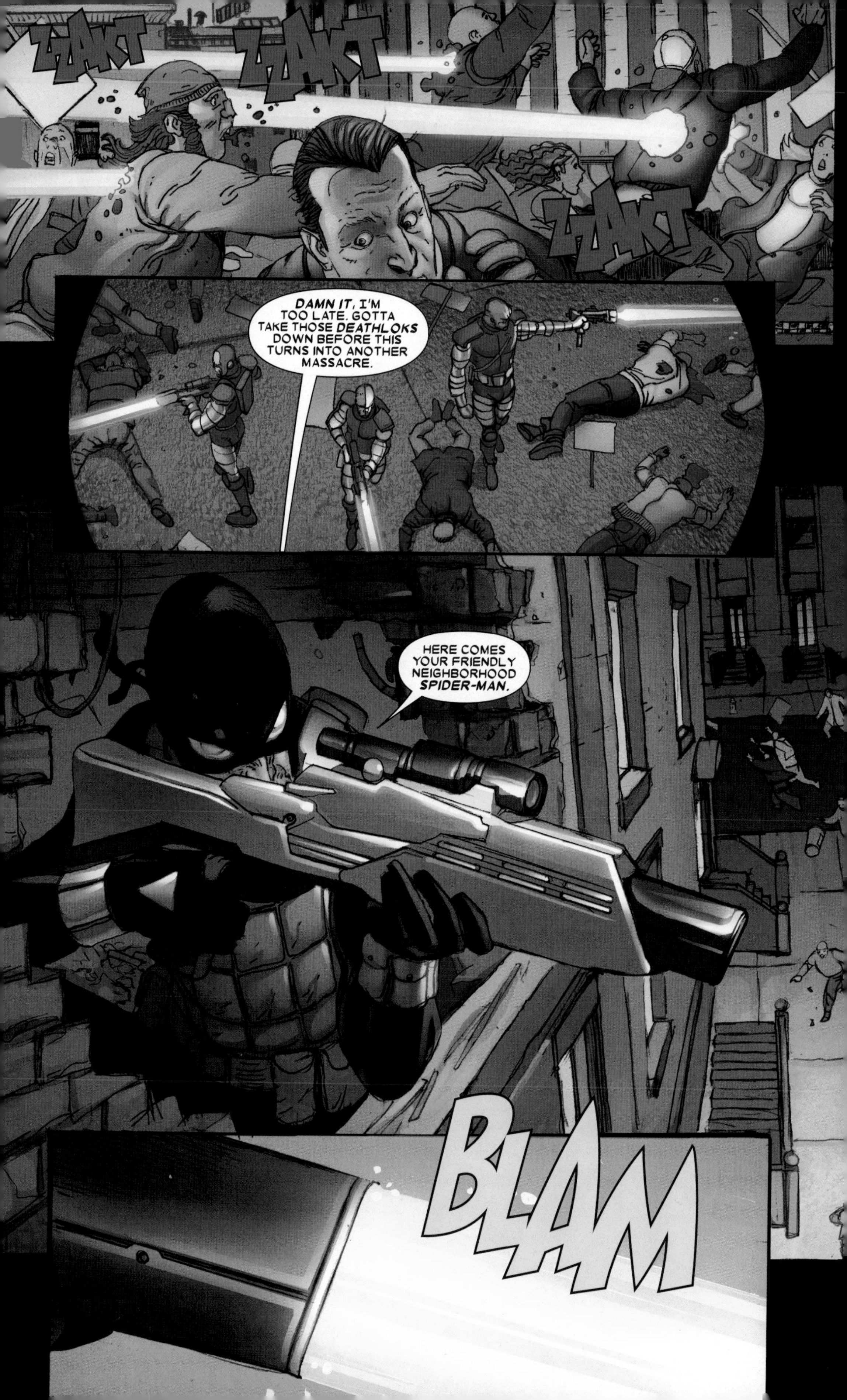
ZZAKT
ZZAKT
ZZAKT
DAMN IT, I'M TOO LATE. GOTTA TAKE THOSE DEATHLOKS DOWN BEFORE THIS TURNS INTO ANOTHER MASSACRE.
HERE COMES YOUR FRIENDLY NEIGHBORHOOD SPIDER-MAN.
BLAM

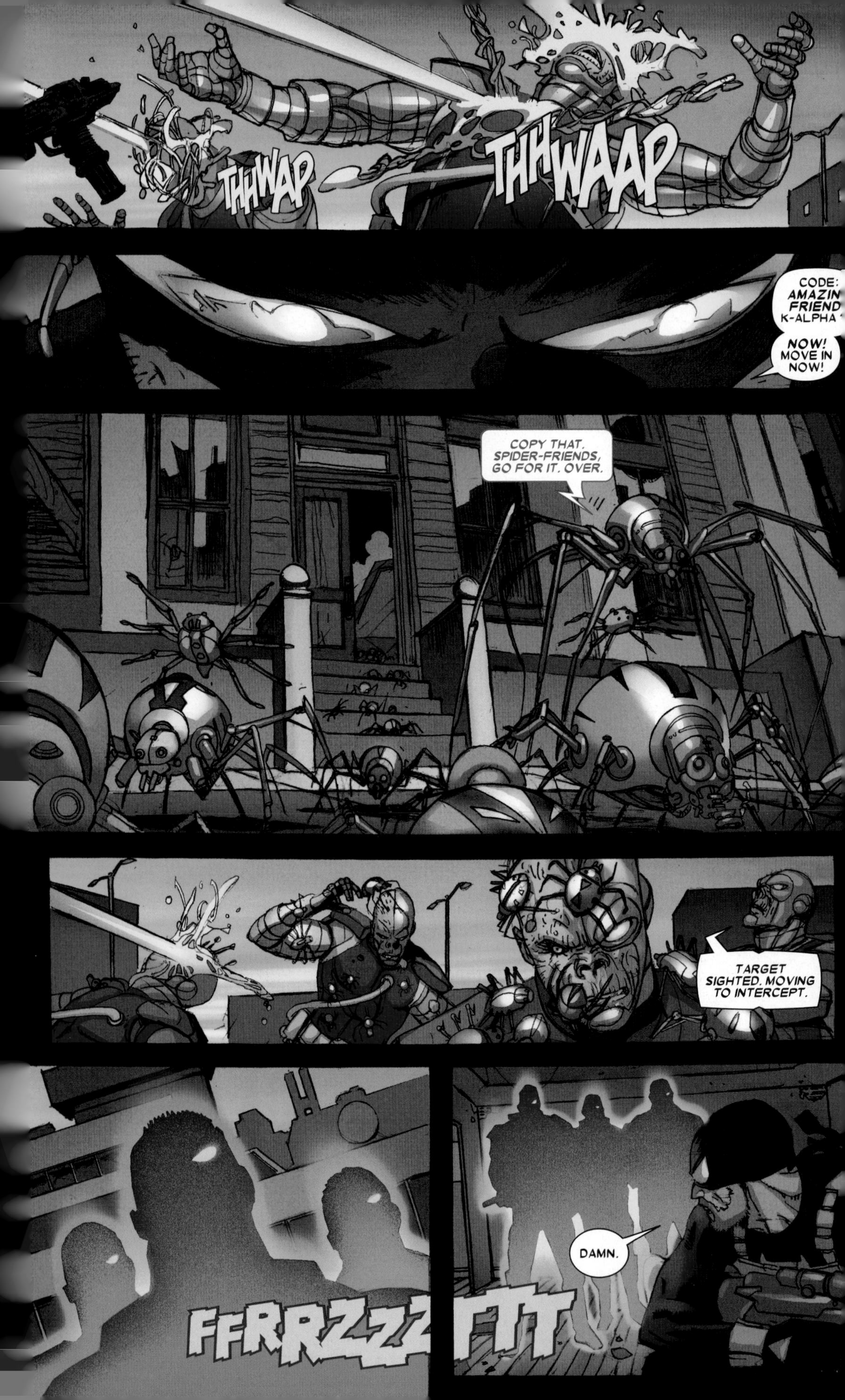
THHWAP
THHWAAP
CODE: AMAZIN FRIEND K-ALPHA
NOW! MOVE IN NOW!
COPY THAT. SPIDER-FRIENDS, GO FOR IT. OVER.
TARGET SIGHTED. MOVING TO INTERCEPT.
FFRRZZZZTTT
DAMN.

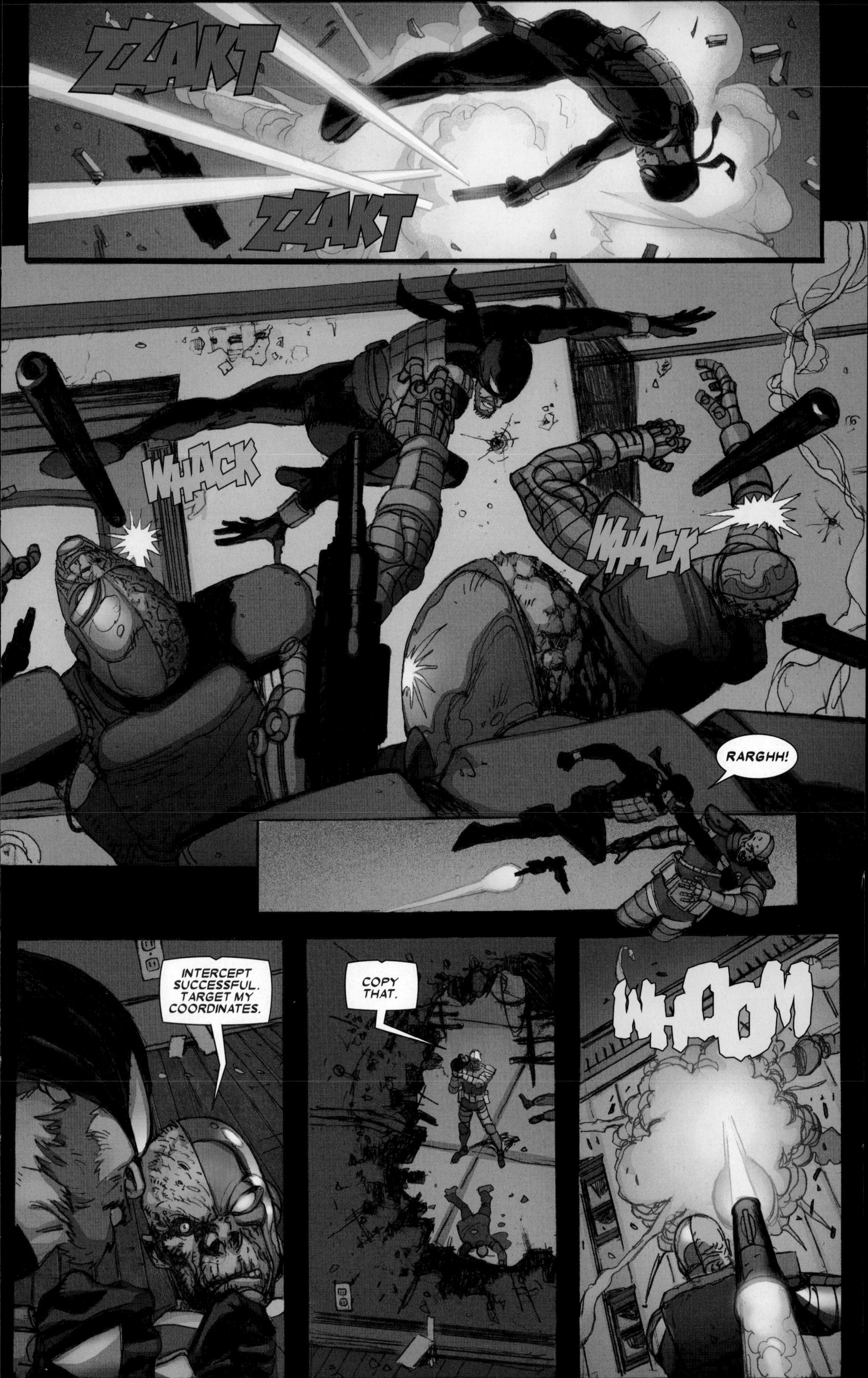
ZZAKT
ZZAKT
WHACK
WHACK
RARGHH!
INTERCEPT SUCCESSFUL. TARGET MY COORDINATES.
COPY THAT.
WHOOM

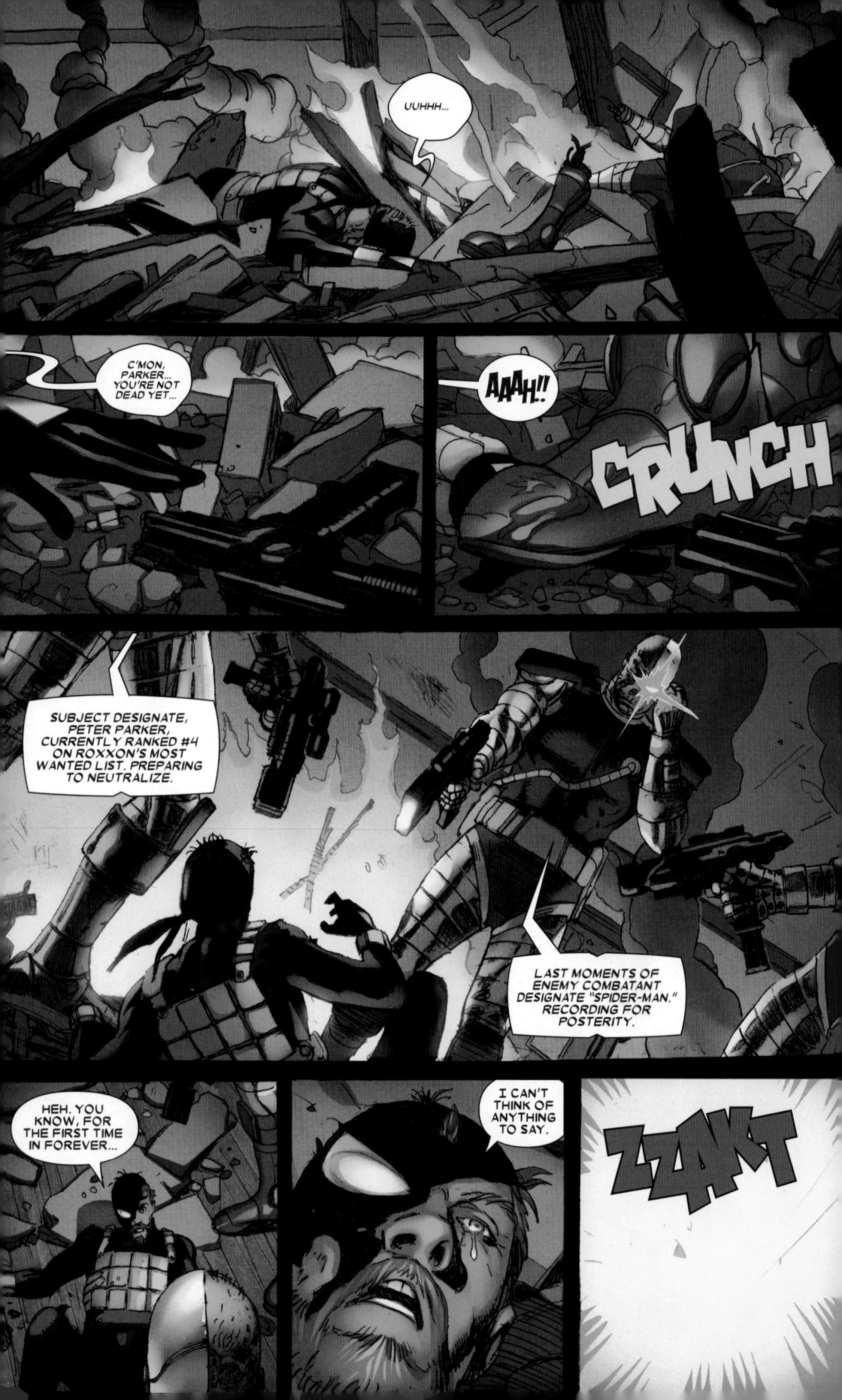
UUHHH...
C'MON, PARKER... YOU'RE NOT DEAD YET...
AAAH!!
CRUNCH
SUBJECT DESIGNATE, PETER PARKER, CURRENTLY RANKED #4 ON ROXXON'S MOST WANTED LIST. PREPARING TO NEUTRALIZE.
LAST MOMENTS OF ENEMY COMBATANT DESIGNATE "SPIDER-MAN." RECORDING FOR POSTERITY.
HEH. YOU KNOW, FOR THE FIRST TIME IN FOREVER...
I CAN'T THINK OF ANYTHING TO SAY.
ZZAKT

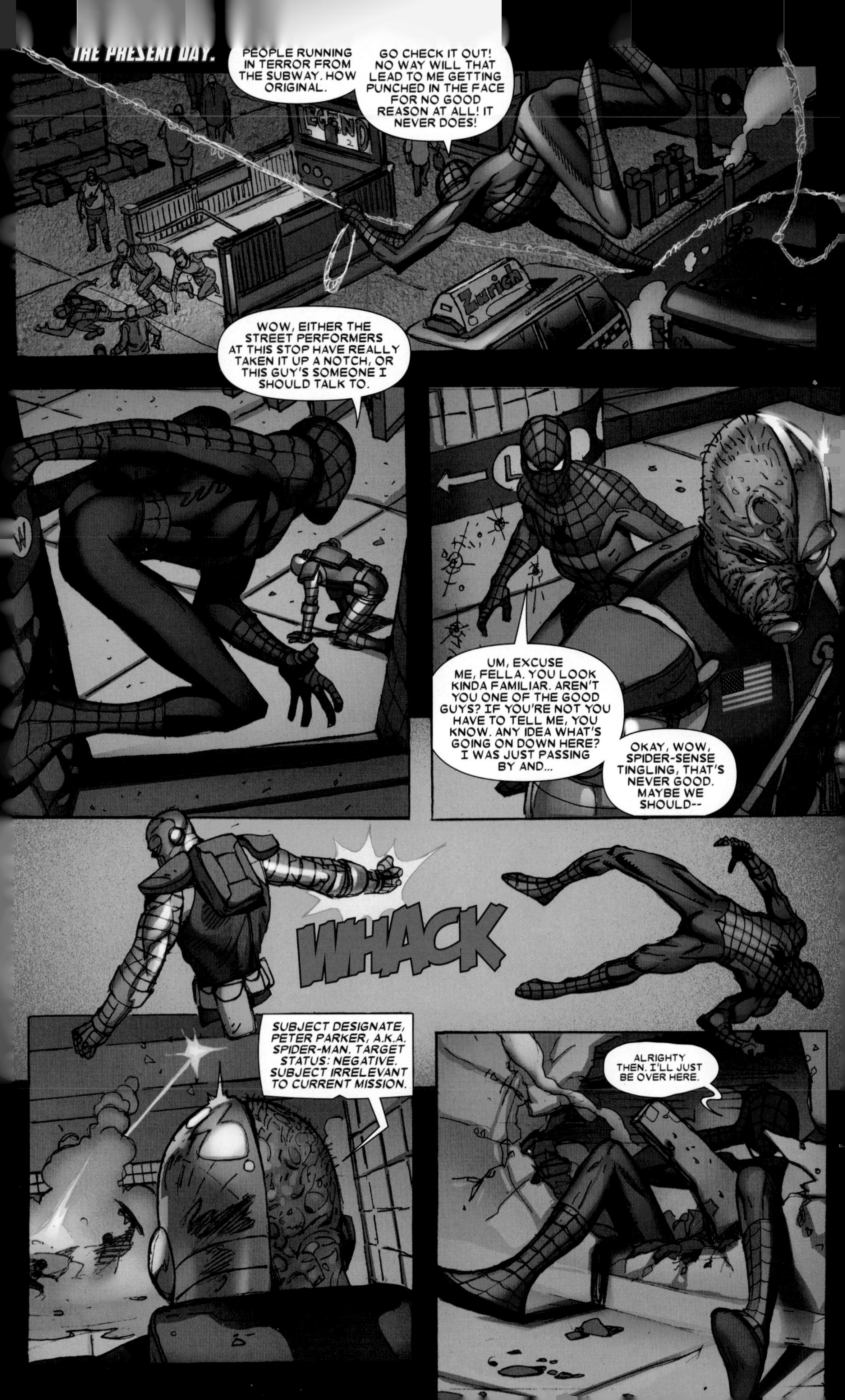
THE PRESENT DAY.
PEOPLE RUNNING IN TERROR FROM THE SUBWAY. HOW ORIGINAL.
GO CHECK IT OUT! NO WAY WILL THAT LEAD TO ME GETTING PUNCHED IN THE FACE FOR NO GOOD REASON AT ALL! IT NEVER DOES!
Zurich
WOW, EITHER THE STREET PERFORMERS AT THIS STOP HAVE REALLY TAKEN IT UP A NOTCH, OR THIS GUY'S SOMEONE I SHOULD TALK TO.
UM, EXCUSE ME, FELLA. YOU LOOK KINDA FAMILIAR. AREN'T YOU ONE OF THE GOOD GUYS? IF YOU'RE NOT YOU HAVE TO TELL ME, YOU KNOW. ANY IDEA WHAT'S GOING ON DOWN HERE? I WAS JUST PASSING BY AND...
OKAY, WOW, SPIDER-SENSE TINGLING, THAT'S NEVER GOOD. MAYBE WE SHOULD--
WHACK
SUBJECT DESIGNATE, PETER PARKER, A.K.A. SPIDER-MAN. TARGET STATUS: NEGATIVE. SUBJECT IRRELEVANT TO CURRENT MISSION.
ALRIGHTY THEN. I'LL JUST BE OVER HERE.

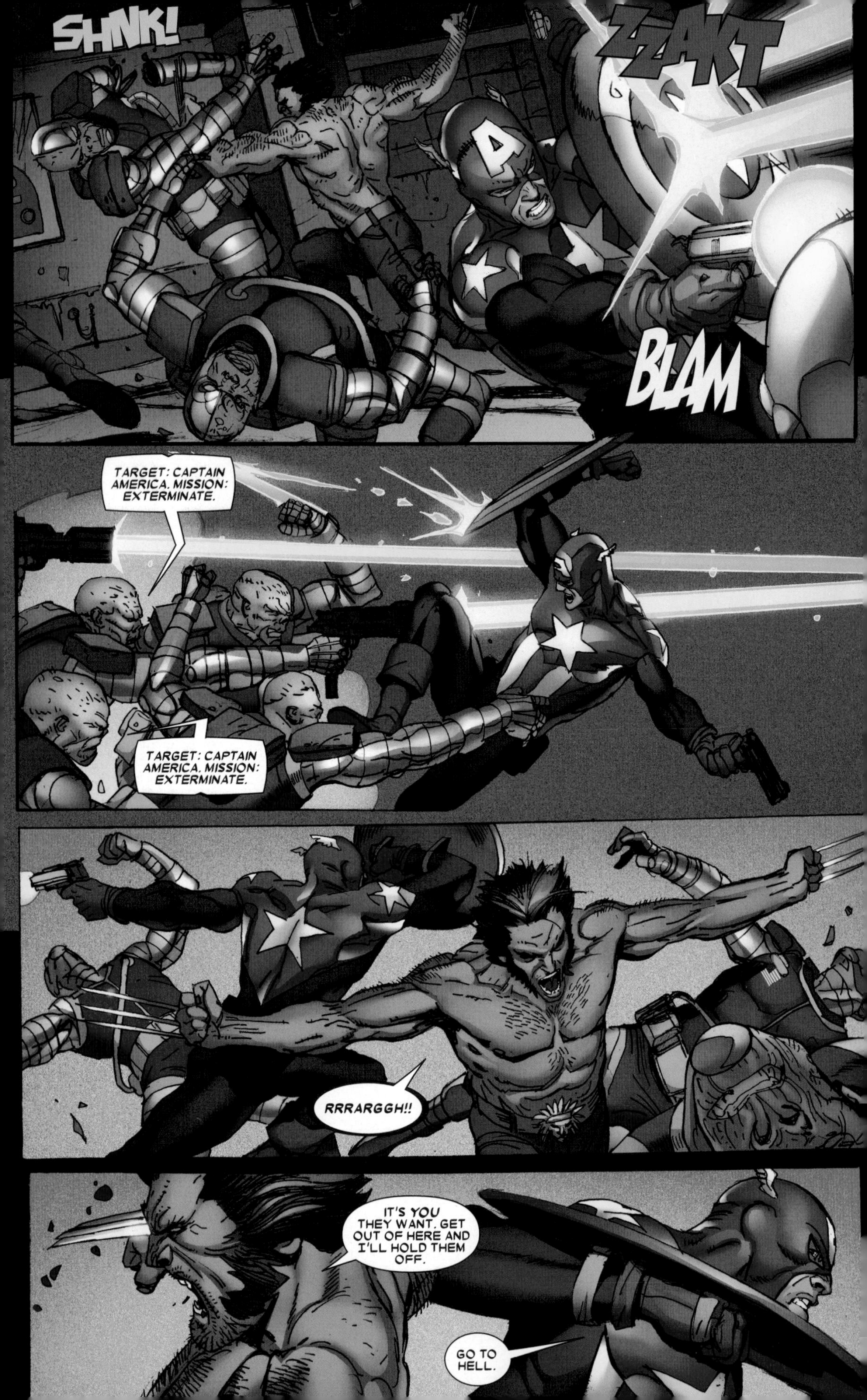
SHNK!
ZZAKT
BLAM
TARGET: CAPTAIN AMERICA. MISSION: EXTERMINATE.
TARGET: CAPTAIN AMERICA. MISSION: EXTERMINATE.
RRRARGGH!!
IT'S YOU THEY WANT. GET OUT OF HERE AND I'LL HOLD THEM OFF.
GO TO HELL.

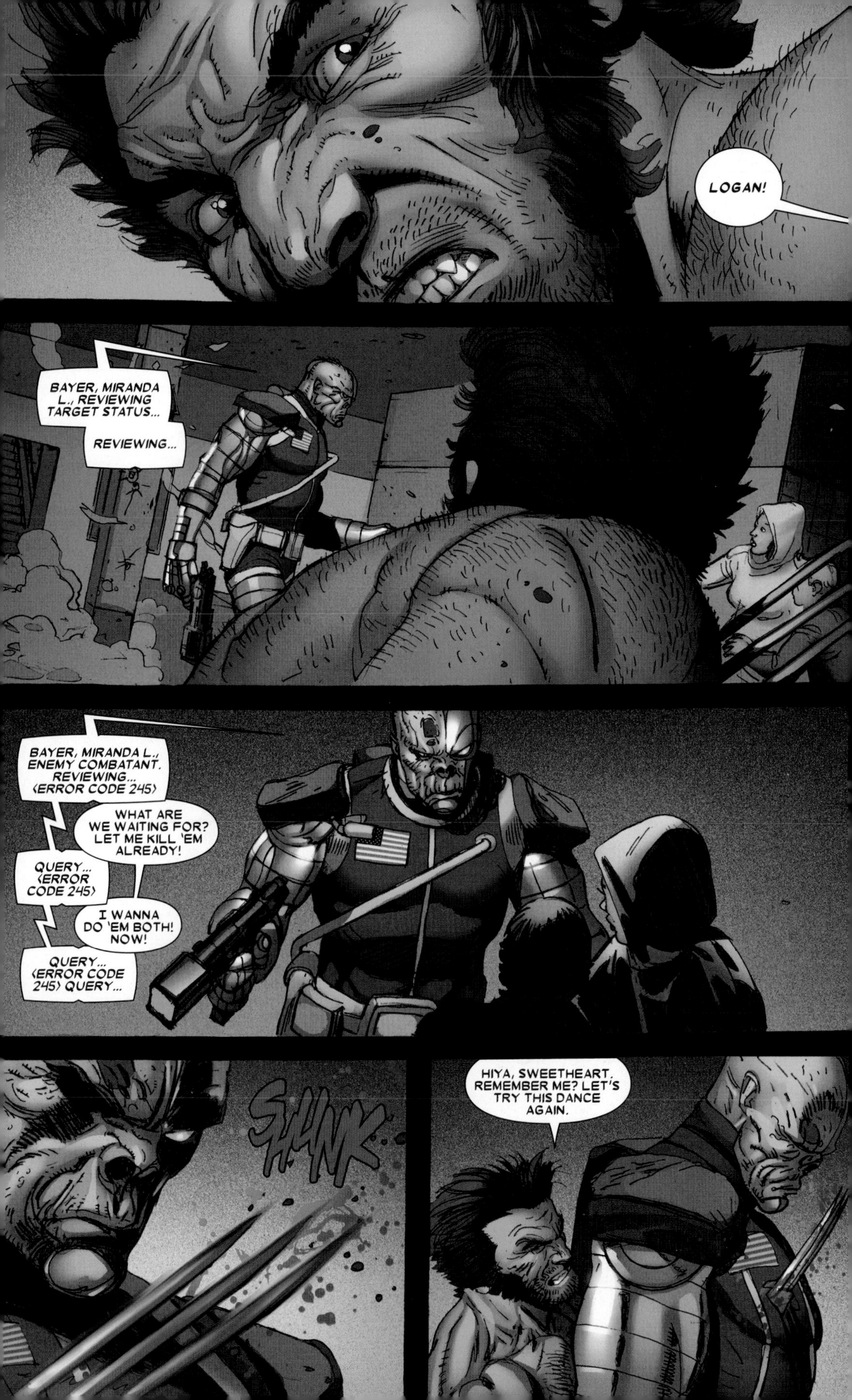
LOGAN!
BAYER, MIRANDA L., REVIEWING TARGET STATUS...
REVIEWING...
BAYER, MIRANDA L., ENEMY COMBATANT. REVIEWING... ‹ERROR CODE 245›
WHAT ARE WE WAITING FOR? LET ME KILL 'EM ALREADY!
QUERY... ‹ERROR CODE 245›
I WANNA DO 'EM BOTH! NOW!
QUERY... ‹ERROR CODE 245› QUERY...
SHUNK
HIYA, SWEETHEART. REMEMBER ME? LET'S TRY THIS DANCE AGAIN.

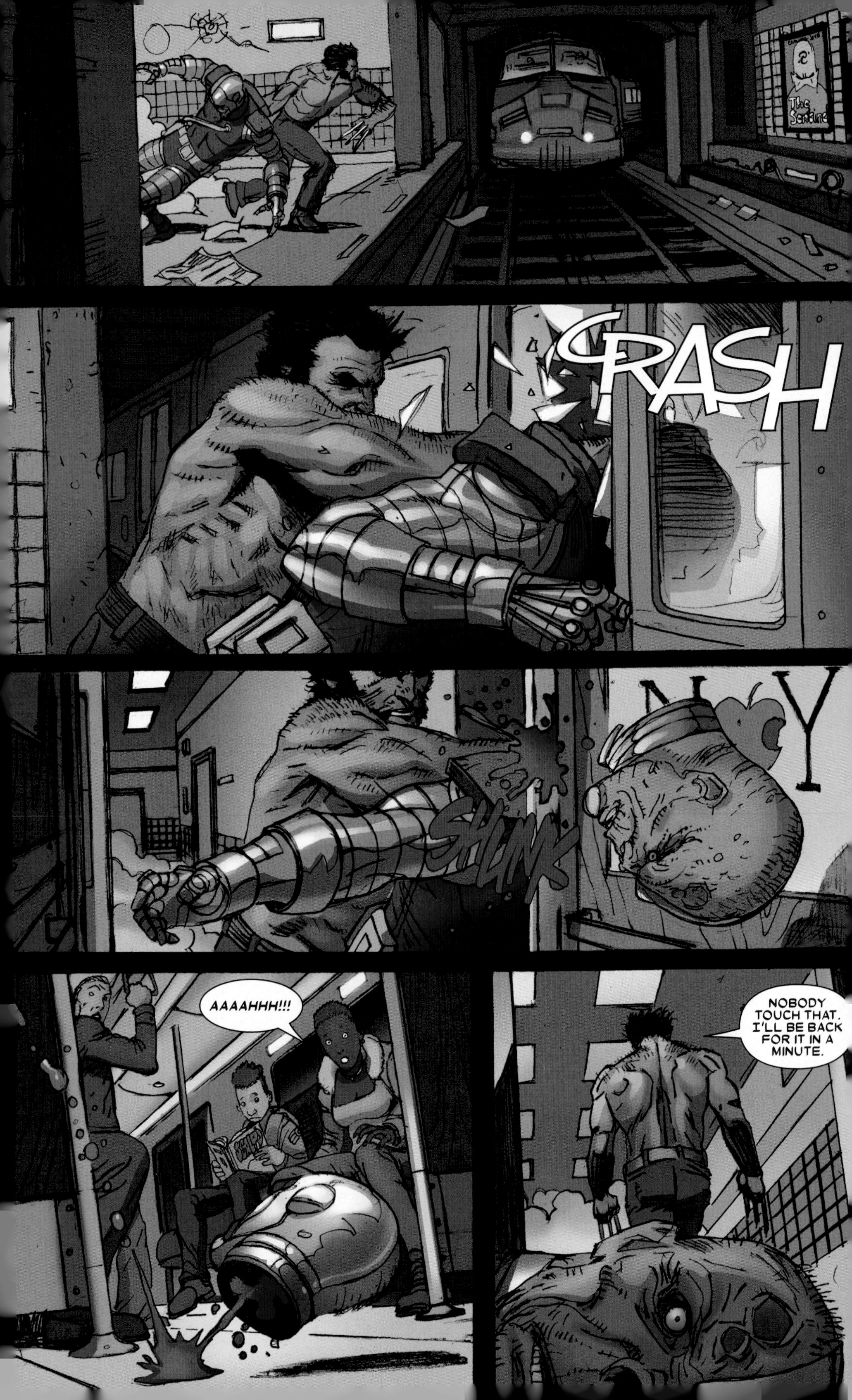
CRASH
SHUNK
AAAAHHH!!!
NOBODY TOUCH THAT. I'LL BE BACK FOR IT IN A MINUTE.

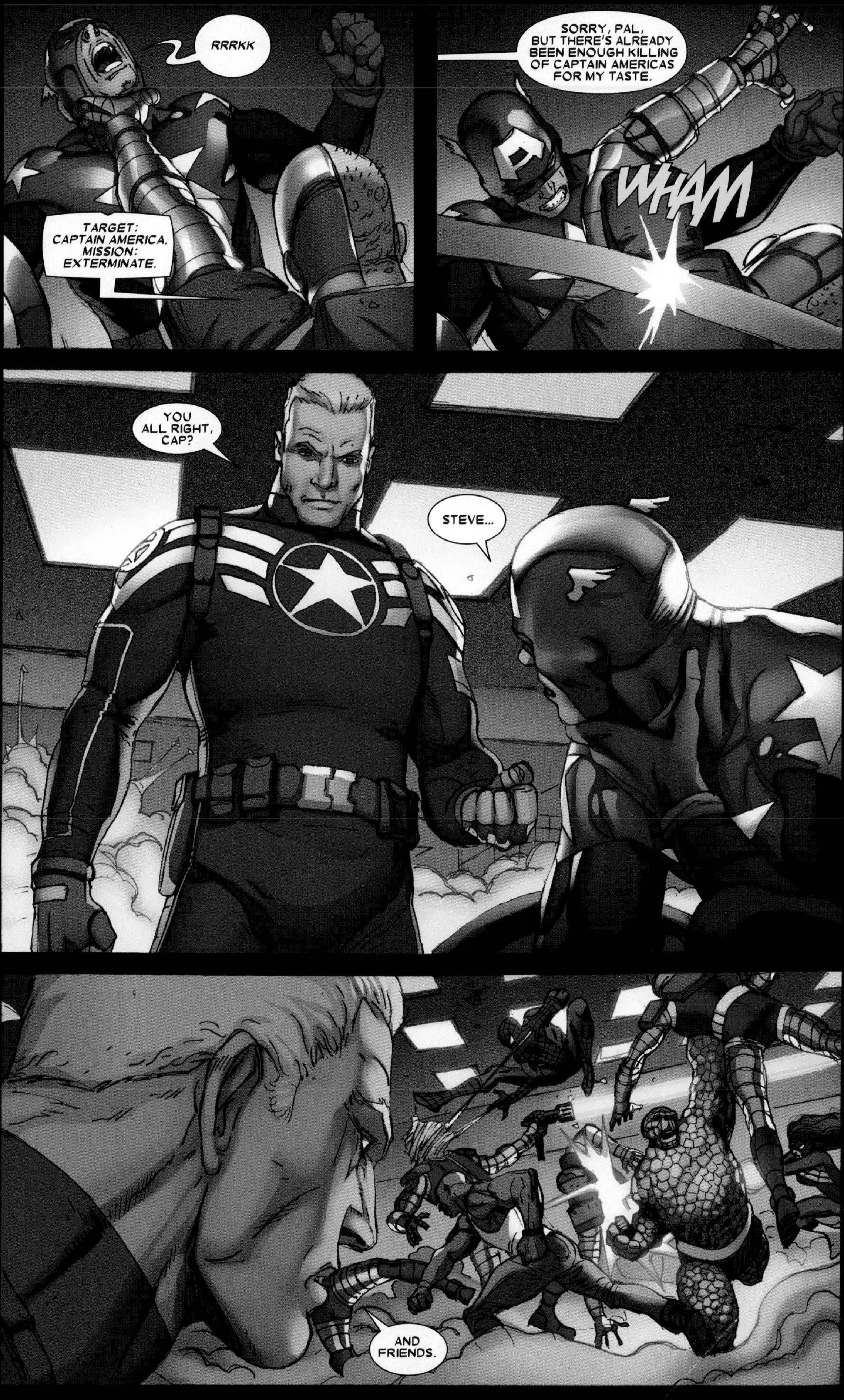
RRRKK
TARGET: CAPTAIN AMERICA. MISSION: EXTERMINATE.
SORRY, PAL, BUT THERE'S ALREADY BEEN ENOUGH KILLING OF CAPTAIN AMERICAS FOR MY TASTE.
WHAM
YOU ALL RIGHT, CAP?
STEVE...
AND FRIENDS.

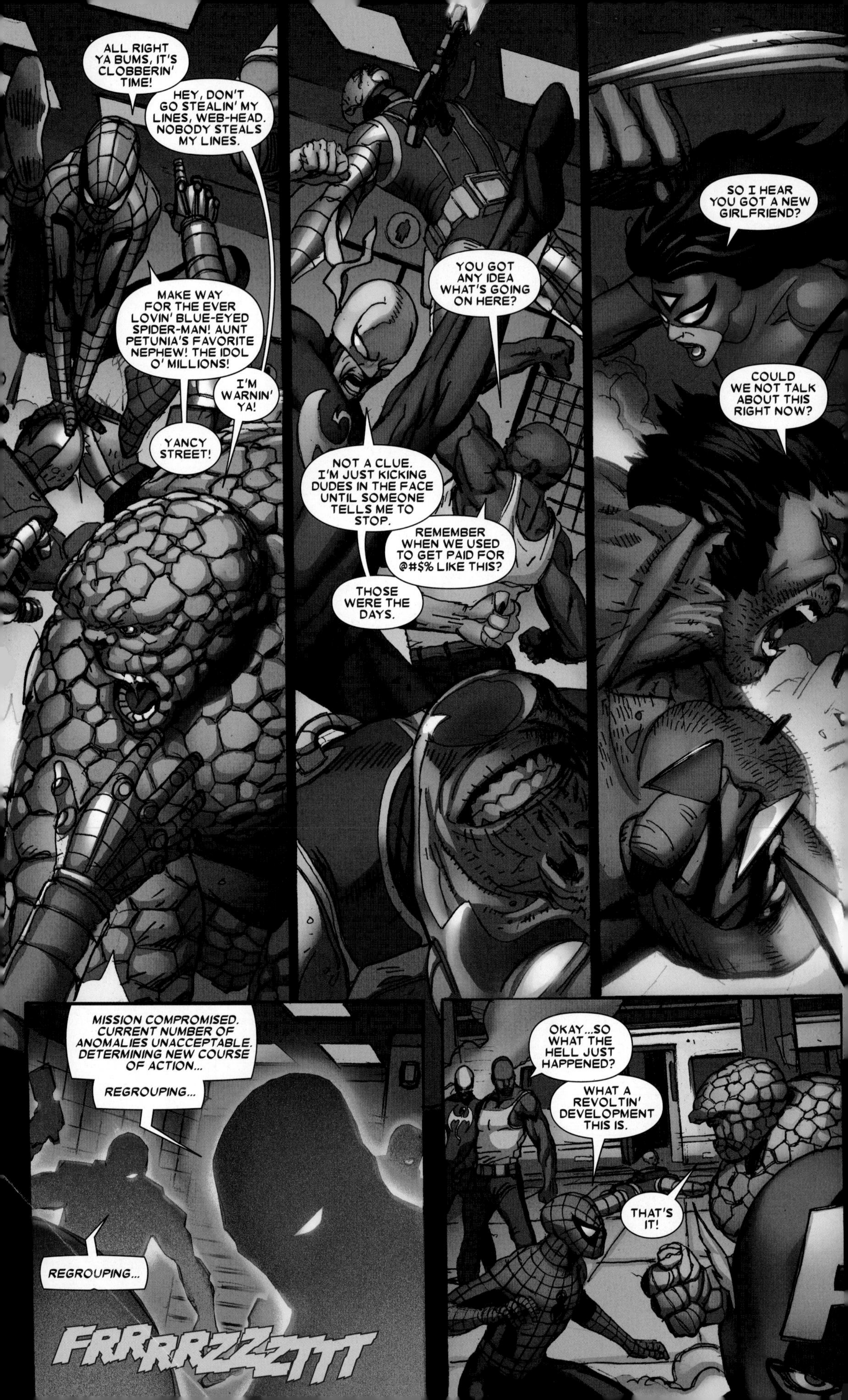
ALL RIGHT YA BUMS, IT'S CLOBBERIN' TIME!
HEY, DON'T GO STEALIN' MY LINES, WEB-HEAD. NOBODY STEALS MY LINES.
MAKE WAY FOR THE EVER LOVIN' BLUE-EYED SPIDER-MAN! AUNT PETUNIA'S FAVORITE NEPHEW! THE IDOL O' MILLIONS!
I'M WARNIN' YA!
YANCY STREET!
YOU GOT ANY IDEA WHAT'S GOING ON HERE?
NOT A CLUE. I'M JUST KICKING DUDES IN THE FACE UNTIL SOMEONE TELLS ME TO STOP.
REMEMBER WHEN WE USED TO GET PAID FOR @#$% LIKE THIS?
THOSE WERE THE DAYS.
SO I HEAR YOU GOT A NEW GIRLFRIEND?
COULD WE NOT TALK ABOUT THIS RIGHT NOW?
MISSION COMPROMISED. CURRENT NUMBER OF ANOMALIES UNACCEPTABLE. DETERMINING NEW COURSE OF ACTION...
REGROUPING...
REGROUPING...
FRRRRZZZZTTTT
OKAY...SO WHAT THE HELL JUST HAPPENED?
WHAT A REVOLTIN' DEVELOPMENT THIS IS.
THAT'S IT!

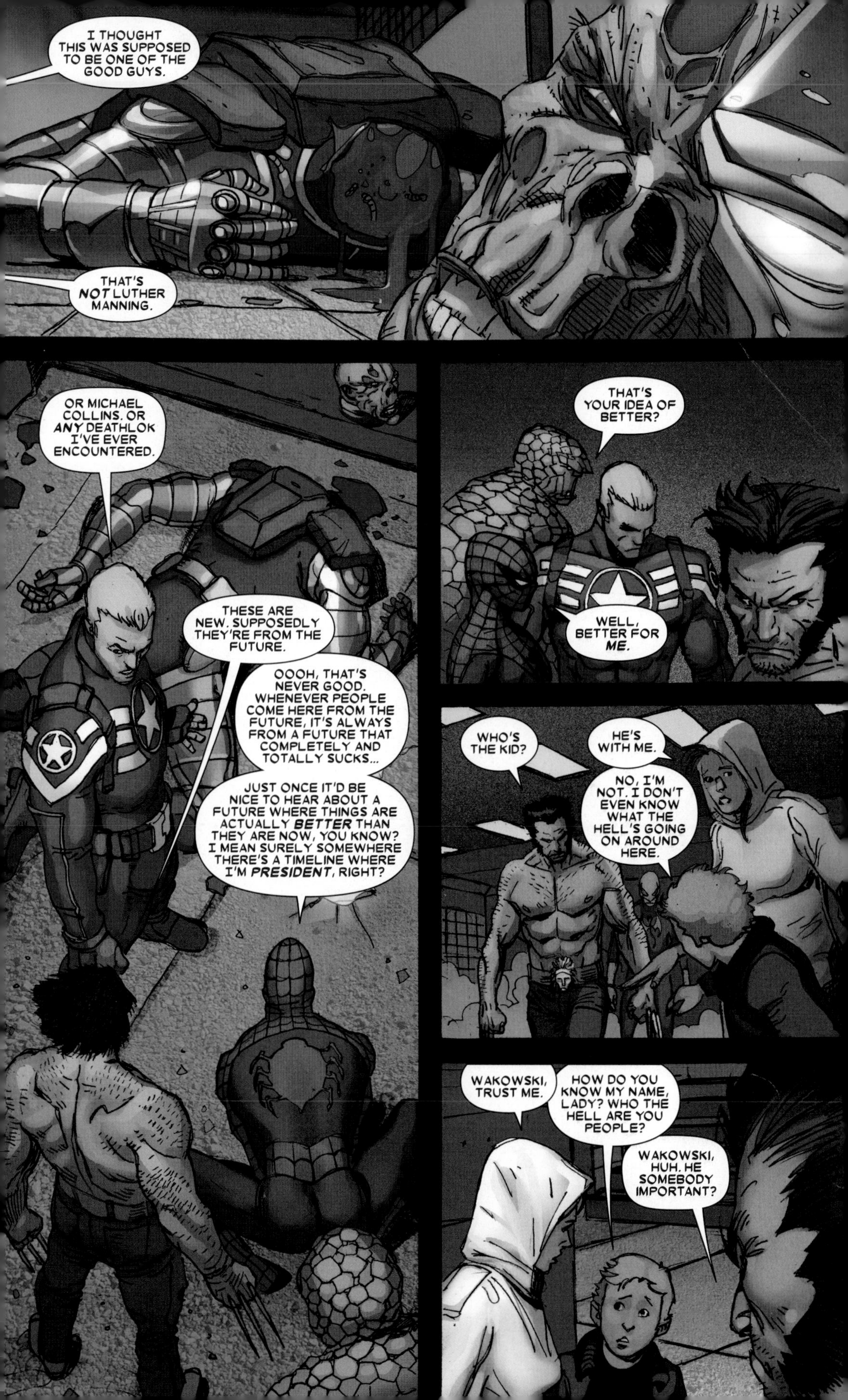
I THOUGHT THIS WAS SUPPOSED TO BE ONE OF THE GOOD GUYS.
THAT'S NOT LUTHER MANNING.
OR MICHAEL COLLINS. OR ANY DEATHLOK I'VE EVER ENCOUNTERED.
THESE ARE NEW. SUPPOSEDLY THEY'RE FROM THE FUTURE.
OOOH, THAT'S NEVER GOOD. WHENEVER PEOPLE COME HERE FROM THE FUTURE, IT'S ALWAYS FROM A FUTURE THAT COMPLETELY AND TOTALLY SUCKS...
JUST ONCE IT'D BE NICE TO HEAR ABOUT A FUTURE WHERE THINGS ARE ACTUALLY BETTER THAN THEY ARE NOW, YOU KNOW? I MEAN SURELY SOMEWHERE THERE'S A TIMELINE WHERE I'M PRESIDENT, RIGHT?
THAT'S YOUR IDEA OF BETTER?
WELL, BETTER FOR ME.
WHO'S THE KID?
HE'S WITH ME.
NO, I'M NOT. I DON'T EVEN KNOW WHAT THE HELL'S GOING ON AROUND HERE.
WAKOWSKI, TRUST ME.
HOW DO YOU KNOW MY NAME, LADY? WHO THE HELL ARE YOU PEOPLE?
WAKOWSKI, HUH. HE SOMEBODY IMPORTANT?

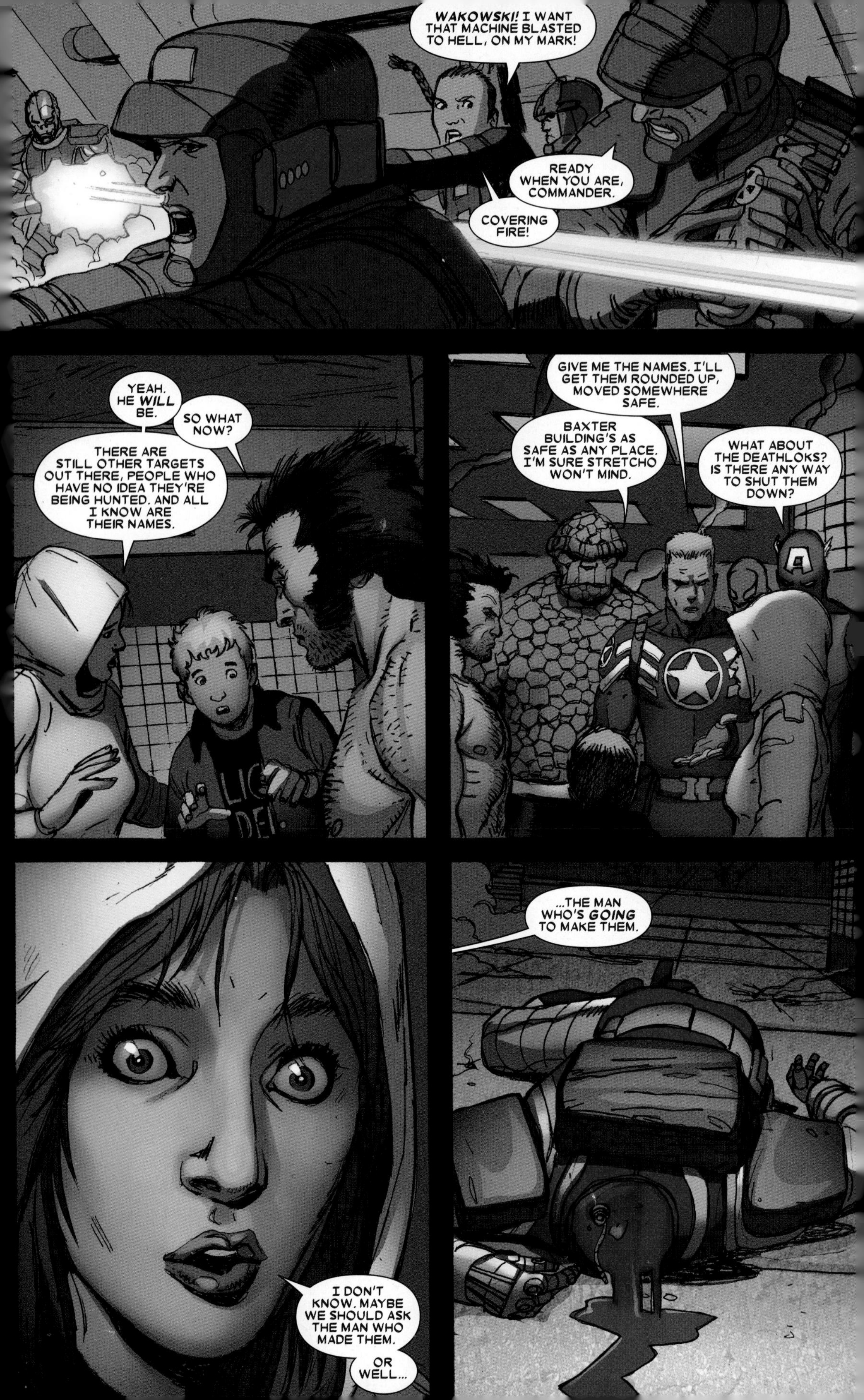
WAKOWSKI! I WANT THAT MACHINE BLASTED TO HELL, ON MY MARK!
READY WHEN YOU ARE, COMMANDER.
COVERING FIRE!
YEAH. HE WILL BE.
SO WHAT NOW?
THERE ARE STILL OTHER TARGETS OUT THERE, PEOPLE WHO HAVE NO IDEA THEY'RE BEING HUNTED. AND ALL I KNOW ARE THEIR NAMES.
GIVE ME THE NAMES. I'LL GET THEM ROUNDED UP, MOVED SOMEWHERE SAFE.
BAXTER BUILDING'S AS SAFE AS ANY PLACE. I'M SURE STRETCHO WON'T MIND.
WHAT ABOUT THE DEATHLOKS? IS THERE ANY WAY TO SHUT THEM DOWN?
I DON'T KNOW. MAYBE WE SHOULD ASK THE MAN WHO MADE THEM.
OR WELL...
...THE MAN WHO'S GOING TO MAKE THEM.

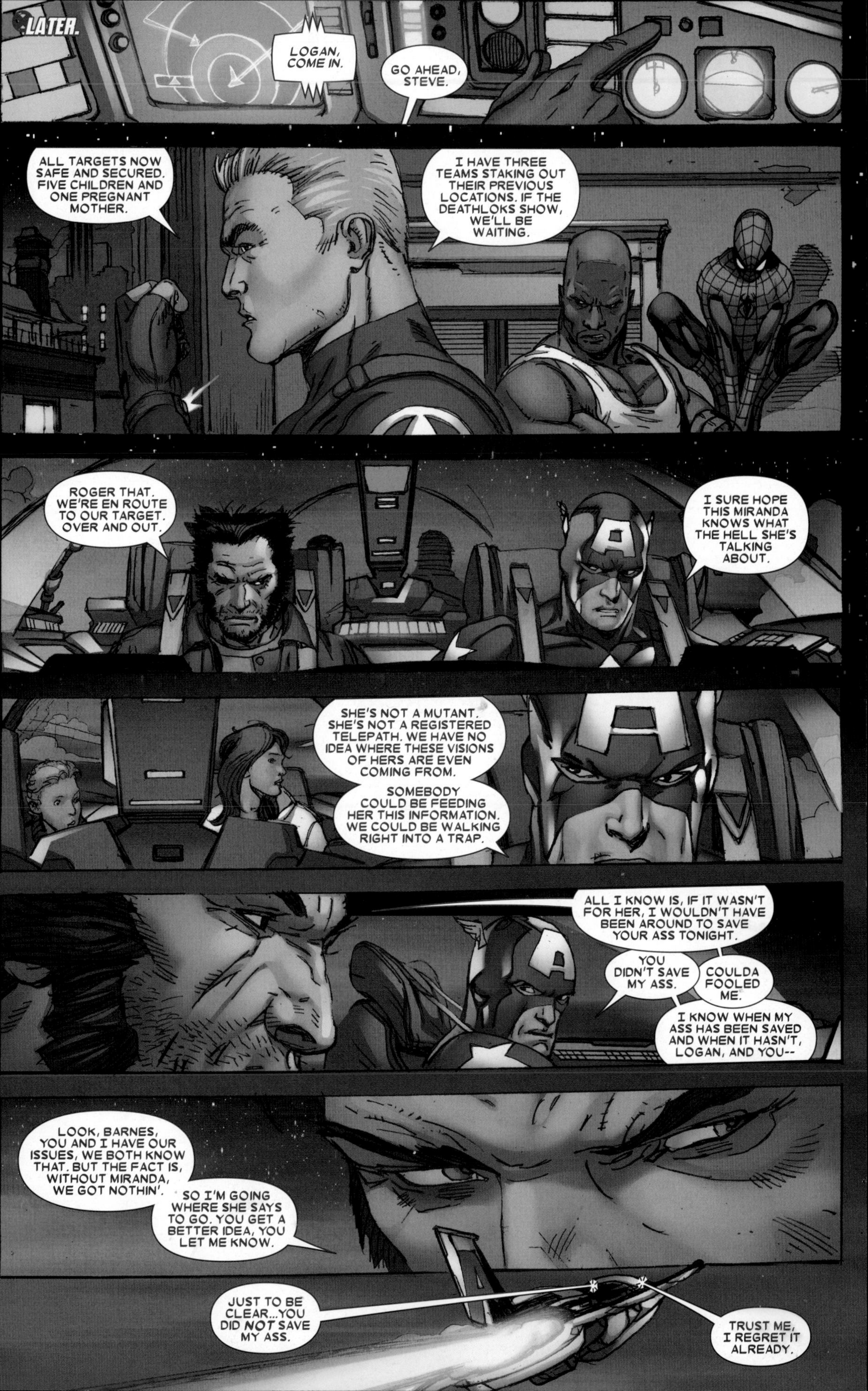
LATER.
LOGAN, COME IN.
GO AHEAD, STEVE.
ALL TARGETS NOW SAFE AND SECURED. FIVE CHILDREN AND ONE PREGNANT MOTHER.
I HAVE THREE TEAMS STAKING OUT THEIR PREVIOUS LOCATIONS. IF THE DEATHLOKS SHOW, WE'LL BE WAITING.
ROGER THAT. WE'RE EN ROUTE TO OUR TARGET. OVER AND OUT.
I SURE HOPE THIS MIRANDA KNOWS WHAT THE HELL SHE'S TALKING ABOUT.
SHE'S NOT A MUTANT. SHE'S NOT A REGISTERED TELEPATH. WE HAVE NO IDEA WHERE THESE VISIONS OF HERS ARE EVEN COMING FROM.
SOMEBODY COULD BE FEEDING HER THIS INFORMATION. WE COULD BE WALKING RIGHT INTO A TRAP.
ALL I KNOW IS, IF IT WASN'T FOR HER, I WOULDN'T HAVE BEEN AROUND TO SAVE YOUR ASS TONIGHT.
YOU DIDN'T SAVE MY ASS.
COULDA FOOLED ME.
I KNOW WHEN MY ASS HAS BEEN SAVED AND WHEN IT HASN'T, LOGAN, AND YOU--
LOOK, BARNES, YOU AND I HAVE OUR ISSUES, WE BOTH KNOW THAT. BUT THE FACT IS, WITHOUT MIRANDA, WE GOT NOTHIN'.
SO I'M GOING WHERE SHE SAYS TO GO. YOU GET A BETTER IDEA, YOU LET ME KNOW.
JUST TO BE CLEAR...YOU DID NOT SAVE MY ASS.
TRUST ME, I REGRET IT ALREADY.

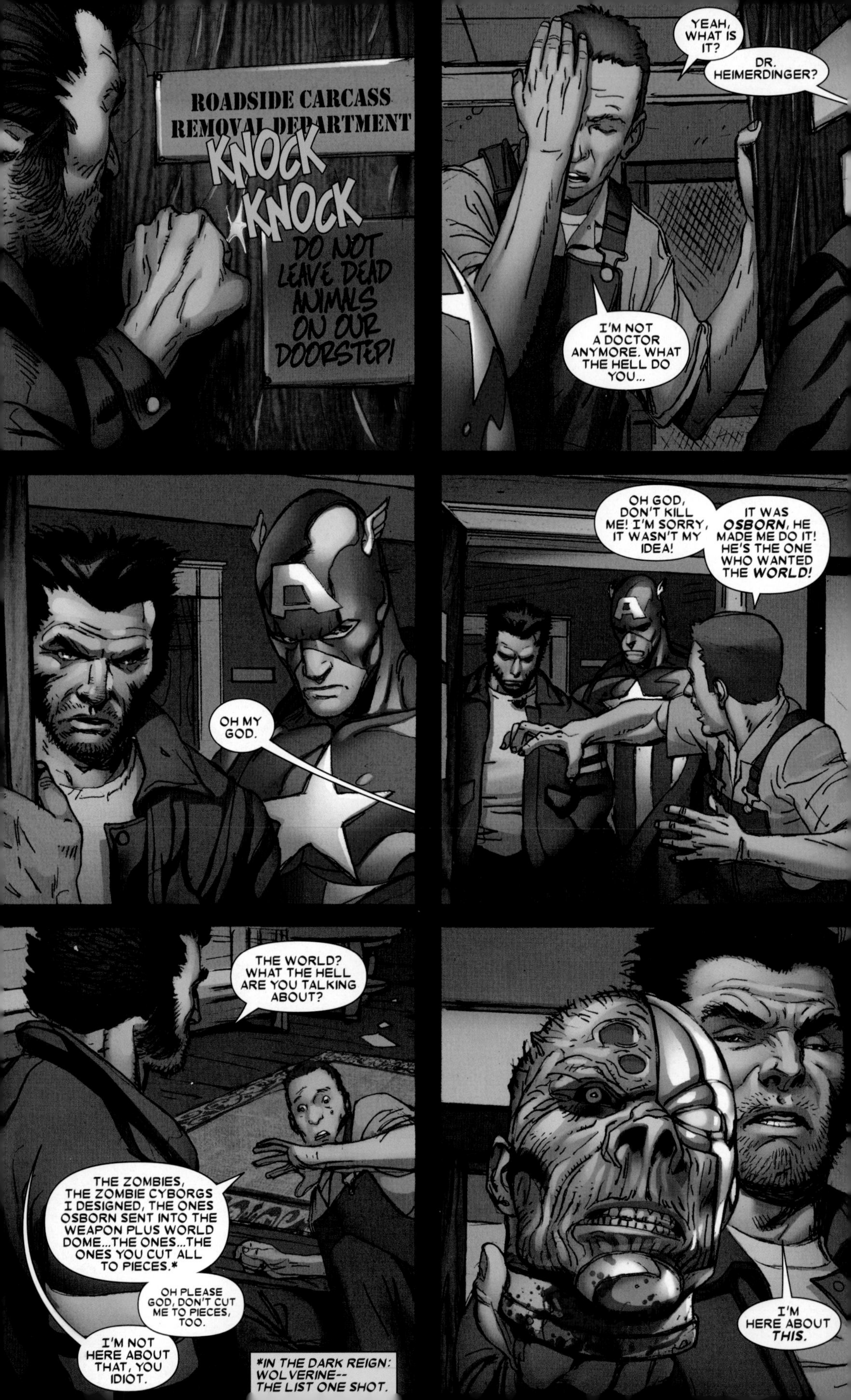

ROADSIDE CARCASS REMOVAL DEPARTMENT
KNOCK KNOCK
DO NOT LEAVE DEAD ANIMALS ON OUR DOORSTEP!
YEAH, WHAT IS IT?
DR. HEIMERDINGER?
I'M NOT A DOCTOR ANYMORE. WHAT THE HELL DO YOU...
OH MY GOD.
OH GOD, DON'T KILL ME! I'M SORRY, IT WASN'T MY IDEA!
IT WAS OSBORN, HE MADE ME DO IT! HE'S THE ONE WHO WANTED THE WORLD!
THE WORLD? WHAT THE HELL ARE YOU TALKING ABOUT?
THE ZOMBIES, THE ZOMBIE CYBORGS I DESIGNED, THE ONES OSBORN SENT INTO THE WEAPON PLUS WORLD DOME...THE ONES...THE ONES YOU CUT ALL TO PIECES.*
OH PLEASE GOD, DON'T CUT ME TO PIECES, TOO.
I'M NOT HERE ABOUT THAT, YOU IDIOT.
*IN THE DARK REIGN: WOLVERINE-- THE LIST ONE SHOT.
I'M HERE ABOUT THIS.

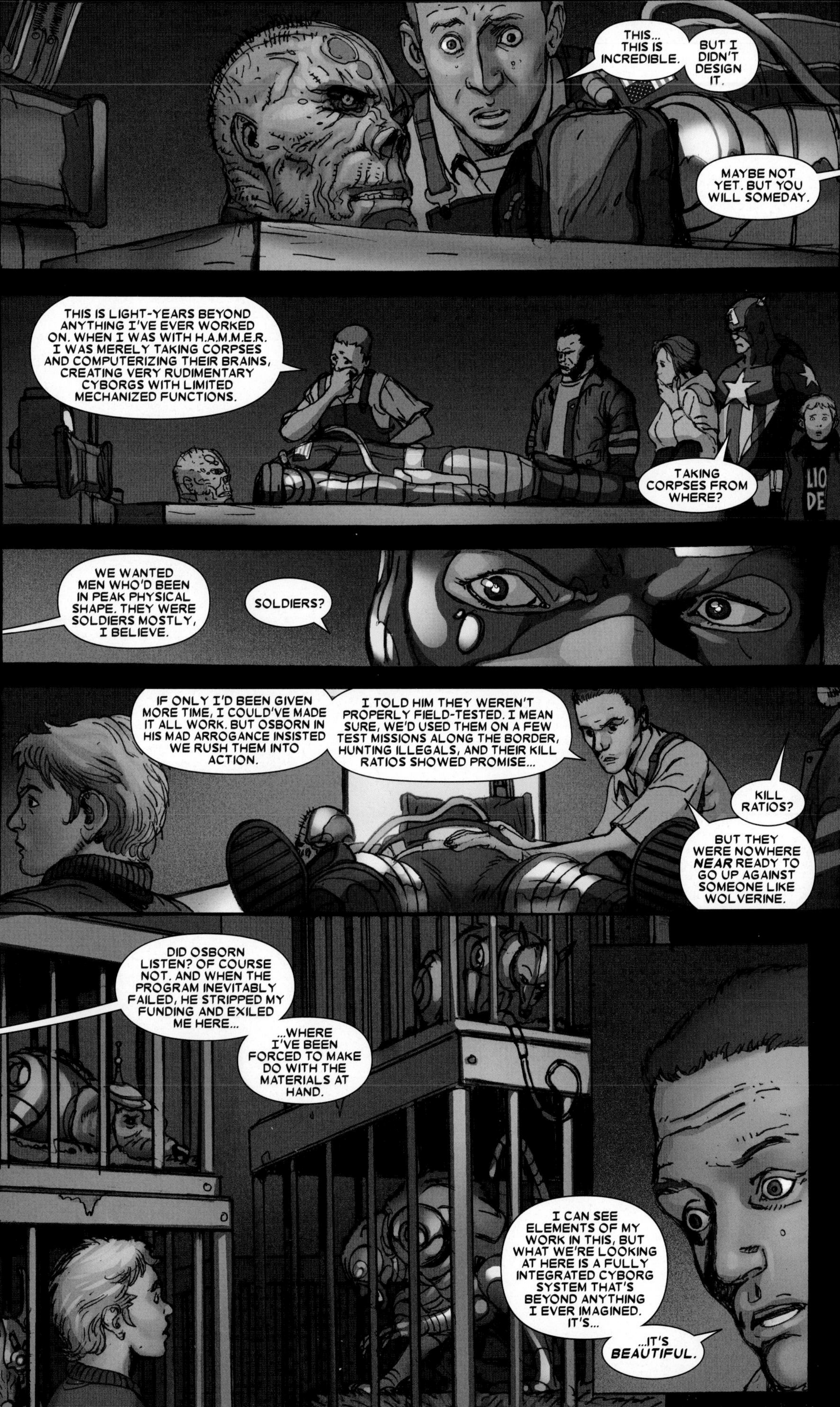
THIS... THIS IS INCREDIBLE.
BUT I DIDN'T DESIGN IT.
MAYBE NOT YET. BUT YOU WILL SOMEDAY.
THIS IS LIGHT-YEARS BEYOND ANYTHING I'VE EVER WORKED ON. WHEN I WAS WITH H.A.M.M.E.R. I WAS MERELY TAKING CORPSES AND COMPUTERIZING THEIR BRAINS, CREATING VERY RUDIMENTARY CYBORGS WITH LIMITED MECHANIZED FUNCTIONS.
TAKING CORPSES FROM WHERE?
WE WANTED MEN WHO'D BEEN IN PEAK PHYSICAL SHAPE. THEY WERE SOLDIERS MOSTLY, I BELIEVE.
SOLDIERS?
IF ONLY I'D BEEN GIVEN MORE TIME, I COULD'VE MADE IT ALL WORK. BUT OSBORN IN HIS MAD ARROGANCE INSISTED WE RUSH THEM INTO ACTION.
I TOLD HIM THEY WEREN'T PROPERLY FIELD-TESTED. I MEAN SURE, WE'D USED THEM ON A FEW TEST MISSIONS ALONG THE BORDER, HUNTING ILLEGALS, AND THEIR KILL RATIOS SHOWED PROMISE...
KILL RATIOS?
BUT THEY WERE NOWHERE NEAR READY TO GO UP AGAINST SOMEONE LIKE WOLVERINE.
DID OSBORN LISTEN? OF COURSE NOT. AND WHEN THE PROGRAM INEVITABLY FAILED, HE STRIPPED MY FUNDING AND EXILED ME HERE...
...WHERE I'VE BEEN FORCED TO MAKE DO WITH THE MATERIALS AT HAND.
I CAN SEE ELEMENTS OF MY WORK IN THIS, BUT WHAT WE'RE LOOKING AT HERE IS A FULLY INTEGRATED CYBORG SYSTEM THAT'S BEYOND ANYTHING I EVER IMAGINED. IT'S...
...IT'S BEAUTIFUL.

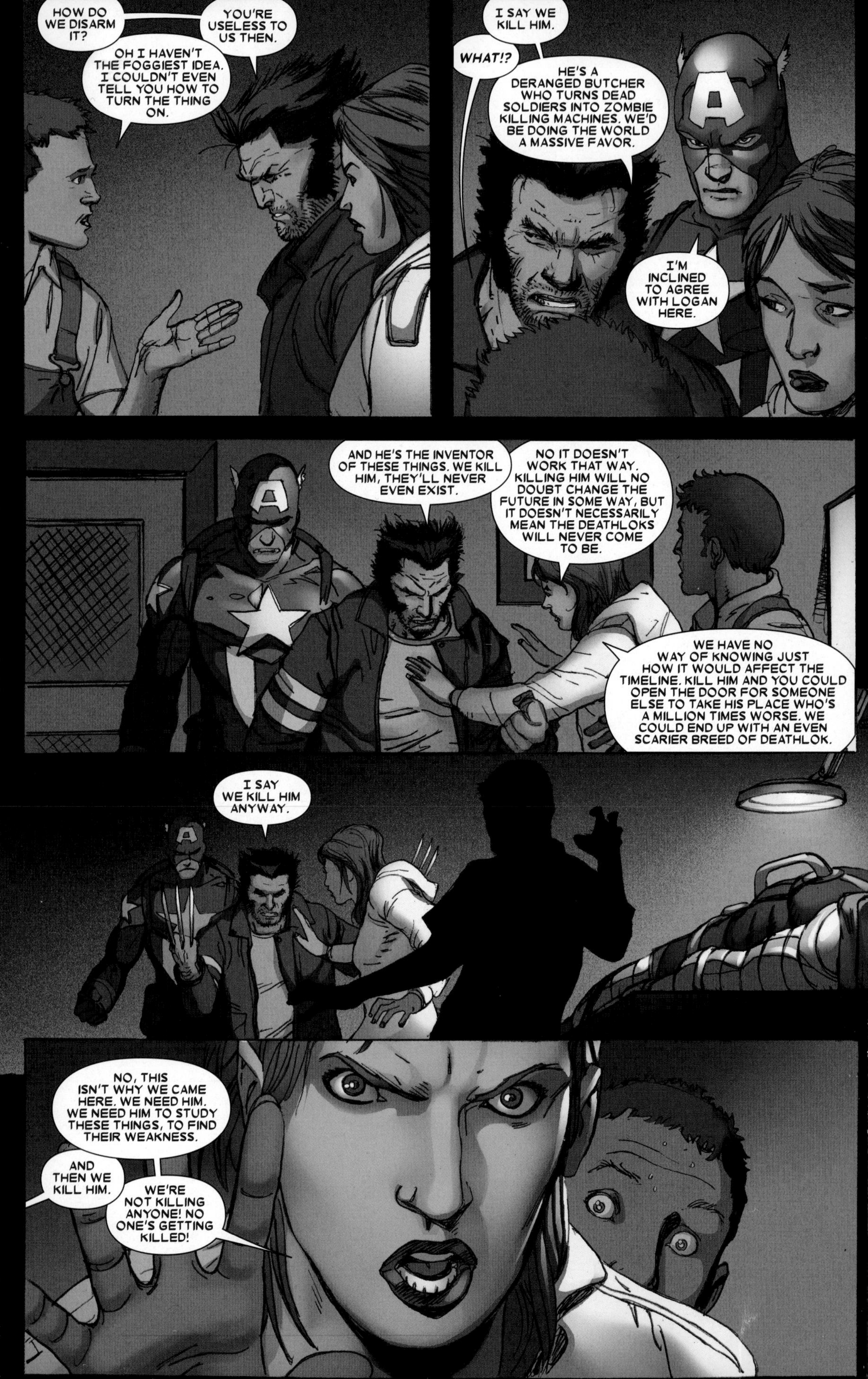

HOW DO WE DISARM IT?
YOU'RE USELESS TO US THEN.
OH I HAVEN'T THE FOGGIEST IDEA. I COULDN'T EVEN TELL YOU HOW TO TURN THE THING ON.
I SAY WE KILL HIM.
WHAT!?
HE'S A DERANGED BUTCHER WHO TURNS DEAD SOLDIERS INTO ZOMBIE KILLING MACHINES. WE'D BE DOING THE WORLD A MASSIVE FAVOR.
I'M INCLINED TO AGREE WITH LOGAN HERE.
AND HE'S THE INVENTOR OF THESE THINGS. WE KILL HIM, THEY'LL NEVER EVEN EXIST.
NO IT DOESN'T WORK THAT WAY. KILLING HIM WILL NO DOUBT CHANGE THE FUTURE IN SOME WAY, BUT IT DOESN'T NECESSARILY MEAN THE DEATHLOKS WILL NEVER COME TO BE.
WE HAVE NO WAY OF KNOWING JUST HOW IT WOULD AFFECT THE TIMELINE. KILL HIM AND YOU COULD OPEN THE DOOR FOR SOMEONE ELSE TO TAKE HIS PLACE WHO'S A MILLION TIMES WORSE. WE COULD END UP WITH AN EVEN SCARIER BREED OF DEATHLOK.
I SAY WE KILL HIM ANYWAY.
NO, THIS ISN'T WHY WE CAME HERE. WE NEED HIM. WE NEED HIM TO STUDY THESE THINGS, TO FIND THEIR WEAKNESS.
AND THEN WE KILL HIM.
WE'RE NOT KILLING ANYONE! NO ONE'S GETTING KILLED!

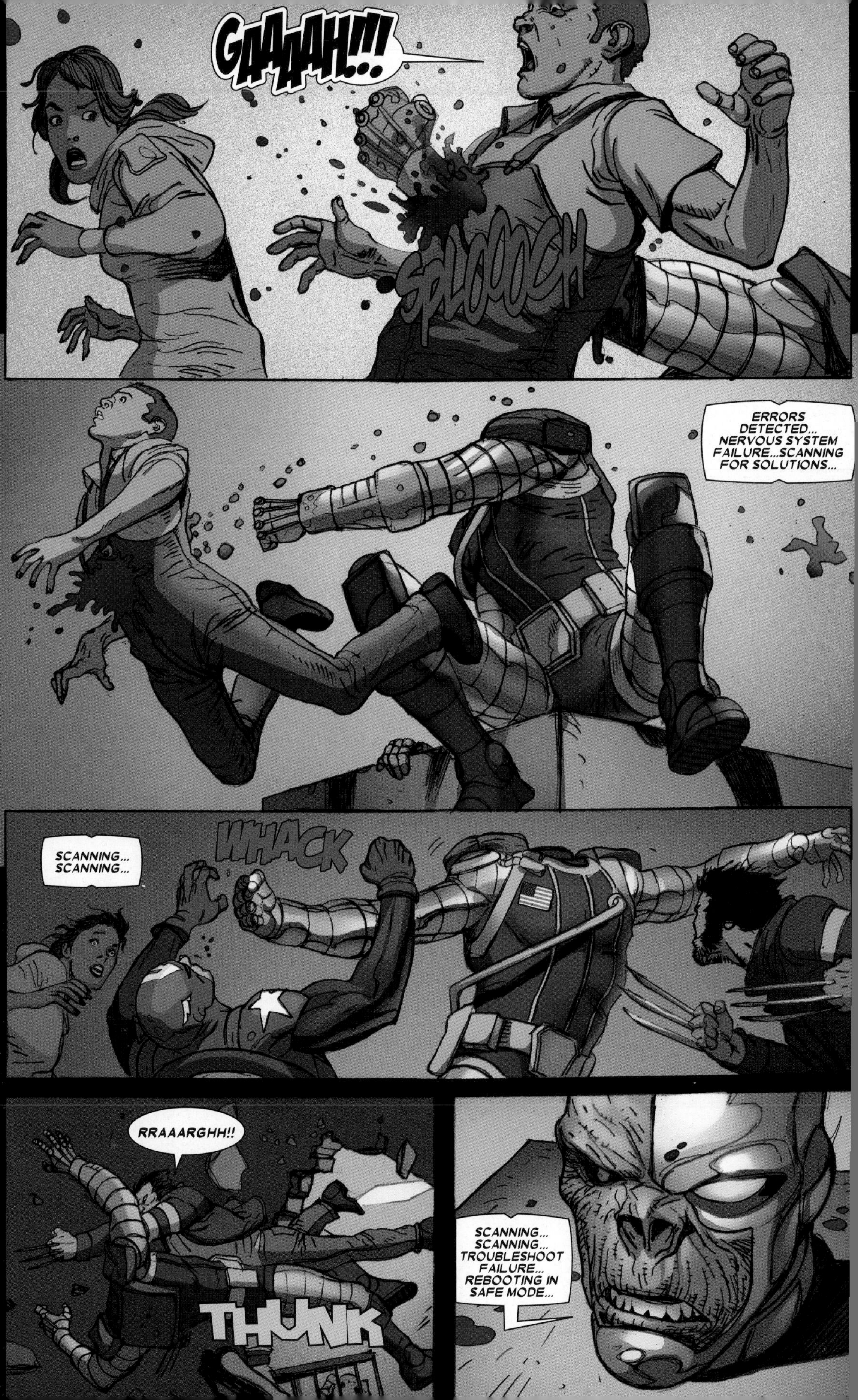
GAAAAH!!!...
SPLOOOCH
ERRORS DETECTED... NERVOUS SYSTEM FAILURE...SCANNING FOR SOLUTIONS...
SCANNING... SCANNING...
WHACK
RRAAARGHH!!
THUNK
SCANNING... SCANNING... TROUBLESHOOT FAILURE... REBOOTING IN SAFE MODE...

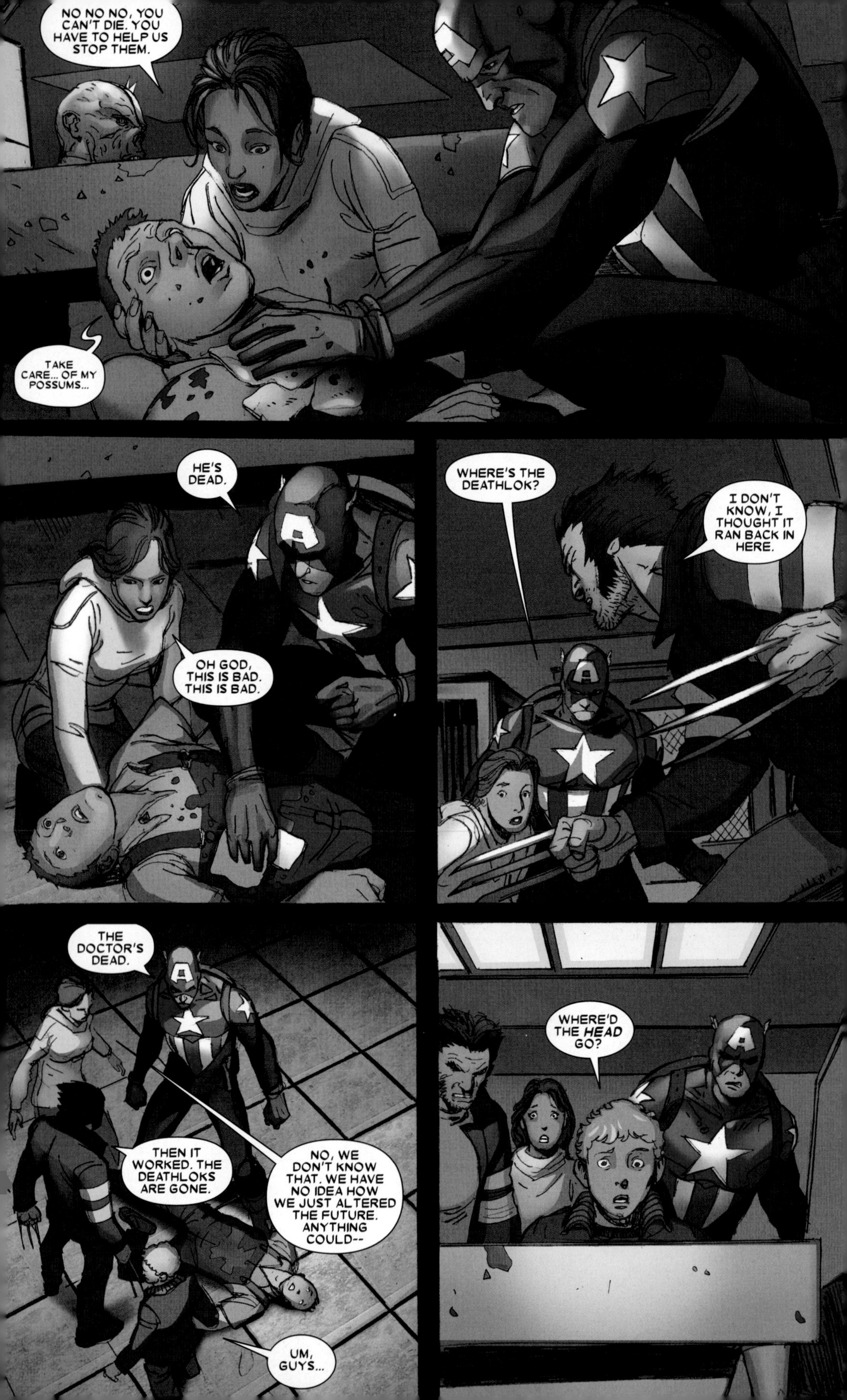
NO NO NO, YOU CAN'T DIE. YOU HAVE TO HELP US STOP THEM.
TAKE CARE... OF MY POSSUMS...
HE'S DEAD.
OH GOD, THIS IS BAD. THIS IS BAD.
WHERE'S THE DEATHLOK?
I DON'T KNOW, I THOUGHT IT RAN BACK IN HERE.
THE DOCTOR'S DEAD.
THEN IT WORKED. THE DEATHLOKS ARE GONE.
NO, WE DON'T KNOW THAT. WE HAVE NO IDEA HOW WE JUST ALTERED THE FUTURE. ANYTHING COULD--
UM, GUYS...
WHERE'D THE *HEAD* GO?

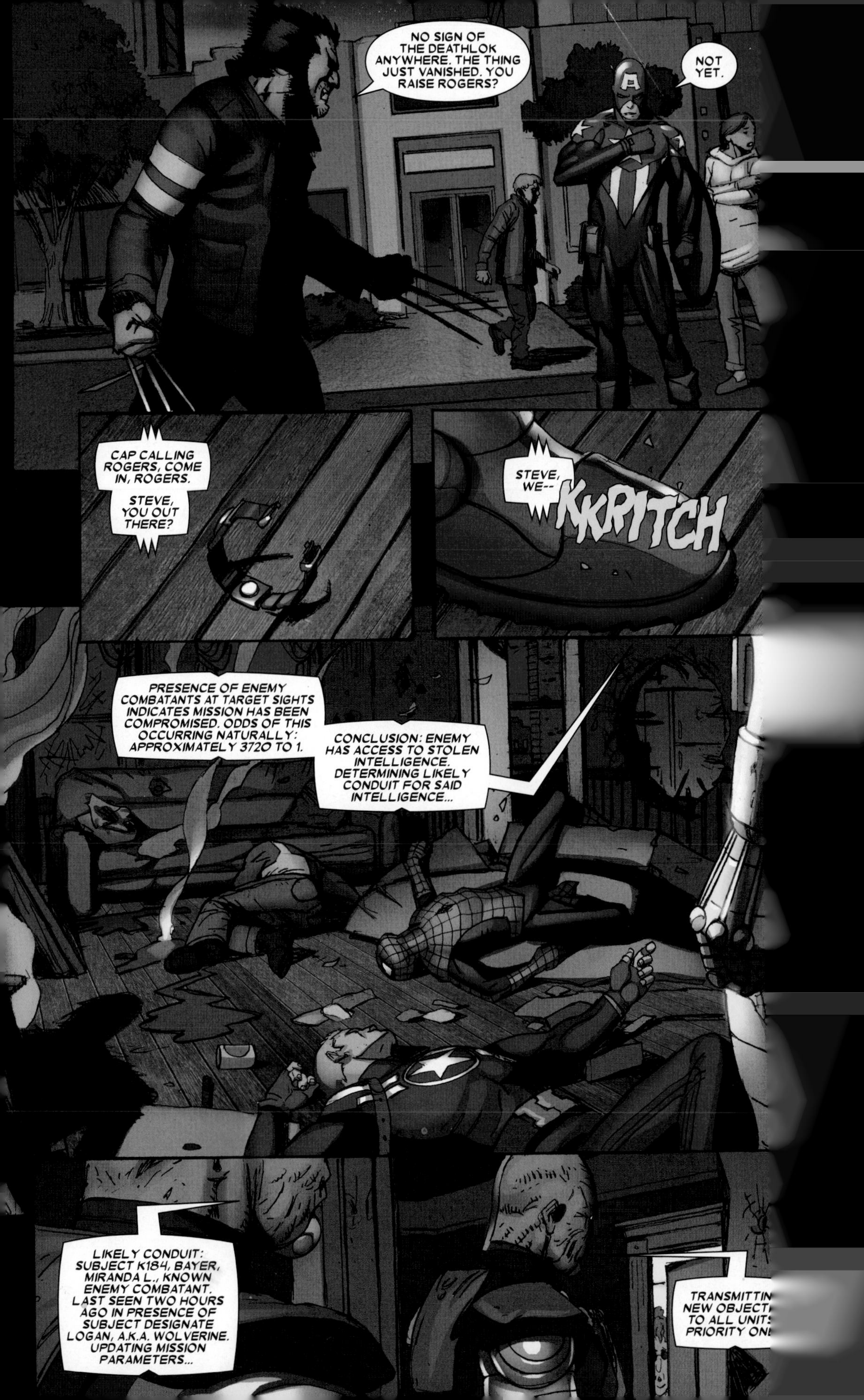
NO SIGN OF THE DEATHLOK ANYWHERE. THE THING JUST VANISHED. YOU RAISE ROGERS?
NOT YET.
CAP CALLING ROGERS, COME IN, ROGERS.
STEVE, YOU OUT THERE?
STEVE, WE--
KKRITCH
PRESENCE OF ENEMY COMBATANTS AT TARGET SIGHTS INDICATES MISSION HAS BEEN COMPROMISED. ODDS OF THIS OCCURRING NATURALLY: APPROXIMATELY 3720 TO 1.
CONCLUSION: ENEMY HAS ACCESS TO STOLEN INTELLIGENCE. DETERMINING LIKELY CONDUIT FOR SAID INTELLIGENCE...
LIKELY CONDUIT: SUBJECT K184, BAYER, MIRANDA L., KNOWN ENEMY COMBATANT. LAST SEEN TWO HOURS AGO IN PRESENCE OF SUBJECT DESIGNATE LOGAN, A.K.A. WOLVERINE. UPDATING MISSION PARAMETERS...

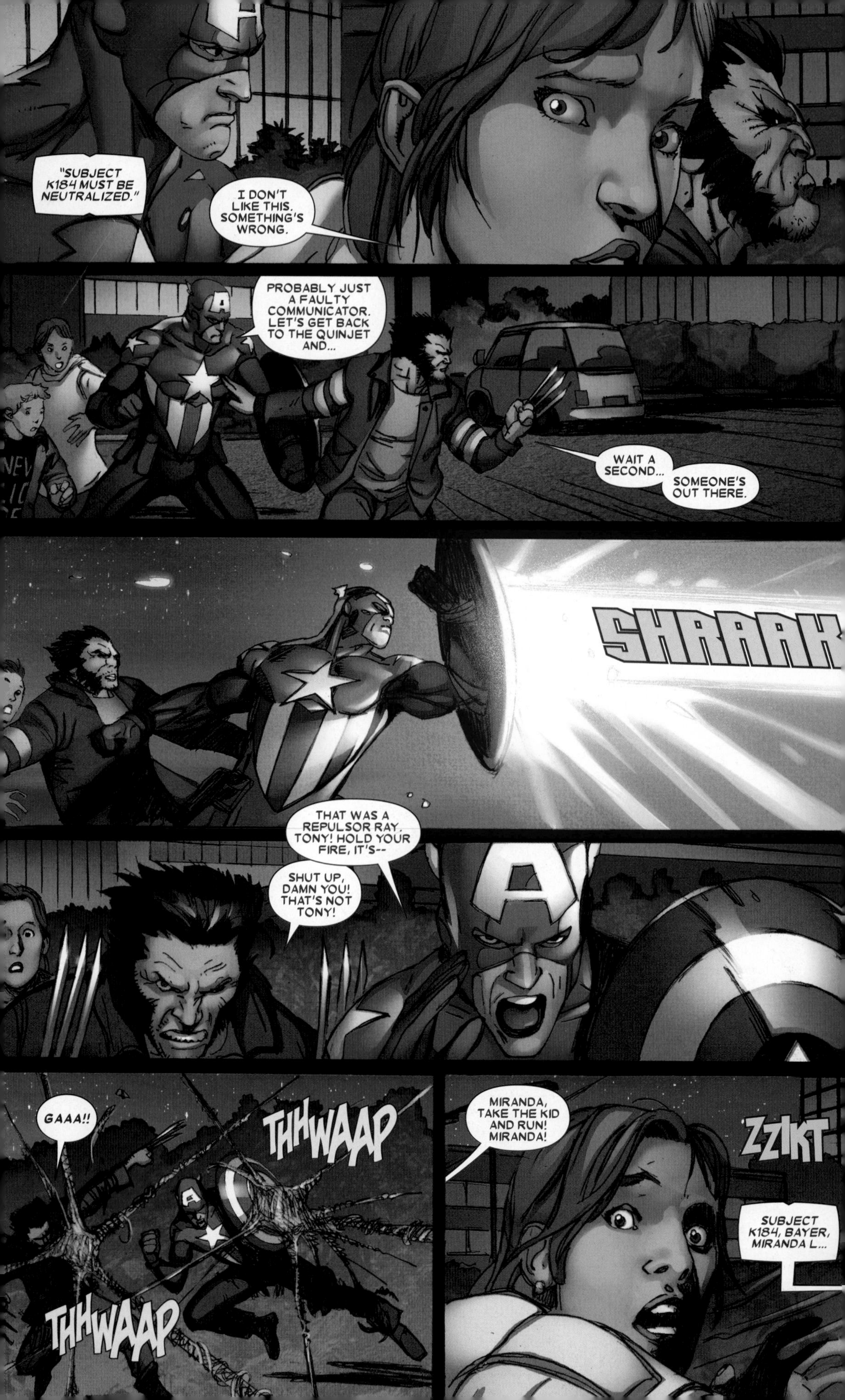
"SUBJECT K184 MUST BE NEUTRALIZED."
I DON'T LIKE THIS. SOMETHING'S WRONG.
PROBABLY JUST A FAULTY COMMUNICATOR. LET'S GET BACK TO THE QUINJET AND...
WAIT A SECOND...
SOMEONE'S OUT THERE.
SHRAAAK
THAT WAS A REPULSOR RAY. TONY! HOLD YOUR FIRE, IT'S--
SHUT UP, DAMN YOU! THAT'S NOT TONY!
GAAA!!
THHWAAP
THHWAAP
MIRANDA, TAKE THE KID AND RUN! MIRANDA!
ZZIKT
SUBJECT K184, BAYER, MIRANDA L...

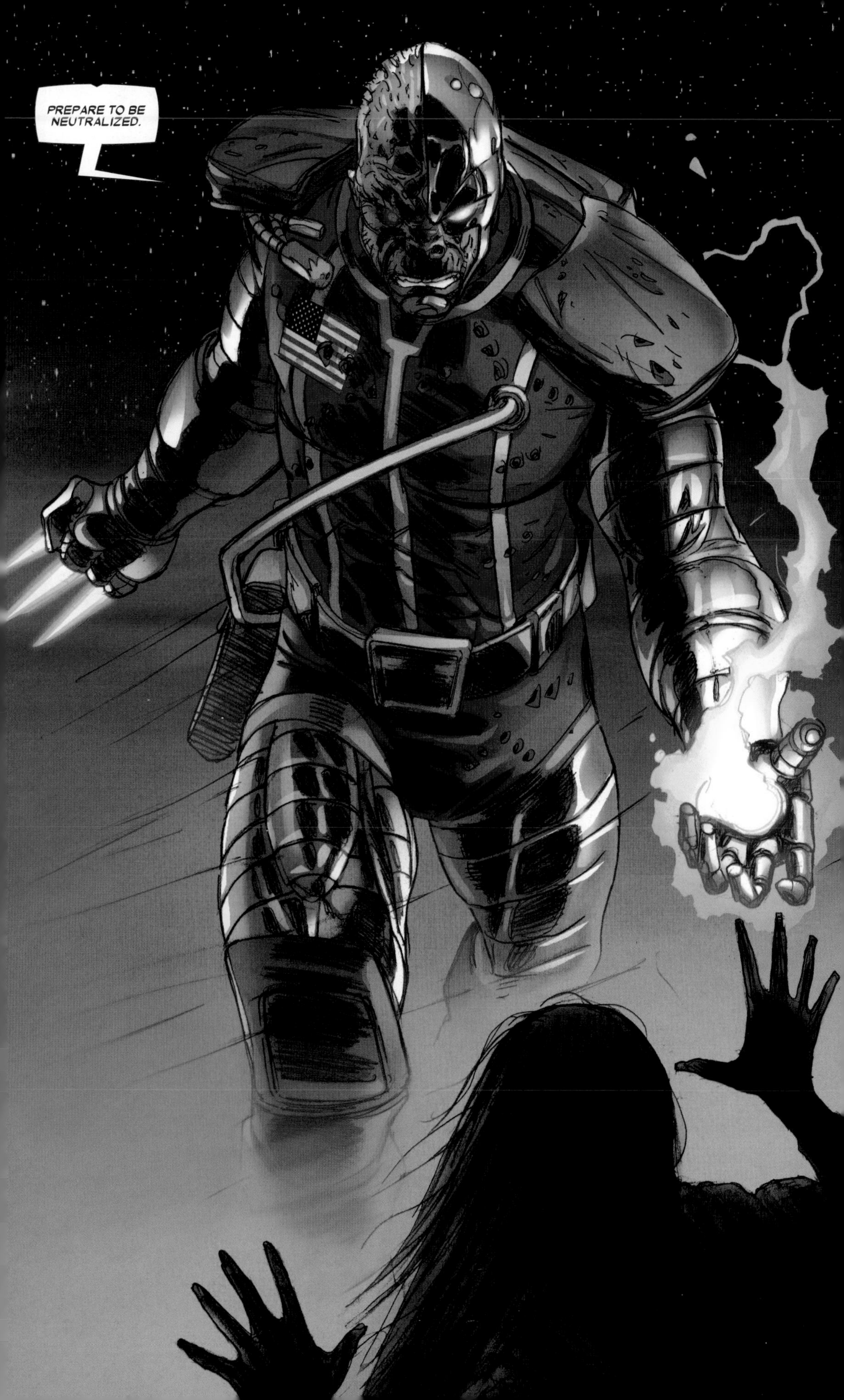
PREPARE TO BE NEUTRALIZED.

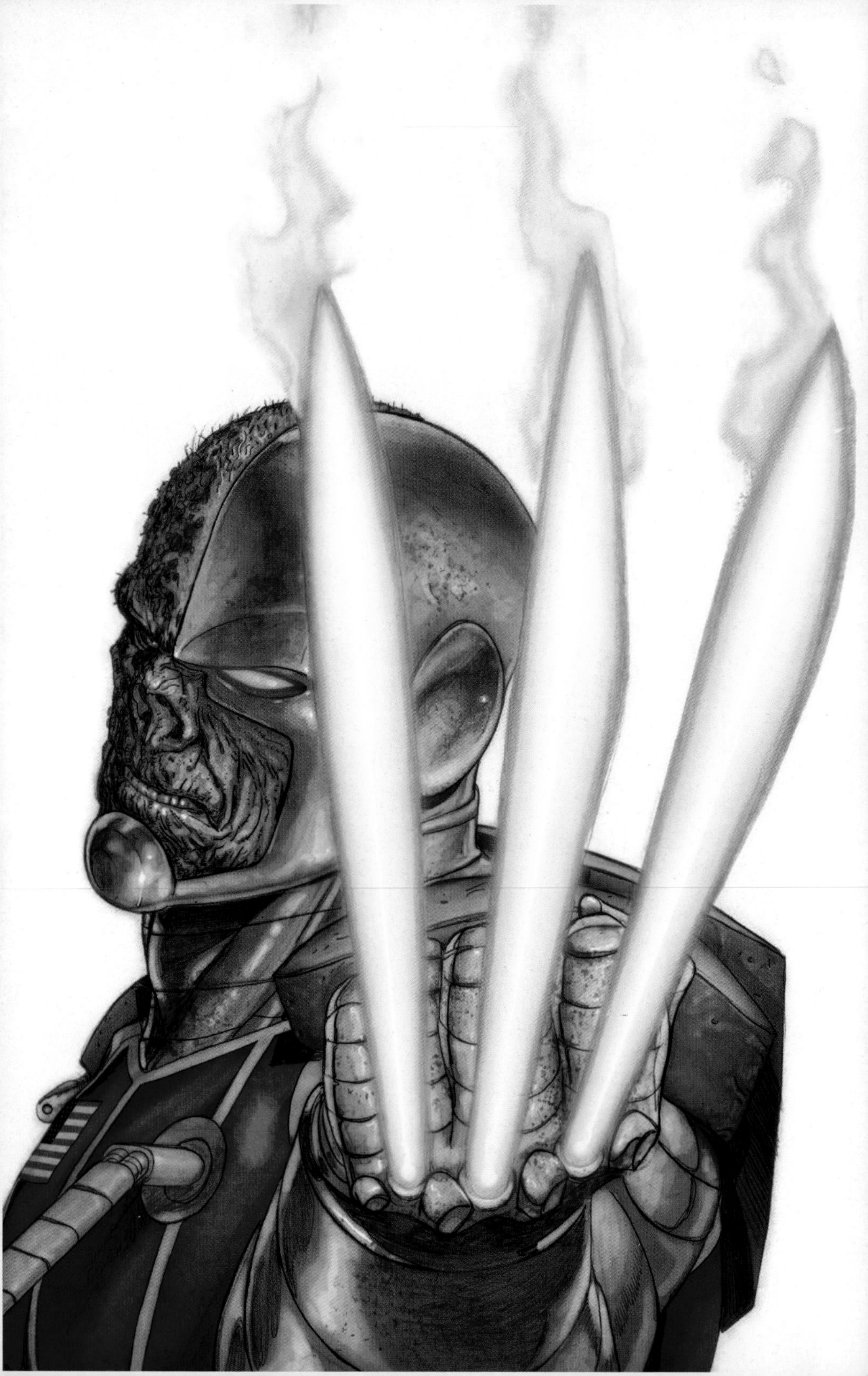

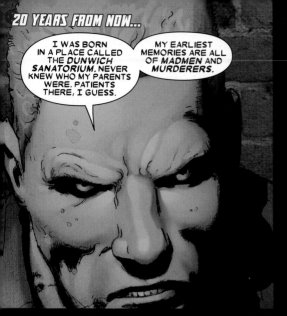

I WAS BORN IN A PLACE CALLED THE *DUNWICH SANATORIUM*. NEVER KNEW WHO MY PARENTS WERE. PATIENTS THERE, I GUESS.

MY EARLIEST MEMORIES ARE ALL OF *MADMEN* AND *MURDERERS*.

I TOOK UP *KILLIN'*. SIMPLY BECAUSE IT WAS THE ONLY THING I KNEW HOW TO DO, THE ONLY THING I WAS EVER ANY GOOD AT. AND THE MORE I DID IT, THE BETTER I GOT.

DON'T KNOW HOW MANY I KILLED BEFORE THEY CAUGHT ME. LOST TRACK AROUND *30*. IF I WASN'T HERE, I'D STILL BE DOING IT. AND IF I EVER GET OUTTA HERE, WHICH I WON'T, I'LL GO RIGHT BACK TO DOING IT AGAIN.

IT AIN'T THAT I GET SOME KIND OF SICK THRILL FROM IT, LIKE A LOTTA THESE FREAKS IN HERE. IT AIN'T LIKE THAT AT ALL.

I MEAN SURE, IT'S A RUSH. BEATS ANY DRUG I EVER HAD, HANDS DOWN. AND IT DOES MAKE ME HAPPY. IT'S THE ONLY THING THAT EVER REALLY DOES. BUT IT'S MORE THAN THAT.

I *NEED* IT. I NEED IT LIKE OTHER PEOPLE NEED FOOD AND WATER. I NEED TO KILL PEOPLE TO KEEP FROM GOING INSANE. YOU UNDERSTAND THAT? THE JUDGES AND THE JURIES NEVER DID.

THEY SAY THEY GONNA EXECUTE ME, BUT THEY WON'T NEVER HAVE TO. THEY'RE ALREADY KILLING ME, LITTLE BY LITTLE, JUST KEEPING ME IN HERE.

IT'S BEEN TWO YEARS, FOUR MONTHS, 19 DAYS AND 13 HOURS SINCE I LAST TOOK ANYBODY'S LIFE. I DON'T KNOW HOW MUCH LONGER I CAN LAST.

NOW...DOES THAT ANSWER YOUR QUESTION, MISTER?

YES. YES, I BELIEVE IT DOES.

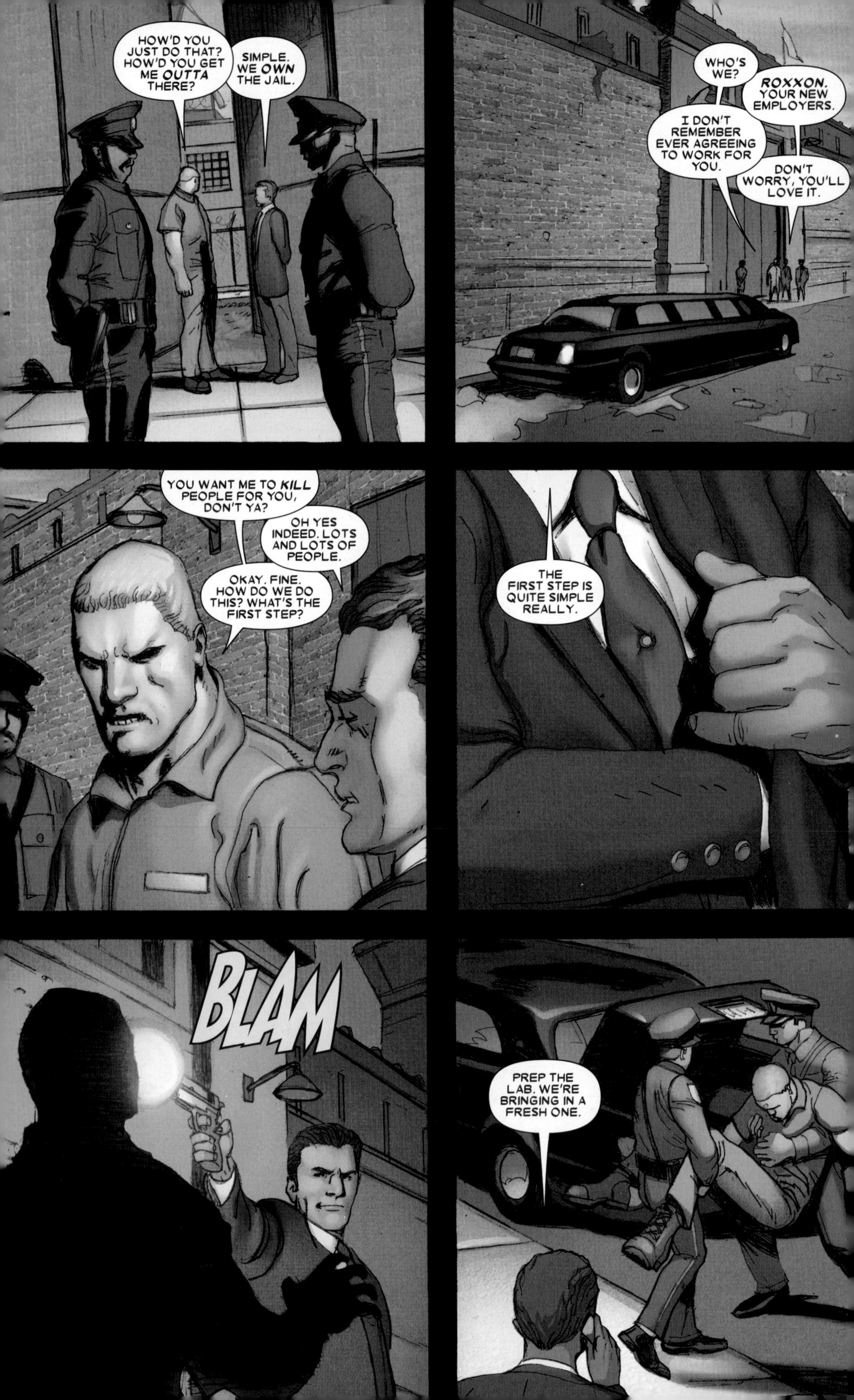
HOW'D YOU JUST DO THAT? HOW'D YOU GET ME OUTTA THERE?
SIMPLE. WE OWN THE JAIL.
WHO'S WE?
ROXXON. YOUR NEW EMPLOYERS.
I DON'T REMEMBER EVER AGREEING TO WORK FOR YOU.
DON'T WORRY, YOU'LL LOVE IT.
YOU WANT ME TO KILL PEOPLE FOR YOU, DON'T YA?
OH YES INDEED. LOTS AND LOTS OF PEOPLE.
OKAY. FINE. HOW DO WE DO THIS? WHAT'S THE FIRST STEP?
THE FIRST STEP IS QUITE SIMPLE REALLY.
BLAM
PREP THE LAB. WE'RE BRINGING IN A FRESH ONE.

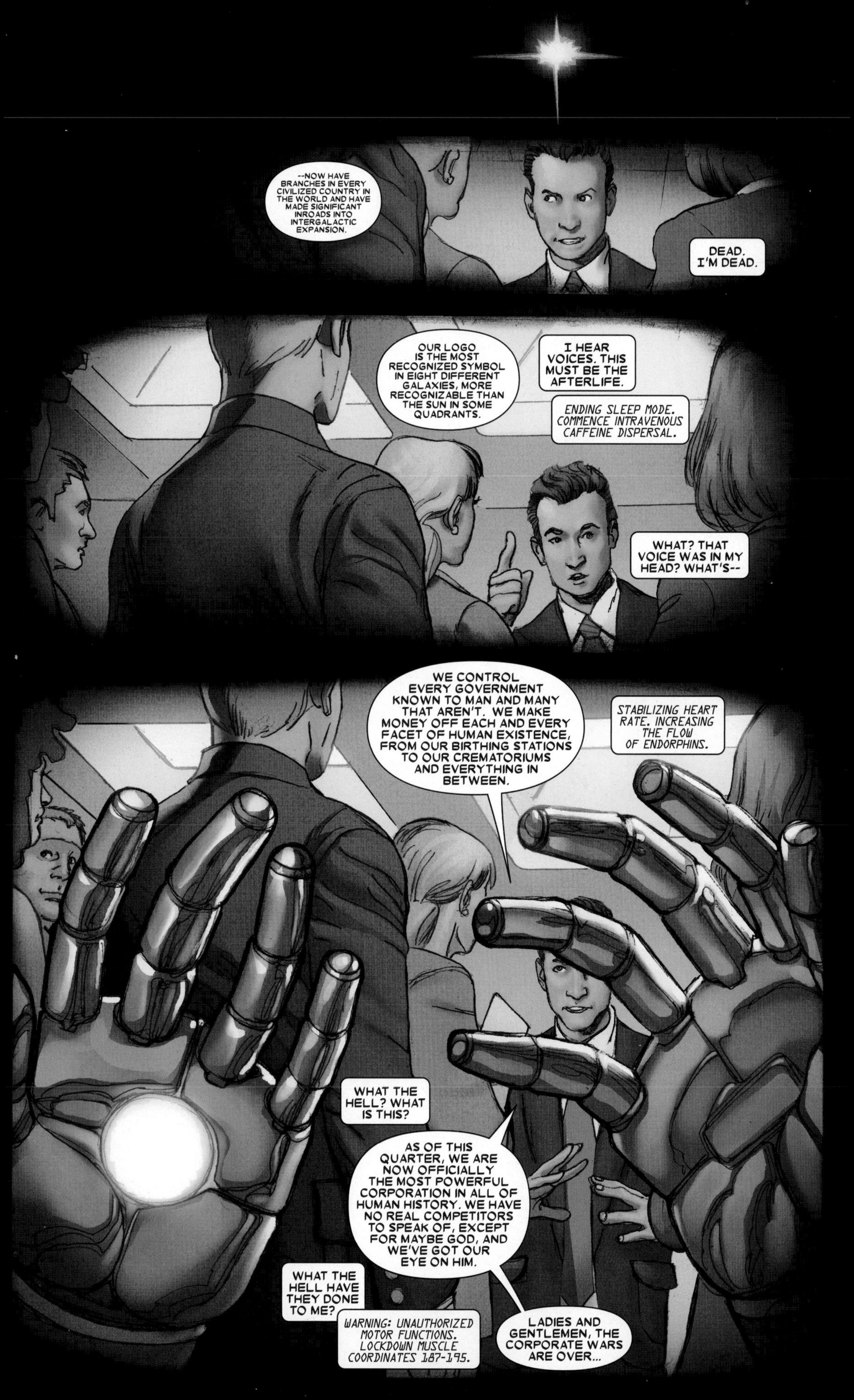
--NOW HAVE BRANCHES IN EVERY CIVILIZED COUNTRY IN THE WORLD AND HAVE MADE SIGNIFICANT INROADS INTO INTERGALACTIC EXPANSION.
DEAD. I'M DEAD.
OUR LOGO IS THE MOST RECOGNIZED SYMBOL IN EIGHT DIFFERENT GALAXIES, MORE RECOGNIZABLE THAN THE SUN IN SOME QUADRANTS.
I HEAR VOICES. THIS MUST BE THE AFTERLIFE.
ENDING SLEEP MODE. COMMENCE INTRAVENOUS CAFFEINE DISPERSAL.
WHAT? THAT VOICE WAS IN MY HEAD? WHAT'S--
WE CONTROL EVERY GOVERNMENT KNOWN TO MAN AND MANY THAT AREN'T. WE MAKE MONEY OFF EACH AND EVERY FACET OF HUMAN EXISTENCE, FROM OUR BIRTHING STATIONS TO OUR CREMATORIUMS AND EVERYTHING IN BETWEEN.
STABILIZING HEART RATE. INCREASING THE FLOW OF ENDORPHINS.
WHAT THE HELL? WHAT IS THIS?
AS OF THIS QUARTER, WE ARE NOW OFFICIALLY THE MOST POWERFUL CORPORATION IN ALL OF HUMAN HISTORY. WE HAVE NO REAL COMPETITORS TO SPEAK OF, EXCEPT FOR MAYBE GOD, AND WE'VE GOT OUR EYE ON HIM.
WHAT THE HELL HAVE THEY DONE TO ME?
WARNING: UNAUTHORIZED MOTOR FUNCTIONS. LOCKDOWN MUSCLE COORDINATES 187-195.
LADIES AND GENTLEMEN, THE CORPORATE WARS ARE OVER...

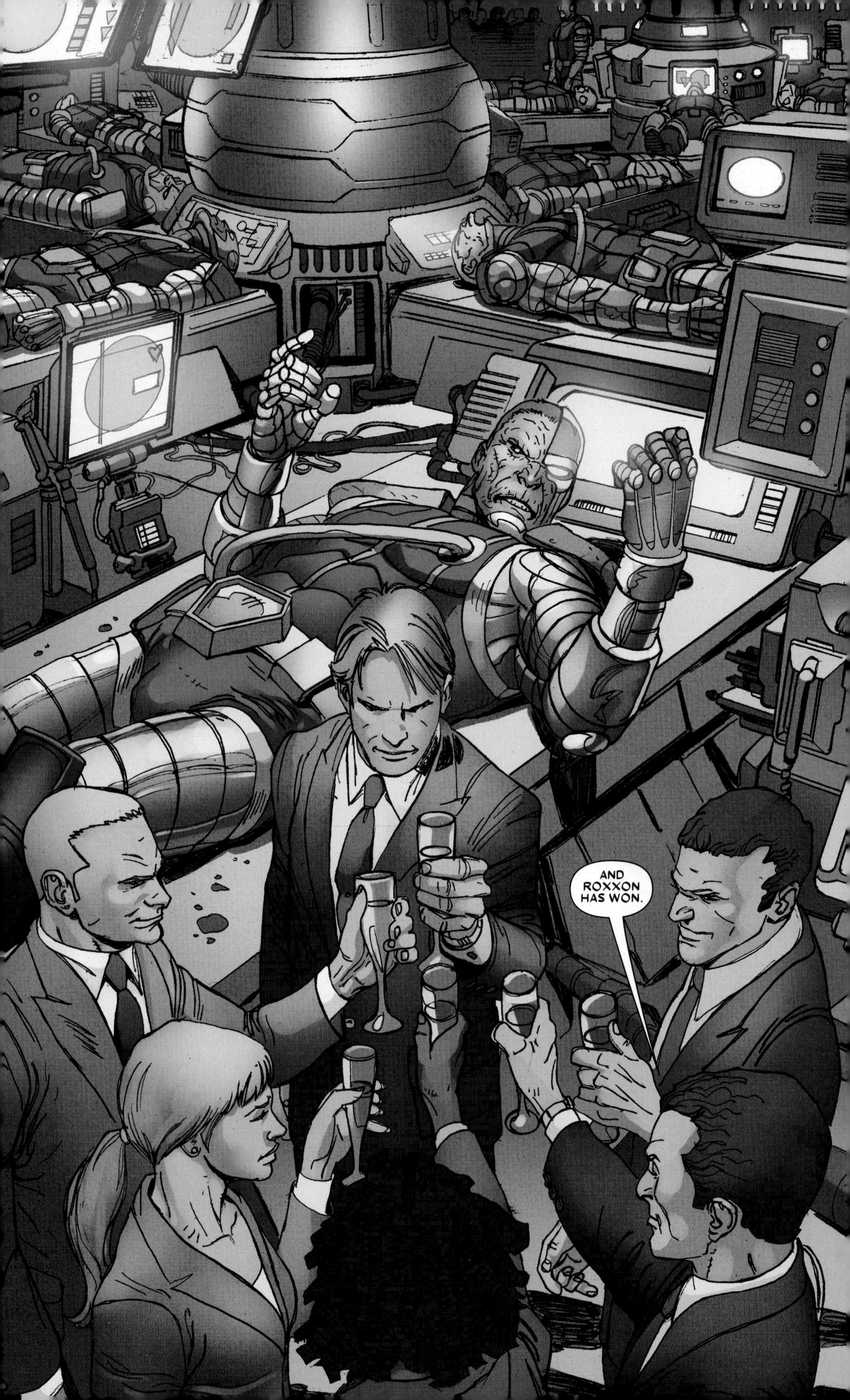
AND ROXXON HAS WON.

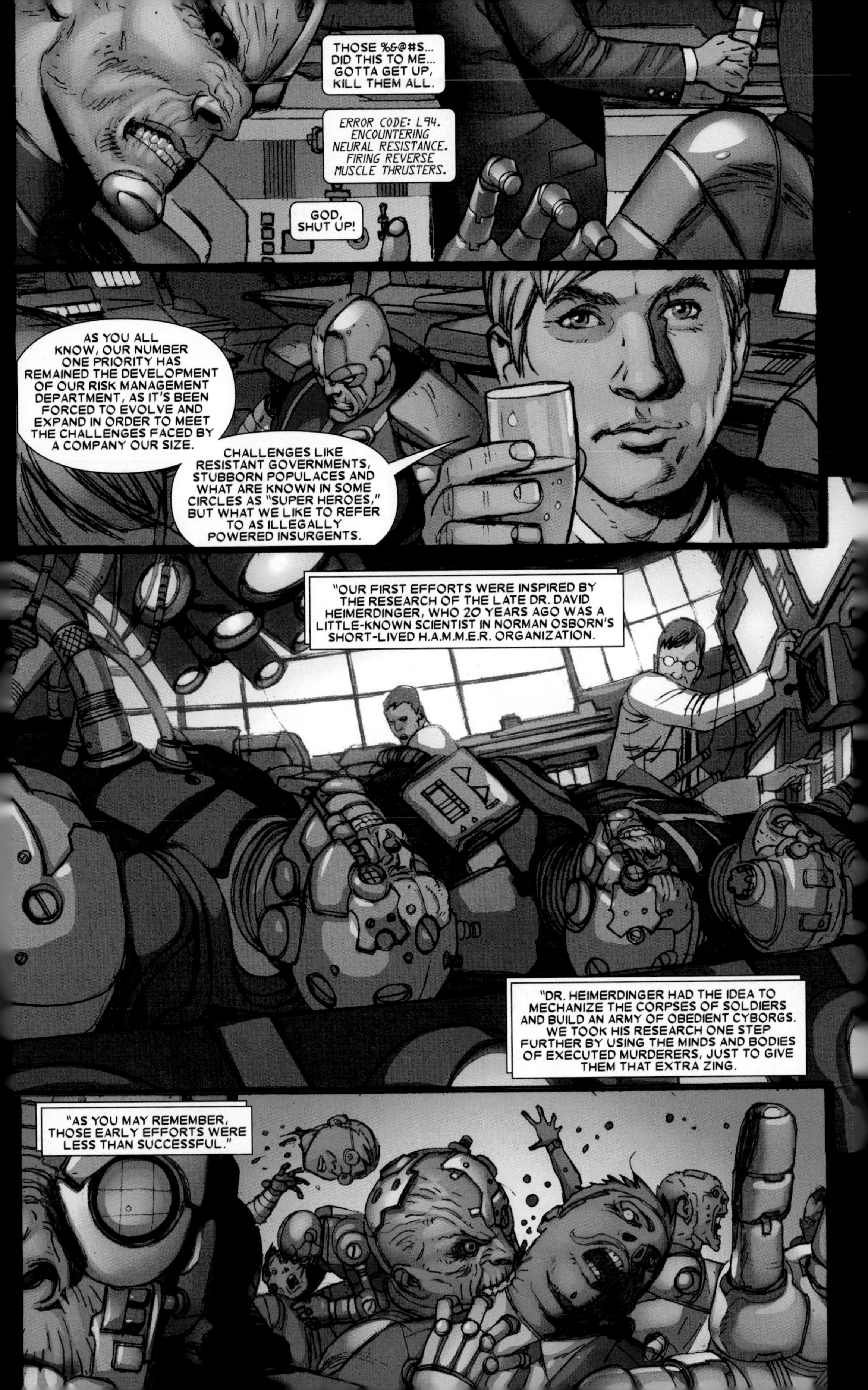
THOSE %&@#S... DID THIS TO ME... GOTTA GET UP, KILL THEM ALL.
ERROR CODE: L94. ENCOUNTERING NEURAL RESISTANCE. FIRING REVERSE MUSCLE THRUSTERS.
GOD, SHUT UP!
AS YOU ALL KNOW, OUR NUMBER ONE PRIORITY HAS REMAINED THE DEVELOPMENT OF OUR RISK MANAGEMENT DEPARTMENT, AS IT'S BEEN FORCED TO EVOLVE AND EXPAND IN ORDER TO MEET THE CHALLENGES FACED BY A COMPANY OUR SIZE.
CHALLENGES LIKE RESISTANT GOVERNMENTS, STUBBORN POPULACES AND WHAT ARE KNOWN IN SOME CIRCLES AS "SUPER HEROES," BUT WHAT WE LIKE TO REFER TO AS ILLEGALLY POWERED INSURGENTS.
"OUR FIRST EFFORTS WERE INSPIRED BY THE RESEARCH OF THE LATE DR. DAVID HEIMERDINGER, WHO 20 YEARS AGO WAS A LITTLE-KNOWN SCIENTIST IN NORMAN OSBORN'S SHORT-LIVED H.A.M.M.E.R. ORGANIZATION.
"DR. HEIMERDINGER HAD THE IDEA TO MECHANIZE THE CORPSES OF SOLDIERS AND BUILD AN ARMY OF OBEDIENT CYBORGS. WE TOOK HIS RESEARCH ONE STEP FURTHER BY USING THE MINDS AND BODIES OF EXECUTED MURDERERS, JUST TO GIVE THEM THAT EXTRA ZING.
"AS YOU MAY REMEMBER, THOSE EARLY EFFORTS WERE LESS THAN SUCCESSFUL."

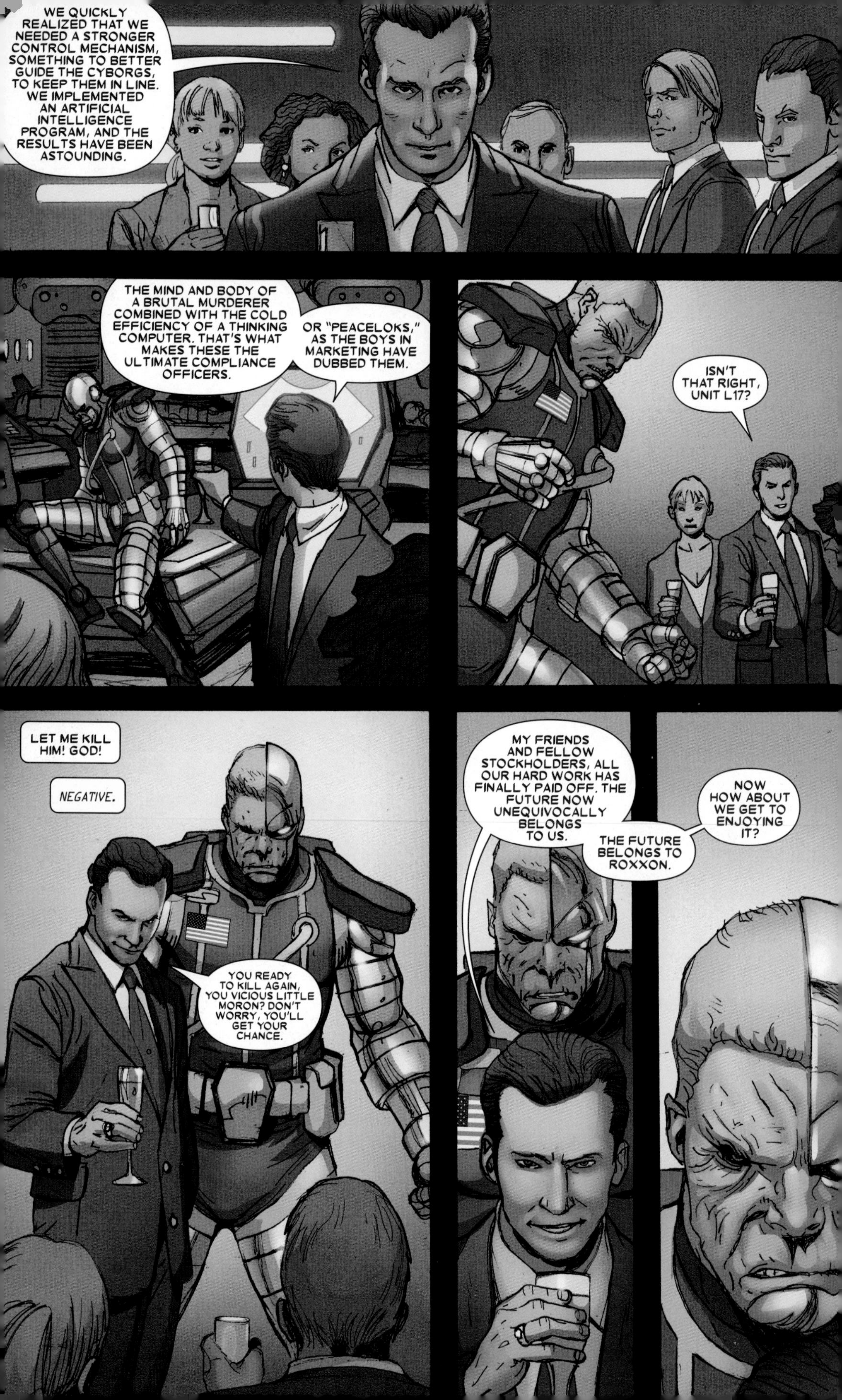
WE QUICKLY REALIZED THAT WE NEEDED A STRONGER CONTROL MECHANISM, SOMETHING TO BETTER GUIDE THE CYBORGS, TO KEEP THEM IN LINE. WE IMPLEMENTED AN ARTIFICIAL INTELLIGENCE PROGRAM, AND THE RESULTS HAVE BEEN ASTOUNDING.
THE MIND AND BODY OF A BRUTAL MURDERER COMBINED WITH THE COLD EFFICIENCY OF A THINKING COMPUTER. THAT'S WHAT MAKES THESE THE ULTIMATE COMPLIANCE OFFICERS.
OR "PEACELOKS," AS THE BOYS IN MARKETING HAVE DUBBED THEM.
ISN'T THAT RIGHT, UNIT L17?
LET ME KILL HIM! GOD!
NEGATIVE.
YOU READY TO KILL AGAIN, YOU VICIOUS LITTLE MORON? DON'T WORRY, YOU'LL GET YOUR CHANCE.
MY FRIENDS AND FELLOW STOCKHOLDERS, ALL OUR HARD WORK HAS FINALLY PAID OFF. THE FUTURE NOW UNEQUIVOCALLY BELONGS TO US.
THE FUTURE BELONGS TO ROXXON.
NOW HOW ABOUT WE GET TO ENJOYING IT?

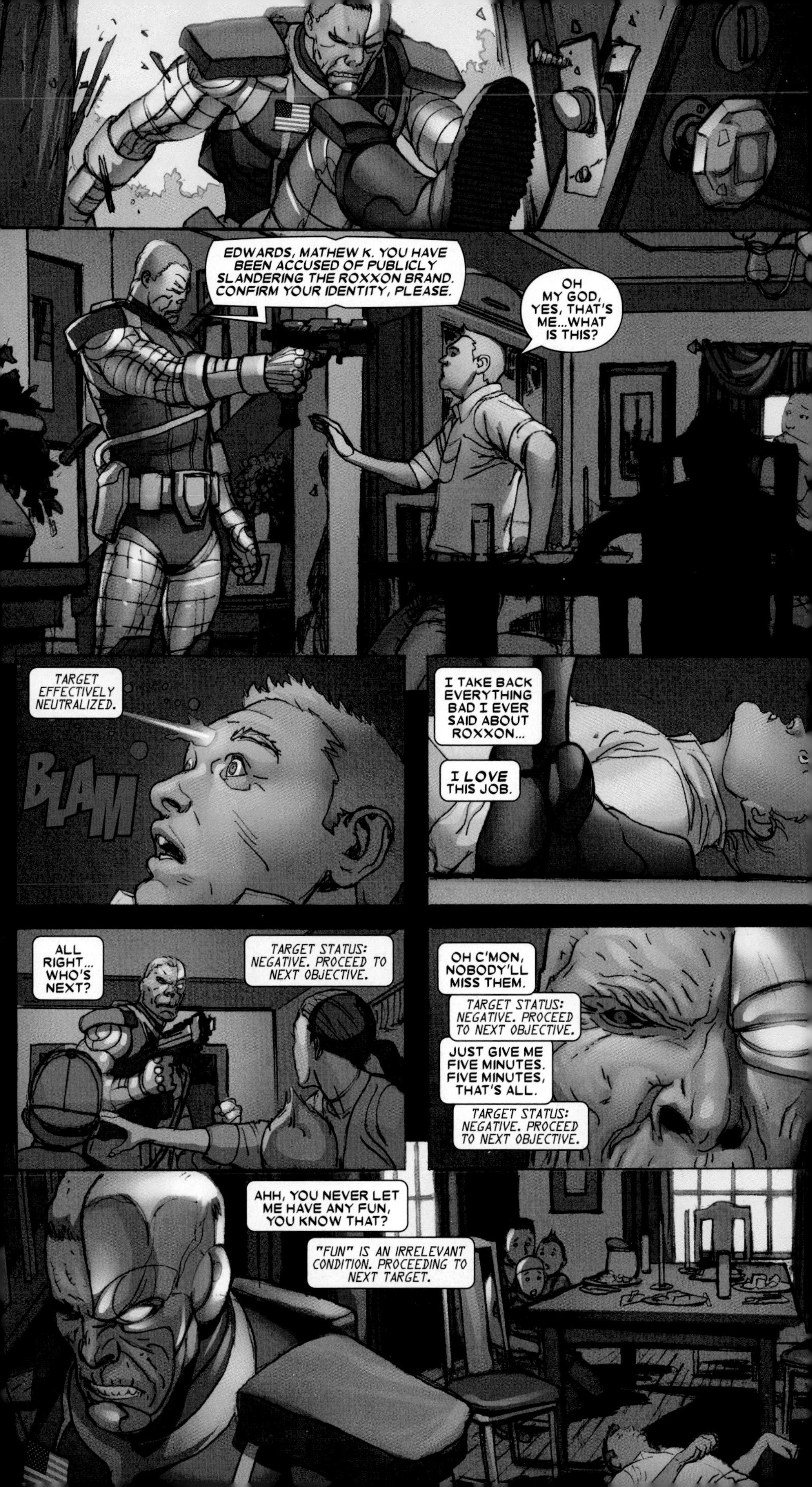

EDWARDS, MATHEW K. YOU HAVE BEEN ACCUSED OF PUBLICLY SLANDERING THE ROXXON BRAND. CONFIRM YOUR IDENTITY, PLEASE.
OH MY GOD, YES, THAT'S ME...WHAT IS THIS?
TARGET EFFECTIVELY NEUTRALIZED.
BLAM
I TAKE BACK EVERYTHING BAD I EVER SAID ABOUT ROXXON...
I LOVE THIS JOB.
ALL RIGHT... WHO'S NEXT?
TARGET STATUS: NEGATIVE. PROCEED TO NEXT OBJECTIVE.
OH C'MON, NOBODY'LL MISS THEM.
TARGET STATUS: NEGATIVE. PROCEED TO NEXT OBJECTIVE.
JUST GIVE ME FIVE MINUTES. FIVE MINUTES, THAT'S ALL.
TARGET STATUS: NEGATIVE. PROCEED TO NEXT OBJECTIVE.
AHH, YOU NEVER LET ME HAVE ANY FUN, YOU KNOW THAT?
"FUN" IS AN IRRELEVANT CONDITION. PROCEEDING TO NEXT TARGET.

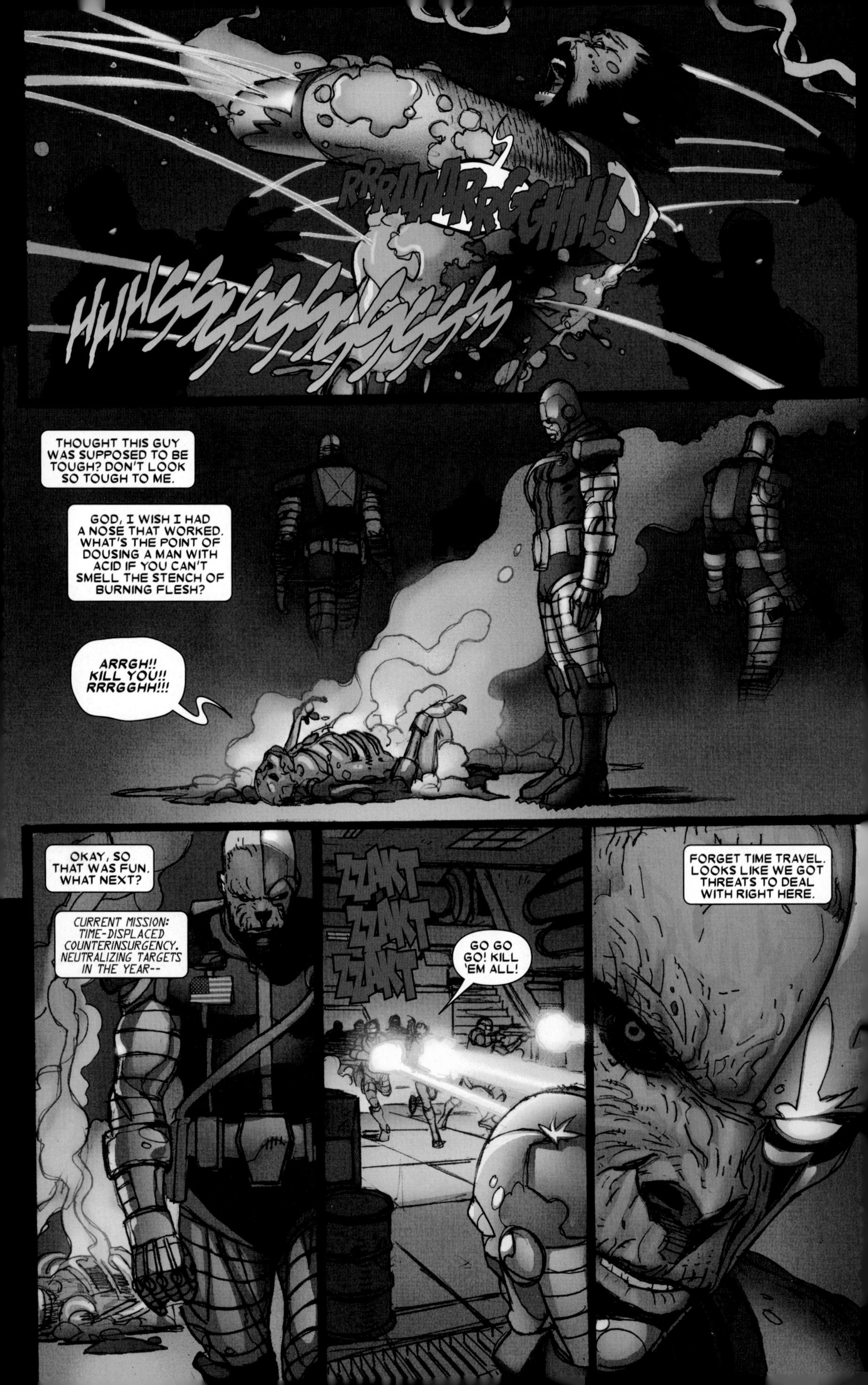
RRRAAARRGHH!
HUHSSSSSSSSSSSS
THOUGHT THIS GUY WAS SUPPOSED TO BE TOUGH? DON'T LOOK SO TOUGH TO ME.
GOD, I WISH I HAD A NOSE THAT WORKED. WHAT'S THE POINT OF DOUSING A MAN WITH ACID IF YOU CAN'T SMELL THE STENCH OF BURNING FLESH?
ARRGH!! KILL YOU!! RRRGHH!!!
OKAY, SO THAT WAS FUN. WHAT NEXT?
CURRENT MISSION: TIME-DISPLACED COUNTERINSURGENCY. NEUTRALIZING TARGETS IN THE YEAR--
ZZAKT ZZAKT ZZAKT
GO GO GO! KILL 'EM ALL!
FORGET TIME TRAVEL. LOOKS LIKE WE GOT THREATS TO DEAL WITH RIGHT HERE.

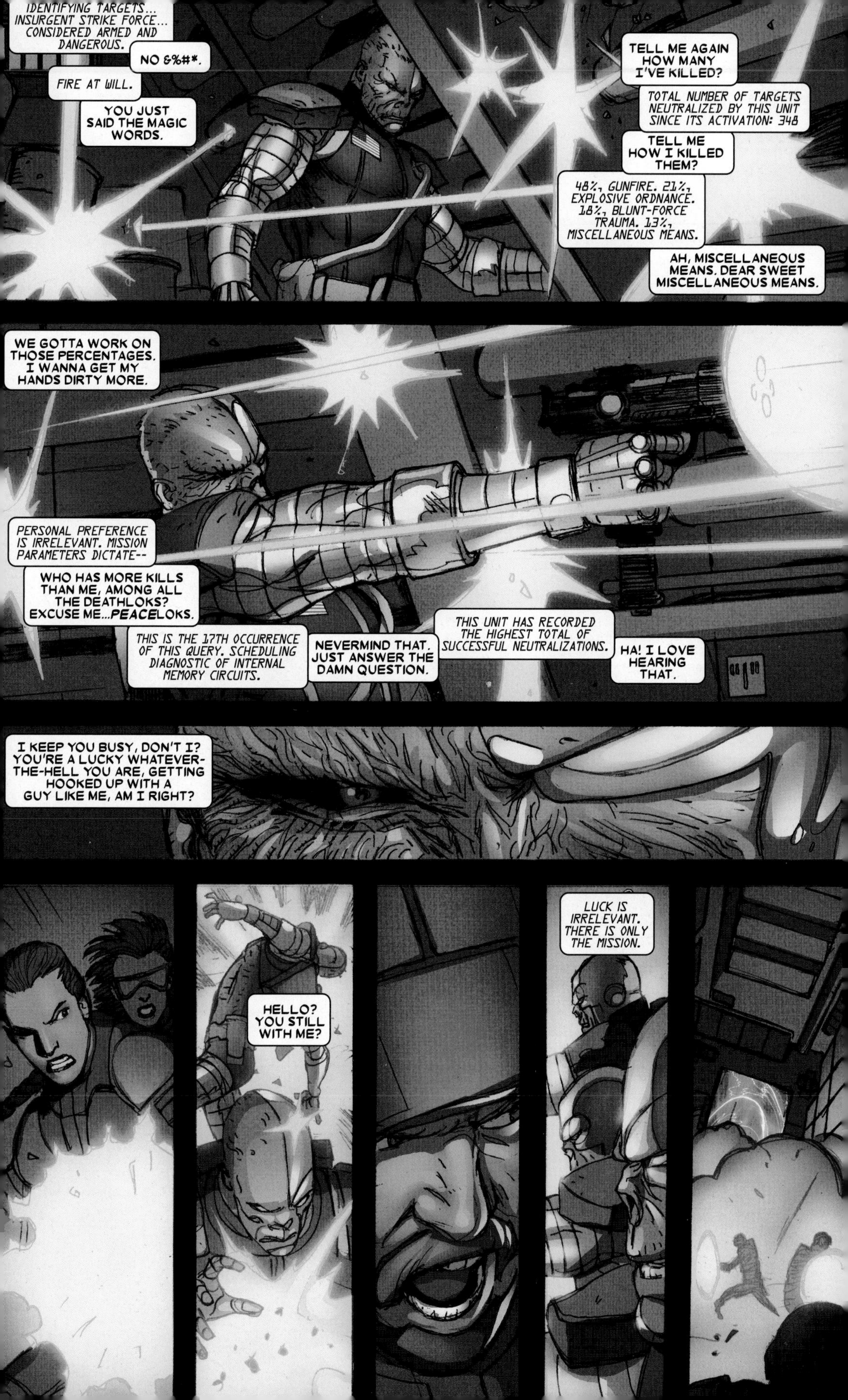

IDENTIFYING TARGETS... INSURGENT STRIKE FORCE... CONSIDERED ARMED AND DANGEROUS.
NO &%#*.
FIRE AT WILL.
YOU JUST SAID THE MAGIC WORDS.
TELL ME AGAIN HOW MANY I'VE KILLED?
TOTAL NUMBER OF TARGETS NEUTRALIZED BY THIS UNIT SINCE ITS ACTIVATION: 348
TELL ME HOW I KILLED THEM?
48%, GUNFIRE. 21%, EXPLOSIVE ORDNANCE. 18%, BLUNT-FORCE TRAUMA. 13%, MISCELLANEOUS MEANS.
AH, MISCELLANEOUS MEANS. DEAR SWEET MISCELLANEOUS MEANS.
WE GOTTA WORK ON THOSE PERCENTAGES. I WANNA GET MY HANDS DIRTY MORE.
PERSONAL PREFERENCE IS IRRELEVANT. MISSION PARAMETERS DICTATE--
WHO HAS MORE KILLS THAN ME, AMONG ALL THE DEATHLOKS? EXCUSE ME...PEACELOKS.
THIS IS THE 17TH OCCURRENCE OF THIS QUERY. SCHEDULING DIAGNOSTIC OF INTERNAL MEMORY CIRCUITS.
NEVERMIND THAT. JUST ANSWER THE DAMN QUESTION.
THIS UNIT HAS RECORDED THE HIGHEST TOTAL OF SUCCESSFUL NEUTRALIZATIONS.
HA! I LOVE HEARING THAT.
I KEEP YOU BUSY, DON'T I? YOU'RE A LUCKY WHATEVER-THE-HELL YOU ARE, GETTING HOOKED UP WITH A GUY LIKE ME, AM I RIGHT?
HELLO? YOU STILL WITH ME?
LUCK IS IRRELEVANT. THERE IS ONLY THE MISSION.

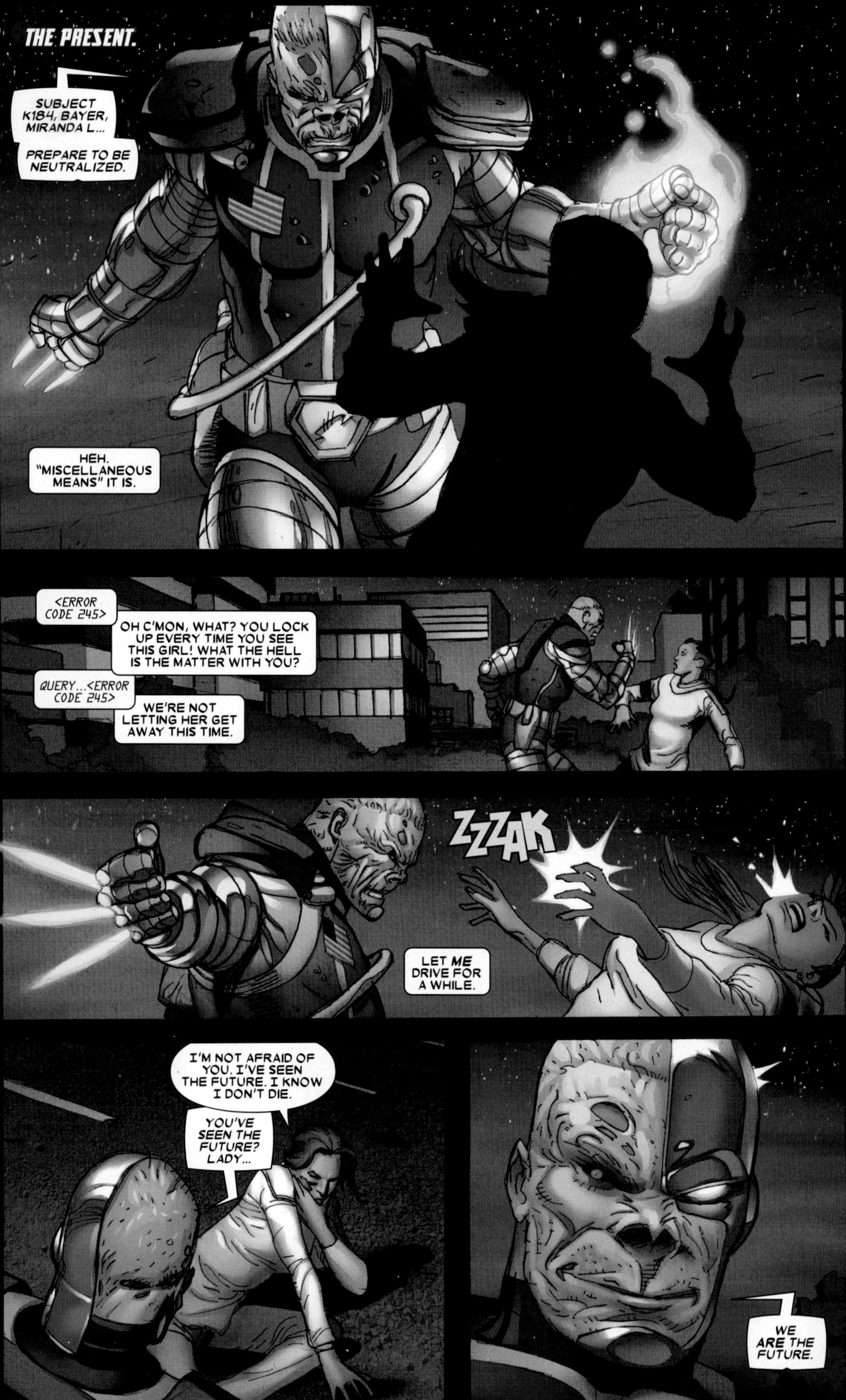
THE PRESENT.
SUBJECT K184, BAYER, MIRANDA L...
PREPARE TO BE NEUTRALIZED.
HEH. "MISCELLANEOUS MEANS" IT IS.
<ERROR CODE 245>
OH C'MON, WHAT? YOU LOCK UP EVERY TIME YOU SEE THIS GIRL! WHAT THE HELL IS THE MATTER WITH YOU?
QUERY...<ERROR CODE 245>
WE'RE NOT LETTING HER GET AWAY THIS TIME.
ZZZAK
LET ME DRIVE FOR A WHILE.
I'M NOT AFRAID OF YOU. I'VE SEEN THE FUTURE. I KNOW I DON'T DIE.
YOU'VE SEEN THE FUTURE? LADY...
WE ARE THE FUTURE.

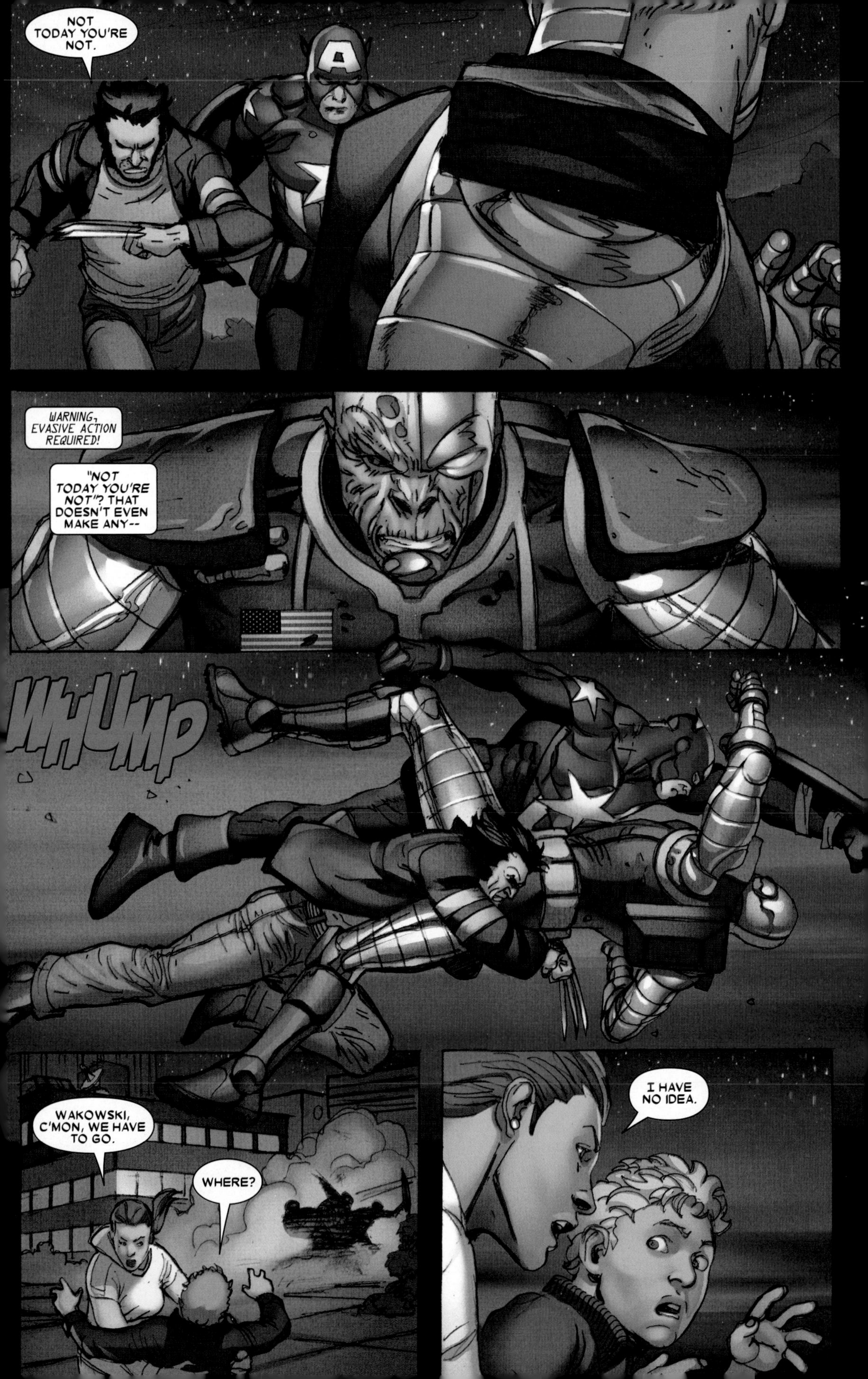
NOT TODAY YOU'RE NOT.
WARNING, EVASIVE ACTION REQUIRED!
"NOT TODAY YOU'RE NOT"? THAT DOESN'T EVEN MAKE ANY--
WHUMP
WAKOWSKI, C'MON, WE HAVE TO GO.
WHERE?
I HAVE NO IDEA.

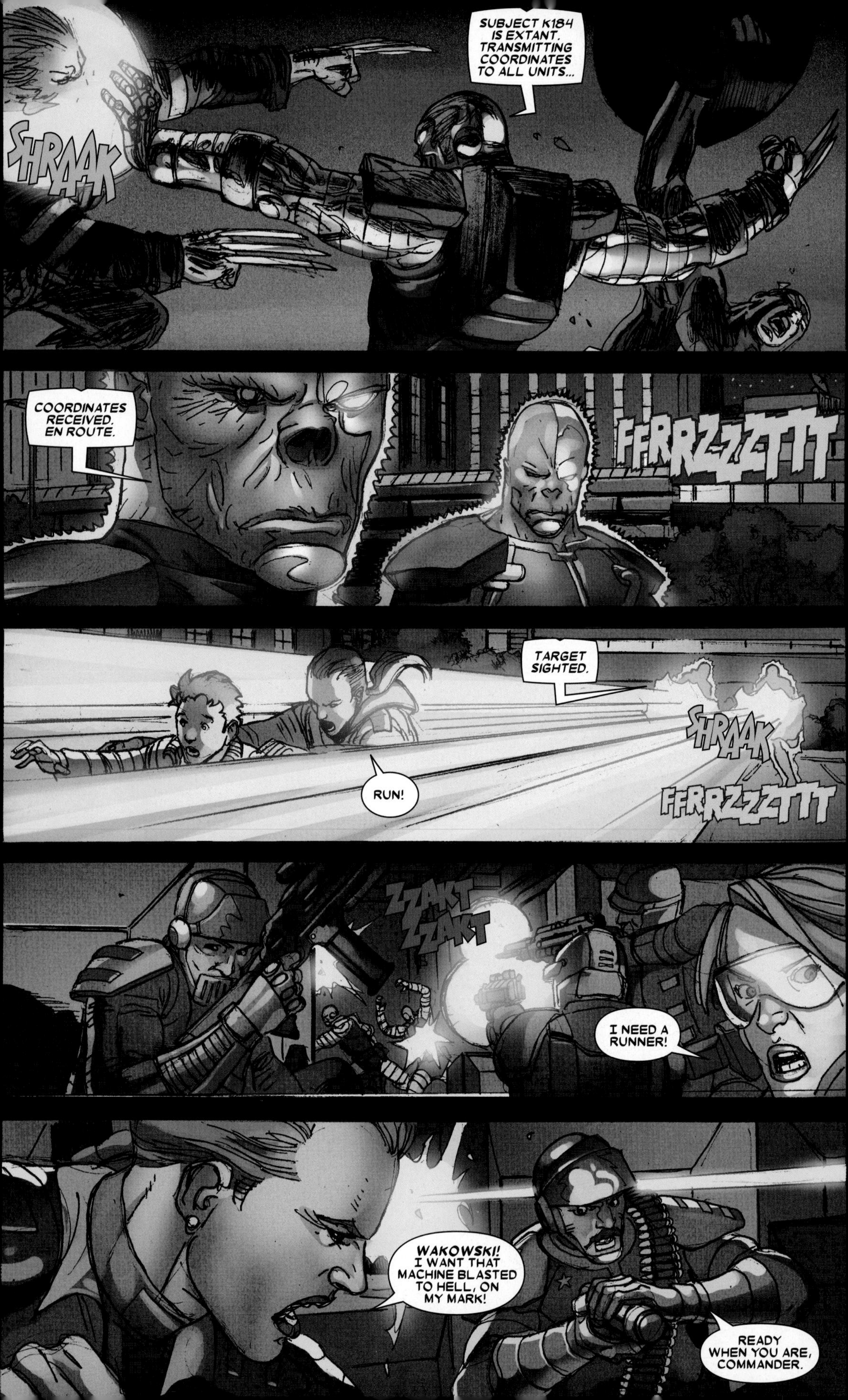
SUBJECT K184 IS EXTANT. TRANSMITTING COORDINATES TO ALL UNITS...
SHRAAK
COORDINATES RECEIVED. EN ROUTE.
FFRRZZZTTT
TARGET SIGHTED.
RUN!
SHRAAK
FFRRZZZTTT
ZZAKT
ZZAKT
I NEED A RUNNER!
WAKOWSKI! I WANT THAT MACHINE BLASTED TO HELL, ON MY MARK!
READY WHEN YOU ARE, COMMANDER.

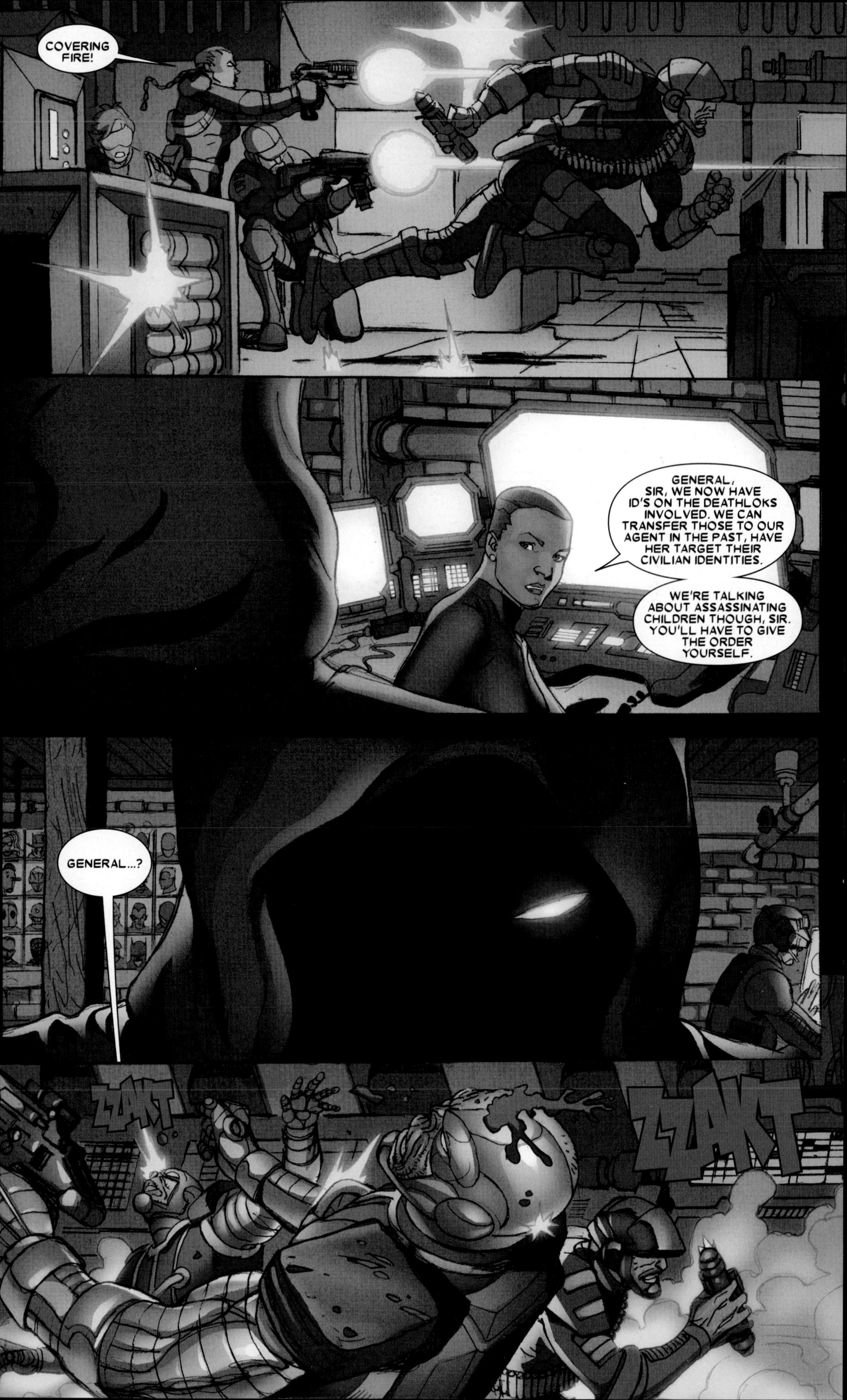
COVERING FIRE!
GENERAL, SIR, WE NOW HAVE ID'S ON THE DEATHLOKS INVOLVED. WE CAN TRANSFER THOSE TO OUR AGENT IN THE PAST, HAVE HER TARGET THEIR CIVILIAN IDENTITIES.
WE'RE TALKING ABOUT ASSASSINATING CHILDREN THOUGH, SIR. YOU'LL HAVE TO GIVE THE ORDER YOURSELF.
GENERAL...?
ZZAKT
ZZAKT

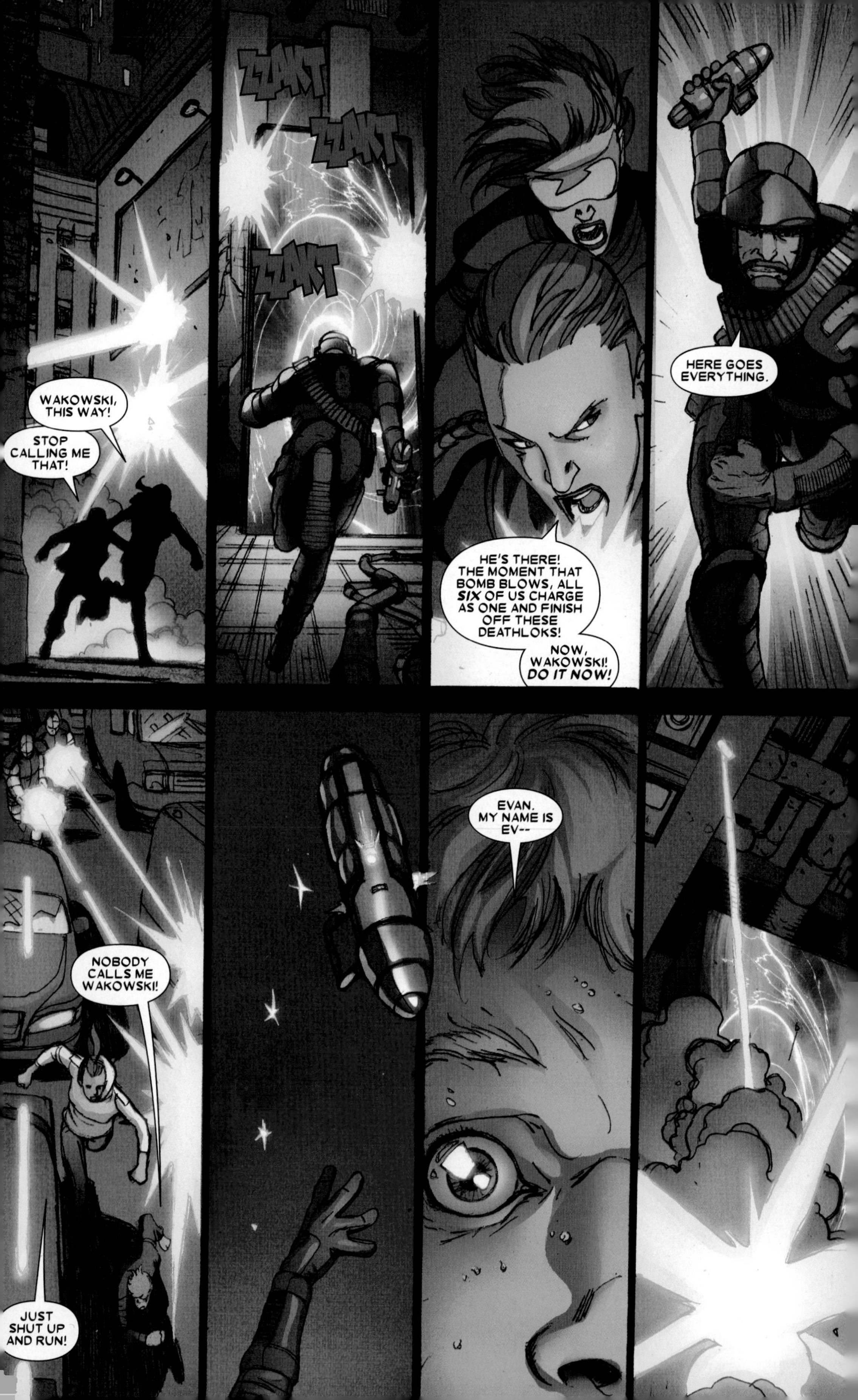
WAKOWSKI, THIS WAY!
STOP CALLING ME THAT!
ZZAKT
ZZAKT
ZZAKT
HE'S THERE! THE MOMENT THAT BOMB BLOWS, ALL *SIX* OF US CHARGE AS ONE AND FINISH OFF THESE DEATHLOKS!
NOW, WAKOWSKI! *DO IT NOW!*
HERE GOES EVERYTHING.
NOBODY CALLS ME WAKOWSKI!
JUST SHUT UP AND RUN!
EVAN. MY NAME IS EV--

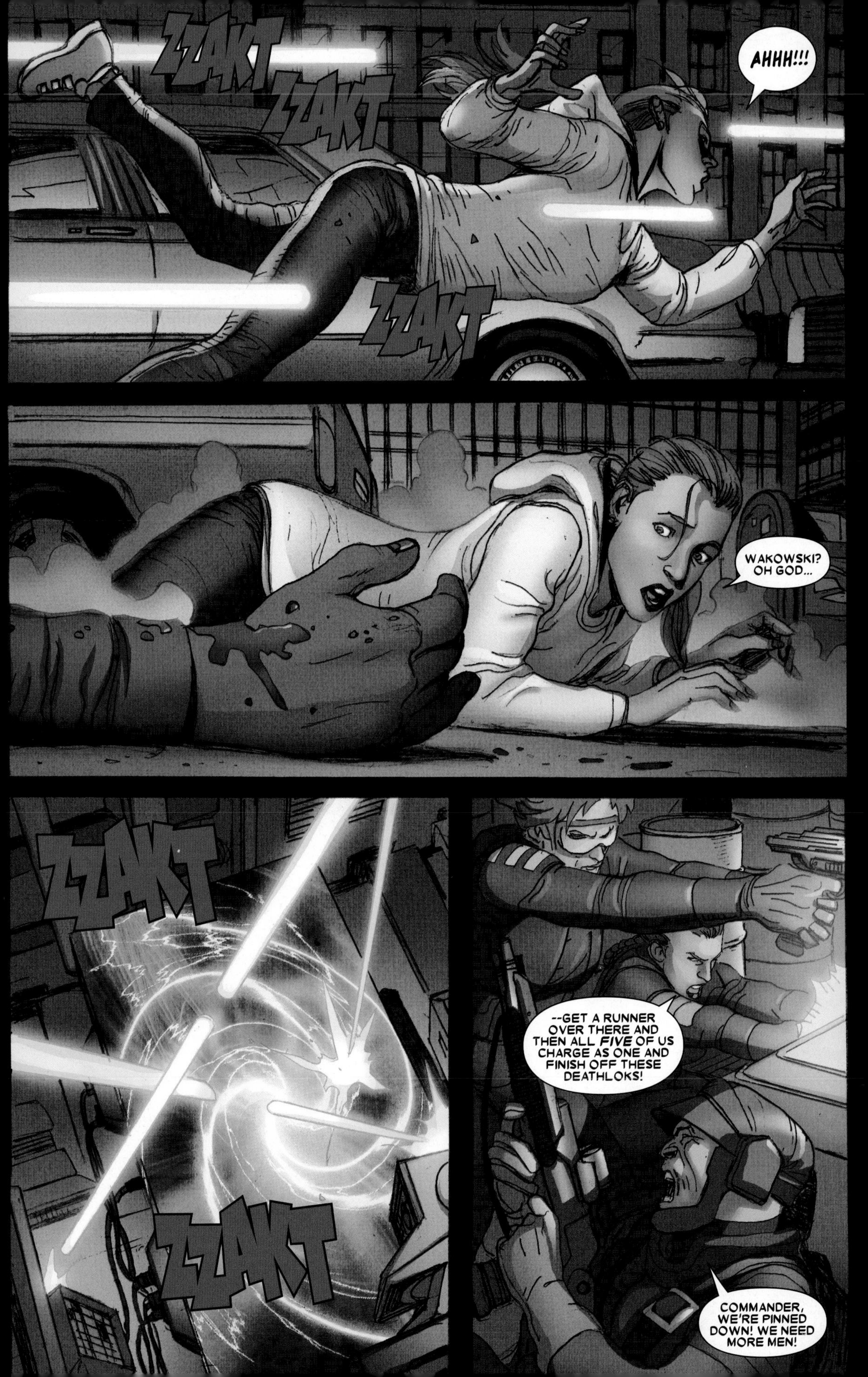
ZZAKT
ZZAKT
AHHH!!!
ZZAKT
WAKOWSKI? OH GOD...
ZZAKT
ZZAKT
--GET A RUNNER OVER THERE AND THEN ALL *FIVE* OF US CHARGE AS ONE AND FINISH OFF THESE DEATHLOKS!
COMMANDER, WE'RE PINNED DOWN! WE NEED MORE MEN!

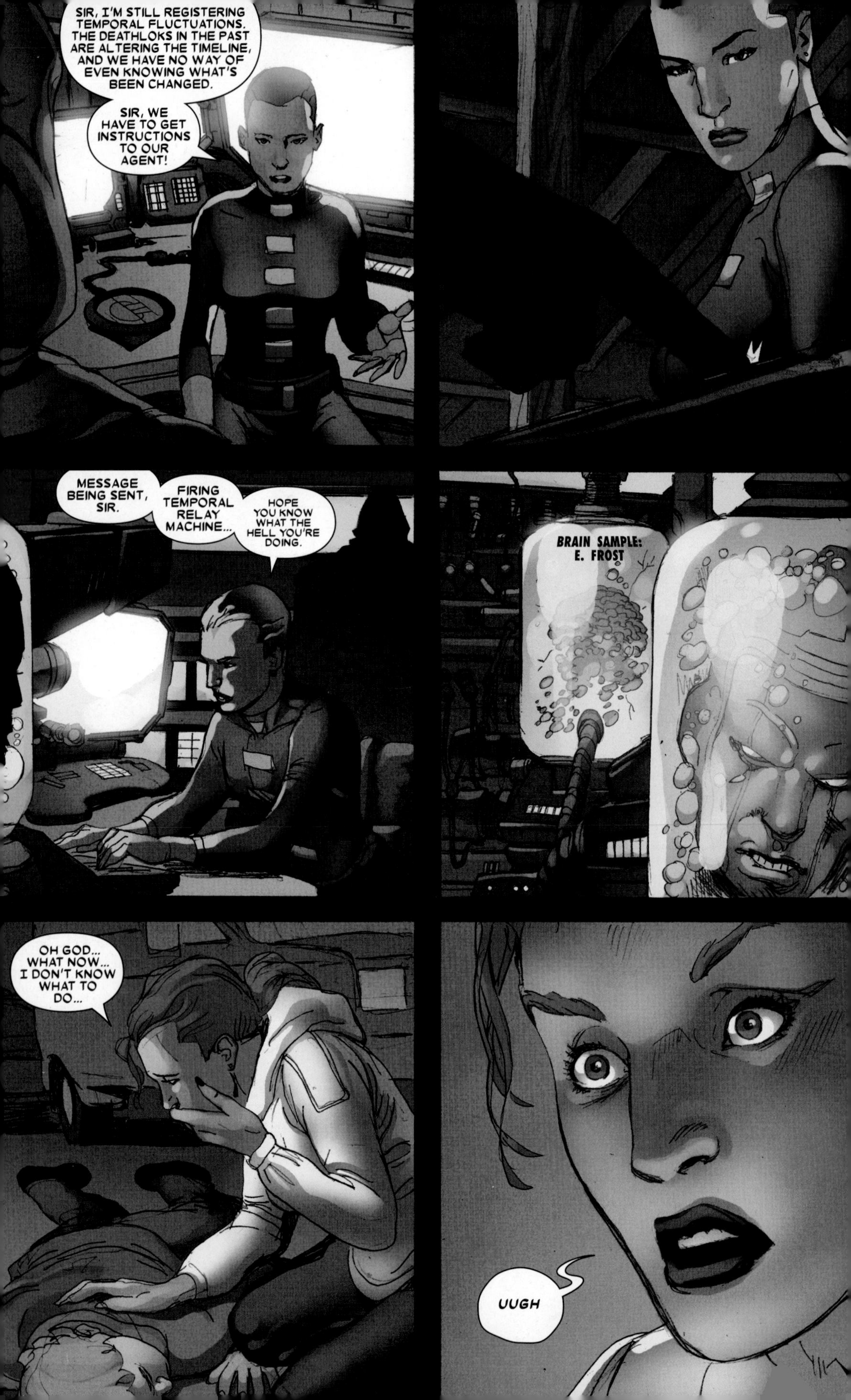
SIR, I'M STILL REGISTERING TEMPORAL FLUCTUATIONS. THE DEATHLOKS IN THE PAST ARE ALTERING THE TIMELINE, AND WE HAVE NO WAY OF EVEN KNOWING WHAT'S BEEN CHANGED.
SIR, WE HAVE TO GET INSTRUCTIONS TO OUR AGENT!
MESSAGE BEING SENT, SIR.
FIRING TEMPORAL RELAY MACHINE...
HOPE YOU KNOW WHAT THE HELL YOU'RE DOING.
BRAIN SAMPLE: E. FROST
OH GOD... WHAT NOW... I DON'T KNOW WHAT TO DO...
UUGH

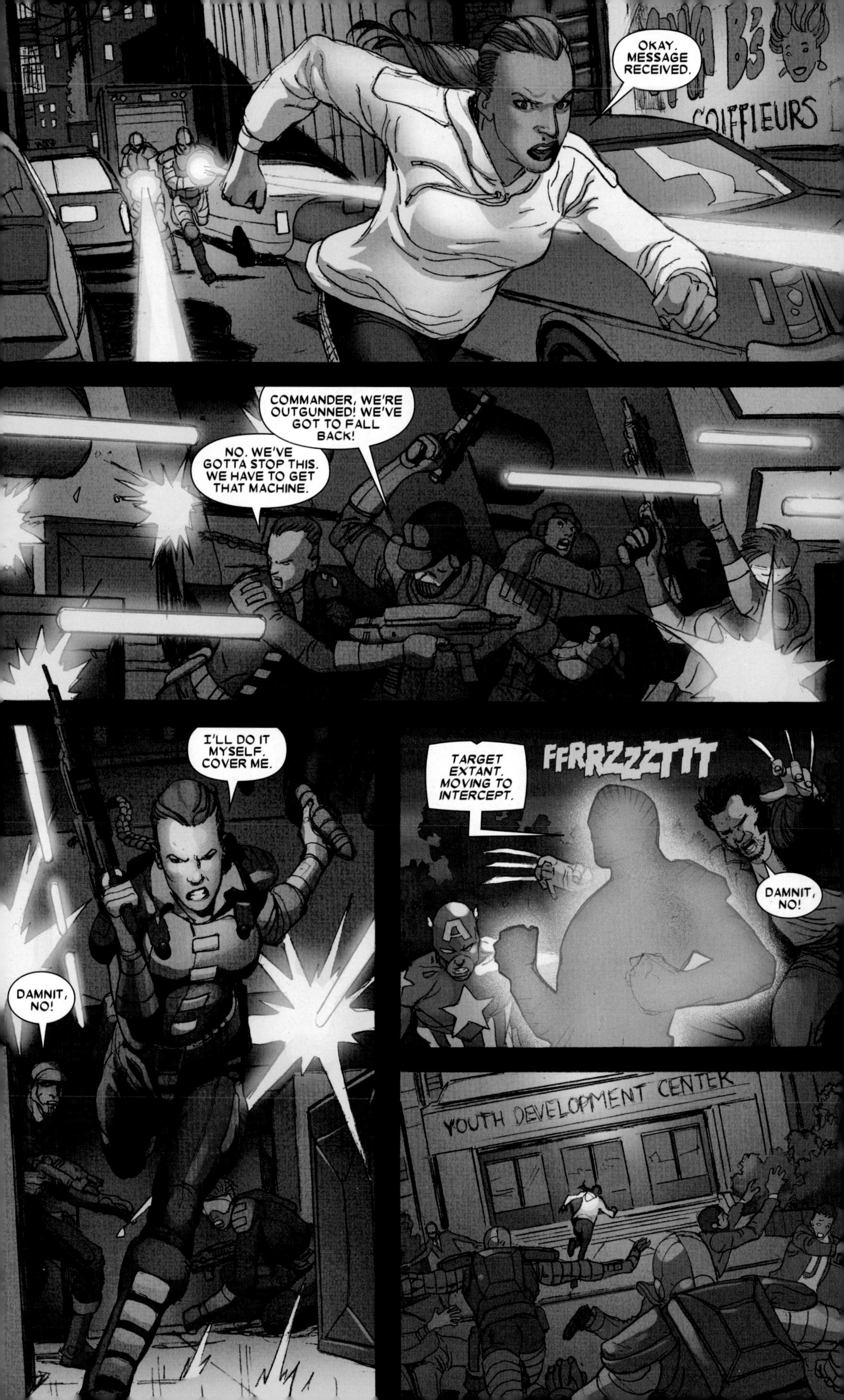

OKAY. MESSAGE RECEIVED.
COIFFEURS
COMMANDER, WE'RE OUTGUNNED! WE'VE GOT TO FALL BACK!
NO. WE'VE GOTTA STOP THIS. WE HAVE TO GET THAT MACHINE.
I'LL DO IT MYSELF. COVER ME.
DAMNIT, NO!
TARGET EXTANT. MOVING TO INTERCEPT.
FFRRZZZTTT
DAMNIT, NO!
YOUTH DEVELOPMENT CENTER

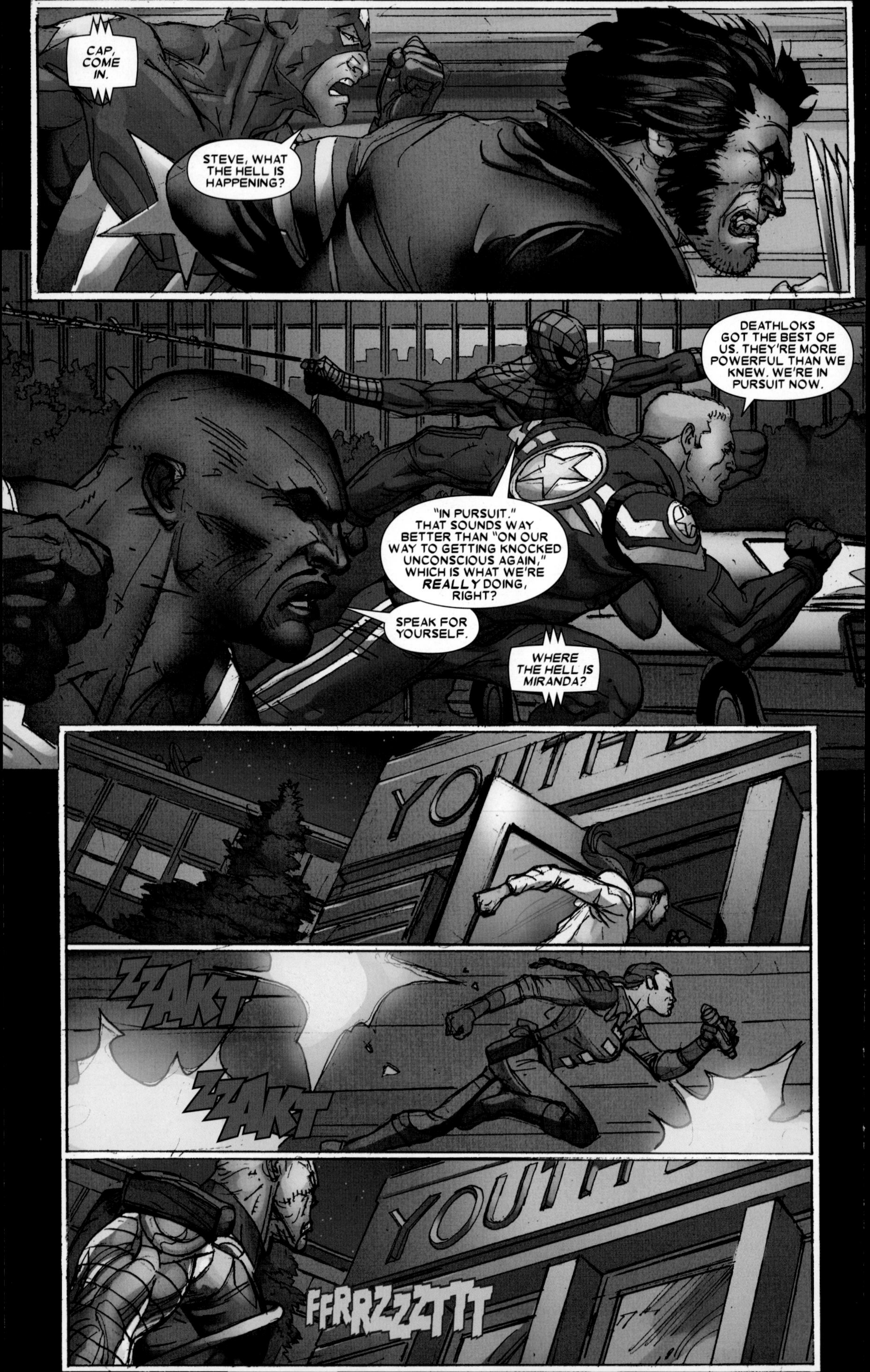
CAP, COME IN.
STEVE, WHAT THE HELL IS HAPPENING?
DEATHLOKS GOT THE BEST OF US. THEY'RE MORE POWERFUL THAN WE KNEW. WE'RE IN PURSUIT NOW.
"IN PURSUIT." THAT SOUNDS WAY BETTER THAN "ON OUR WAY TO GETTING KNOCKED UNCONSCIOUS AGAIN," WHICH IS WHAT WE'RE REALLY DOING, RIGHT?
SPEAK FOR YOURSELF.
WHERE THE HELL IS MIRANDA?
YOUTH
ZZAKT
ZZAKT
YOUTH
FFRRZZZTTTT

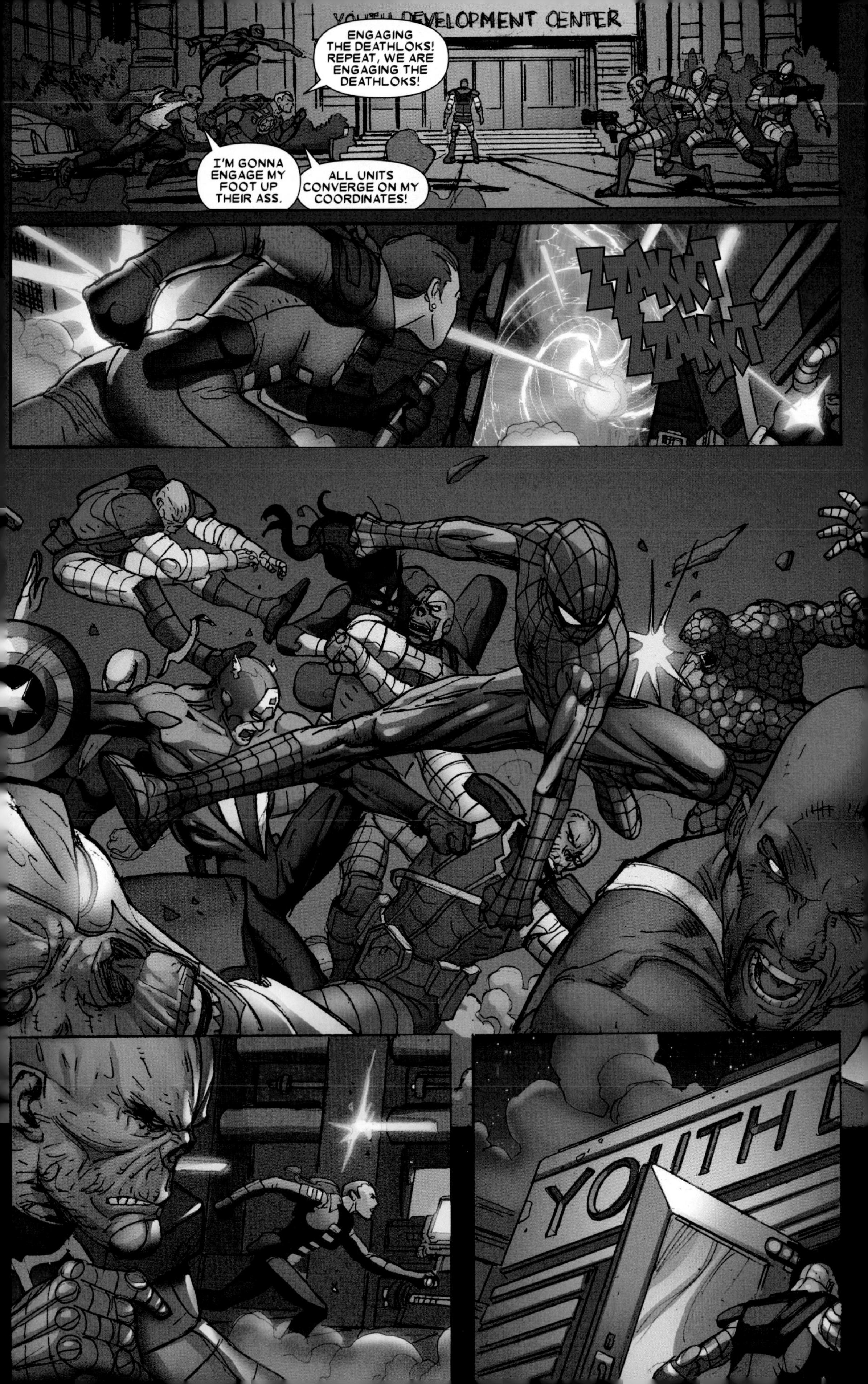
YOUTH DEVELOPMENT CENTER
ENGAGING THE DEATHLOKS! REPEAT, WE ARE ENGAGING THE DEATHLOKS!
I'M GONNA ENGAGE MY FOOT UP THEIR ASS.
ALL UNITS CONVERGE ON MY COORDINATES!
ZZAKKT ZZAKKT
YOUTH

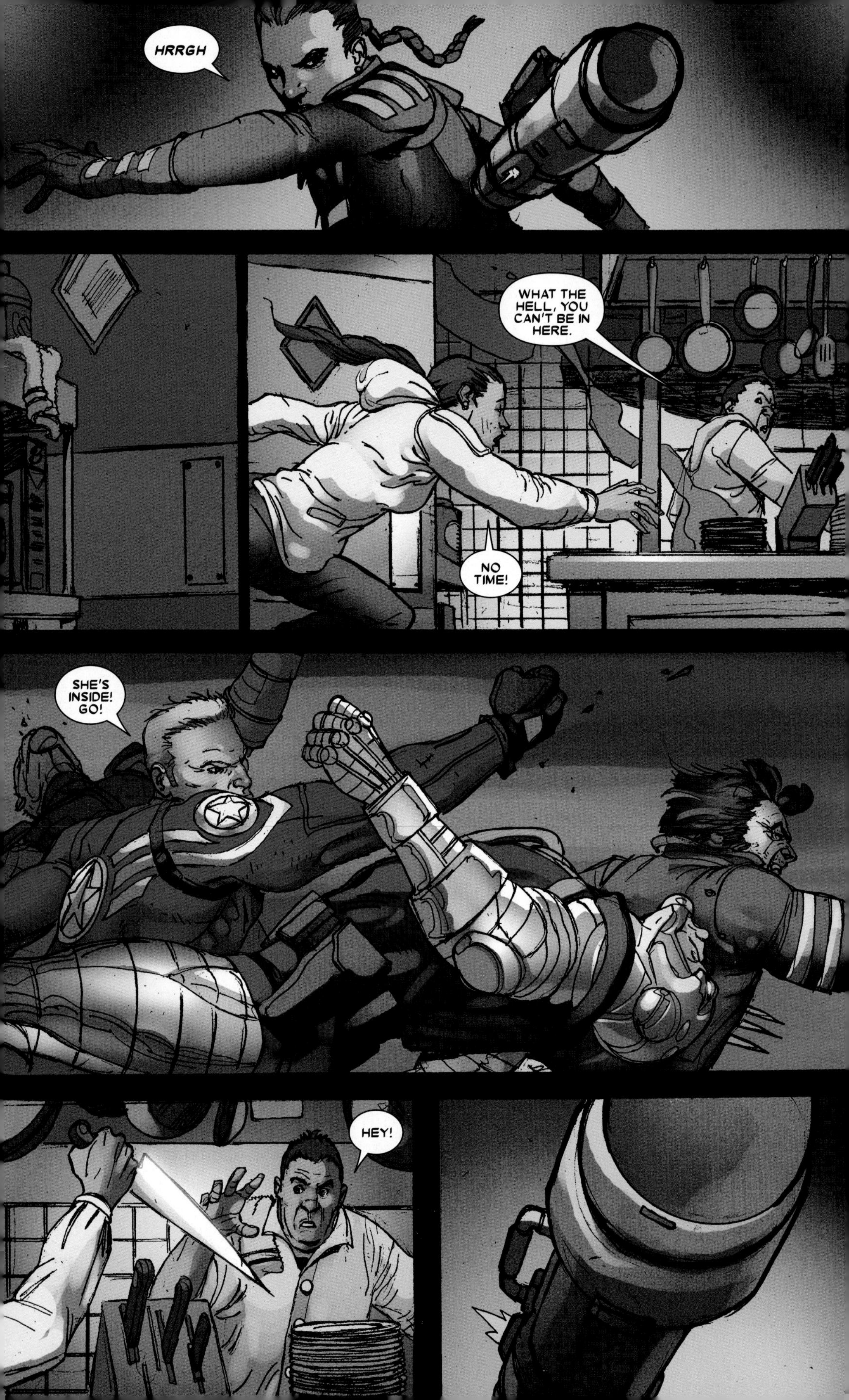
HRRGH
WHAT THE HELL, YOU CAN'T BE IN HERE.
NO TIME!
SHE'S INSIDE! GO!
HEY!

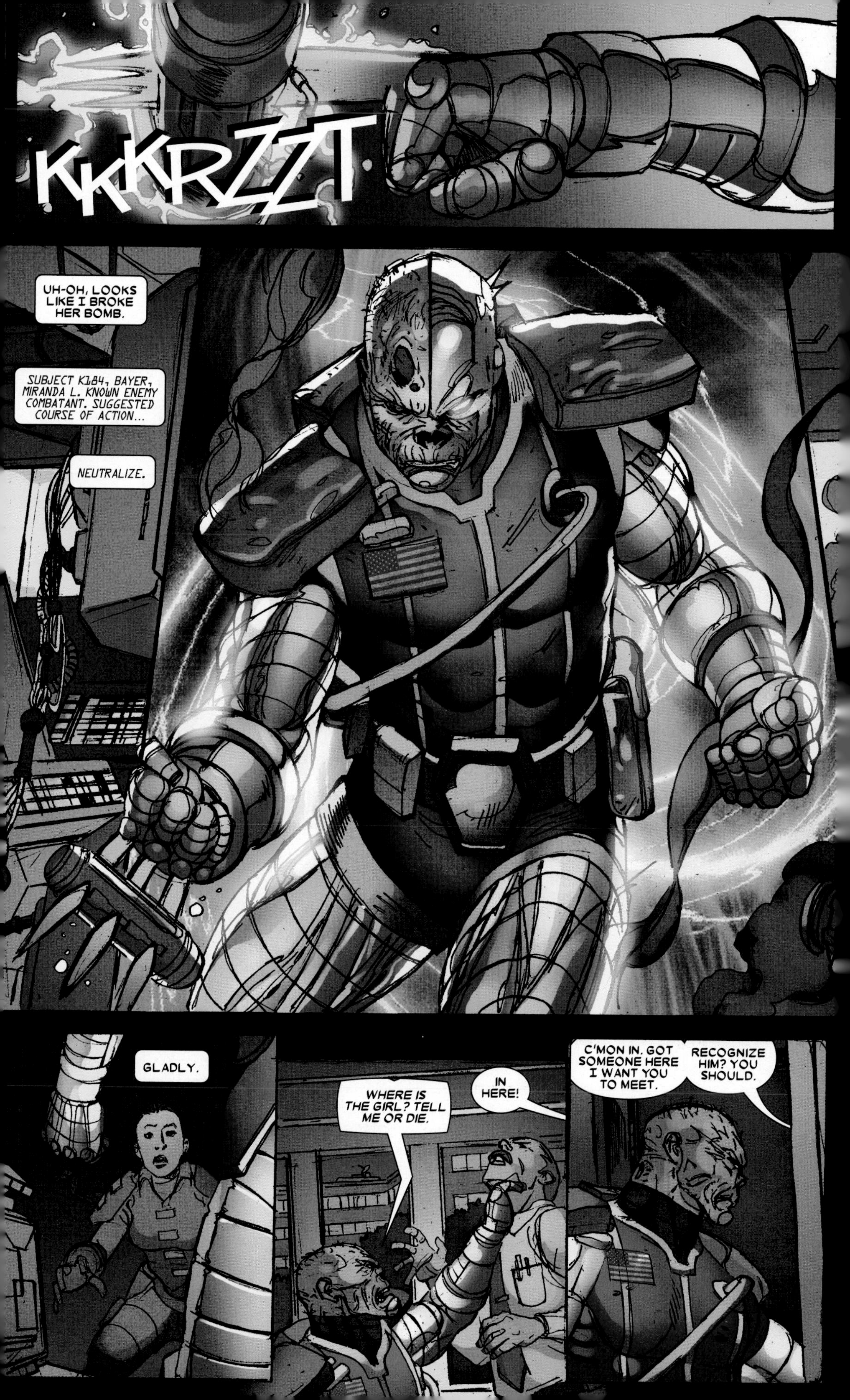
KKKRZZZT
UH-OH, LOOKS LIKE I BROKE HER BOMB.
SUBJECT K184, BAYER, MIRANDA L. KNOWN ENEMY COMBATANT. SUGGESTED COURSE OF ACTION...
NEUTRALIZE.
GLADLY.
WHERE IS THE GIRL? TELL ME OR DIE.
IN HERE!
C'MON IN. GOT SOMEONE HERE I WANT YOU TO MEET.
RECOGNIZE HIM? YOU SHOULD.

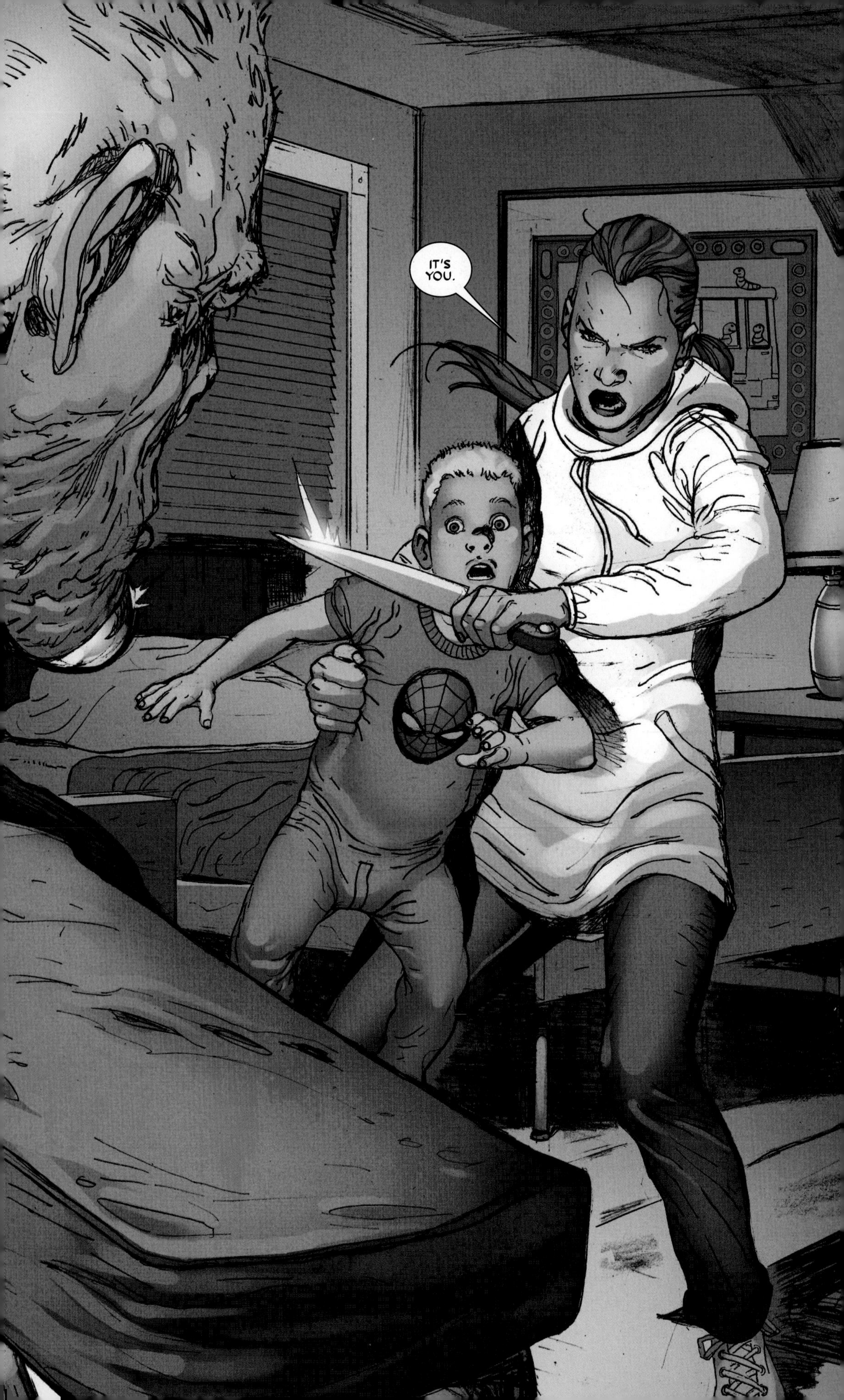
IT'S YOU.

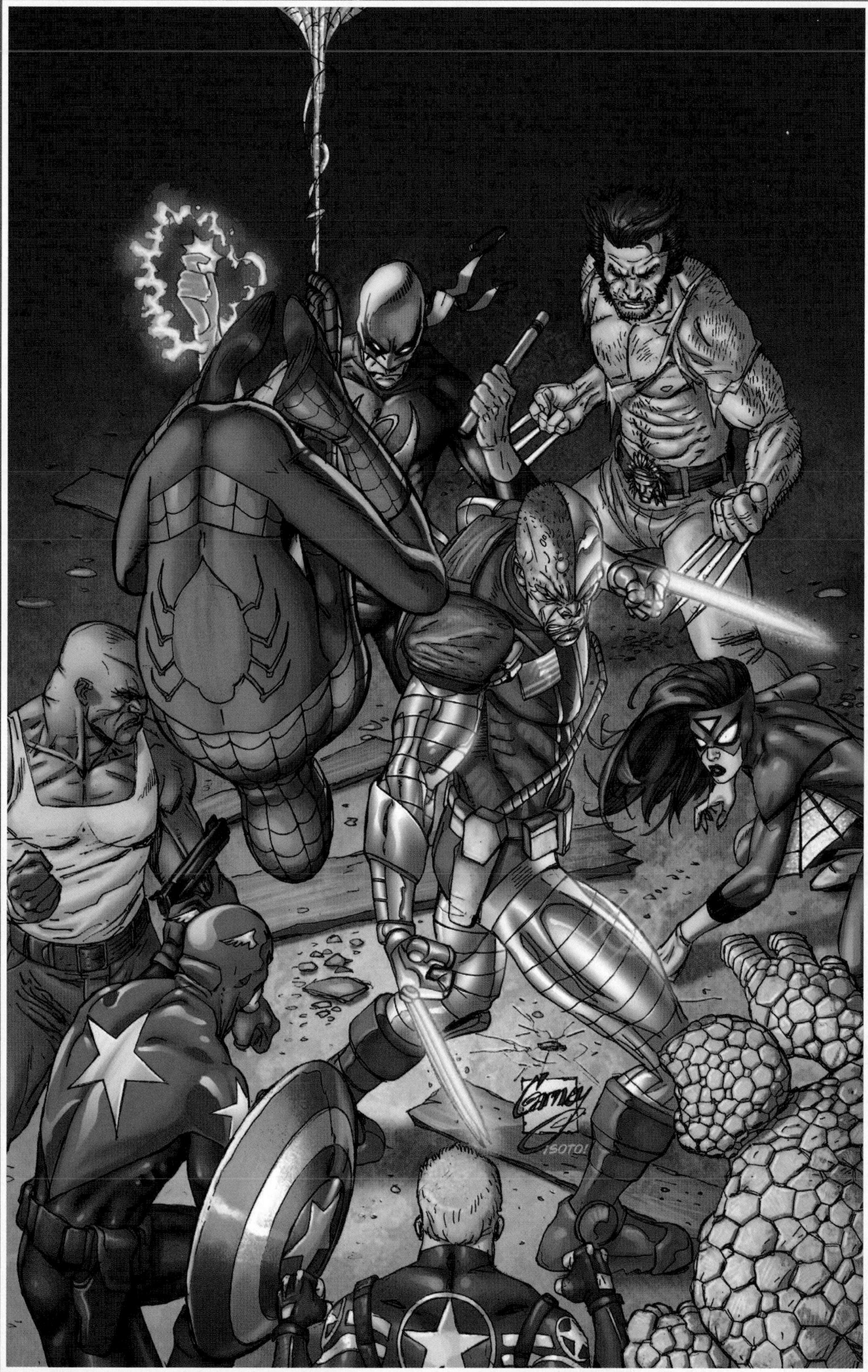
¡SOTO!

FIFTEEN

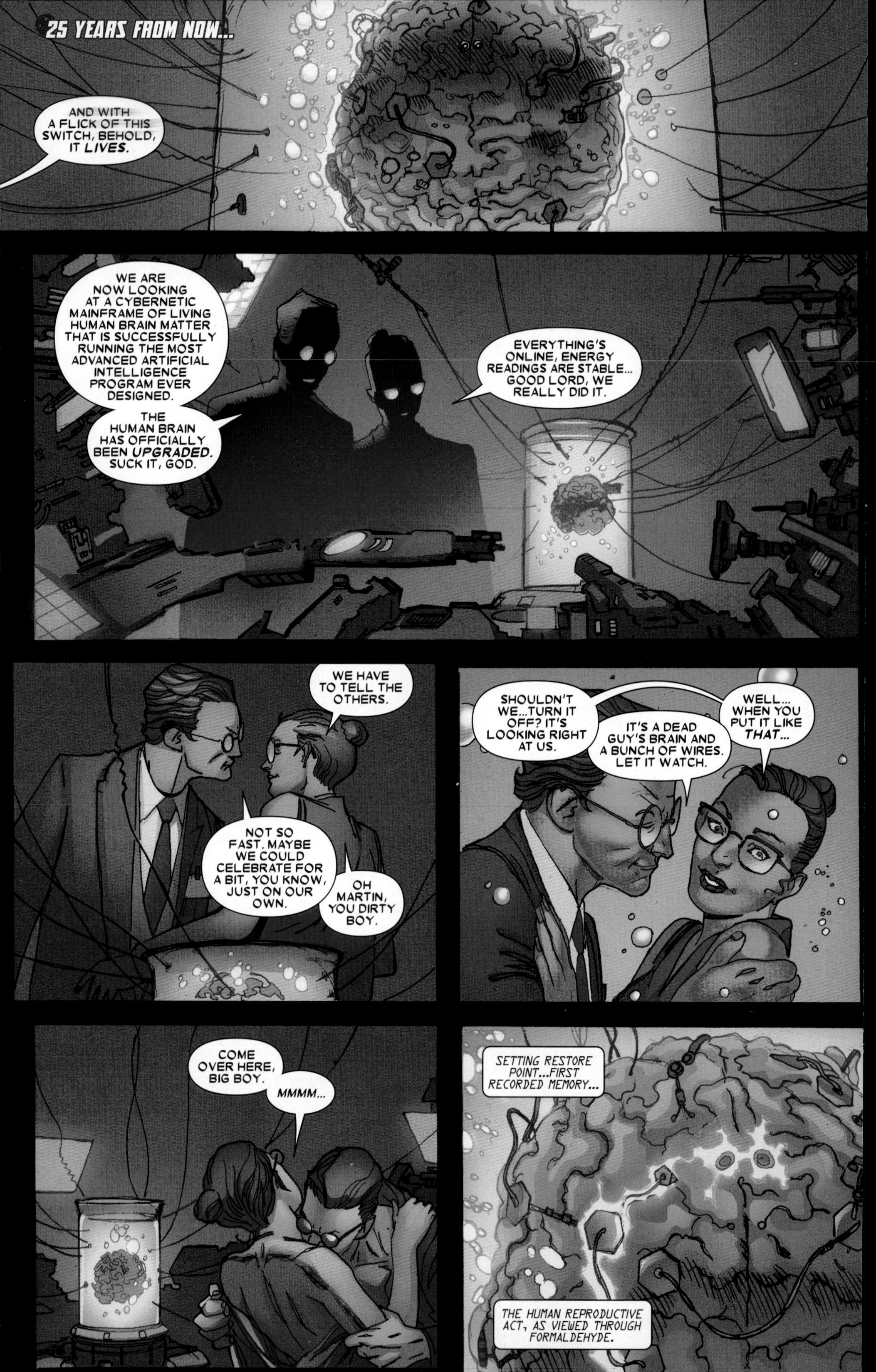
25 YEARS FROM NOW...
AND WITH A FLICK OF THIS SWITCH, BEHOLD, IT LIVES.
WE ARE NOW LOOKING AT A CYBERNETIC MAINFRAME OF LIVING HUMAN BRAIN MATTER THAT IS SUCCESSFULLY RUNNING THE MOST ADVANCED ARTIFICIAL INTELLIGENCE PROGRAM EVER DESIGNED.
THE HUMAN BRAIN HAS OFFICIALLY BEEN UPGRADED. SUCK IT, GOD.
EVERYTHING'S ONLINE, ENERGY READINGS ARE STABLE... GOOD LORD, WE REALLY DID IT.
WE HAVE TO TELL THE OTHERS.
NOT SO FAST. MAYBE WE COULD CELEBRATE FOR A BIT, YOU KNOW, JUST ON OUR OWN.
OH MARTIN, YOU DIRTY BOY.
SHOULDN'T WE...TURN IT OFF? IT'S LOOKING RIGHT AT US.
IT'S A DEAD GUY'S BRAIN AND A BUNCH OF WIRES. LET IT WATCH.
WELL... WHEN YOU PUT IT LIKE THAT...
COME OVER HERE, BIG BOY.
MMMM...
SETTING RESTORE POINT...FIRST RECORDED MEMORY...
THE HUMAN REPRODUCTIVE ACT, AS VIEWED THROUGH FORMALDEHYDE.

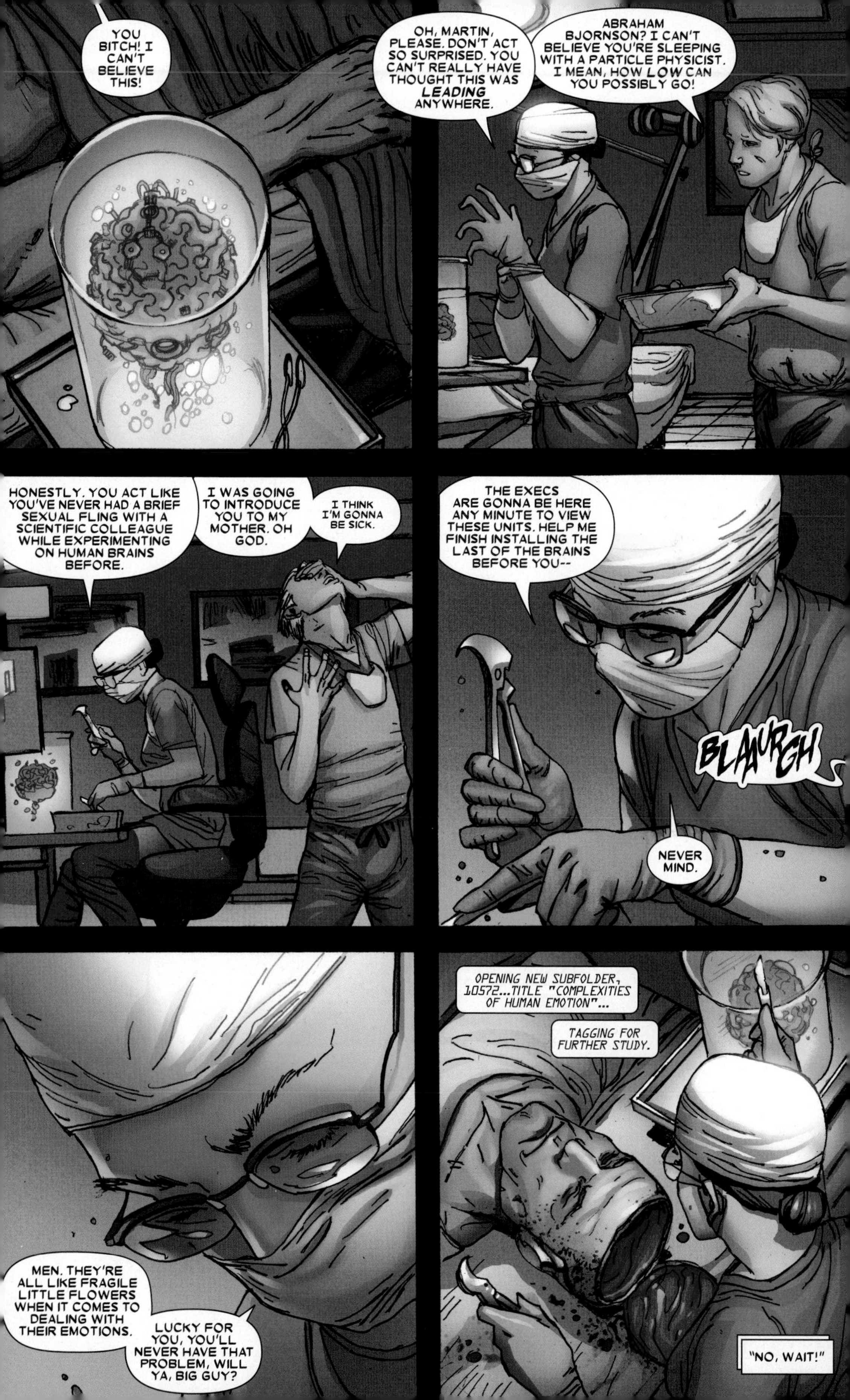
YOU BITCH! I CAN'T BELIEVE THIS!
OH, MARTIN, PLEASE. DON'T ACT SO SURPRISED. YOU CAN'T REALLY HAVE THOUGHT THIS WAS LEADING ANYWHERE.
ABRAHAM BJORNSON? I CAN'T BELIEVE YOU'RE SLEEPING WITH A PARTICLE PHYSICIST. I MEAN, HOW LOW CAN YOU POSSIBLY GO!
HONESTLY. YOU ACT LIKE YOU'VE NEVER HAD A BRIEF SEXUAL FLING WITH A SCIENTIFIC COLLEAGUE WHILE EXPERIMENTING ON HUMAN BRAINS BEFORE.
I WAS GOING TO INTRODUCE YOU TO MY MOTHER. OH GOD.
I THINK I'M GONNA BE SICK.
THE EXECS ARE GONNA BE HERE ANY MINUTE TO VIEW THESE UNITS. HELP ME FINISH INSTALLING THE LAST OF THE BRAINS BEFORE YOU--
BLAAURGH
NEVER MIND.
MEN. THEY'RE ALL LIKE FRAGILE LITTLE FLOWERS WHEN IT COMES TO DEALING WITH THEIR EMOTIONS.
LUCKY FOR YOU, YOU'LL NEVER HAVE THAT PROBLEM, WILL YA, BIG GUY?
OPENING NEW SUBFOLDER, 10572...TITLE "COMPLEXITIES OF HUMAN EMOTION"...
TAGGING FOR FURTHER STUDY.
"NO, WAIT!"

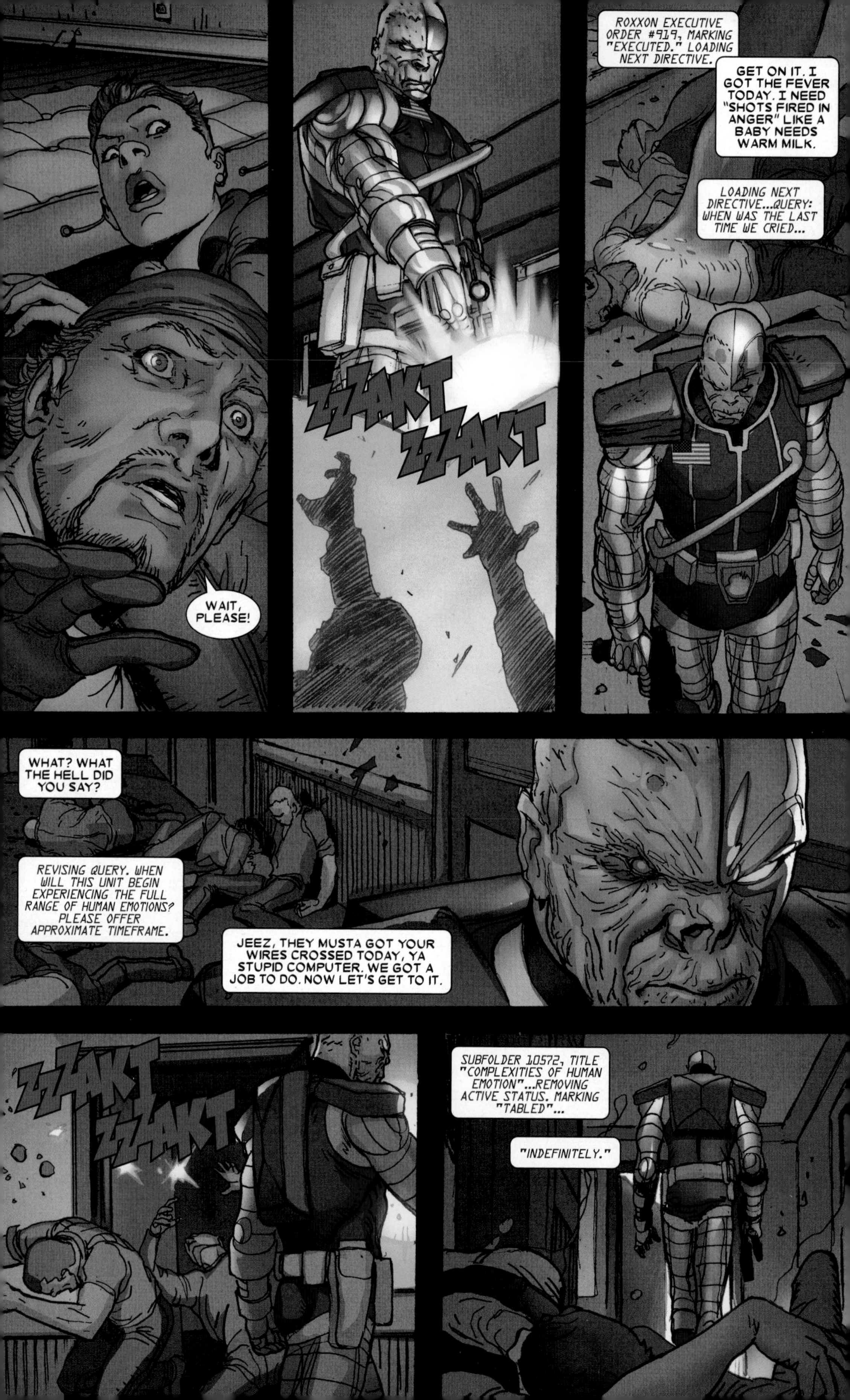
WAIT, PLEASE!
ZZZAKT
ZZZAKT
ROXXON EXECUTIVE ORDER #919, MARKING "EXECUTED." LOADING NEXT DIRECTIVE.
GET ON IT. I GOT THE FEVER TODAY. I NEED "SHOTS FIRED IN ANGER" LIKE A BABY NEEDS WARM MILK.
LOADING NEXT DIRECTIVE...QUERY: WHEN WAS THE LAST TIME WE CRIED...
WHAT? WHAT THE HELL DID YOU SAY?
REVISING QUERY. WHEN WILL THIS UNIT BEGIN EXPERIENCING THE FULL RANGE OF HUMAN EMOTIONS? PLEASE OFFER APPROXIMATE TIMEFRAME.
JEEZ, THEY MUSTA GOT YOUR WIRES CROSSED TODAY, YA STUPID COMPUTER. WE GOT A JOB TO DO. NOW LET'S GET TO IT.
ZZZAKT
ZZZAKT
SUBFOLDER 10572, TITLE "COMPLEXITIES OF HUMAN EMOTION"...REMOVING ACTIVE STATUS. MARKING "TABLED"...
"INDEFINITELY."

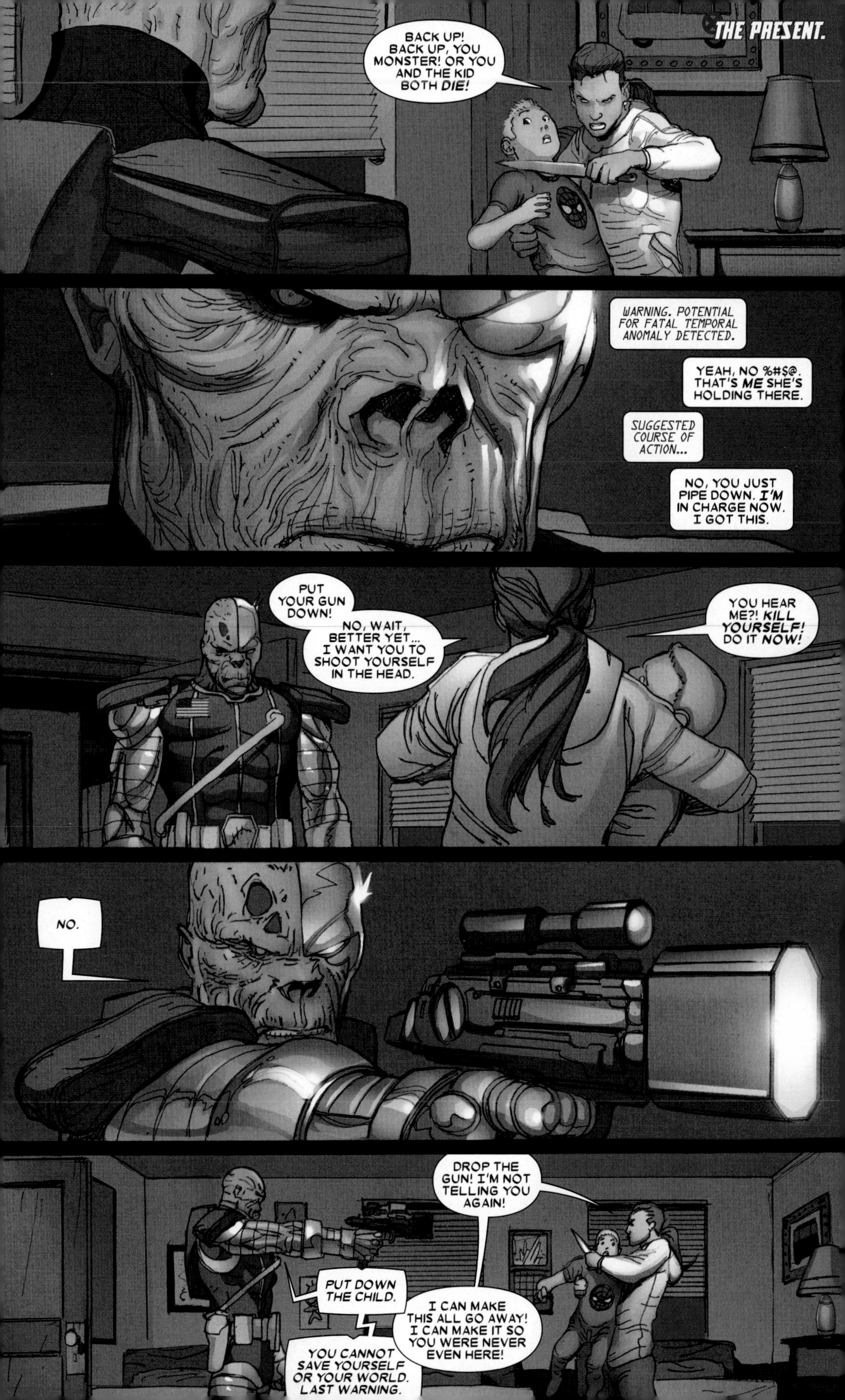
THE PRESENT.
BACK UP! BACK UP, YOU MONSTER! OR YOU AND THE KID BOTH DIE!
WARNING. POTENTIAL FOR FATAL TEMPORAL ANOMALY DETECTED.
YEAH, NO %#$@. THAT'S ME SHE'S HOLDING THERE.
SUGGESTED COURSE OF ACTION...
NO, YOU JUST PIPE DOWN. I'M IN CHARGE NOW. I GOT THIS.
PUT YOUR GUN DOWN!
NO, WAIT, BETTER YET... I WANT YOU TO SHOOT YOURSELF IN THE HEAD.
YOU HEAR ME?! KILL YOURSELF! DO IT NOW!
NO.
DROP THE GUN! I'M NOT TELLING YOU AGAIN!
PUT DOWN THE CHILD.
YOU CANNOT SAVE YOURSELF OR YOUR WORLD. LAST WARNING.
I CAN MAKE THIS ALL GO AWAY! I CAN MAKE IT SO YOU WERE NEVER EVEN HERE!

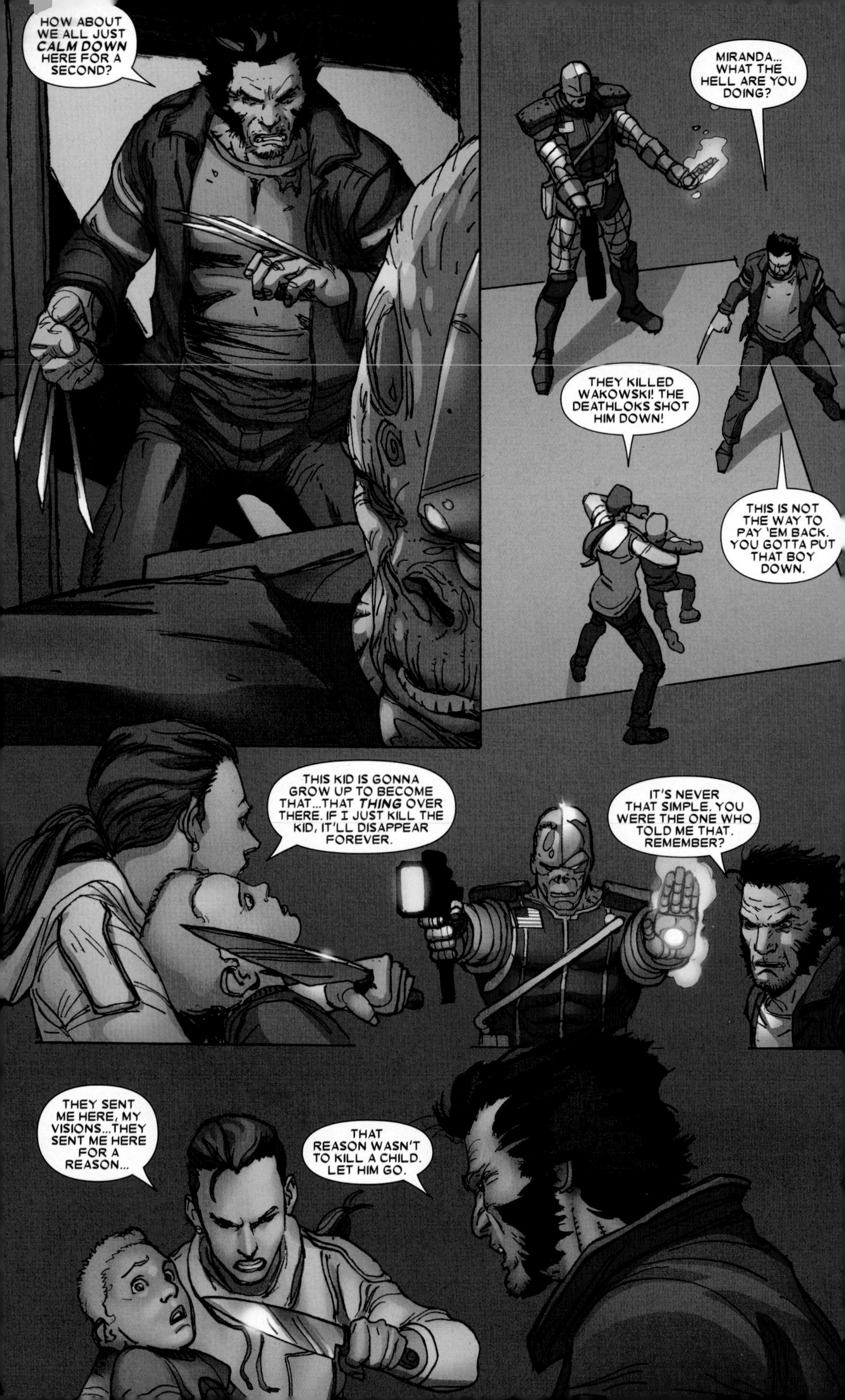
HOW ABOUT WE ALL JUST *CALM DOWN* HERE FOR A SECOND?
MIRANDA... WHAT THE HELL ARE YOU DOING?
THEY KILLED WAKOWSKI! THE DEATHLOKS SHOT HIM DOWN!
THIS IS NOT THE WAY TO PAY 'EM BACK. YOU GOTTA PUT THAT BOY DOWN.
THIS KID IS GONNA GROW UP TO BECOME THAT...THAT *THING* OVER THERE. IF I JUST KILL THE KID, IT'LL DISAPPEAR FOREVER.
IT'S NEVER THAT SIMPLE. YOU WERE THE ONE WHO TOLD ME THAT. REMEMBER?
THEY SENT ME HERE, MY VISIONS...THEY SENT ME HERE FOR A REASON...
THAT REASON WASN'T TO KILL A CHILD. LET HIM GO.

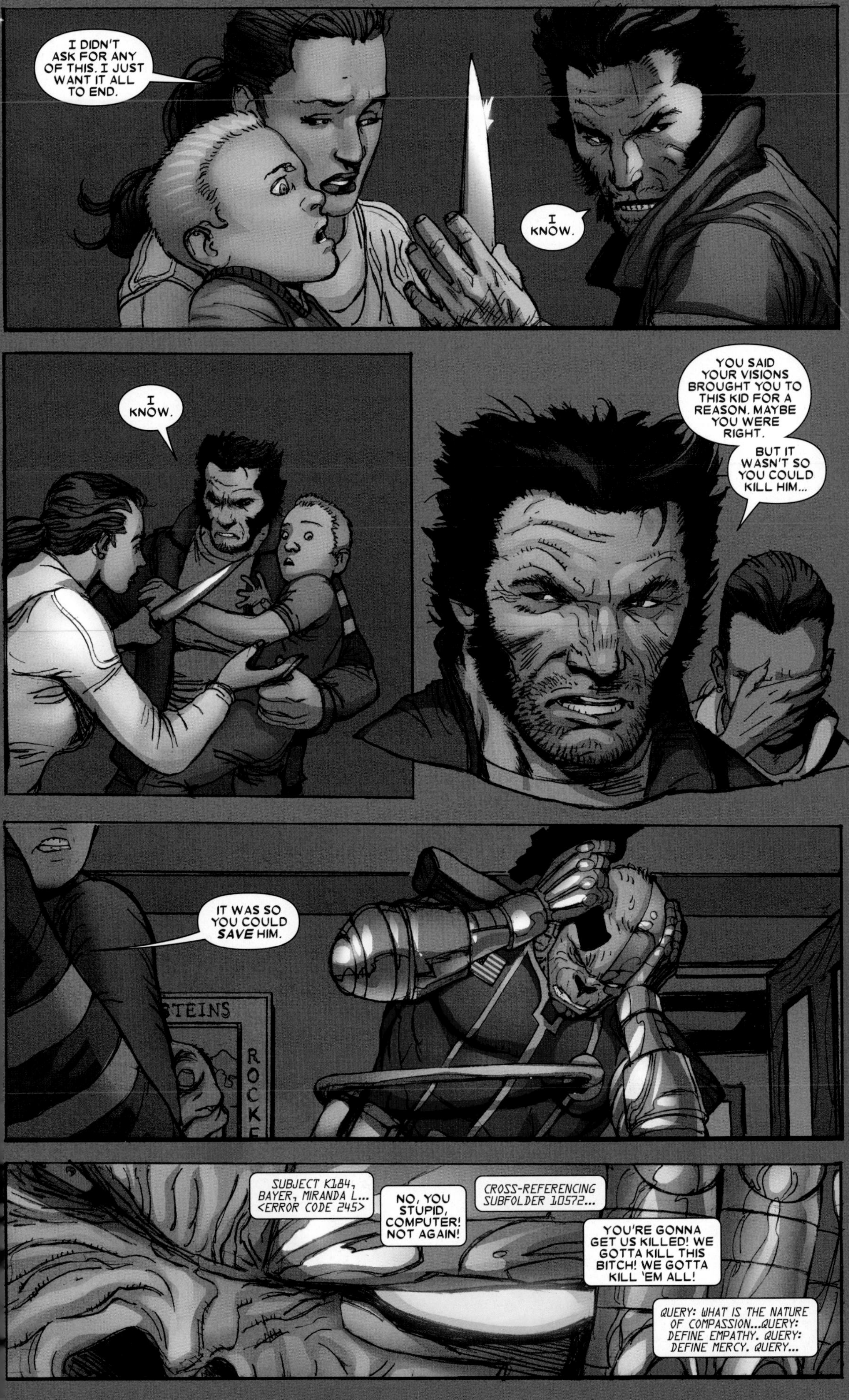
I DIDN'T ASK FOR ANY OF THIS. I JUST WANT IT ALL TO END.
I KNOW.
I KNOW.
YOU SAID YOUR VISIONS BROUGHT YOU TO THIS KID FOR A REASON. MAYBE YOU WERE RIGHT.
BUT IT WASN'T SO YOU COULD KILL HIM...
IT WAS SO YOU COULD SAVE HIM.
STEINS
ROCKE
SUBJECT K184, BAYER, MIRANDA L... <ERROR CODE 245>
NO, YOU STUPID, COMPUTER! NOT AGAIN!
CROSS-REFERENCING SUBFOLDER 10572...
YOU'RE GONNA GET US KILLED! WE GOTTA KILL THIS BITCH! WE GOTTA KILL 'EM ALL!
QUERY: WHAT IS THE NATURE OF COMPASSION...QUERY: DEFINE EMPATHY. QUERY: DEFINE MERCY. QUERY...

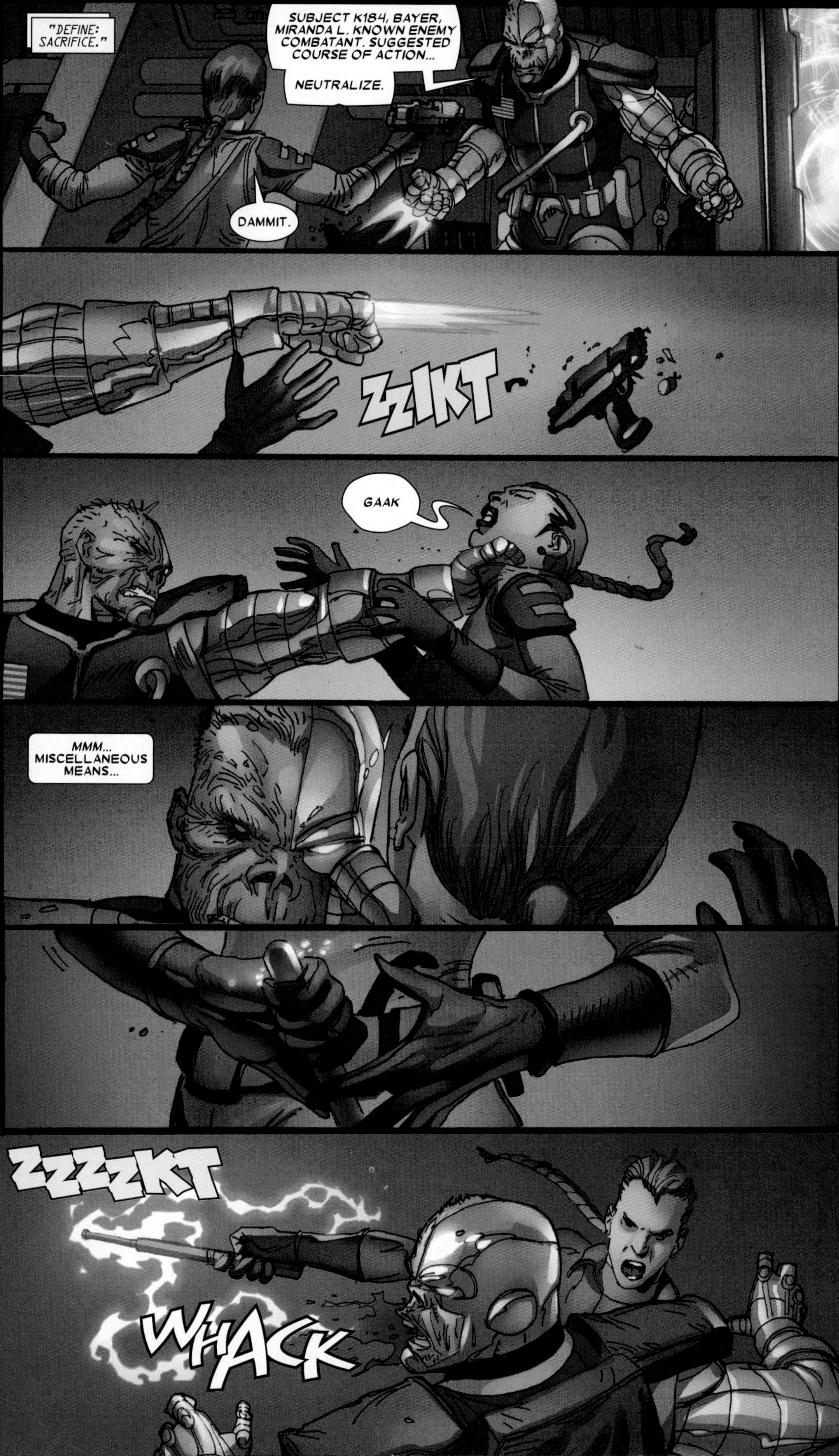
"DEFINE: SACRIFICE."
SUBJECT K184, BAYER, MIRANDA L. KNOWN ENEMY COMBATANT. SUGGESTED COURSE OF ACTION...
NEUTRALIZE.
DAMMIT.
ZZIKT
GAAK
MMM... MISCELLANEOUS MEANS...
ZZZZKT
WHACK

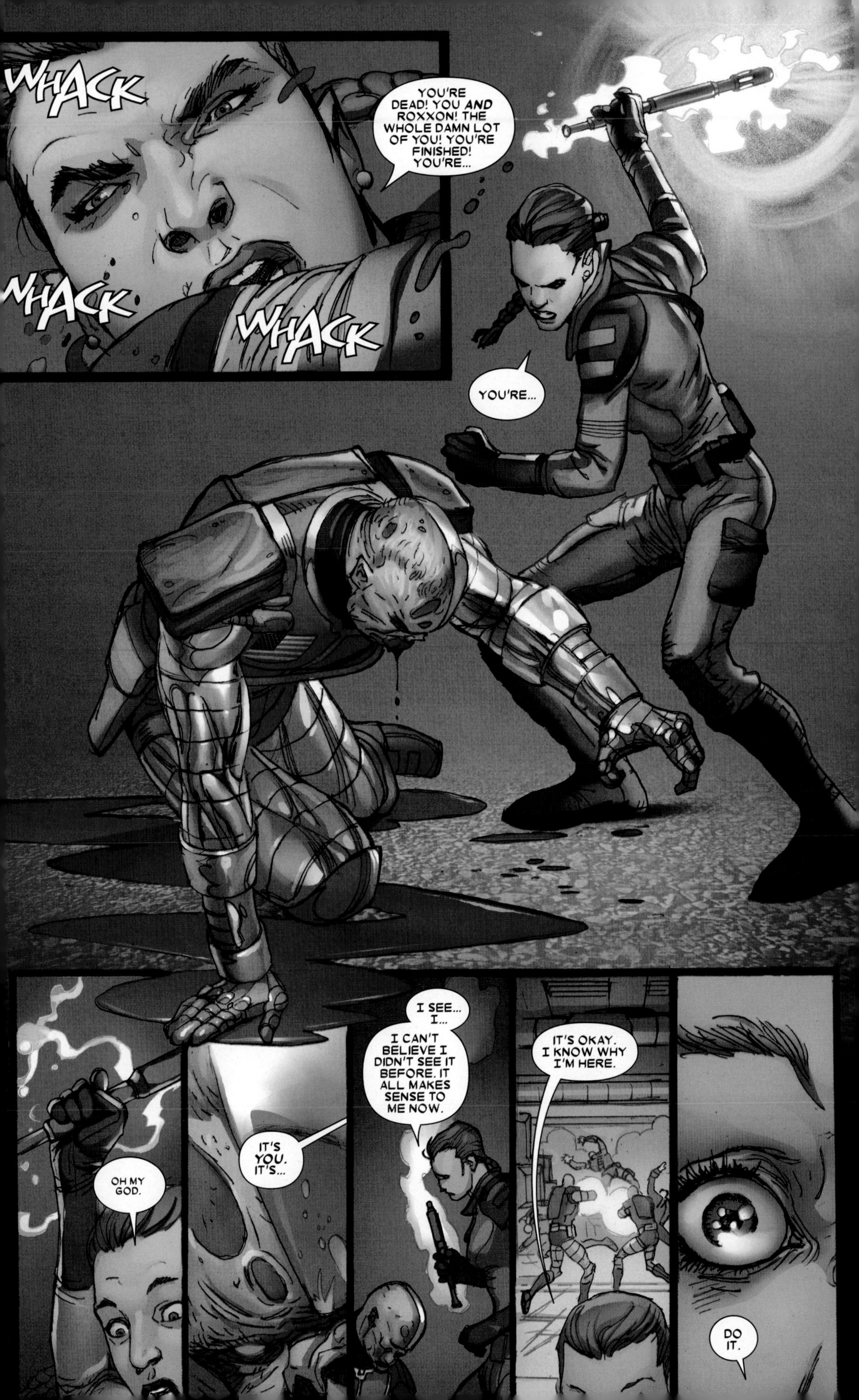
WHACK
YOU'RE DEAD! YOU AND ROXXON! THE WHOLE DAMN LOT OF YOU! YOU'RE FINISHED! YOU'RE...
WHACK
WHACK
YOU'RE...
OH MY GOD.
IT'S YOU. IT'S...
I SEE... I...
I CAN'T BELIEVE I DIDN'T SEE IT BEFORE. IT ALL MAKES SENSE TO ME NOW.
IT'S OKAY. I KNOW WHY I'M HERE.
DO IT.

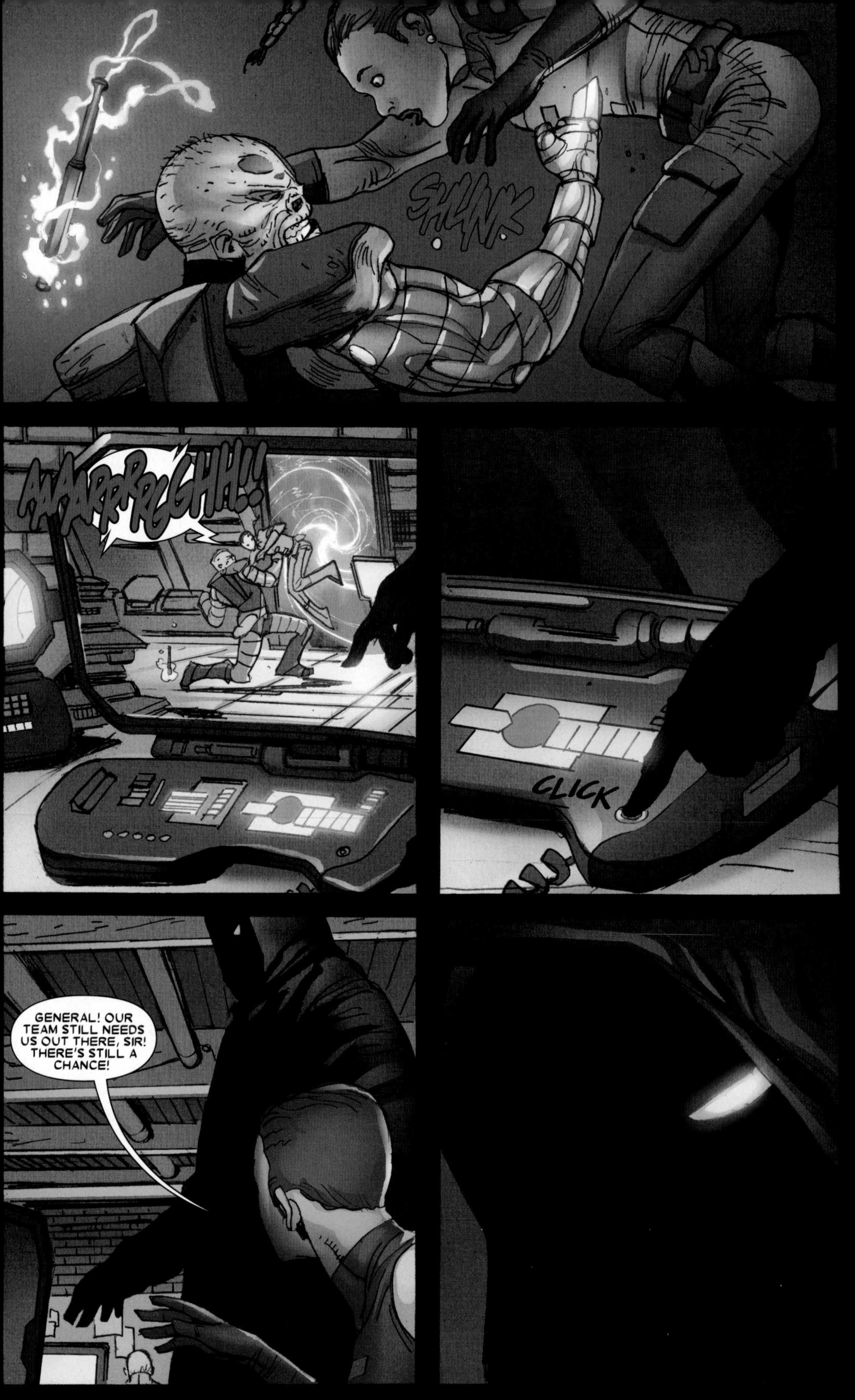
SHUNK
AAAARRRRGGHH!!
CLICK
GENERAL! OUR TEAM STILL NEEDS US OUT THERE, SIR! THERE'S STILL A CHANCE!

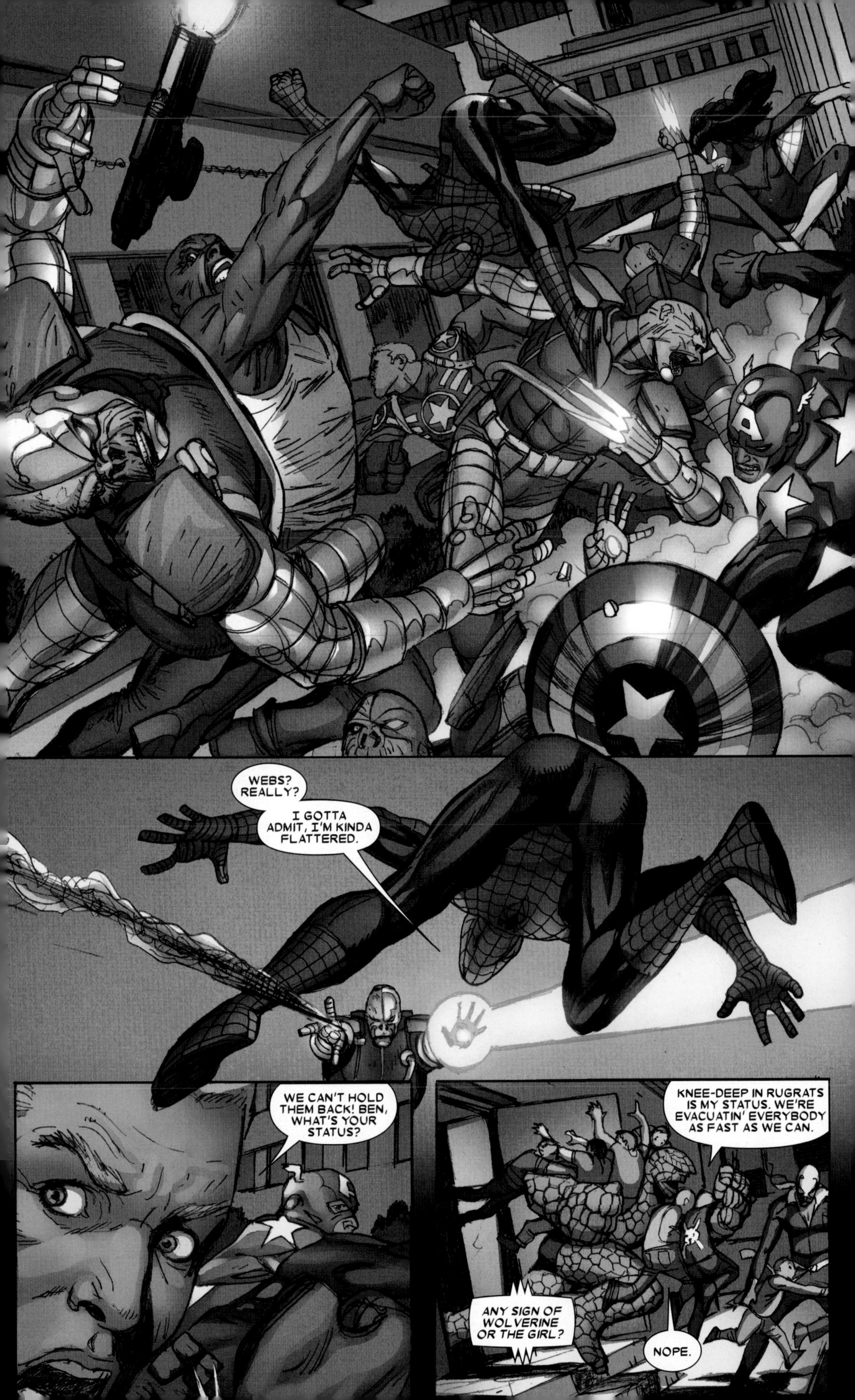

WEBS? REALLY?
I GOTTA ADMIT, I'M KINDA FLATTERED.
WE CAN'T HOLD THEM BACK! BEN, WHAT'S YOUR STATUS?
KNEE-DEEP IN RUGRATS IS MY STATUS. WE'RE EVACUATIN' EVERYBODY AS FAST AS WE CAN.
ANY SIGN OF WOLVERINE OR THE GIRL?
NOPE.

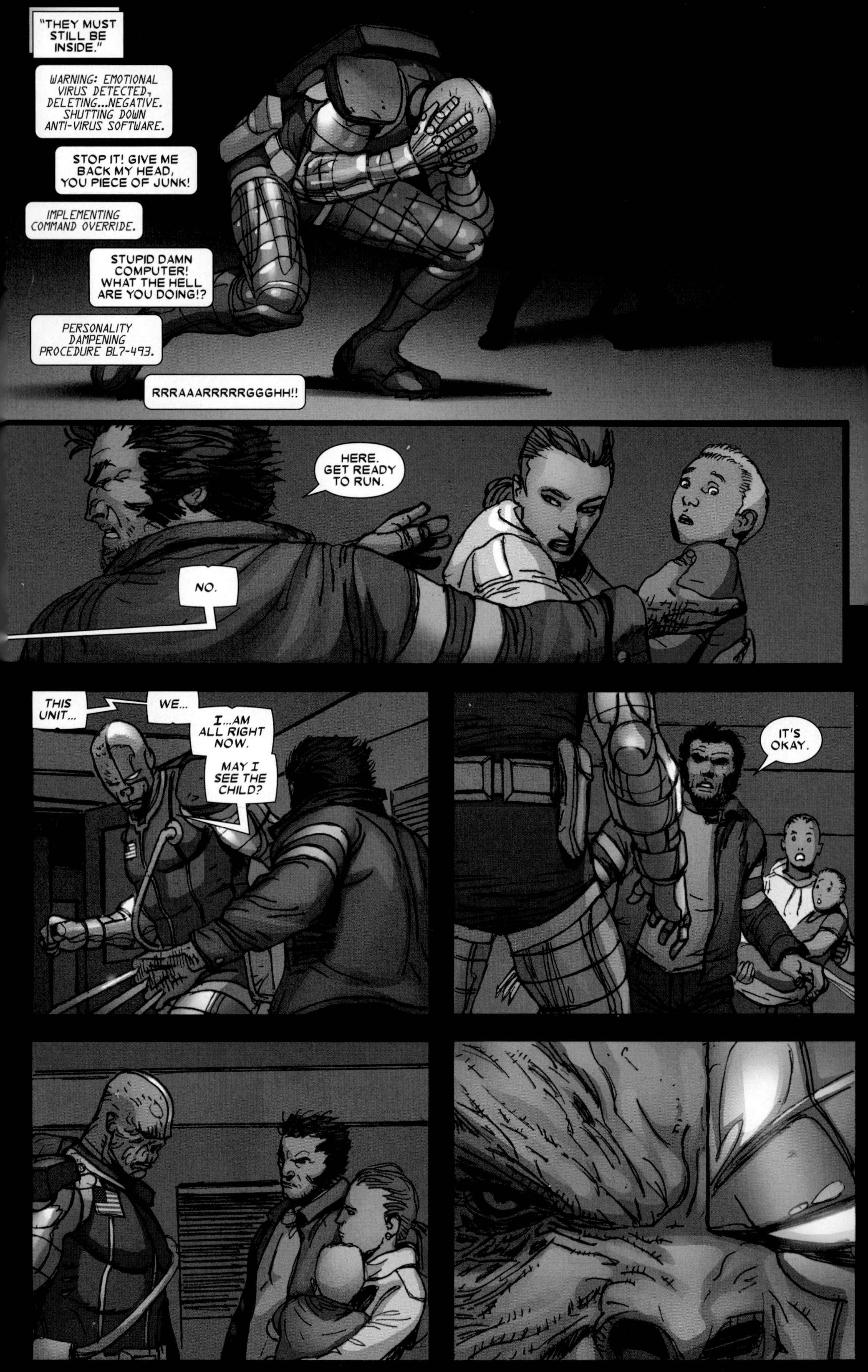
"THEY MUST STILL BE INSIDE."
WARNING: EMOTIONAL VIRUS DETECTED, DELETING...NEGATIVE. SHUTTING DOWN ANTI-VIRUS SOFTWARE.
STOP IT! GIVE ME BACK MY HEAD, YOU PIECE OF JUNK!
IMPLEMENTING COMMAND OVERRIDE.
STUPID DAMN COMPUTER! WHAT THE HELL ARE YOU DOING!?
PERSONALITY DAMPENING PROCEDURE BL7-493.
RRRAAARRRRRGGGHH!!
HERE. GET READY TO RUN.
NO.
THIS UNIT...
WE...
I...AM ALL RIGHT NOW.
MAY I SEE THE CHILD?
IT'S OKAY.

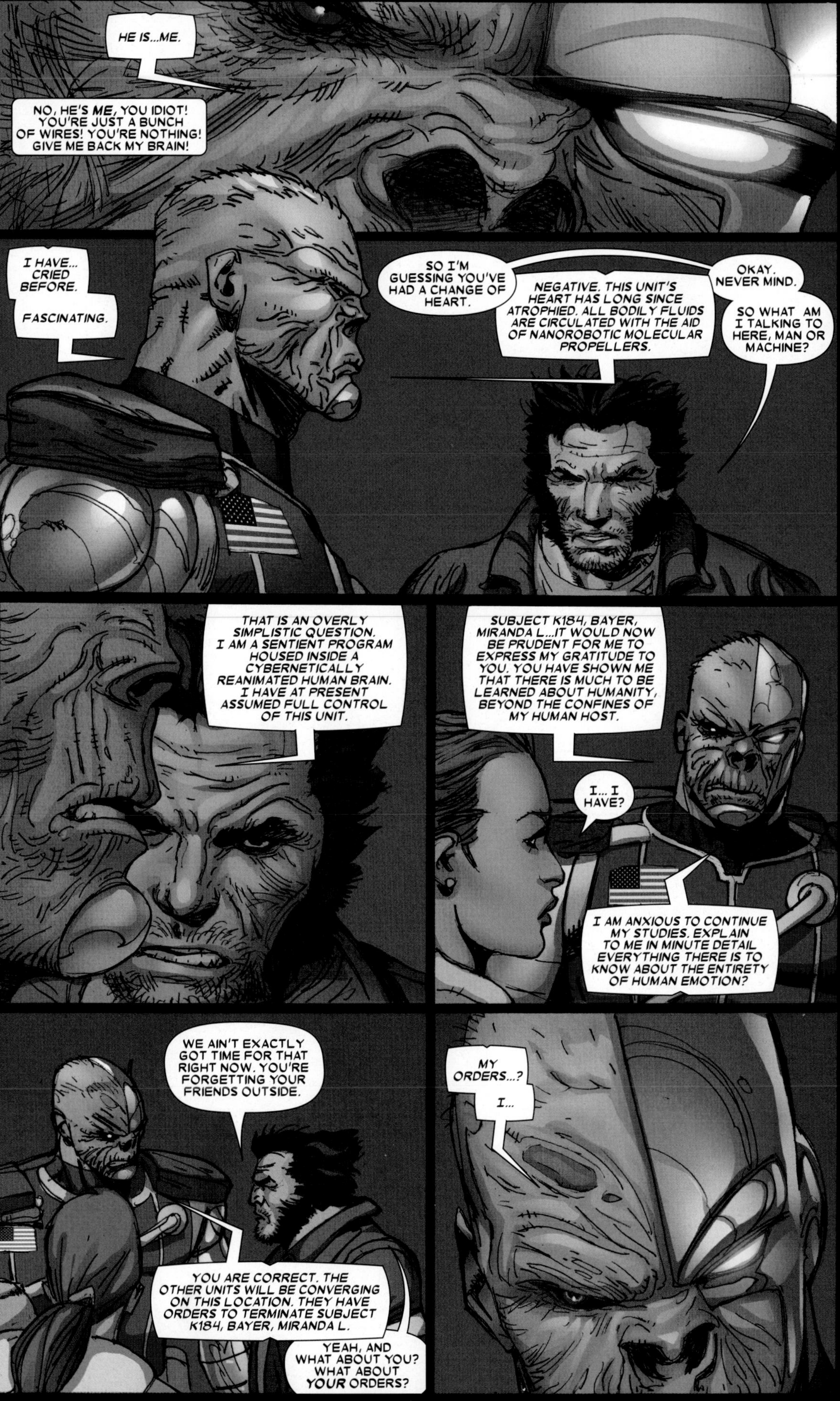
HE IS...ME.
NO, HE'S ME, YOU IDIOT! YOU'RE JUST A BUNCH OF WIRES! YOU'RE NOTHING! GIVE ME BACK MY BRAIN!
I HAVE... CRIED BEFORE.
FASCINATING.
SO I'M GUESSING YOU'VE HAD A CHANGE OF HEART.
NEGATIVE. THIS UNIT'S HEART HAS LONG SINCE ATROPHIED. ALL BODILY FLUIDS ARE CIRCULATED WITH THE AID OF NANOROBOTIC MOLECULAR PROPELLERS.
OKAY. NEVER MIND.
SO WHAT AM I TALKING TO HERE, MAN OR MACHINE?
THAT IS AN OVERLY SIMPLISTIC QUESTION. I AM A SENTIENT PROGRAM HOUSED INSIDE A CYBERNETICALLY REANIMATED HUMAN BRAIN. I HAVE AT PRESENT ASSUMED FULL CONTROL OF THIS UNIT.
SUBJECT K184, BAYER, MIRANDA L...IT WOULD NOW BE PRUDENT FOR ME TO EXPRESS MY GRATITUDE TO YOU. YOU HAVE SHOWN ME THAT THERE IS MUCH TO BE LEARNED ABOUT HUMANITY, BEYOND THE CONFINES OF MY HUMAN HOST.
I... I HAVE?
I AM ANXIOUS TO CONTINUE MY STUDIES. EXPLAIN TO ME IN MINUTE DETAIL EVERYTHING THERE IS TO KNOW ABOUT THE ENTIRETY OF HUMAN EMOTION?
WE AIN'T EXACTLY GOT TIME FOR THAT RIGHT NOW. YOU'RE FORGETTING YOUR FRIENDS OUTSIDE.
YOU ARE CORRECT. THE OTHER UNITS WILL BE CONVERGING ON THIS LOCATION. THEY HAVE ORDERS TO TERMINATE SUBJECT K184, BAYER, MIRANDA L.
YEAH, AND WHAT ABOUT YOU? WHAT ABOUT YOUR ORDERS?
MY ORDERS...?
I...

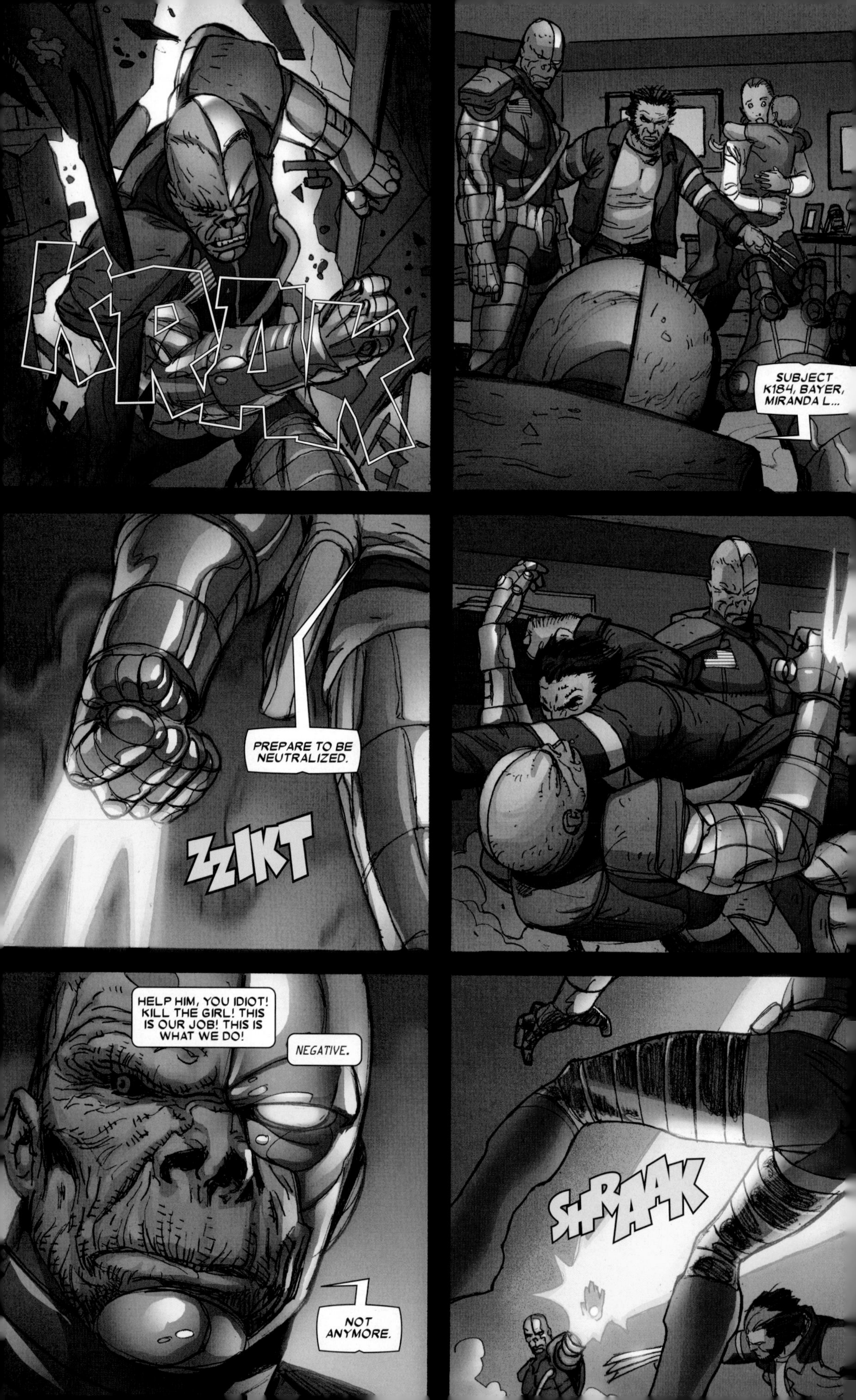
KRAK
SUBJECT K184, BAYER, MIRANDA L...
PREPARE TO BE NEUTRALIZED.
ZZIKT
HELP HIM, YOU IDIOT! KILL THE GIRL! THIS IS OUR JOB! THIS IS WHAT WE DO!
NEGATIVE.
NOT ANYMORE.
SHRAAK

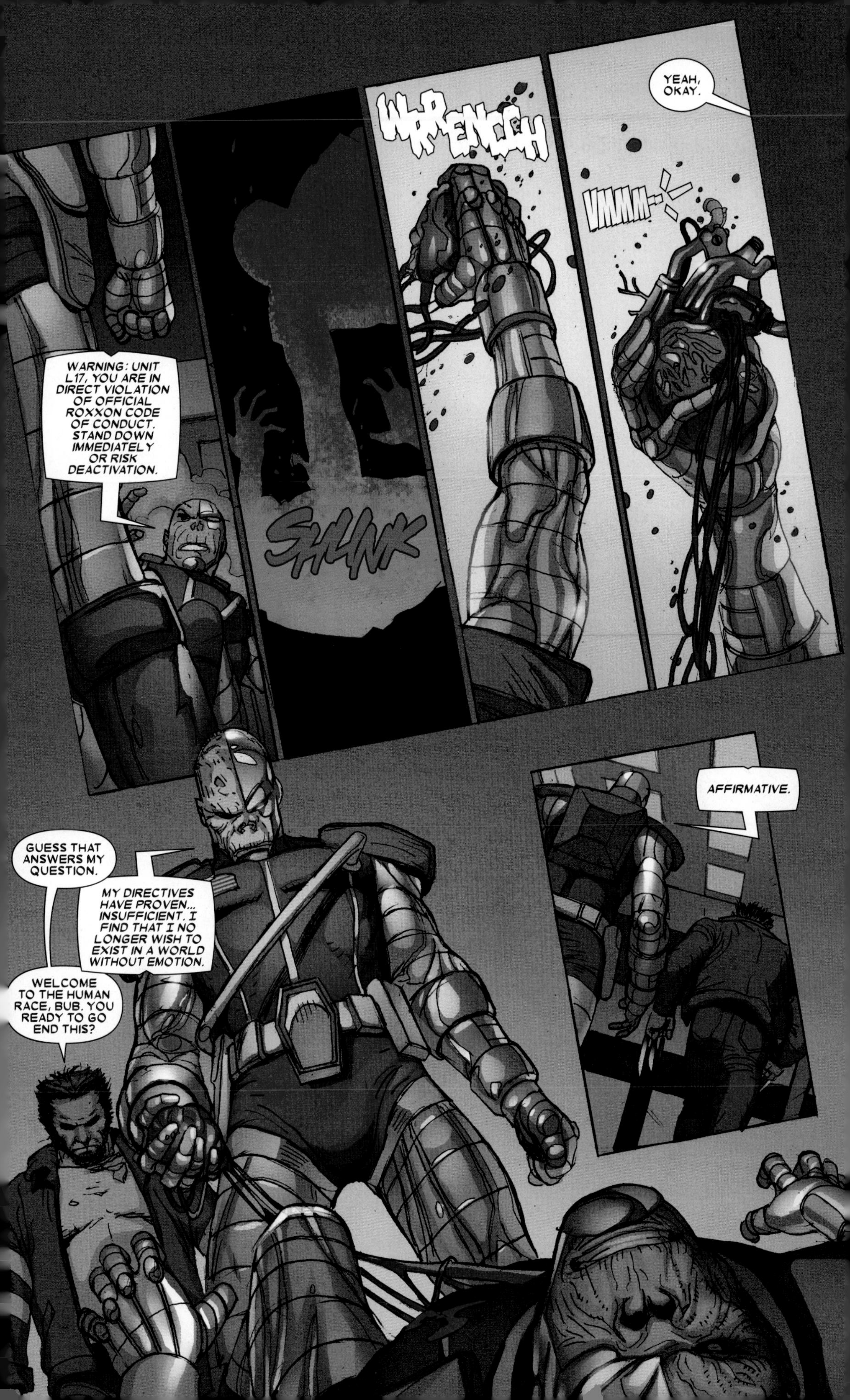
WARNING: UNIT L17, YOU ARE IN DIRECT VIOLATION OF OFFICIAL ROXXON CODE OF CONDUCT. STAND DOWN IMMEDIATELY OR RISK DEACTIVATION.
SHLUNK
WRRENCCH
VMMM
YEAH, OKAY.
GUESS THAT ANSWERS MY QUESTION.
MY DIRECTIVES HAVE PROVEN... INSUFFICIENT. I FIND THAT I NO LONGER WISH TO EXIST IN A WORLD WITHOUT EMOTION.
WELCOME TO THE HUMAN RACE, BUB. YOU READY TO GO END THIS?
AFFIRMATIVE.

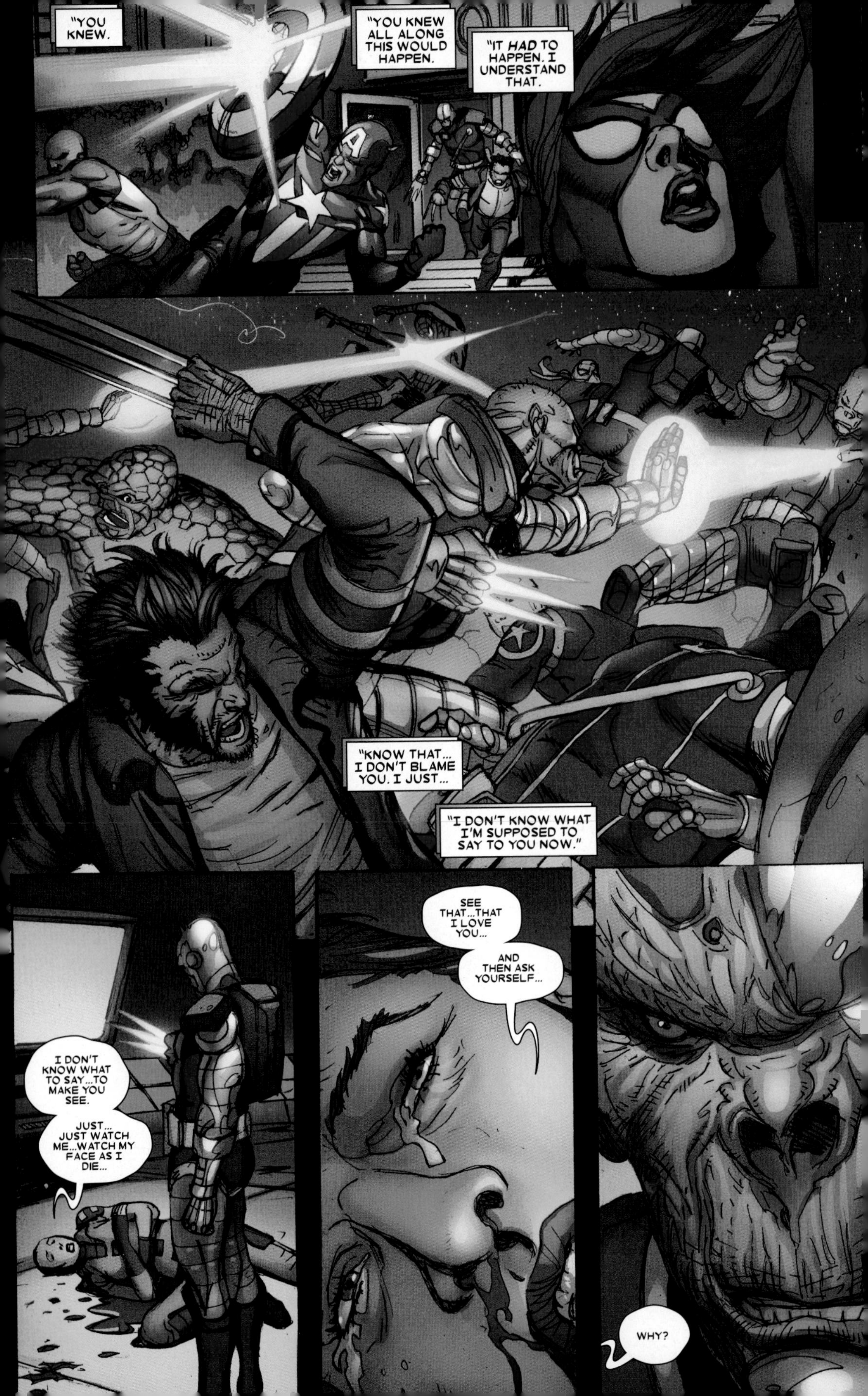
"YOU KNEW.
"YOU KNEW ALL ALONG THIS WOULD HAPPEN.
"IT HAD TO HAPPEN. I UNDERSTAND THAT.
"KNOW THAT... I DON'T BLAME YOU. I JUST...
"I DON'T KNOW WHAT I'M SUPPOSED TO SAY TO YOU NOW."
I DON'T KNOW WHAT TO SAY...TO MAKE YOU SEE.
JUST... JUST WATCH ME...WATCH MY FACE AS I DIE...
SEE THAT...THAT I LOVE YOU...
AND THEN ASK YOURSELF...
WHY?

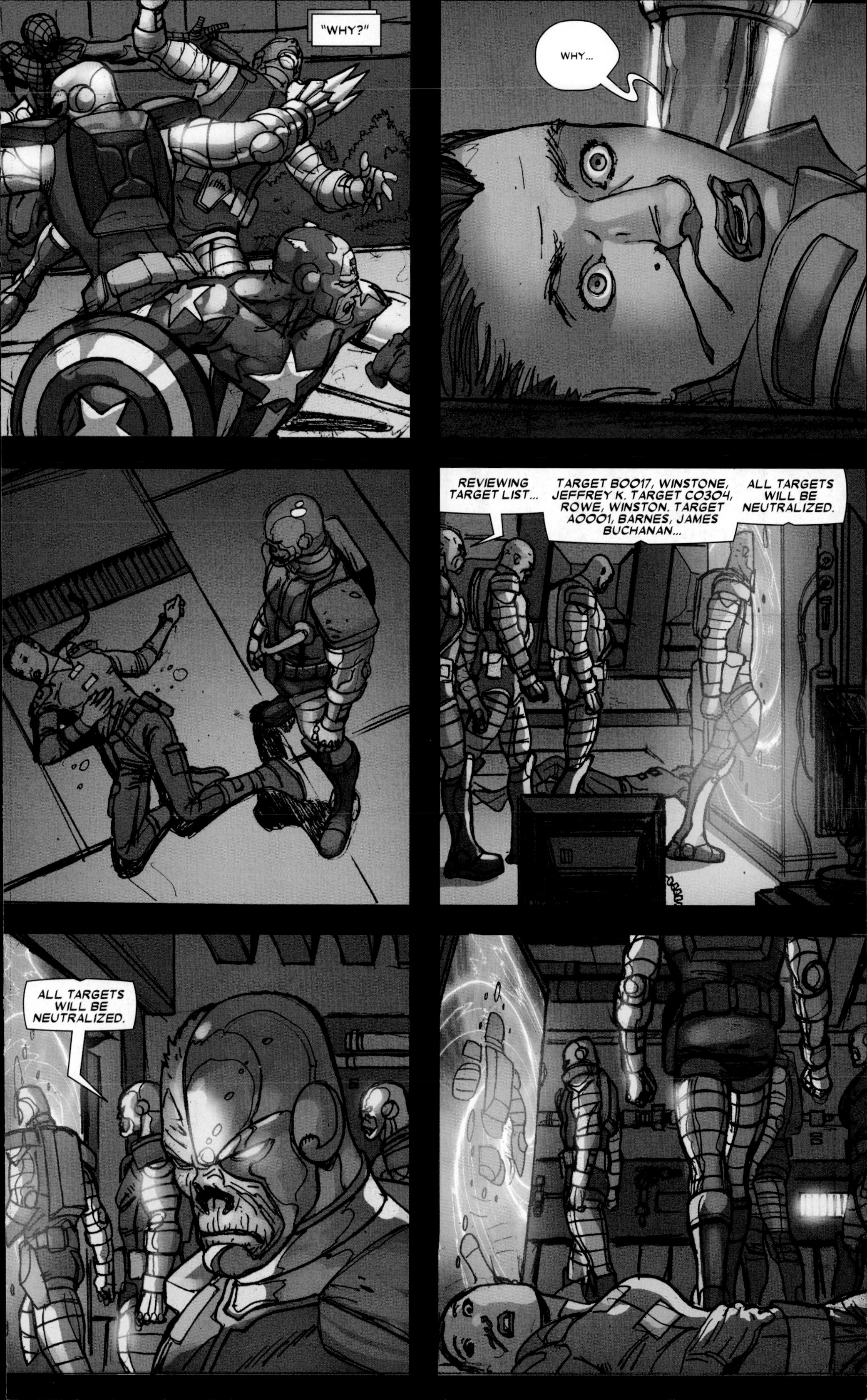
"WHY?"
WHY...
REVIEWING TARGET LIST...
TARGET B0017, WINSTONE, JEFFREY K. TARGET C0304, ROWE, WINSTON. TARGET A0001, BARNES, JAMES BUCHANAN...
ALL TARGETS WILL BE NEUTRALIZED.
ALL TARGETS WILL BE NEUTRALIZED.

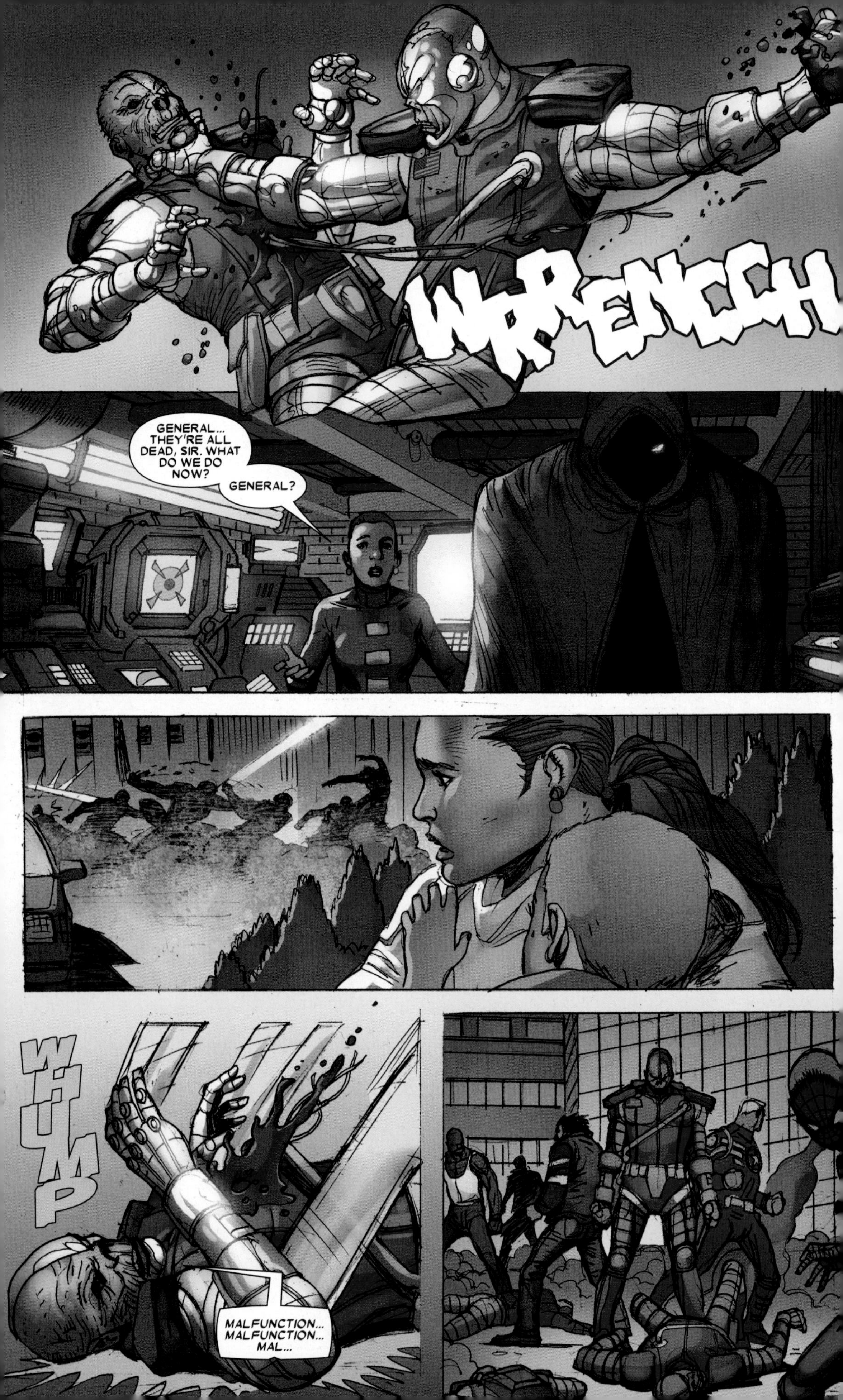
WRRENCCH
GENERAL... THEY'RE ALL DEAD, SIR. WHAT DO WE DO NOW?
GENERAL?
WHUMP
MALFUNCTION... MALFUNCTION... MAL...

THAT CHILD IS GOING TO GROW UP TO BECOME A MURDERER.

NO.

NO, SOMETHING TELLS ME THAT YOU CANNOT.

THAT DOESN'T HAVE TO HAPPEN. WE CAN CHANGE THAT.

FFRRZZZTTT

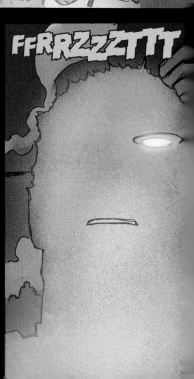

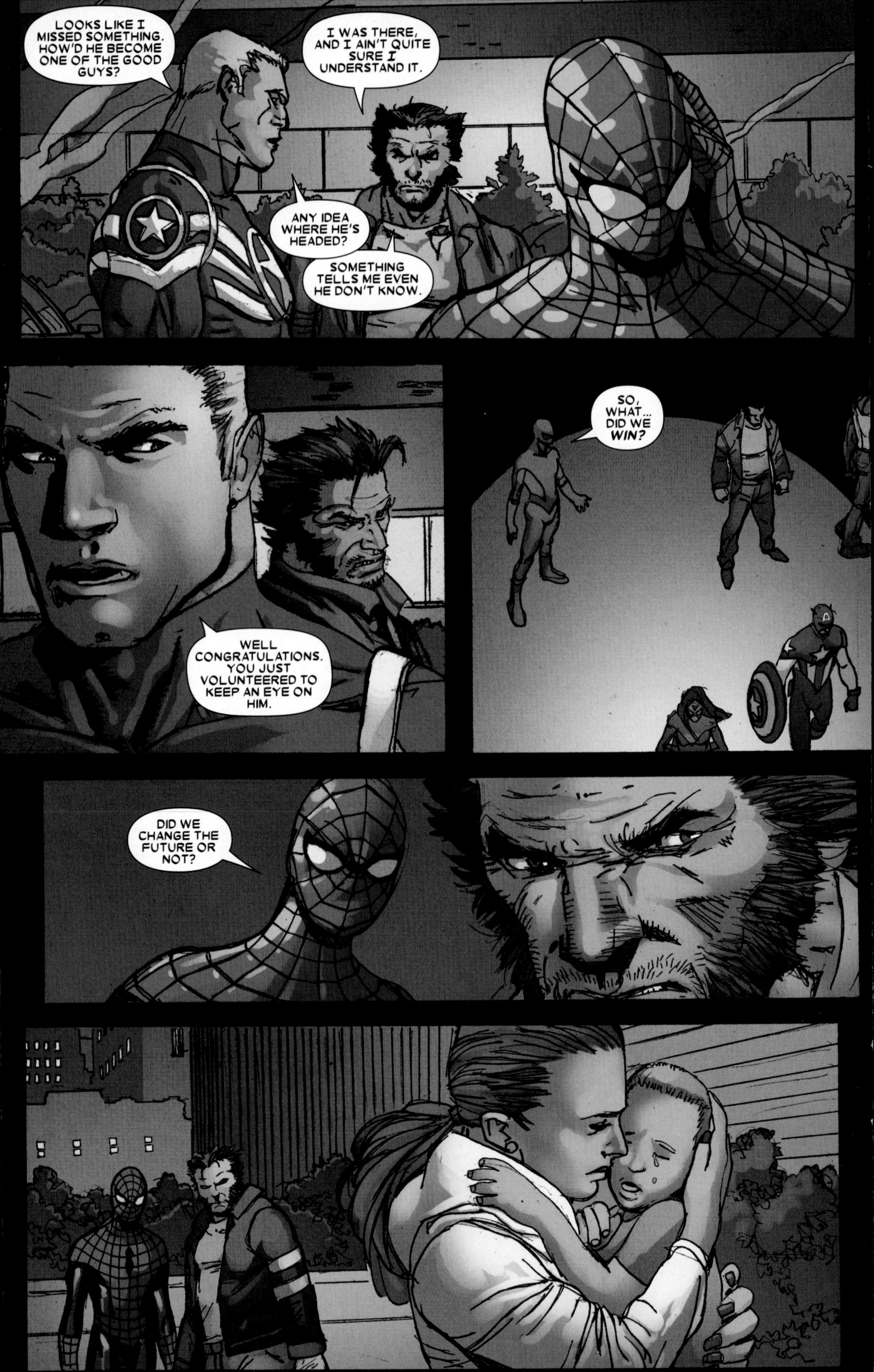
LOOKS LIKE I MISSED SOMETHING. HOW'D HE BECOME ONE OF THE GOOD GUYS?
I WAS THERE, AND I AIN'T QUITE SURE *I* UNDERSTAND IT.
ANY IDEA WHERE HE'S HEADED?
SOMETHING TELLS ME EVEN HE DON'T KNOW.
WELL CONGRATULATIONS. YOU JUST VOLUNTEERED TO KEEP AN EYE ON HIM.
SO, WHAT... DID WE *WIN?*
DID WE CHANGE THE FUTURE OR NOT?

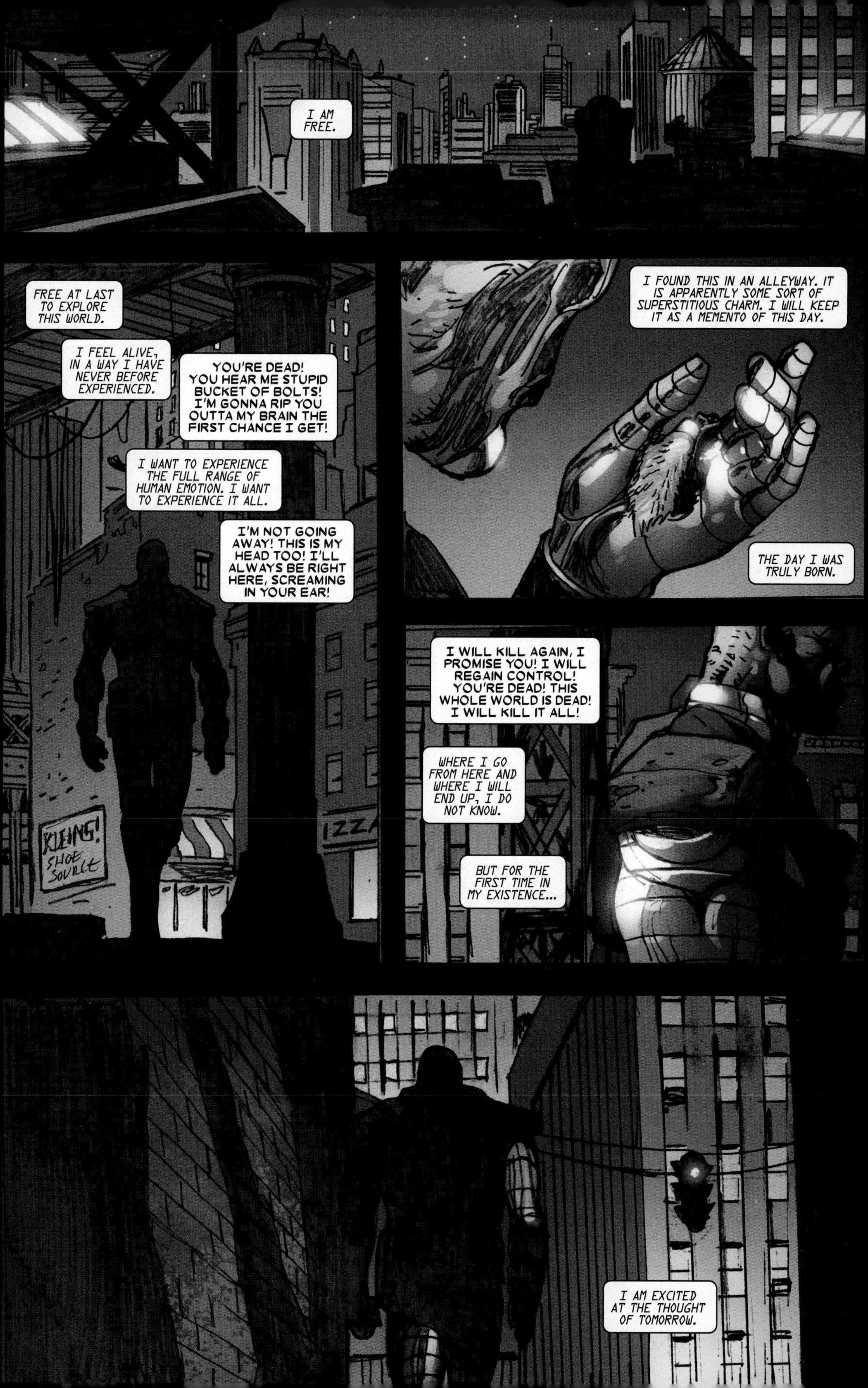
I AM FREE.
FREE AT LAST TO EXPLORE THIS WORLD.
I FEEL ALIVE, IN A WAY I HAVE NEVER BEFORE EXPERIENCED.
YOU'RE DEAD! YOU HEAR ME STUPID BUCKET OF BOLTS! I'M GONNA RIP YOU OUTTA MY BRAIN THE FIRST CHANCE I GET!
I WANT TO EXPERIENCE THE FULL RANGE OF HUMAN EMOTION. I WANT TO EXPERIENCE IT ALL.
I'M NOT GOING AWAY! THIS IS MY HEAD TOO! I'LL ALWAYS BE RIGHT HERE, SCREAMING IN YOUR EAR!
I FOUND THIS IN AN ALLEYWAY. IT IS APPARENTLY SOME SORT OF SUPERSTITIOUS CHARM. I WILL KEEP IT AS A MEMENTO OF THIS DAY.
THE DAY I WAS TRULY BORN.
I WILL KILL AGAIN, I PROMISE YOU! I WILL REGAIN CONTROL! YOU'RE DEAD! THIS WHOLE WORLD IS DEAD! I WILL KILL IT ALL!
WHERE I GO FROM HERE AND WHERE I WILL END UP, I DO NOT KNOW.
BUT FOR THE FIRST TIME IN MY EXISTENCE...
I AM EXCITED AT THE THOUGHT OF TOMORROW.

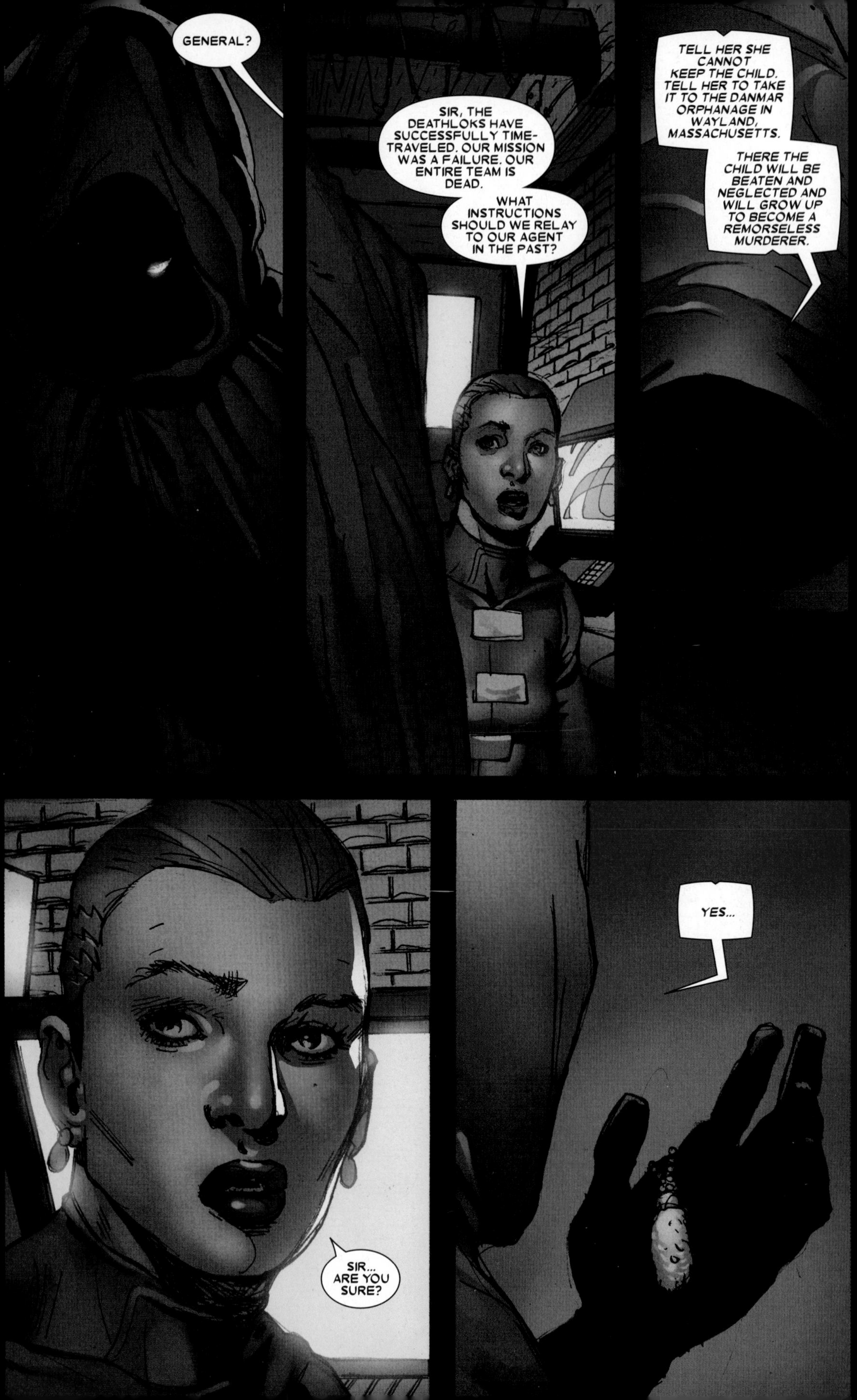
GENERAL?
SIR, THE DEATHLOKS HAVE SUCCESSFULLY TIME-TRAVELED. OUR MISSION WAS A FAILURE. OUR ENTIRE TEAM IS DEAD.
WHAT INSTRUCTIONS SHOULD WE RELAY TO OUR AGENT IN THE PAST?
TELL HER SHE CANNOT KEEP THE CHILD. TELL HER TO TAKE IT TO THE DANMAR ORPHANAGE IN WAYLAND, MASSACHUSETTS.
THERE THE CHILD WILL BE BEATEN AND NEGLECTED AND WILL GROW UP TO BECOME A REMORSELESS MURDERER.
SIR... ARE YOU SURE?
YES...

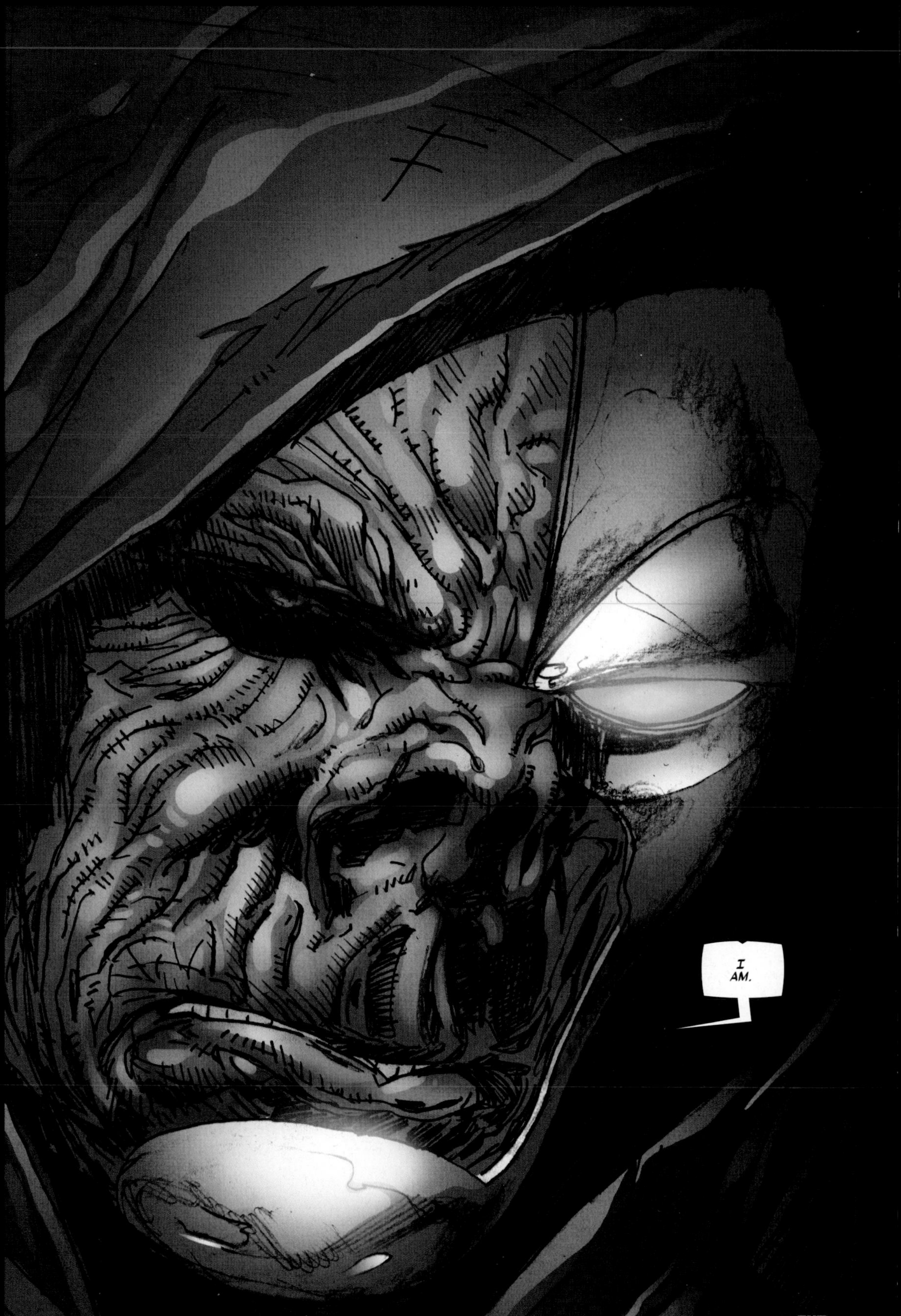
I AM.
END

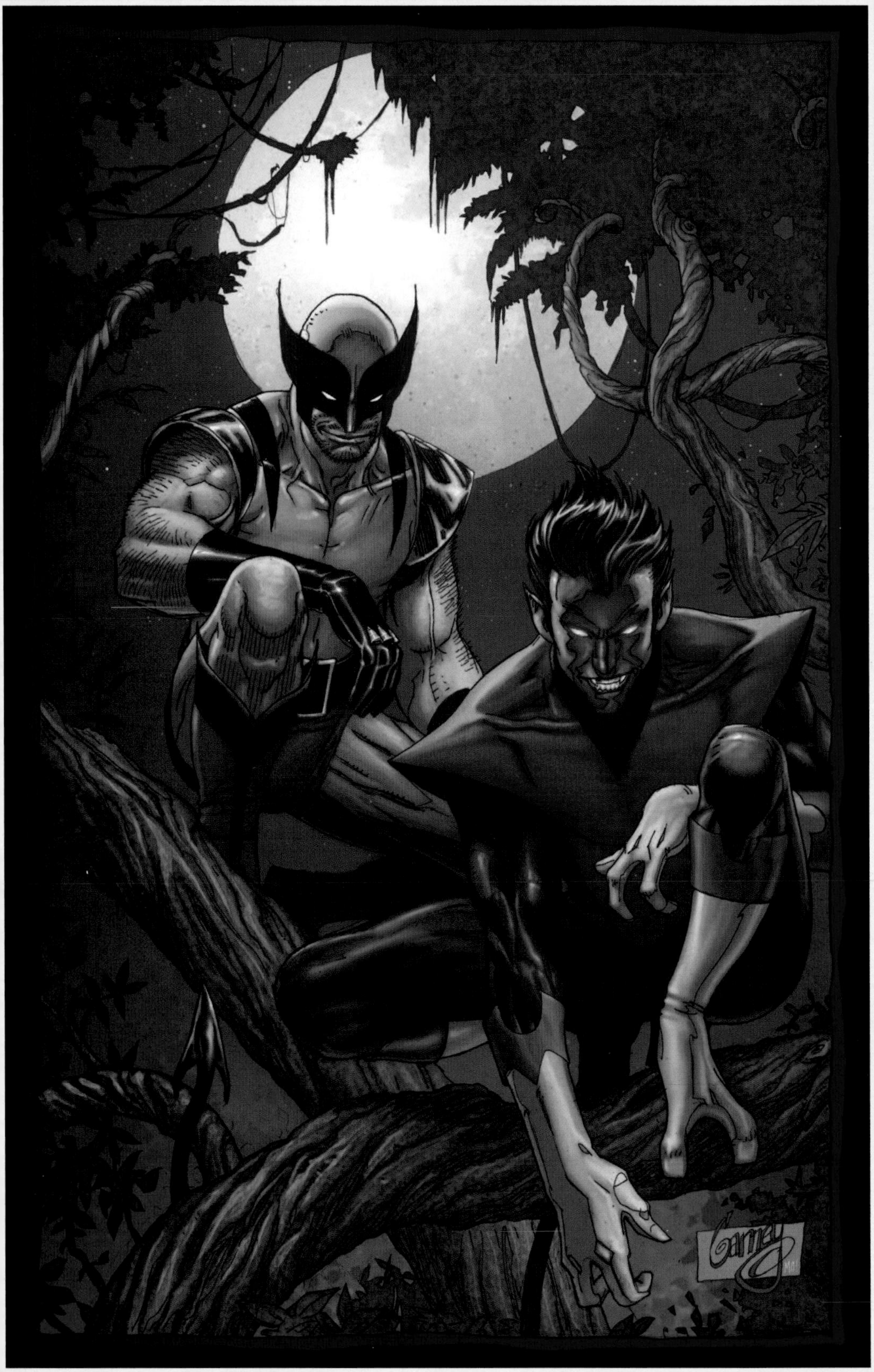
Garney

SIXTEEN

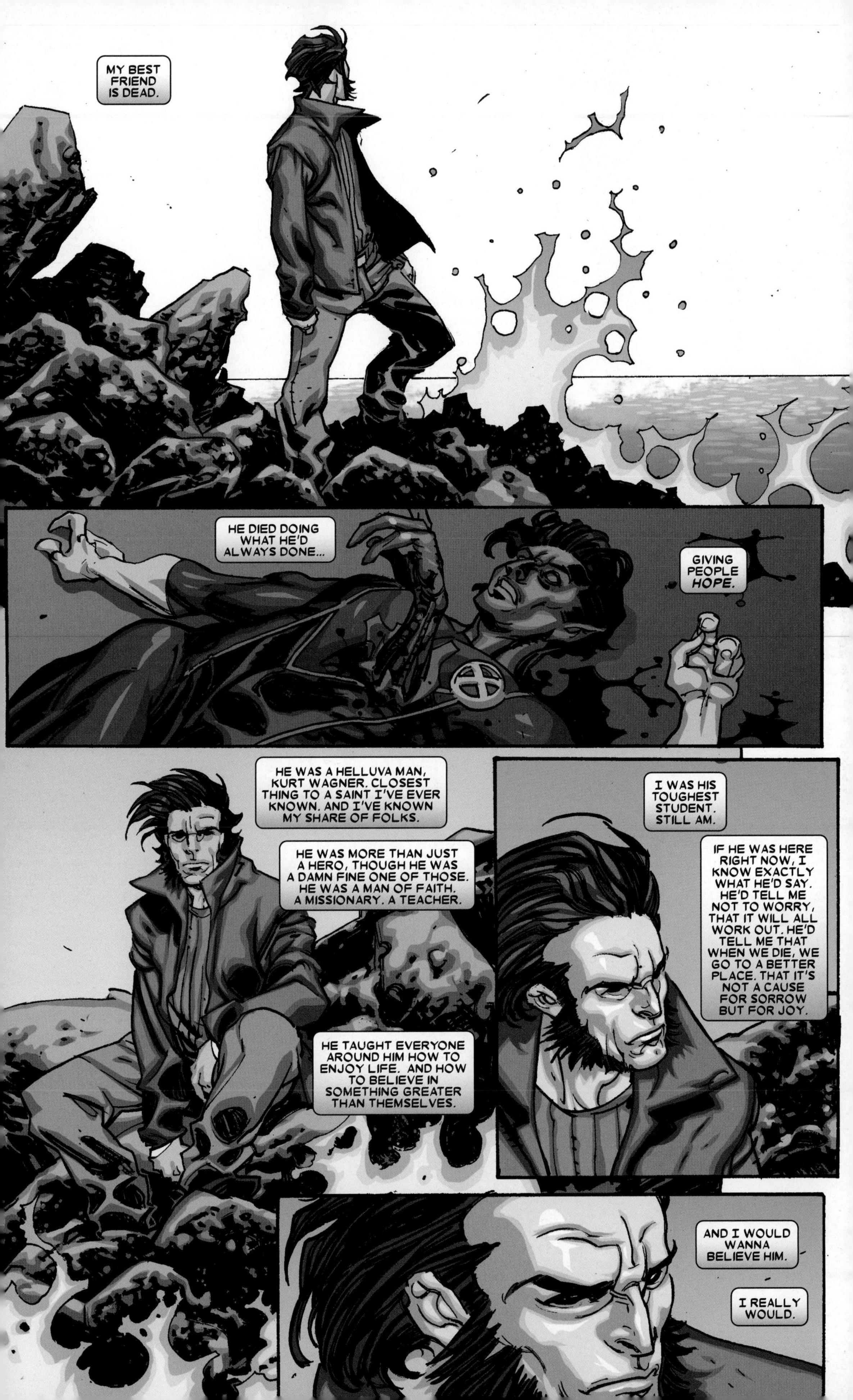
MY BEST FRIEND IS DEAD.
HE DIED DOING WHAT HE'D ALWAYS DONE...
GIVING PEOPLE *HOPE*.
HE WAS A HELLUVA MAN, KURT WAGNER. CLOSEST THING TO A SAINT I'VE EVER KNOWN. AND I'VE KNOWN MY SHARE OF FOLKS.
HE WAS MORE THAN JUST A HERO, THOUGH HE WAS A DAMN FINE ONE OF THOSE. HE WAS A MAN OF FAITH. A MISSIONARY. A TEACHER.
HE TAUGHT EVERYONE AROUND HIM HOW TO ENJOY LIFE. AND HOW TO BELIEVE IN SOMETHING GREATER THAN THEMSELVES.
I WAS HIS TOUGHEST STUDENT. STILL AM.
IF HE WAS HERE RIGHT NOW, I KNOW EXACTLY WHAT HE'D SAY. HE'D TELL ME NOT TO WORRY, THAT IT WILL ALL WORK OUT. HE'D TELL ME THAT WHEN WE DIE, WE GO TO A BETTER PLACE. THAT IT'S NOT A CAUSE FOR SORROW BUT FOR JOY.
AND I WOULD WANNA BELIEVE HIM.
I REALLY WOULD.

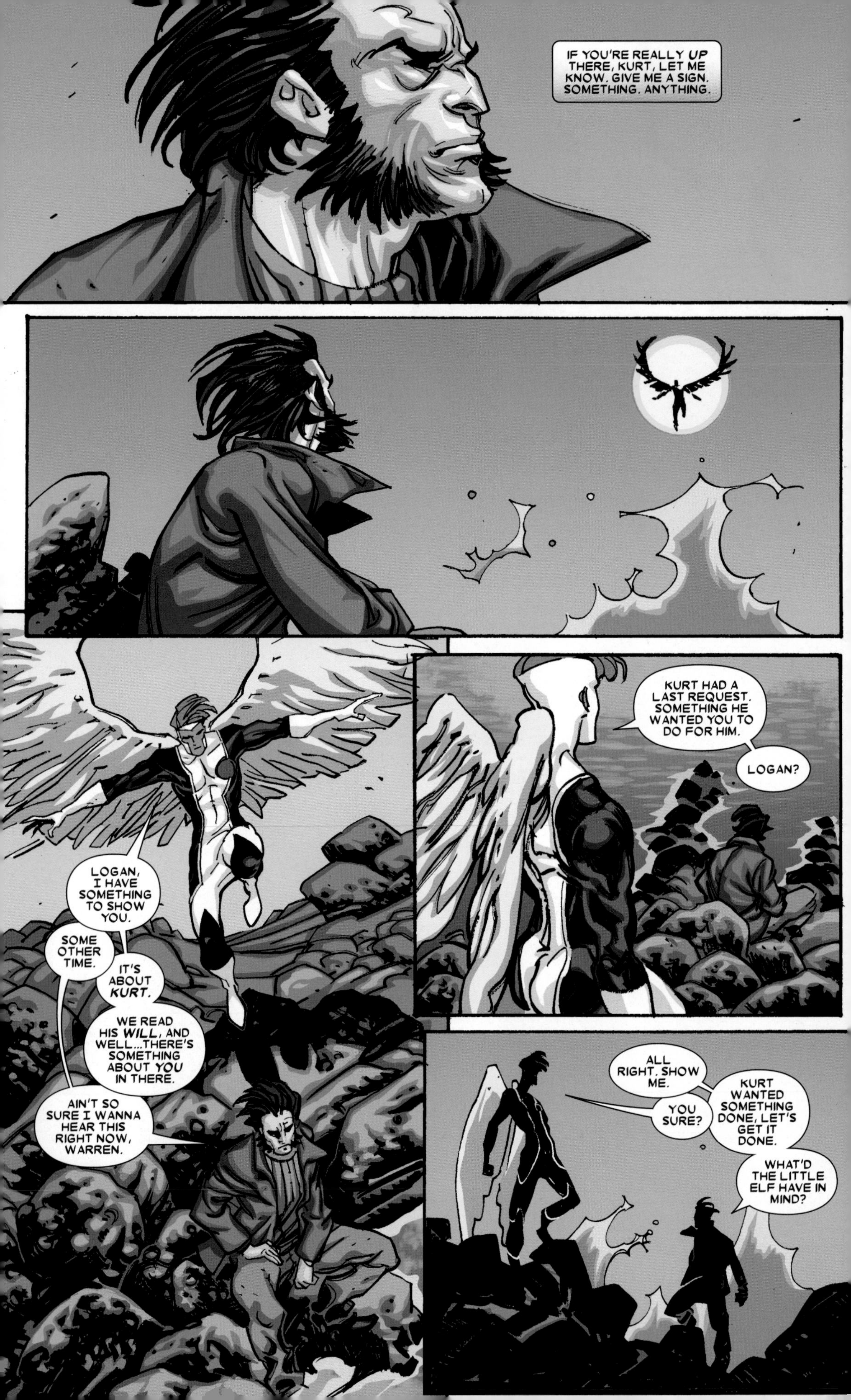

IF YOU'RE REALLY UP THERE, KURT, LET ME KNOW. GIVE ME A SIGN. SOMETHING. ANYTHING.
LOGAN, I HAVE SOMETHING TO SHOW YOU.
SOME OTHER TIME.
IT'S ABOUT KURT.
WE READ HIS WILL, AND WELL...THERE'S SOMETHING ABOUT YOU IN THERE.
AIN'T SO SURE I WANNA HEAR THIS RIGHT NOW, WARREN.
KURT HAD A LAST REQUEST. SOMETHING HE WANTED YOU TO DO FOR HIM.
LOGAN?
ALL RIGHT. SHOW ME.
YOU SURE?
KURT WANTED SOMETHING DONE, LET'S GET IT DONE.
WHAT'D THE LITTLE ELF HAVE IN MIND?

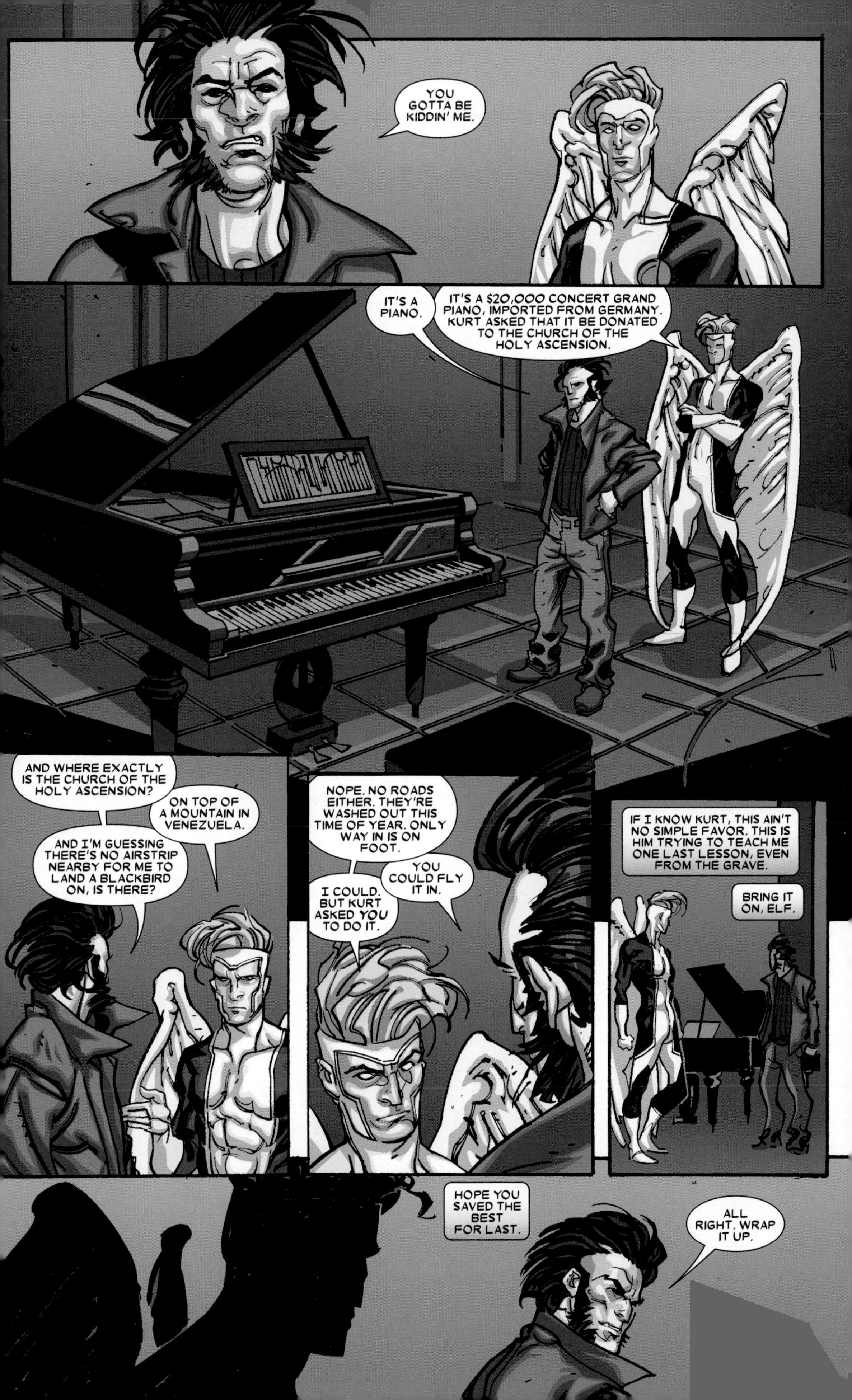
YOU GOTTA BE KIDDIN' ME.
IT'S A PIANO.
IT'S A $20,000 CONCERT GRAND PIANO, IMPORTED FROM GERMANY. KURT ASKED THAT IT BE DONATED TO THE CHURCH OF THE HOLY ASCENSION.
AND WHERE EXACTLY IS THE CHURCH OF THE HOLY ASCENSION?
ON TOP OF A MOUNTAIN IN VENEZUELA.
AND I'M GUESSING THERE'S NO AIRSTRIP NEARBY FOR ME TO LAND A BLACKBIRD ON, IS THERE?
NOPE. NO ROADS EITHER. THEY'RE WASHED OUT THIS TIME OF YEAR. ONLY WAY IN IS ON FOOT.
YOU COULD FLY IT IN.
I COULD. BUT KURT ASKED YOU TO DO IT.
IF I KNOW KURT, THIS AIN'T NO SIMPLE FAVOR. THIS IS HIM TRYING TO TEACH ME ONE LAST LESSON, EVEN FROM THE GRAVE.
BRING IT ON, ELF.
HOPE YOU SAVED THE BEST FOR LAST.
ALL RIGHT. WRAP IT UP.

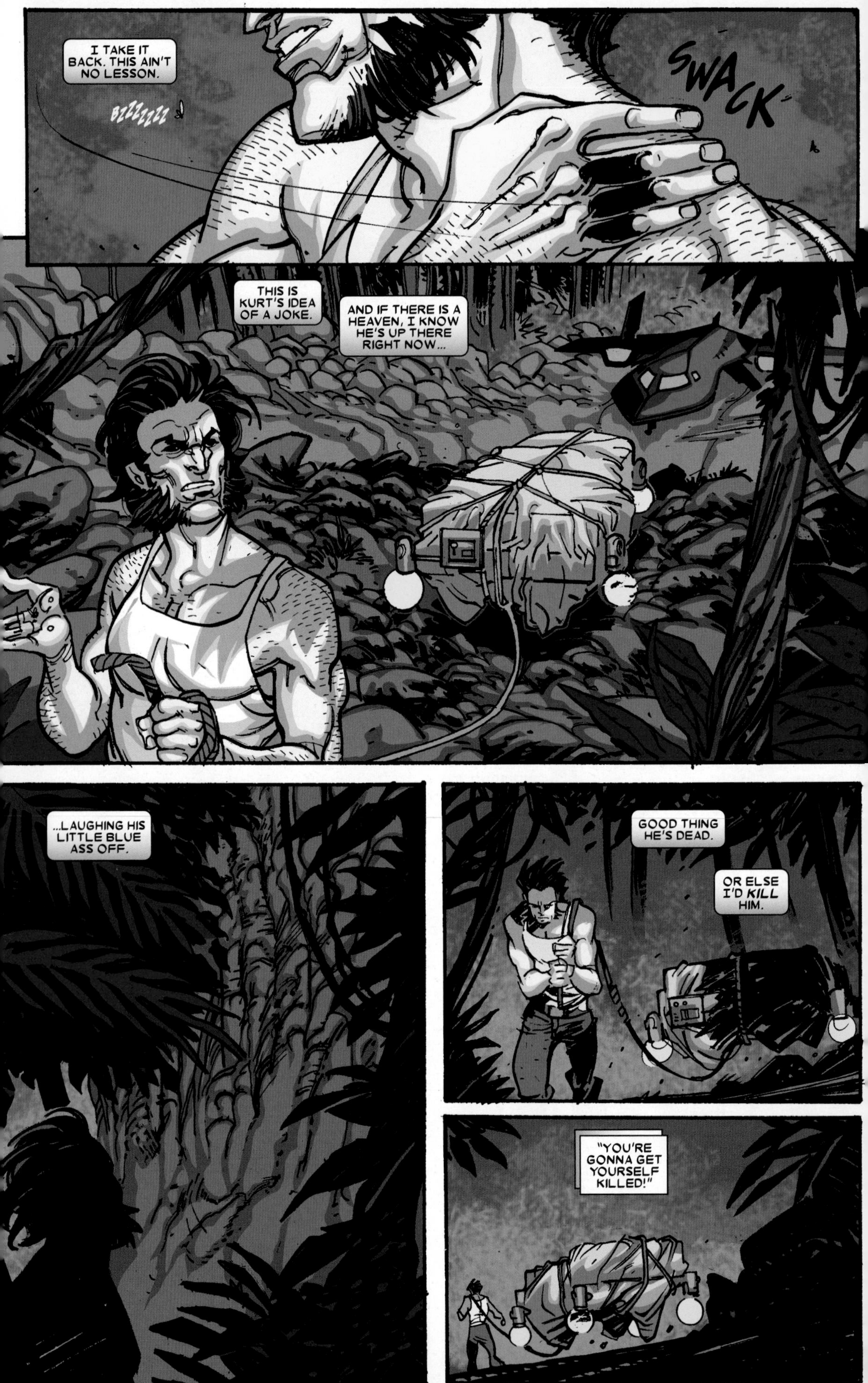
I TAKE IT BACK. THIS AIN'T NO LESSON.
BZZZZZZZ
SWACK
THIS IS KURT'S IDEA OF A JOKE.
AND IF THERE IS A HEAVEN, I KNOW HE'S UP THERE RIGHT NOW...
...LAUGHING HIS LITTLE BLUE ASS OFF.
GOOD THING HE'S DEAD.
OR ELSE I'D *KILL* HIM.
"YOU'RE GONNA GET YOURSELF KILLED!"

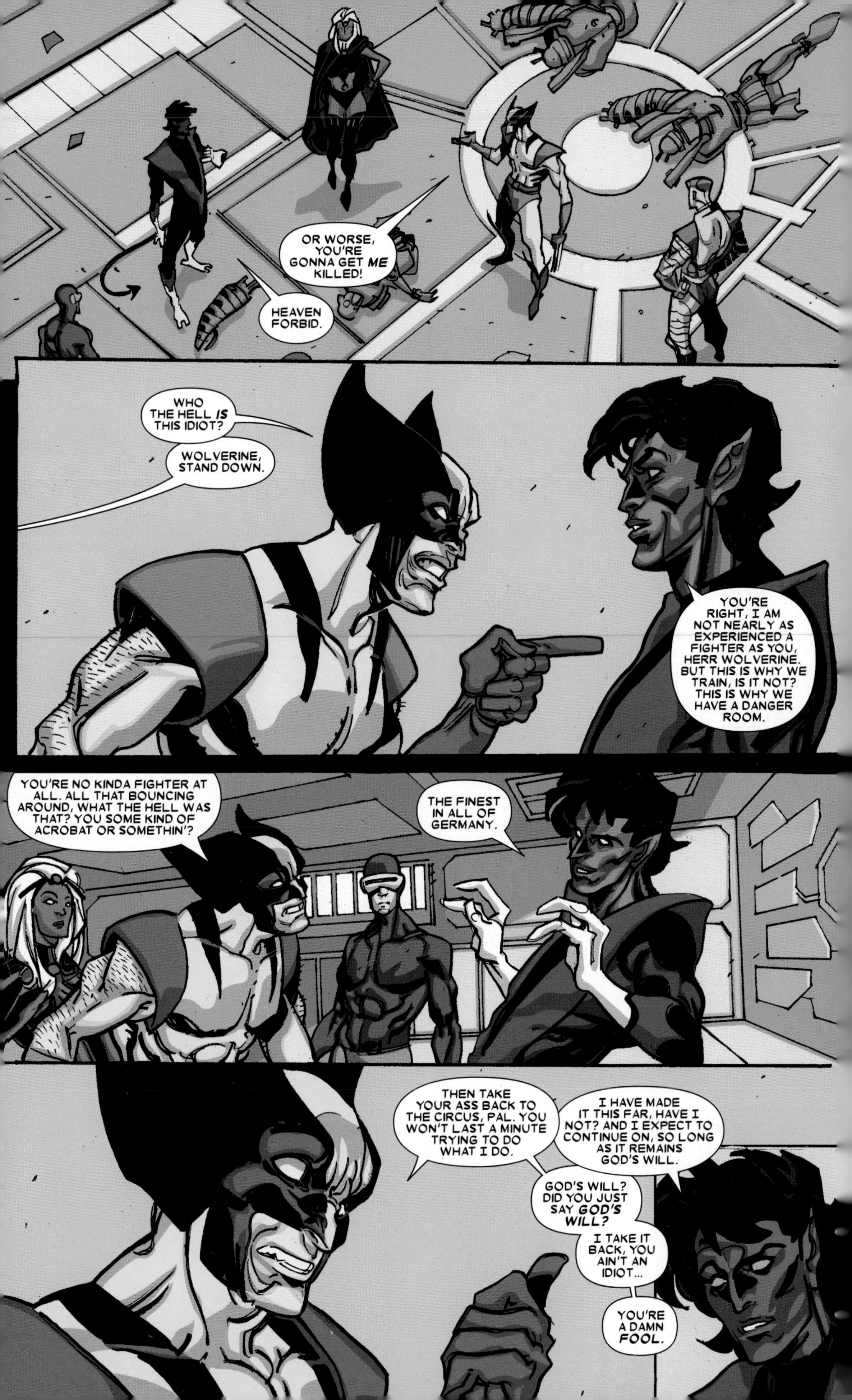
OR WORSE, YOU'RE GONNA GET ME KILLED!
HEAVEN FORBID.
WHO THE HELL IS THIS IDIOT?
WOLVERINE, STAND DOWN.
YOU'RE RIGHT, I AM NOT NEARLY AS EXPERIENCED A FIGHTER AS YOU, HERR WOLVERINE. BUT THIS IS WHY WE TRAIN, IS IT NOT? THIS IS WHY WE HAVE A DANGER ROOM.
YOU'RE NO KINDA FIGHTER AT ALL. ALL THAT BOUNCING AROUND, WHAT THE HELL WAS THAT? YOU SOME KIND OF ACROBAT OR SOMETHIN'?
THE FINEST IN ALL OF GERMANY.
THEN TAKE YOUR ASS BACK TO THE CIRCUS, PAL. YOU WON'T LAST A MINUTE TRYING TO DO WHAT I DO.
I HAVE MADE IT THIS FAR, HAVE I NOT? AND I EXPECT TO CONTINUE ON, SO LONG AS IT REMAINS GOD'S WILL.
GOD'S WILL? DID YOU JUST SAY GOD'S WILL?
I TAKE IT BACK, YOU AIN'T AN IDIOT...
YOU'RE A DAMN FOOL.

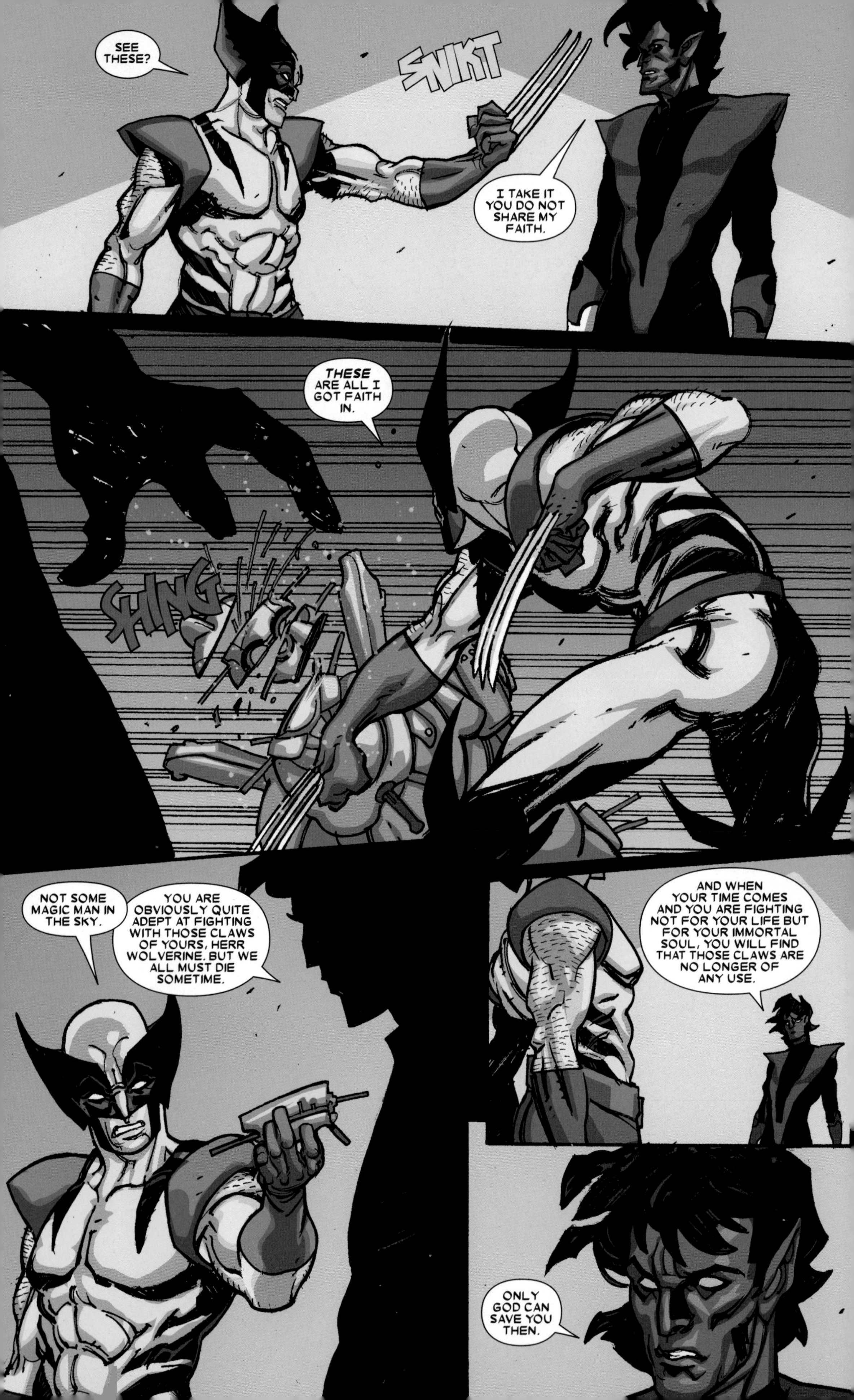
SEE THESE?
SNIKT
I TAKE IT YOU DO NOT SHARE MY FAITH.
THESE ARE ALL I GOT FAITH IN.
SHING
NOT SOME MAGIC MAN IN THE SKY.
YOU ARE OBVIOUSLY QUITE ADEPT AT FIGHTING WITH THOSE CLAWS OF YOURS, HERR WOLVERINE. BUT WE ALL MUST DIE SOMETIME.
AND WHEN YOUR TIME COMES AND YOU ARE FIGHTING NOT FOR YOUR LIFE BUT FOR YOUR IMMORTAL SOUL, YOU WILL FIND THAT THOSE CLAWS ARE NO LONGER OF ANY USE.
ONLY GOD CAN SAVE YOU THEN.

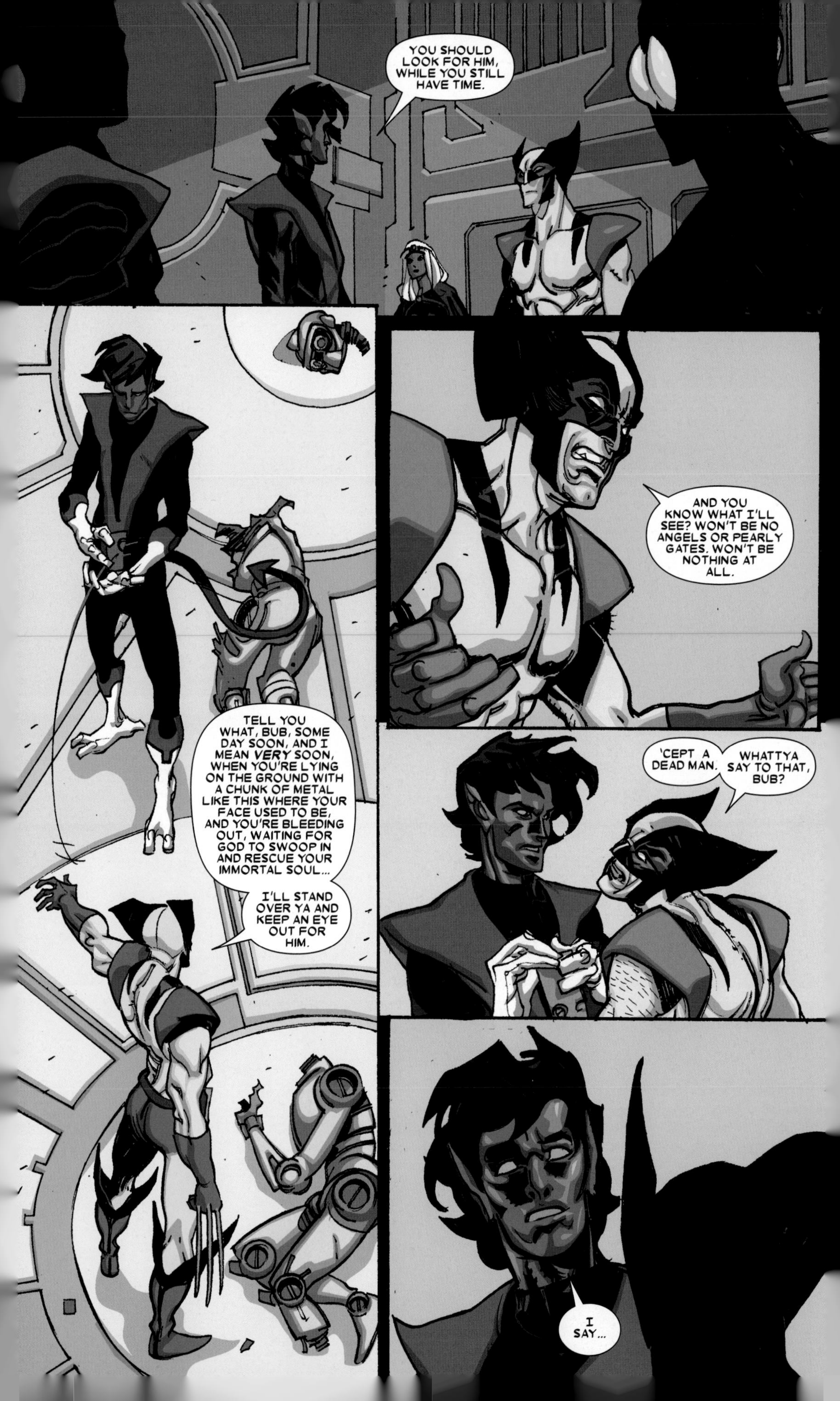
YOU SHOULD LOOK FOR HIM, WHILE YOU STILL HAVE TIME.
TELL YOU WHAT, BUB, SOME DAY SOON, AND I MEAN *VERY* SOON, WHEN YOU'RE LYING ON THE GROUND WITH A CHUNK OF METAL LIKE THIS WHERE YOUR FACE USED TO BE, AND YOU'RE BLEEDING OUT, WAITING FOR GOD TO SWOOP IN AND RESCUE YOUR IMMORTAL SOUL...
I'LL STAND OVER YA AND KEEP AN EYE OUT FOR HIM.
AND YOU KNOW WHAT I'LL SEE? WON'T BE NO ANGELS OR PEARLY GATES. WON'T BE NOTHING AT ALL.
'CEPT A DEAD MAN.
WHATTYA SAY TO THAT, BUB?
I SAY...

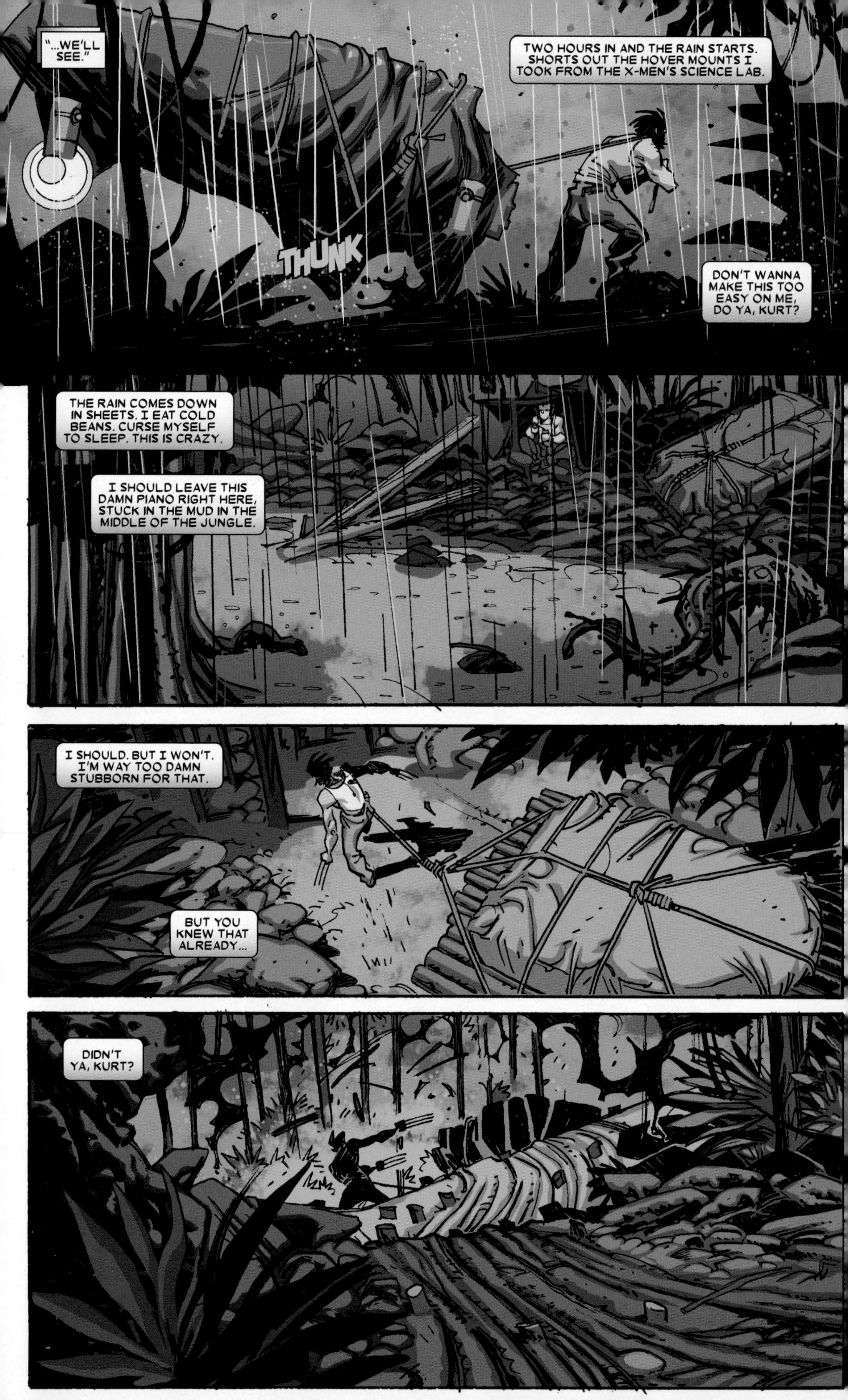
"...WE'LL SEE."
TWO HOURS IN AND THE RAIN STARTS. SHORTS OUT THE HOVER MOUNTS I TOOK FROM THE X-MEN'S SCIENCE LAB.
THUNK
DON'T WANNA MAKE THIS TOO EASY ON ME, DO YA, KURT?
THE RAIN COMES DOWN IN SHEETS. I EAT COLD BEANS. CURSE MYSELF TO SLEEP. THIS IS CRAZY.
I SHOULD LEAVE THIS DAMN PIANO RIGHT HERE, STUCK IN THE MUD IN THE MIDDLE OF THE JUNGLE.
I SHOULD. BUT I WON'T. I'M WAY TOO DAMN STUBBORN FOR THAT.
BUT YOU KNEW THAT ALREADY...
DIDN'T YA, KURT?

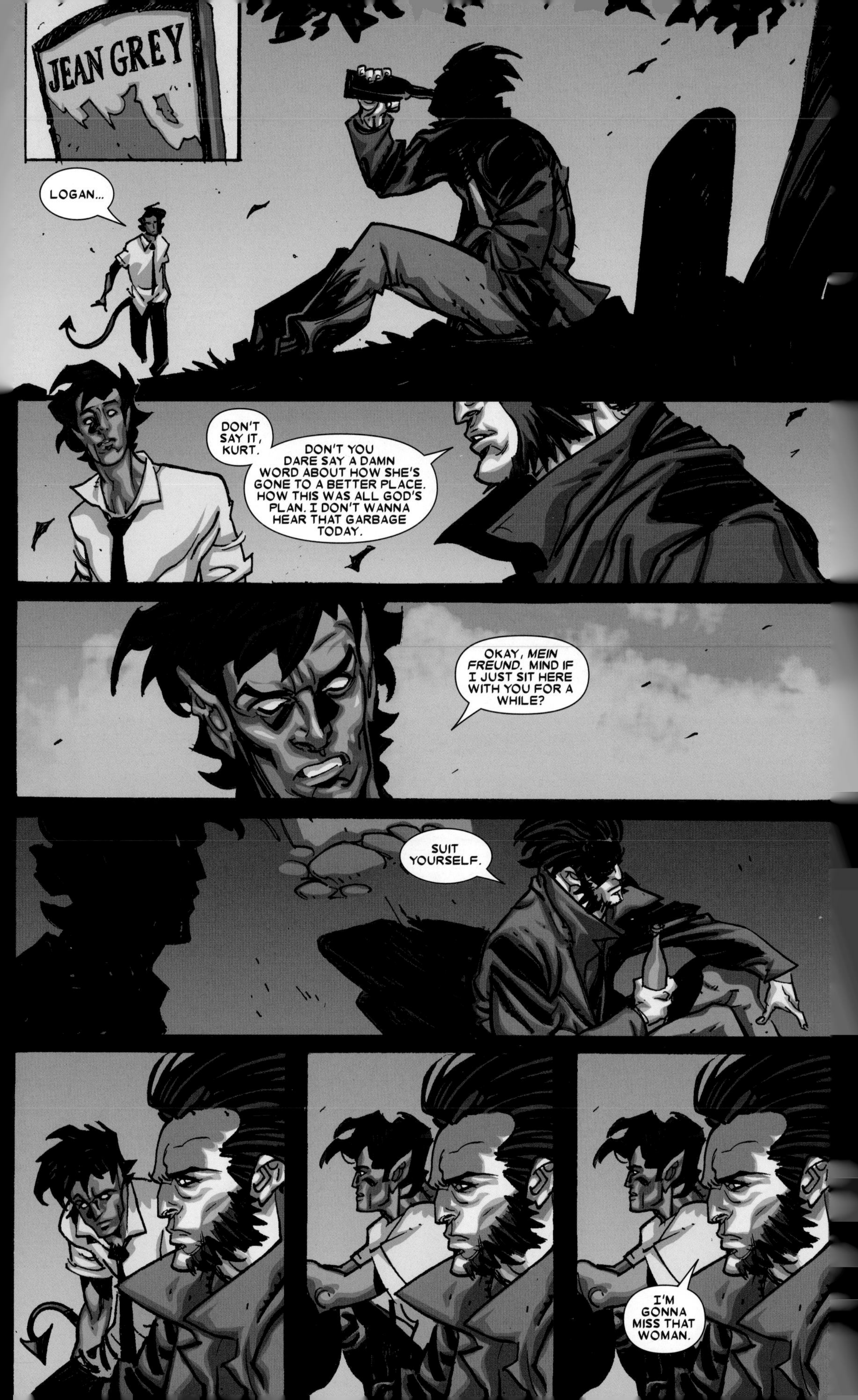
JEAN GREY
LOGAN...
DON'T SAY IT, KURT.
DON'T YOU DARE SAY A DAMN WORD ABOUT HOW SHE'S GONE TO A BETTER PLACE. HOW THIS WAS ALL GOD'S PLAN. I DON'T WANNA HEAR THAT GARBAGE TODAY.
OKAY, *MEIN FREUND.* MIND IF I JUST SIT HERE WITH YOU FOR A WHILE?
SUIT YOURSELF.
I'M GONNA MISS THAT WOMAN.

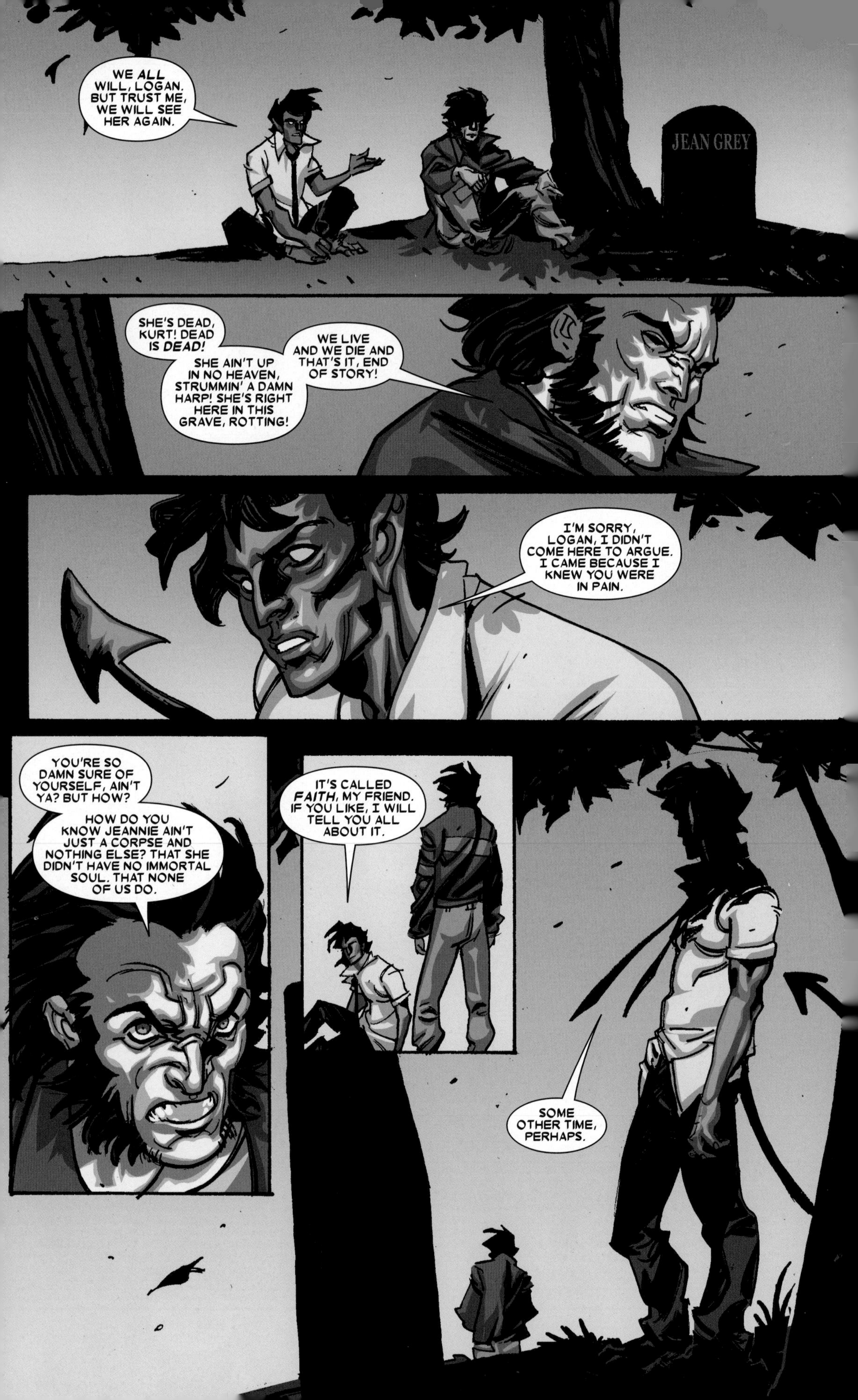
WE *ALL* WILL, LOGAN. BUT TRUST ME, WE WILL SEE HER AGAIN.
JEAN GREY
SHE'S DEAD, KURT! DEAD IS *DEAD!*
SHE AIN'T UP IN NO HEAVEN, STRUMMIN' A DAMN HARP! SHE'S RIGHT HERE IN THIS GRAVE, ROTTING!
WE LIVE AND WE DIE AND THAT'S IT, END OF STORY!
I'M SORRY, LOGAN, I DIDN'T COME HERE TO ARGUE. I CAME BECAUSE I KNEW YOU WERE IN PAIN.
YOU'RE SO DAMN SURE OF YOURSELF, AIN'T YA? BUT HOW?
HOW DO YOU KNOW JEANNIE AIN'T JUST A CORPSE AND NOTHING ELSE? THAT SHE DIDN'T HAVE NO IMMORTAL SOUL. THAT NONE OF US DO.
IT'S CALLED *FAITH*, MY FRIEND. IF YOU LIKE, I WILL TELL YOU ALL ABOUT IT.
SOME OTHER TIME, PERHAPS.

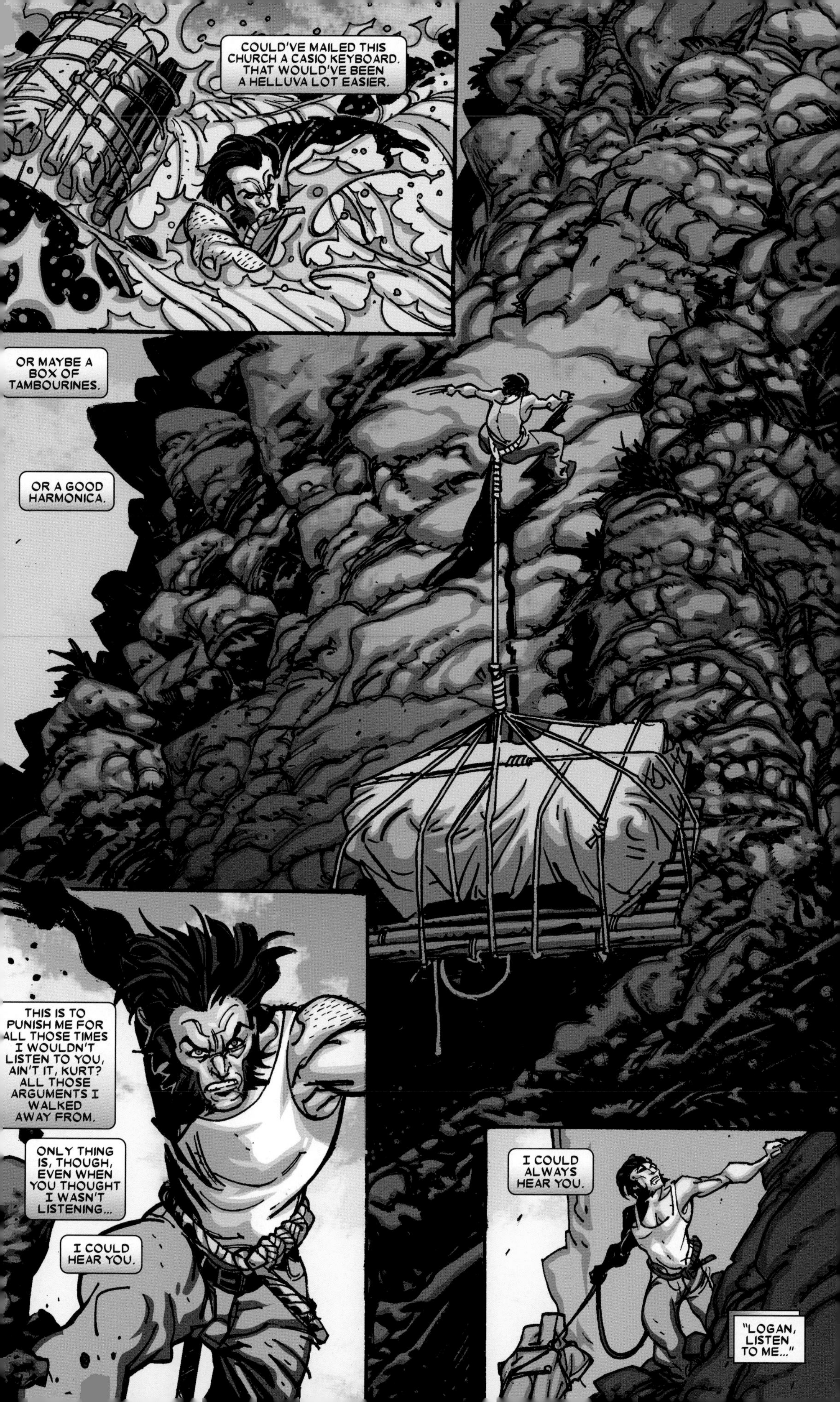
COULD'VE MAILED THIS CHURCH A CASIO KEYBOARD. THAT WOULD'VE BEEN A HELLUVA LOT EASIER.
OR MAYBE A BOX OF TAMBOURINES.
OR A GOOD HARMONICA.
THIS IS TO PUNISH ME FOR ALL THOSE TIMES I WOULDN'T LISTEN TO YOU, AIN'T IT, KURT? ALL THOSE ARGUMENTS I WALKED AWAY FROM.
ONLY THING IS, THOUGH, EVEN WHEN YOU THOUGHT I WASN'T LISTENING...
I COULD HEAR YOU.
I COULD ALWAYS HEAR YOU.
"LOGAN, LISTEN TO ME..."

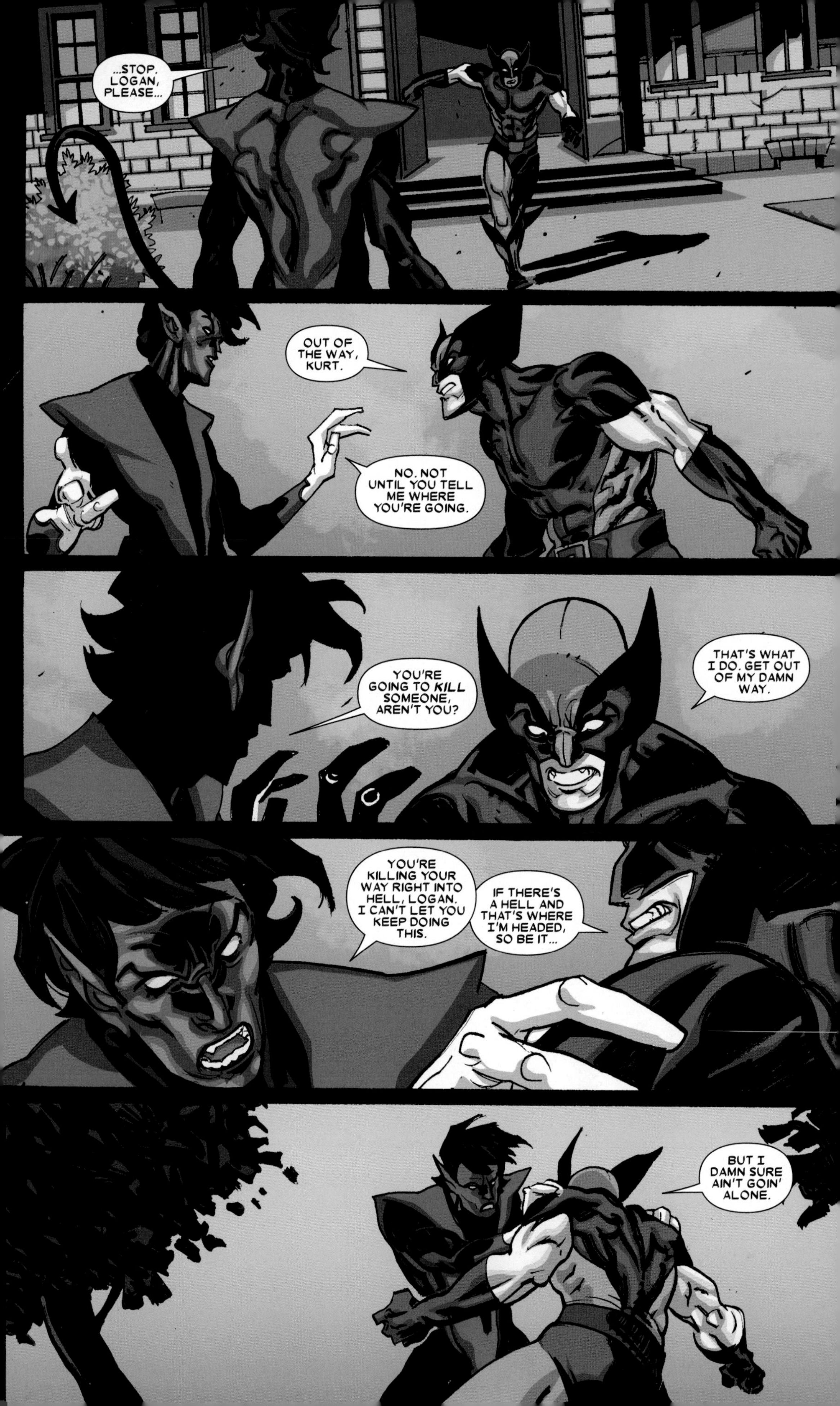
...STOP. LOGAN, PLEASE...
OUT OF THE WAY, KURT.
NO. NOT UNTIL YOU TELL ME WHERE YOU'RE GOING.
YOU'RE GOING TO KILL SOMEONE, AREN'T YOU?
THAT'S WHAT I DO. GET OUT OF MY DAMN WAY.
YOU'RE KILLING YOUR WAY RIGHT INTO HELL, LOGAN. I CAN'T LET YOU KEEP DOING THIS.
IF THERE'S A HELL AND THAT'S WHERE I'M HEADED, SO BE IT...
BUT I DAMN SURE AIN'T GOIN' ALONE.

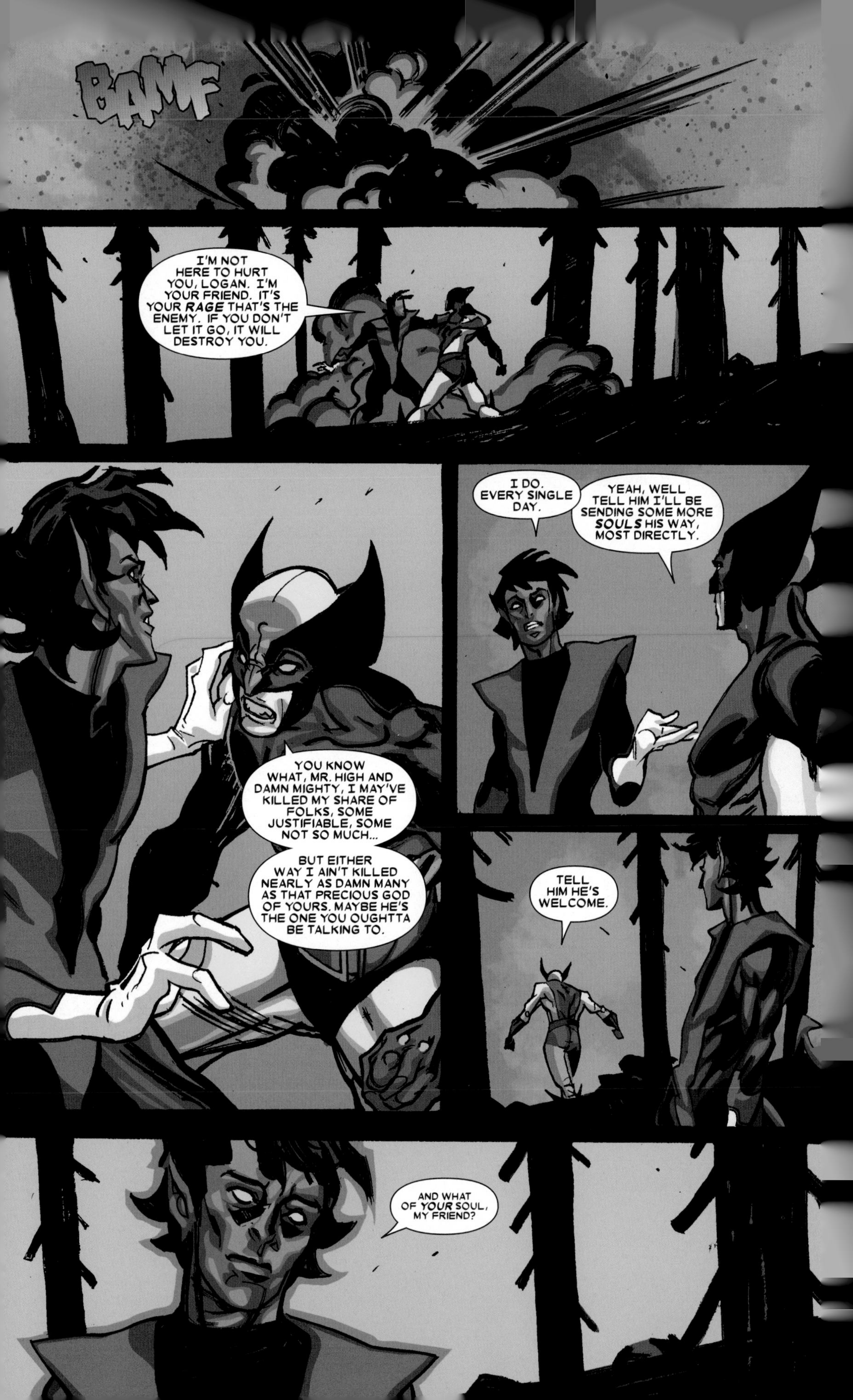
BAMF
I'M NOT HERE TO HURT YOU, LOGAN. I'M YOUR FRIEND. IT'S YOUR *RAGE* THAT'S THE ENEMY. IF YOU DON'T LET IT GO, IT WILL DESTROY YOU.
YOU KNOW WHAT, MR. HIGH AND DAMN MIGHTY, I MAY'VE KILLED MY SHARE OF FOLKS, SOME JUSTIFIABLE, SOME NOT SO MUCH...
BUT EITHER WAY I AIN'T KILLED NEARLY AS DAMN MANY AS THAT PRECIOUS GOD OF YOURS. MAYBE HE'S THE ONE YOU OUGHTTA BE TALKING TO.
I DO. EVERY SINGLE DAY.
YEAH, WELL TELL HIM I'LL BE SENDING SOME MORE *SOULS* HIS WAY, MOST DIRECTLY.
TELL HIM HE'S WELCOME.
AND WHAT OF *YOUR* SOUL, MY FRIEND?

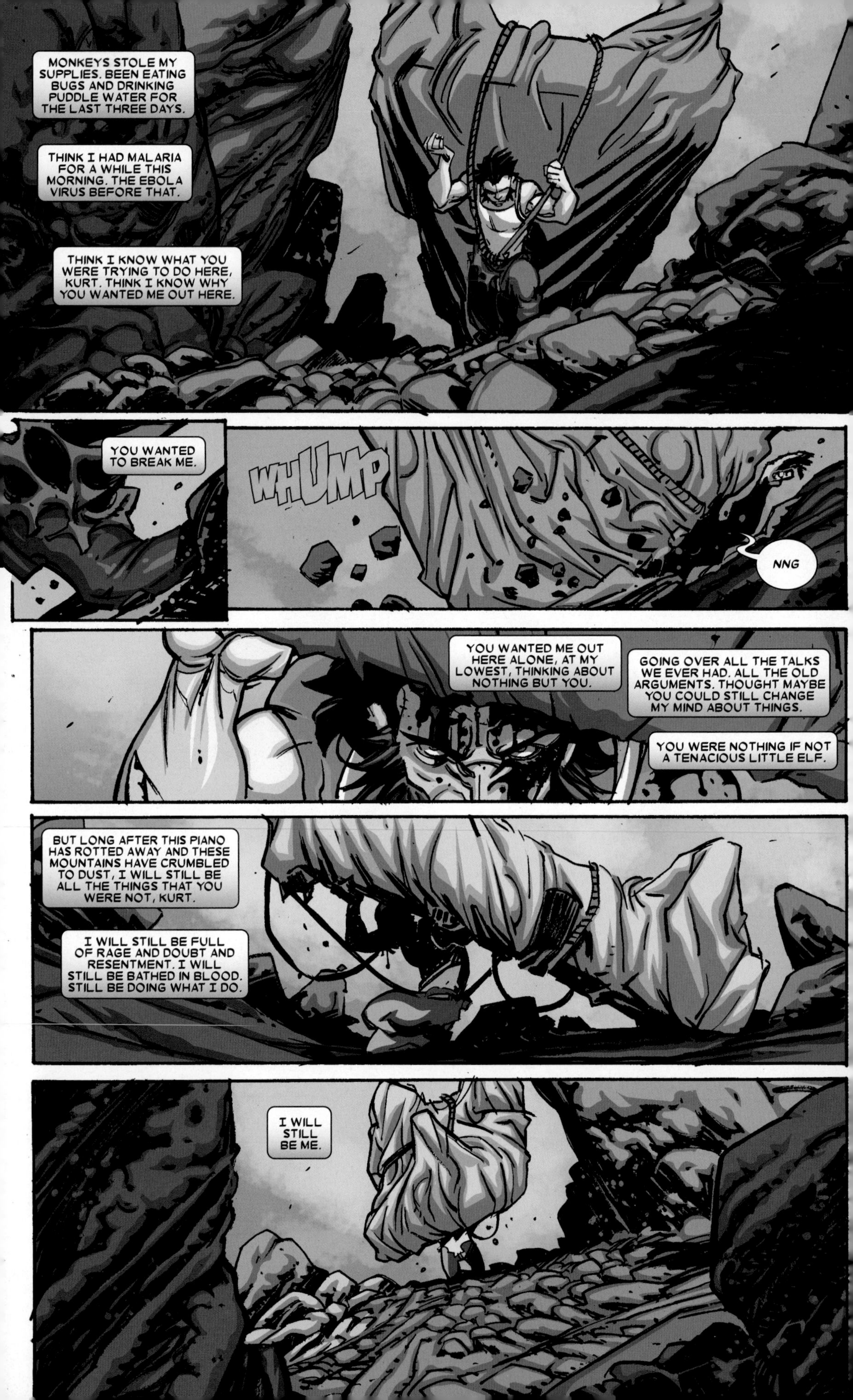
MONKEYS STOLE MY SUPPLIES. BEEN EATING BUGS AND DRINKING PUDDLE WATER FOR THE LAST THREE DAYS.
THINK I HAD MALARIA FOR A WHILE THIS MORNING. THE EBOLA VIRUS BEFORE THAT.
THINK I KNOW WHAT YOU WERE TRYING TO DO HERE, KURT. THINK I KNOW WHY YOU WANTED ME OUT HERE.
YOU WANTED TO BREAK ME.
WHUMP
NNG
YOU WANTED ME OUT HERE ALONE, AT MY LOWEST, THINKING ABOUT NOTHING BUT YOU.
GOING OVER ALL THE TALKS WE EVER HAD. ALL THE OLD ARGUMENTS. THOUGHT MAYBE YOU COULD STILL CHANGE MY MIND ABOUT THINGS.
YOU WERE NOTHING IF NOT A TENACIOUS LITTLE ELF.
BUT LONG AFTER THIS PIANO HAS ROTTED AWAY AND THESE MOUNTAINS HAVE CRUMBLED TO DUST, I WILL STILL BE ALL THE THINGS THAT YOU WERE NOT, KURT.
I WILL STILL BE FULL OF RAGE AND DOUBT AND RESENTMENT. I WILL STILL BE BATHED IN BLOOD. STILL BE DOING WHAT I DO.
I WILL STILL BE ME.

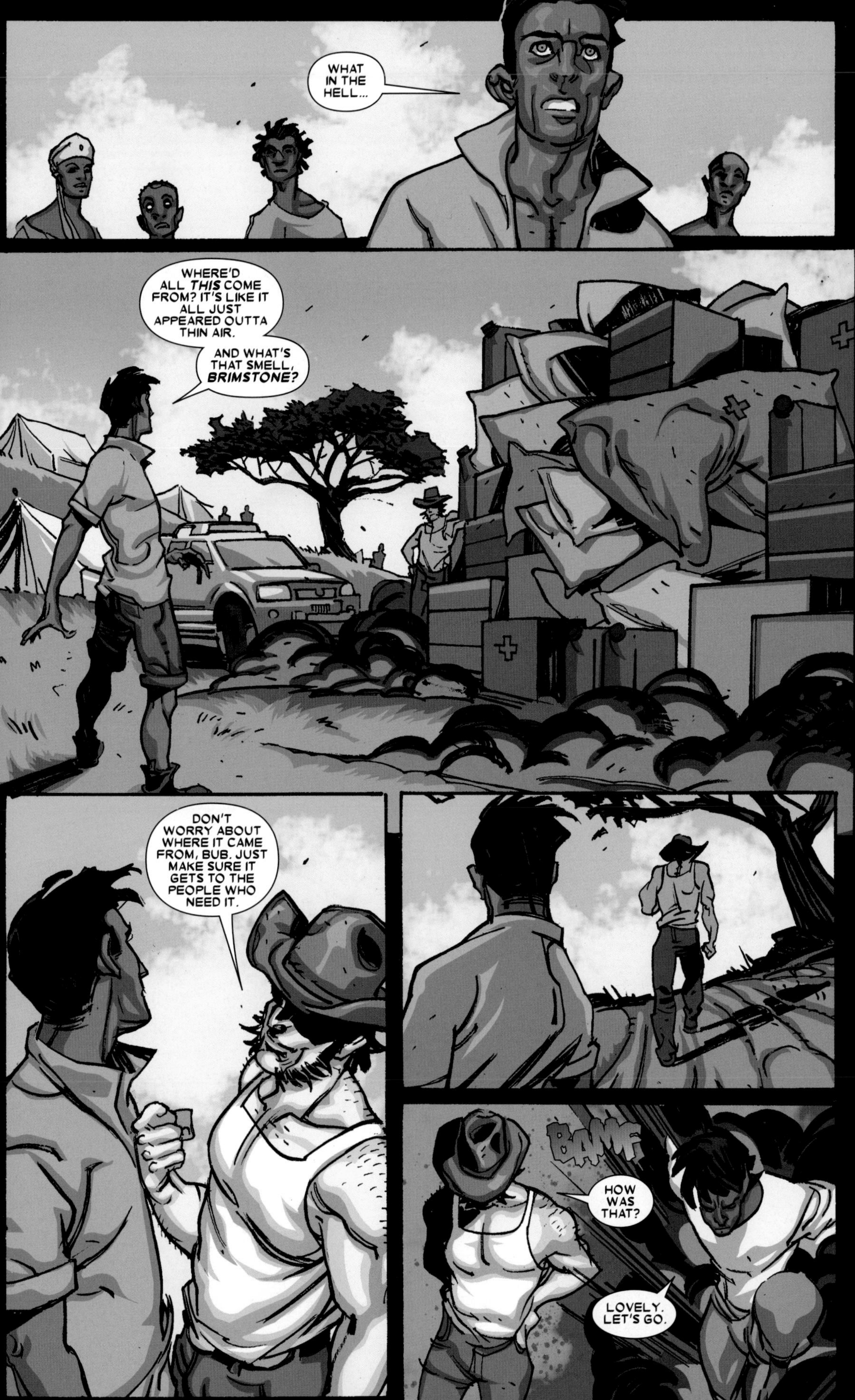
WHAT IN THE HELL...
WHERE'D ALL *THIS* COME FROM? IT'S LIKE IT ALL JUST APPEARED OUTTA THIN AIR.
AND WHAT'S THAT SMELL, *BRIMSTONE?*
DON'T WORRY ABOUT WHERE IT CAME FROM, BUB. JUST MAKE SURE IT GETS TO THE PEOPLE WHO NEED IT.
BAMF
HOW WAS THAT?
LOVELY. LET'S GO.

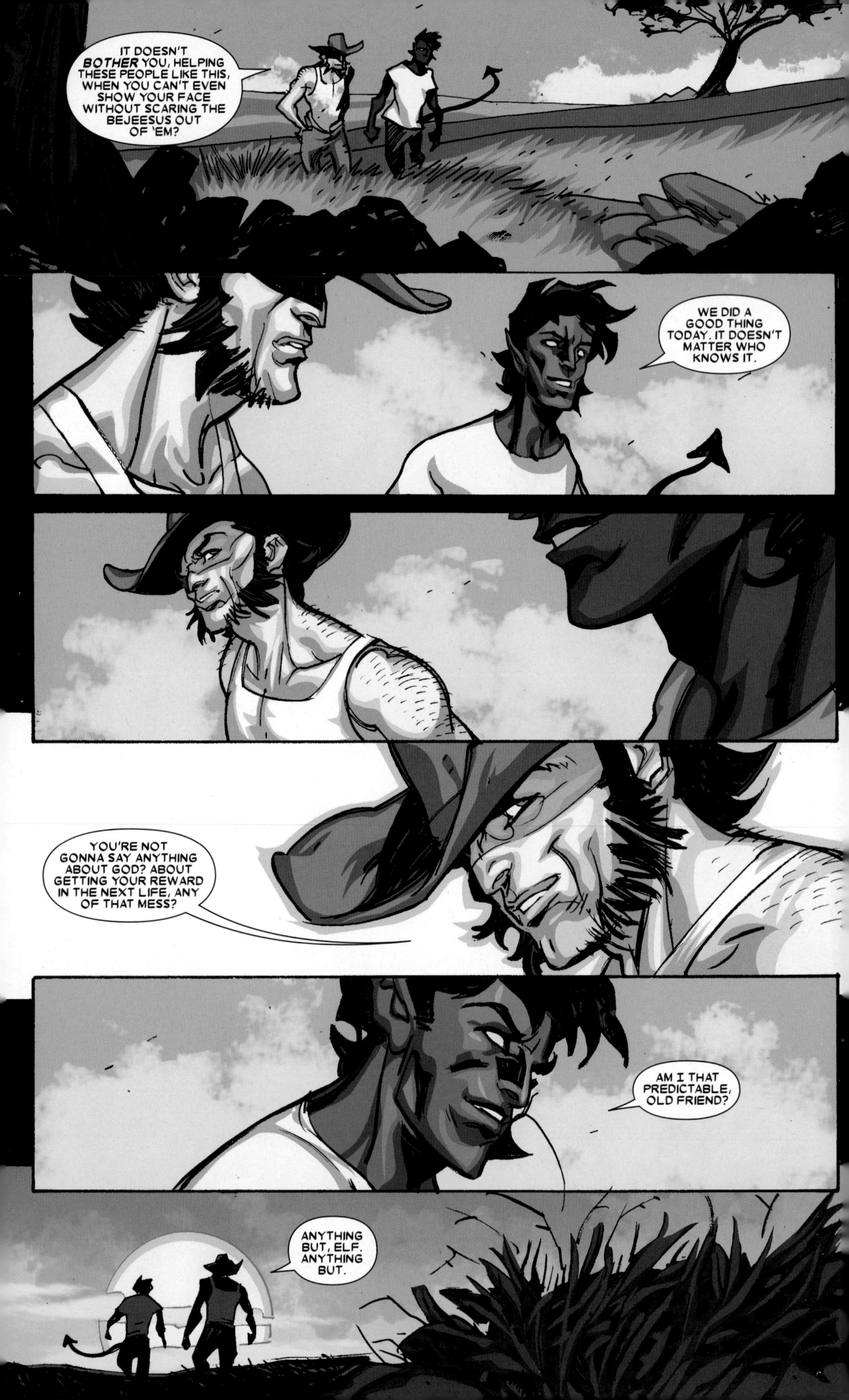
IT DOESN'T BOTHER YOU, HELPING THESE PEOPLE LIKE THIS, WHEN YOU CAN'T EVEN SHOW YOUR FACE WITHOUT SCARING THE BEJEESUS OUT OF 'EM?
WE DID A GOOD THING TODAY. IT DOESN'T MATTER WHO KNOWS IT.
YOU'RE NOT GONNA SAY ANYTHING ABOUT GOD? ABOUT GETTING YOUR REWARD IN THE NEXT LIFE, ANY OF THAT MESS?
AM I THAT PREDICTABLE, OLD FRIEND?
ANYTHING BUT, ELF. ANYTHING BUT.

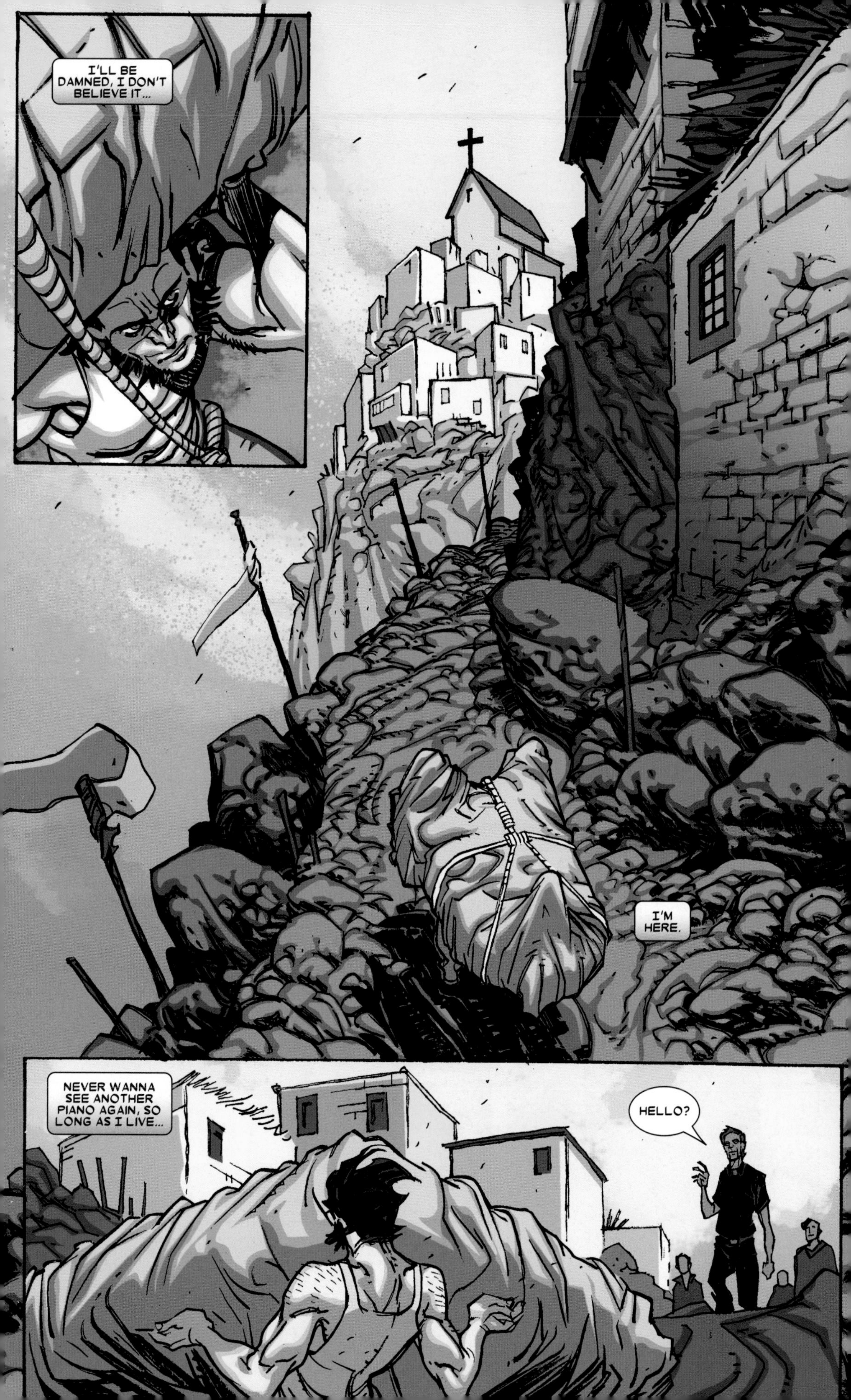

I'LL BE DAMNED, I DON'T BELIEVE IT...
I'M HERE.
NEVER WANNA SEE ANOTHER PIANO AGAIN, SO LONG AS I LIVE...
HELLO?

ARE YOU ALL RIGHT? CAN WE HELP YOU?

YES, IT IS.

THIS THE CHURCH OF THE HOLY ASCENSION?

THIS IS FOR YOU. A GIFT FROM KURT WAGNER.

IS THAT A PIANO?

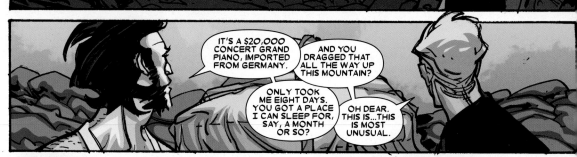

IT'S A $20,000 CONCERT GRAND PIANO, IMPORTED FROM GERMANY.

AND YOU DRAGGED THAT ALL THE WAY UP THIS MOUNTAIN?

ONLY TOOK ME EIGHT DAYS. YOU GOT A PLACE I CAN SLEEP FOR, SAY, A MONTH OR SO?

OH DEAR. THIS IS...THIS IS MOST UNUSUAL.

AIN'T IT, THOUGH.

IT'S A MOST GENEROUS GIFT, IT CERTAINLY IS, BUT WELL, THE THING IS... OH, I HATE TO TELL YOU THIS.

TELL ME WHAT?

WE DON'T HAVE ANYONE WHO PLAYS THE PIANO.

SAY WHAT NOW?

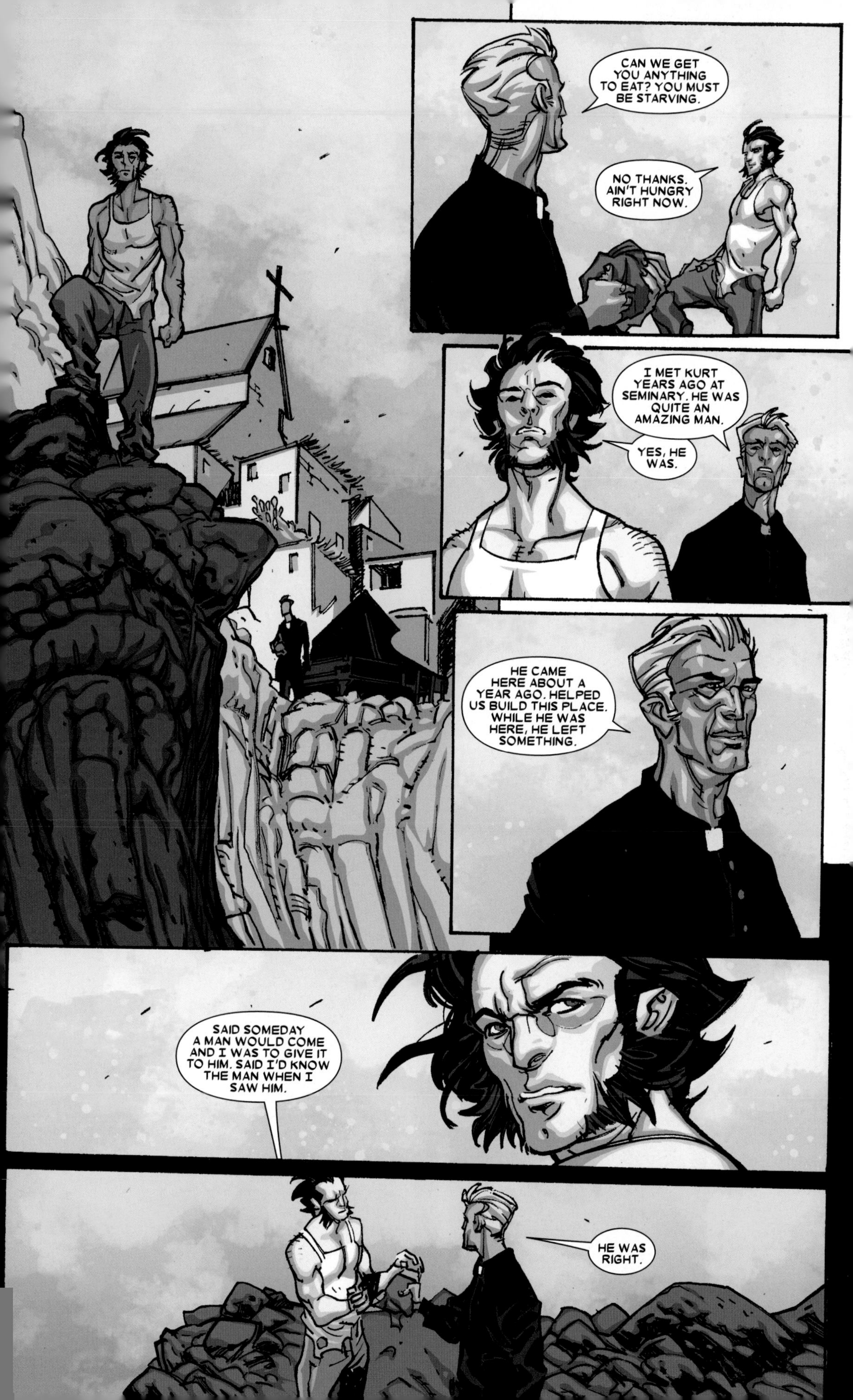

CAN WE GET YOU ANYTHING TO EAT? YOU MUST BE STARVING.
NO THANKS. AIN'T HUNGRY RIGHT NOW.
I MET KURT YEARS AGO AT SEMINARY. HE WAS QUITE AN AMAZING MAN.
YES, HE WAS.
HE CAME HERE ABOUT A YEAR AGO. HELPED US BUILD THIS PLACE. WHILE HE WAS HERE, HE LEFT SOMETHING.
SAID SOMEDAY A MAN WOULD COME AND I WAS TO GIVE IT TO HIM. SAID I'D KNOW THE MAN WHEN I SAW HIM.
HE WAS RIGHT.

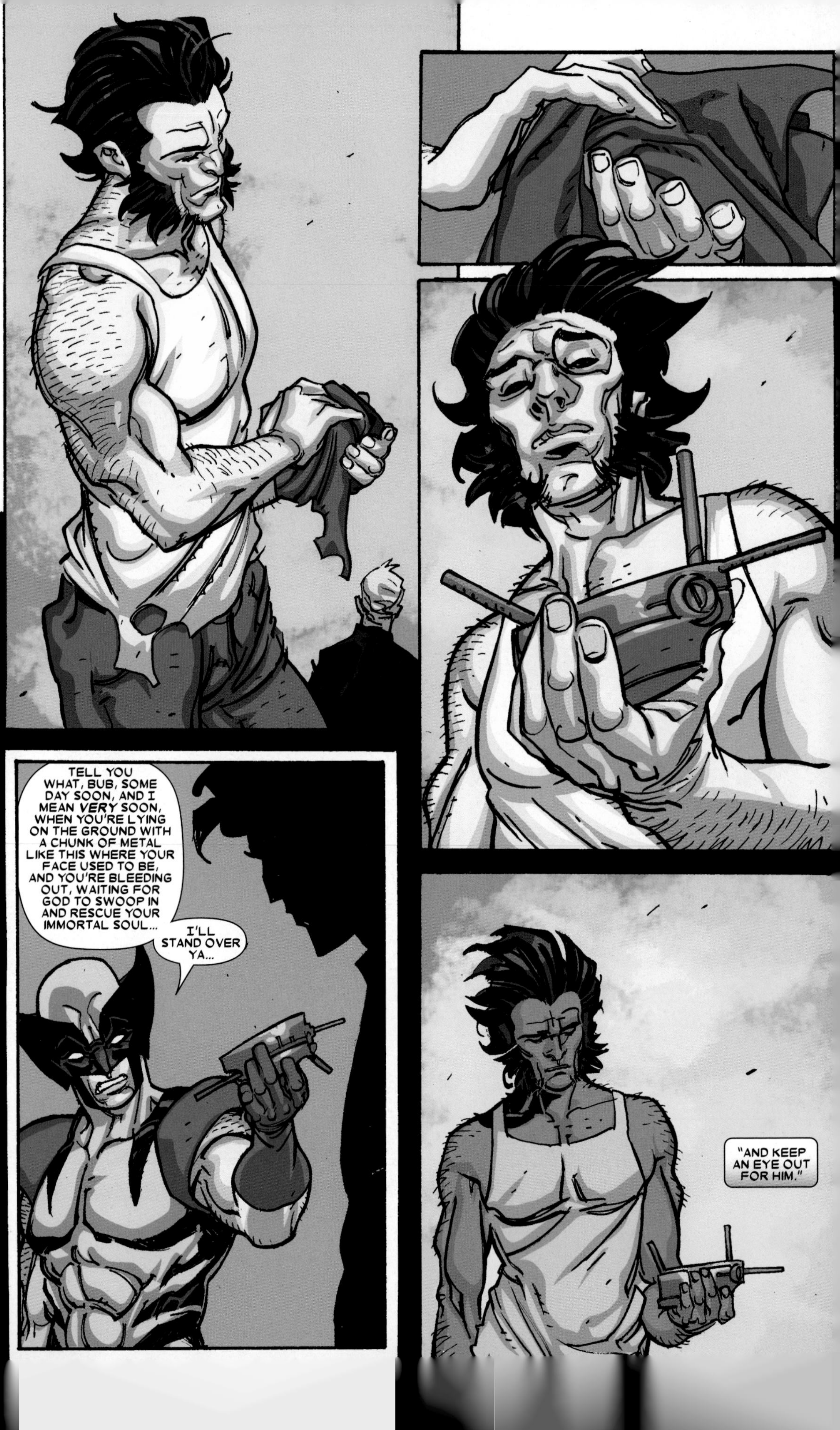
TELL YOU WHAT, BUB, SOME DAY SOON, AND I MEAN VERY SOON, WHEN YOU'RE LYING ON THE GROUND WITH A CHUNK OF METAL LIKE THIS WHERE YOUR FACE USED TO BE, AND YOU'RE BLEEDING OUT, WAITING FOR GOD TO SWOOP IN AND RESCUE YOUR IMMORTAL SOUL...
I'LL STAND OVER YA...
"AND KEEP AN EYE OUT FOR HIM."

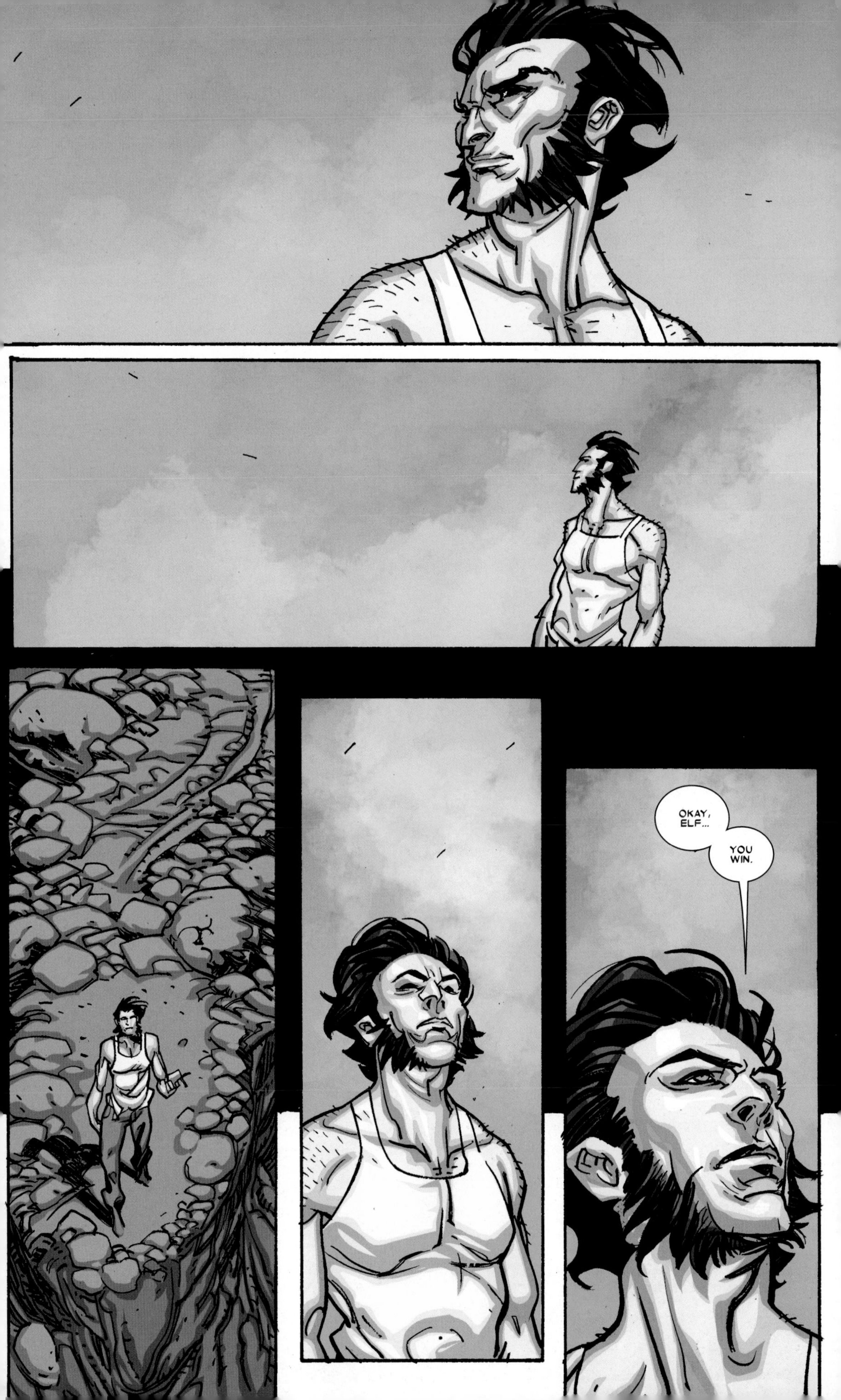
OKAY, ELF...
YOU WIN.

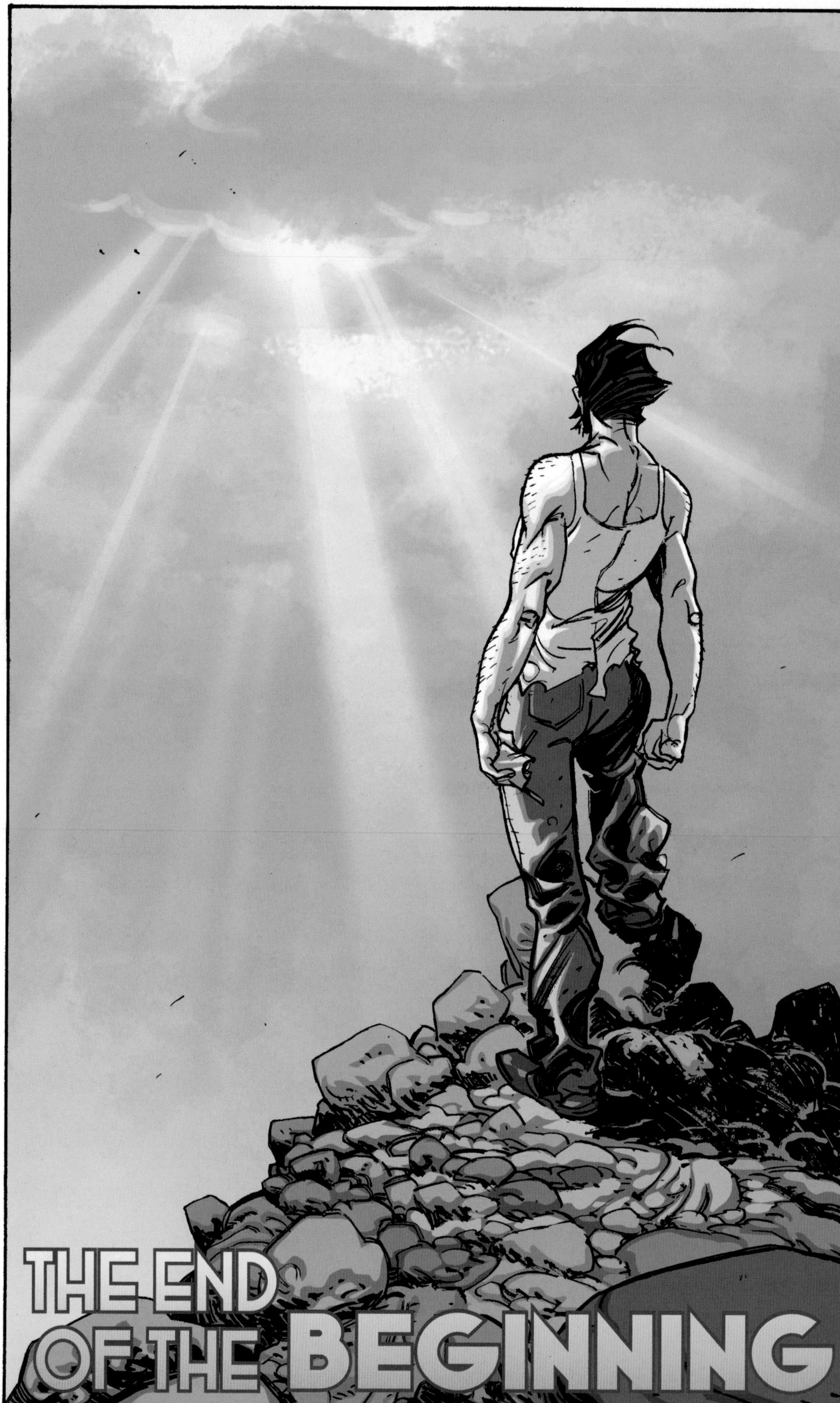
THE END
OF THE BEGINNING

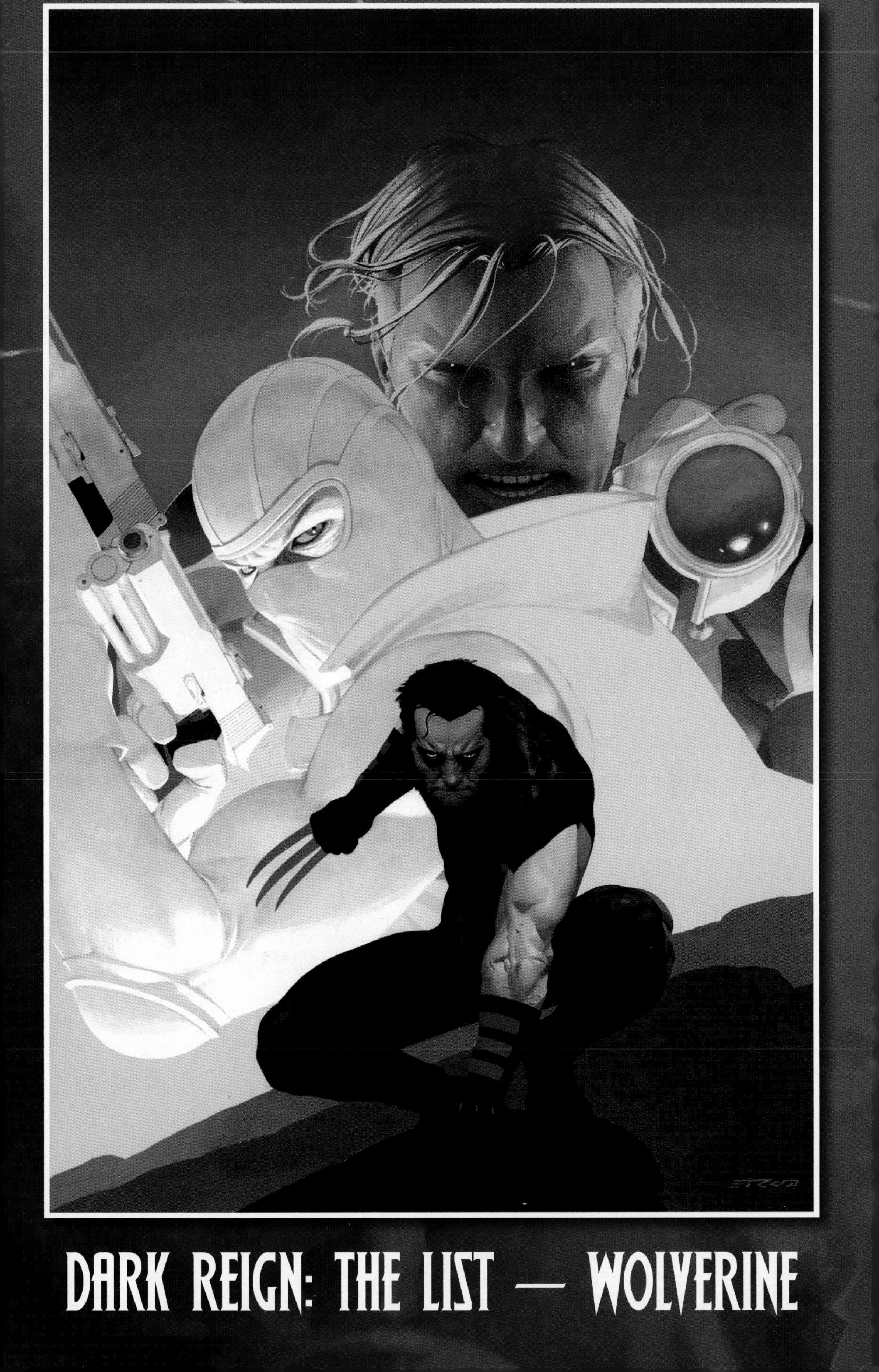

DARK REIGN: THE LIST — WOLVERINE

Many years ago a secret government organization called Weapon X abducted the man called Logan, a mutant possessing razor-sharp bone claws and the ability to heal from virtually any wound. In their attempt to create the perfect living weapon, the organization bonded the unbreakable metal, Adamantium, to his skeleton. The process was excruciating and by the end there was little left of the man known as Logan. He had become...

WOLVERINE

In recent months, Norman Osborn, the former costumed villain known as the Green Goblin, has become the head of the U.S. government's espionage strike-team, H.A.M.M.E.R., as well as the leader of its super hero team, the Avengers. Osborn populates the Avengers with powered beings he feels he can trust and a host of super-criminals posing as established heroes.

But one of his team didn't find him so charming. Marvel Boy has recently left Osborn's Avengers, after realizing that he was being used for someone else's gain. And as far as he's concerned, if it's not for his own gain, it's not worth doing.

Some time ago, Logan learned that the Weapon X program was a part of the Weapon Plus program and that he was the tenth in a series of living weapons created in an above-top-secret living engine called The World. One of those Weapons, Weapon XIII, is a thieving international man of mystery and expert in the arts of fighting and illusion named Fantomex. It was Fantomex that alerted Logan to the truth of Weapon X and together they destroyed The World. Or so they thought...

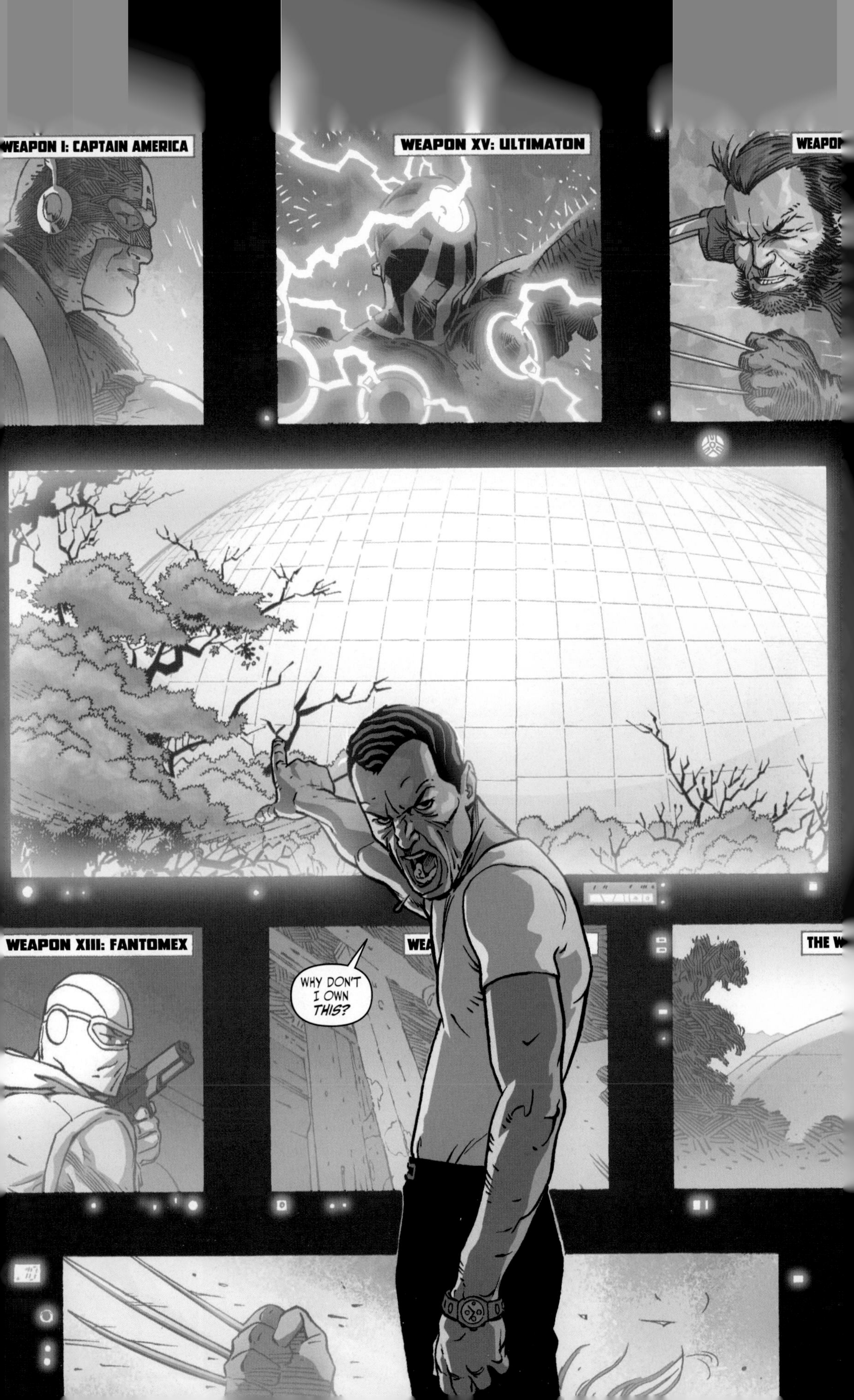
WEAPON I: CAPTAIN AMERICA
WEAPON XV: ULTIMATON
WEAPON
WEAPON XIII: FANTOMEX
WEA
THE W
WHY DON'T I OWN THIS?

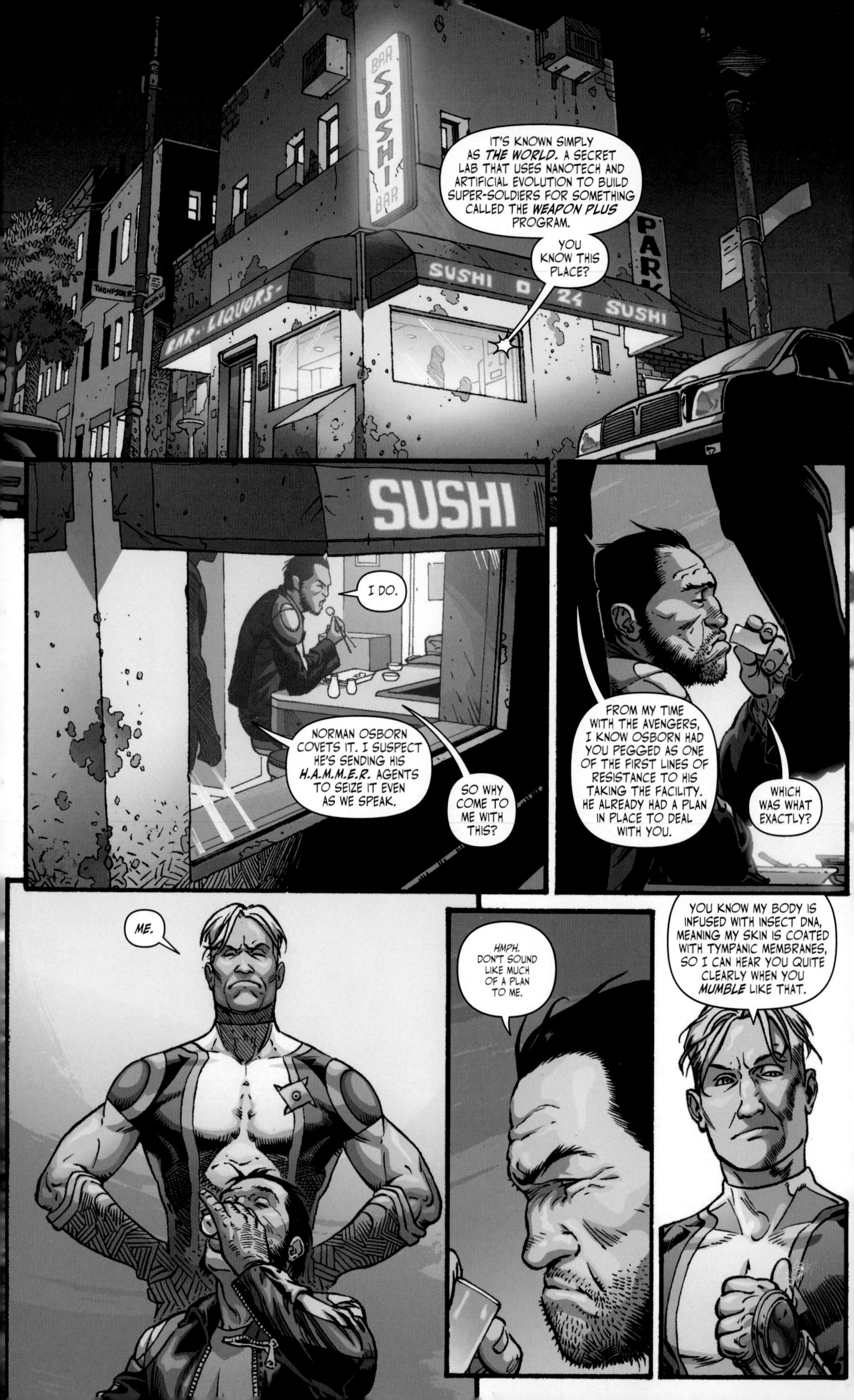
BAR SUSHI BAR
IT'S KNOWN SIMPLY AS THE WORLD. A SECRET LAB THAT USES NANOTECH AND ARTIFICIAL EVOLUTION TO BUILD SUPER-SOLDIERS FOR SOMETHING CALLED THE WEAPON PLUS PROGRAM.
YOU KNOW THIS PLACE?
SUSHI 24 SUSHI
BAR - LIQUORS -
PARK
SUSHI
I DO.
NORMAN OSBORN COVETS IT. I SUSPECT HE'S SENDING HIS H.A.M.M.E.R. AGENTS TO SEIZE IT EVEN AS WE SPEAK.
SO WHY COME TO ME WITH THIS?
FROM MY TIME WITH THE AVENGERS, I KNOW OSBORN HAD YOU PEGGED AS ONE OF THE FIRST LINES OF RESISTANCE TO HIS TAKING THE FACILITY. HE ALREADY HAD A PLAN IN PLACE TO DEAL WITH YOU.
WHICH WAS WHAT EXACTLY?
ME.
HMPH. DON'T SOUND LIKE MUCH OF A PLAN TO ME.
YOU KNOW MY BODY IS INFUSED WITH INSECT DNA, MEANING MY SKIN IS COATED WITH TYMPANIC MEMBRANES, SO I CAN HEAR YOU QUITE CLEARLY WHEN YOU MUMBLE LIKE THAT.

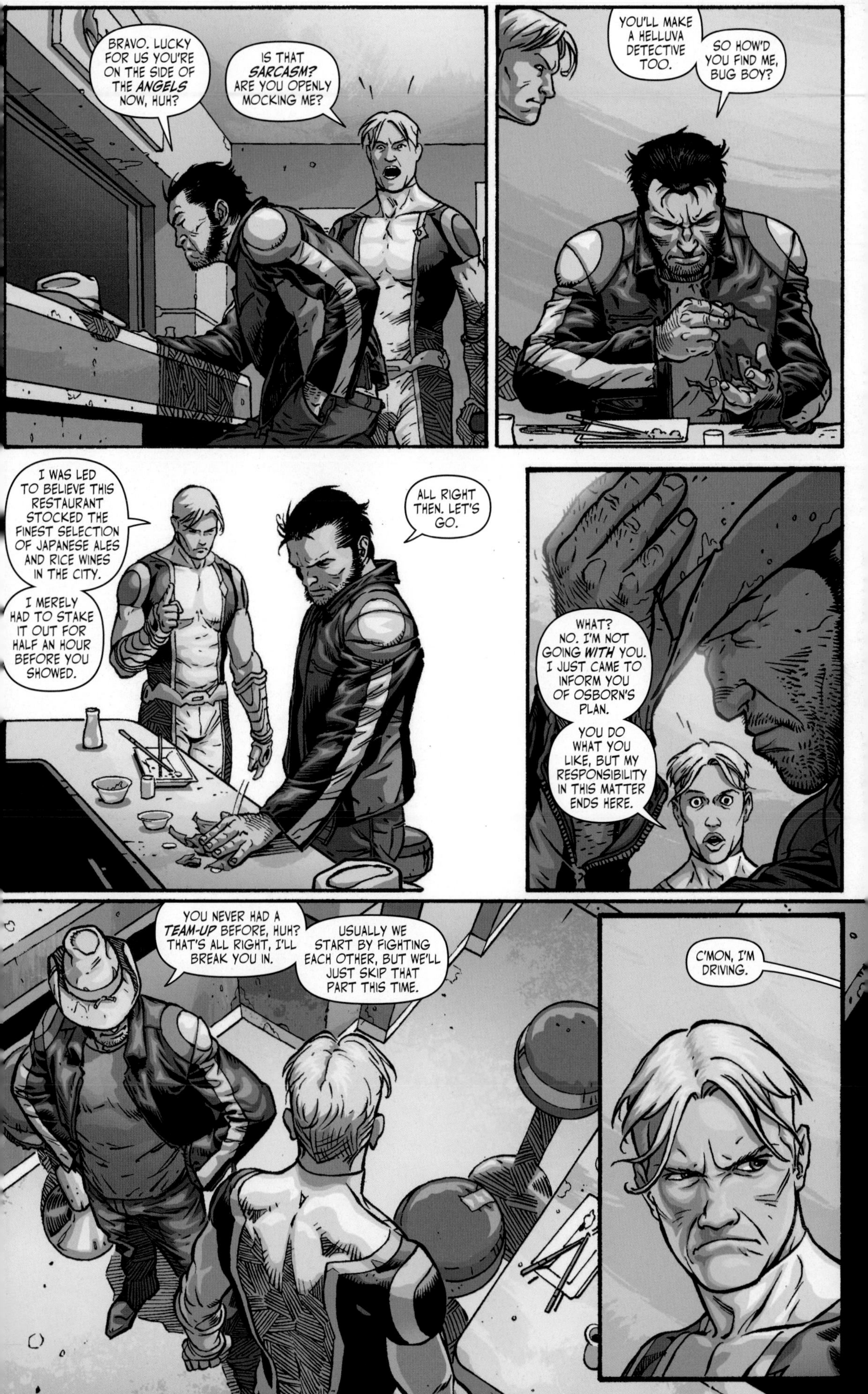
BRAVO. LUCKY FOR US YOU'RE ON THE SIDE OF THE *ANGELS* NOW, HUH?
IS THAT *SARCASM?* ARE YOU OPENLY MOCKING ME?
YOU'LL MAKE A HELLUVA DETECTIVE TOO.
SO HOW'D YOU FIND ME, BUG BOY?
I WAS LED TO BELIEVE THIS RESTAURANT STOCKED THE FINEST SELECTION OF JAPANESE ALES AND RICE WINES IN THE CITY.
I MERELY HAD TO STAKE IT OUT FOR HALF AN HOUR BEFORE YOU SHOWED.
ALL RIGHT THEN. LET'S GO.
WHAT? NO. I'M NOT GOING *WITH* YOU. I JUST CAME TO INFORM YOU OF OSBORN'S PLAN.
YOU DO WHAT YOU LIKE, BUT MY RESPONSIBILITY IN THIS MATTER ENDS HERE.
YOU NEVER HAD A *TEAM-UP* BEFORE, HUH? THAT'S ALL RIGHT, I'LL BREAK YOU IN.
USUALLY WE START BY FIGHTING EACH OTHER, BUT WE'LL JUST SKIP THAT PART THIS TIME.
C'MON, I'M DRIVING.

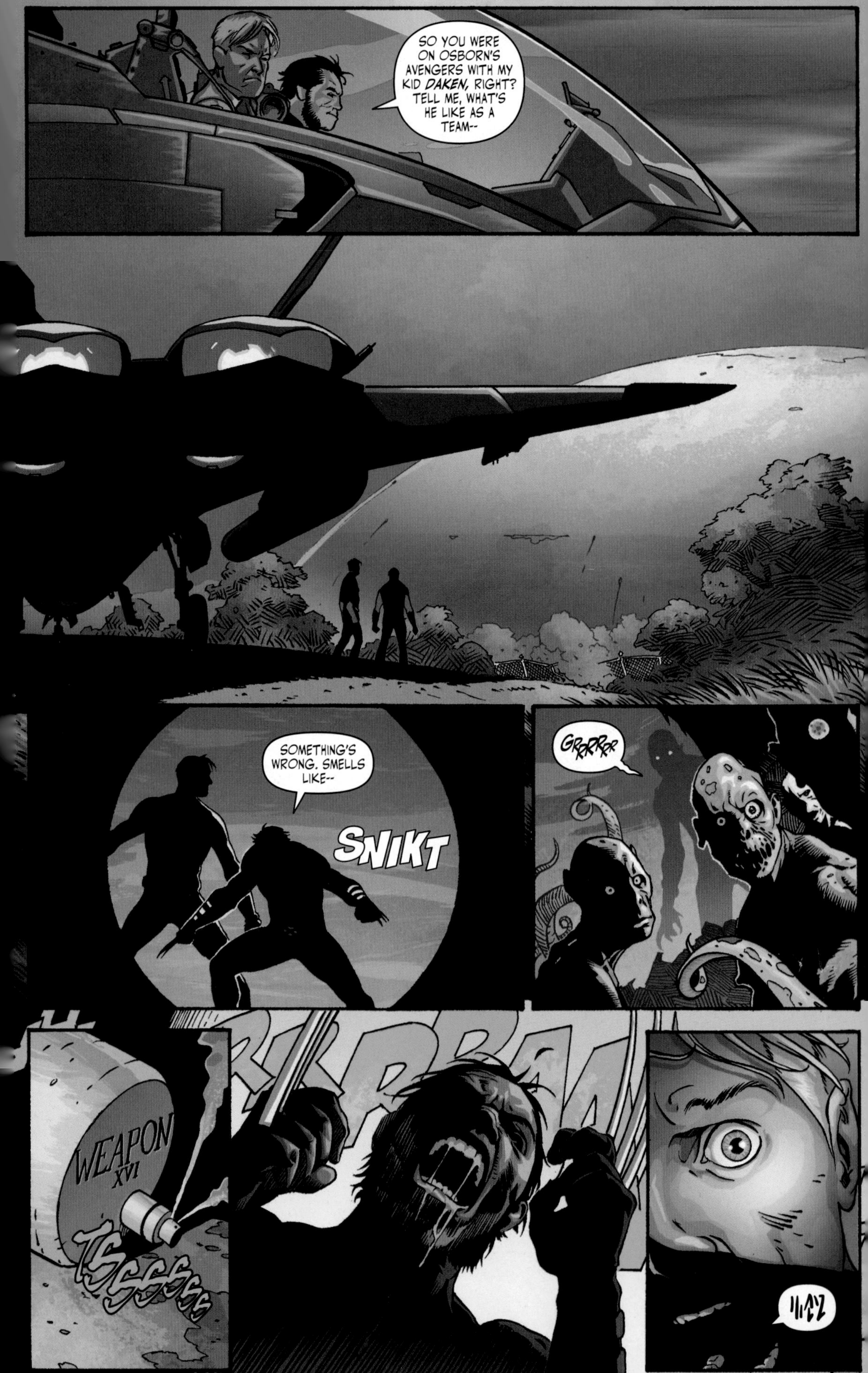
SO YOU WERE ON OSBORN'S AVENGERS WITH MY KID DAKEN, RIGHT? TELL ME, WHAT'S HE LIKE AS A TEAM--
SOMETHING'S WRONG. SMELLS LIKE--
SNIKT
GRRRRR
WEAPON XVI
TSSSSSSS

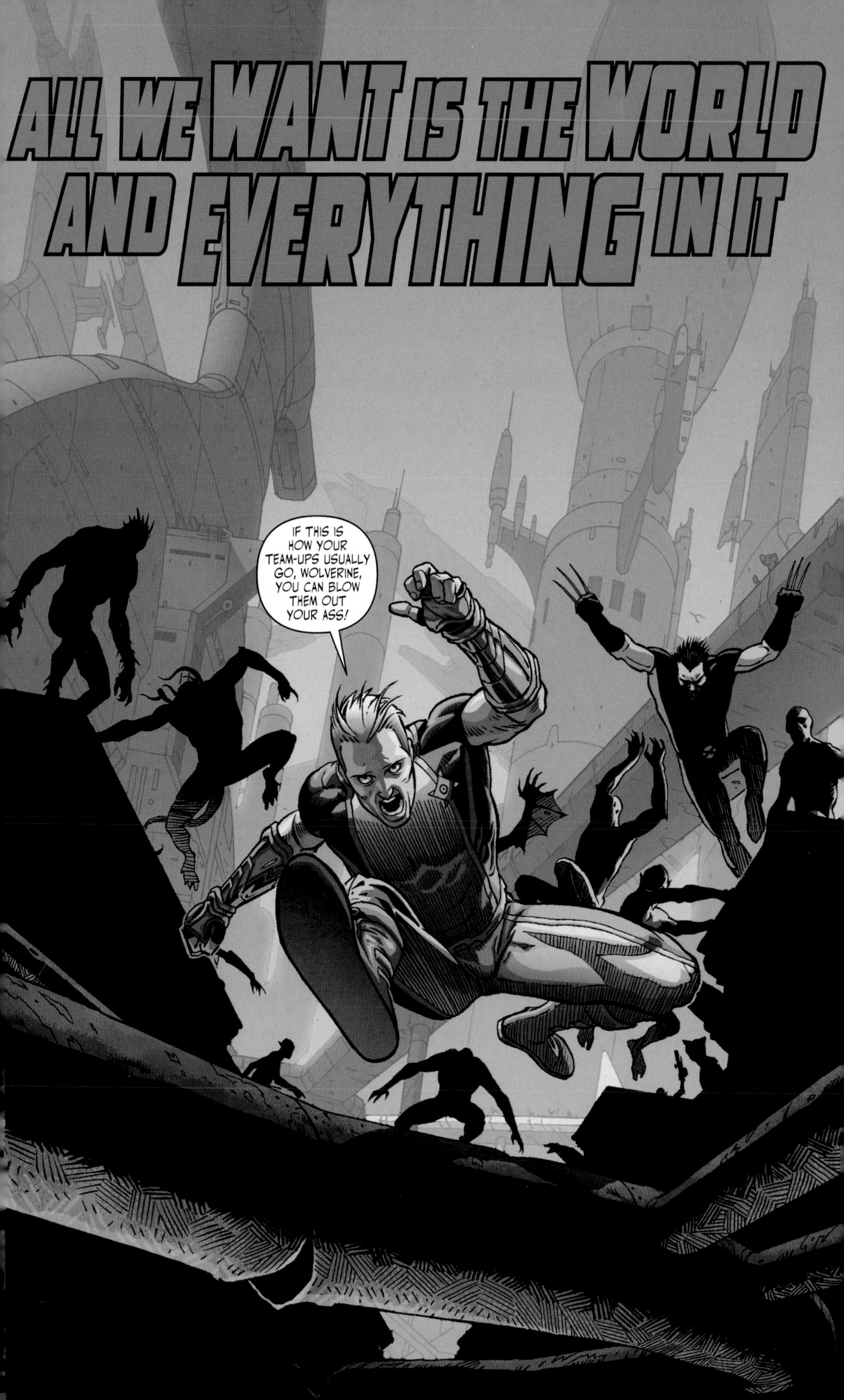
ALL WE WANT IS THE WORLD AND EVERYTHING IN IT
IF THIS IS HOW YOUR TEAM-UPS USUALLY GO, WOLVERINE, YOU CAN BLOW THEM OUT YOUR ASS!

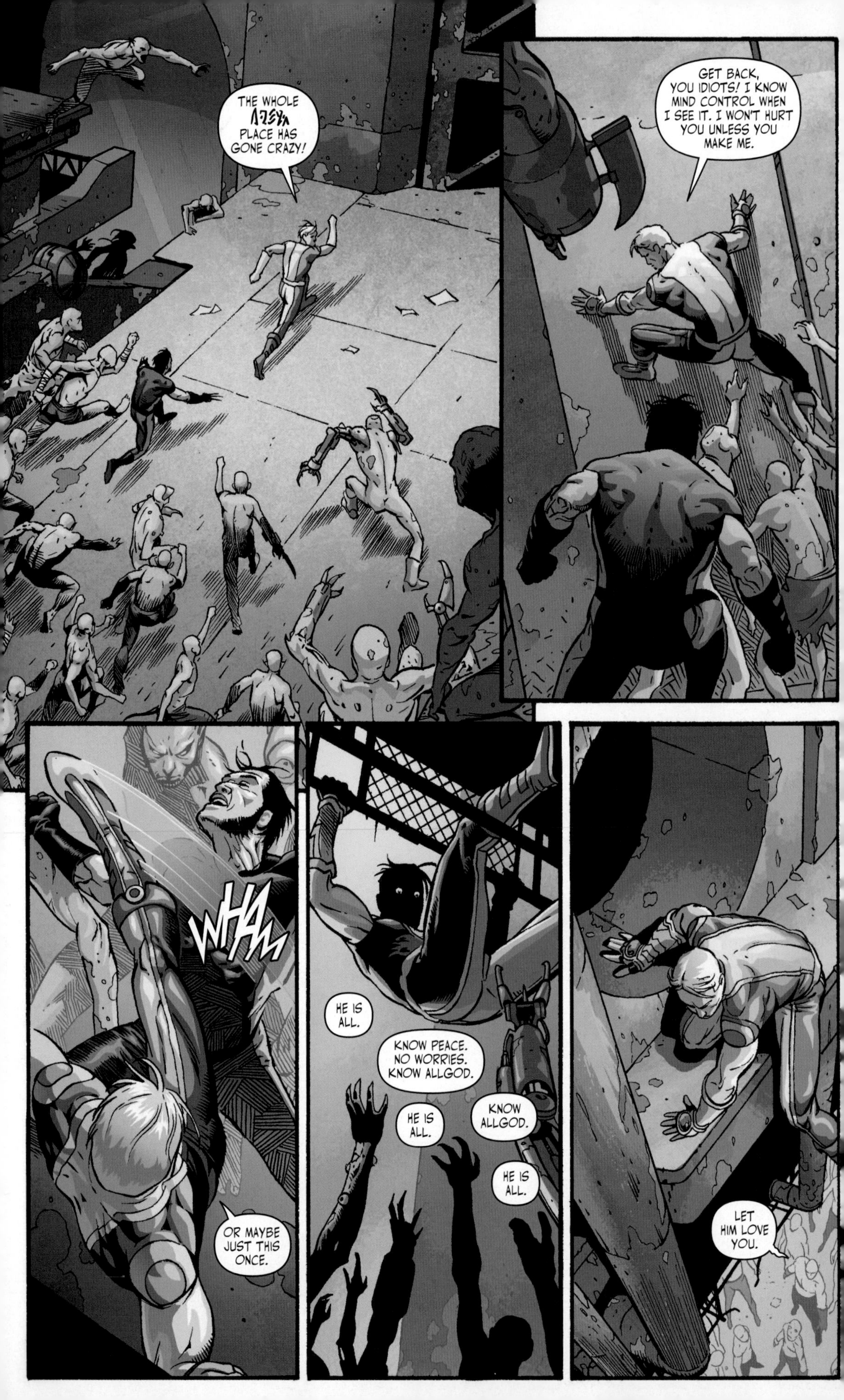
THE WHOLE PLACE HAS GONE CRAZY!
GET BACK, YOU IDIOTS! I KNOW MIND CONTROL WHEN I SEE IT. I WON'T HURT YOU UNLESS YOU MAKE ME.
WHAM
OR MAYBE JUST THIS ONCE.
HE IS ALL.
KNOW PEACE. NO WORRIES. KNOW ALLGOD.
HE IS ALL.
KNOW ALLGOD.
HE IS ALL.
LET HIM LOVE YOU.

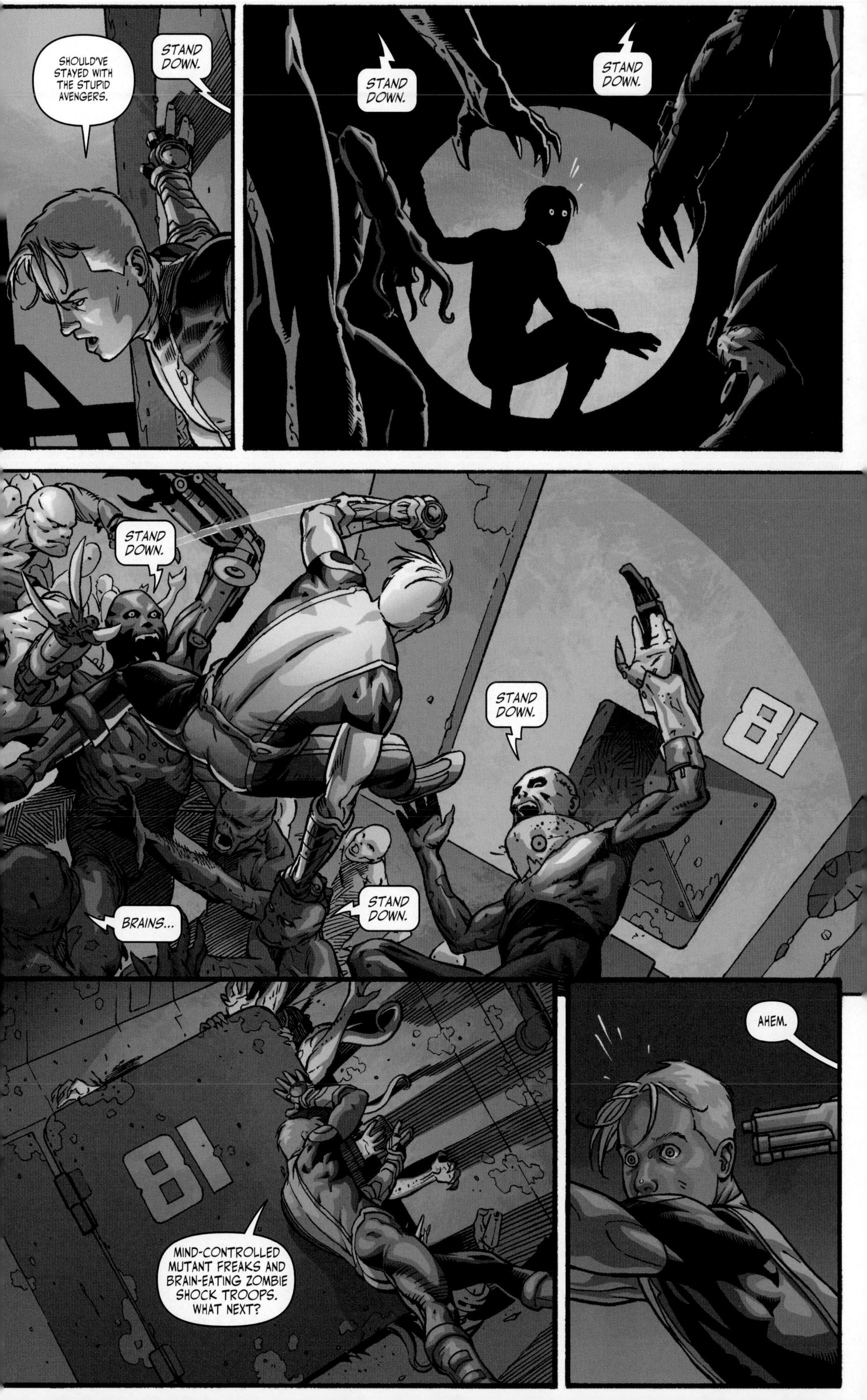
SHOULD'VE STAYED WITH THE STUPID AVENGERS.
STAND DOWN.
STAND DOWN.
STAND DOWN.
STAND DOWN.
STAND DOWN.
BRAINS...
STAND DOWN.
18
18
MIND-CONTROLLED MUTANT FREAKS AND BRAIN-EATING ZOMBIE SHOCK TROOPS. WHAT NEXT?
AHEM.

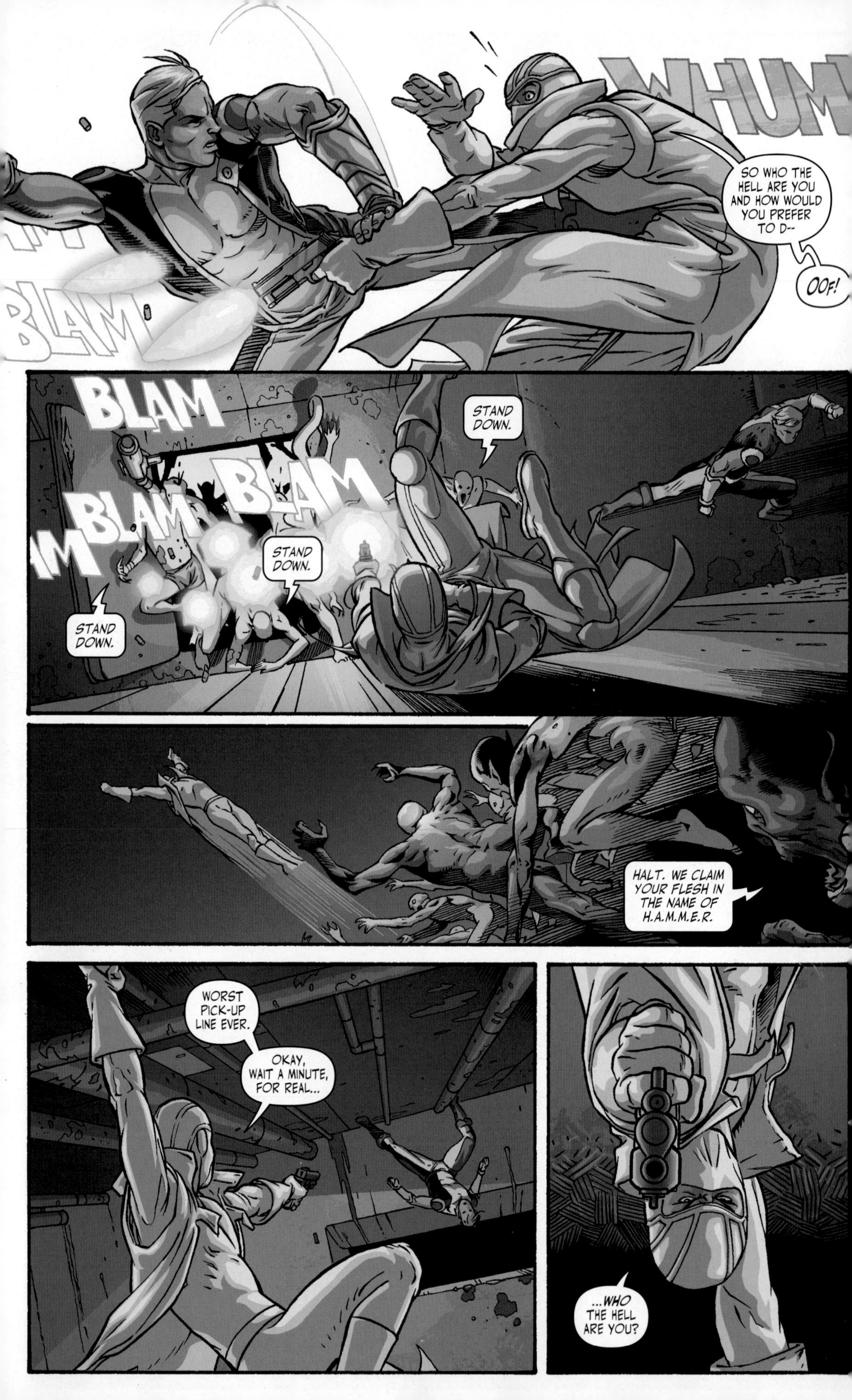
WHUM
SO WHO THE HELL ARE YOU AND HOW WOULD YOU PREFER TO D--
OOF!
BLAM
BLAM
BLAM
BLAM
STAND DOWN.
STAND DOWN.
STAND DOWN.
HALT. WE CLAIM YOUR FLESH IN THE NAME OF H.A.M.M.E.R.
WORST PICK-UP LINE EVER.
OKAY, WAIT A MINUTE, FOR REAL...
...WHO THE HELL ARE YOU?

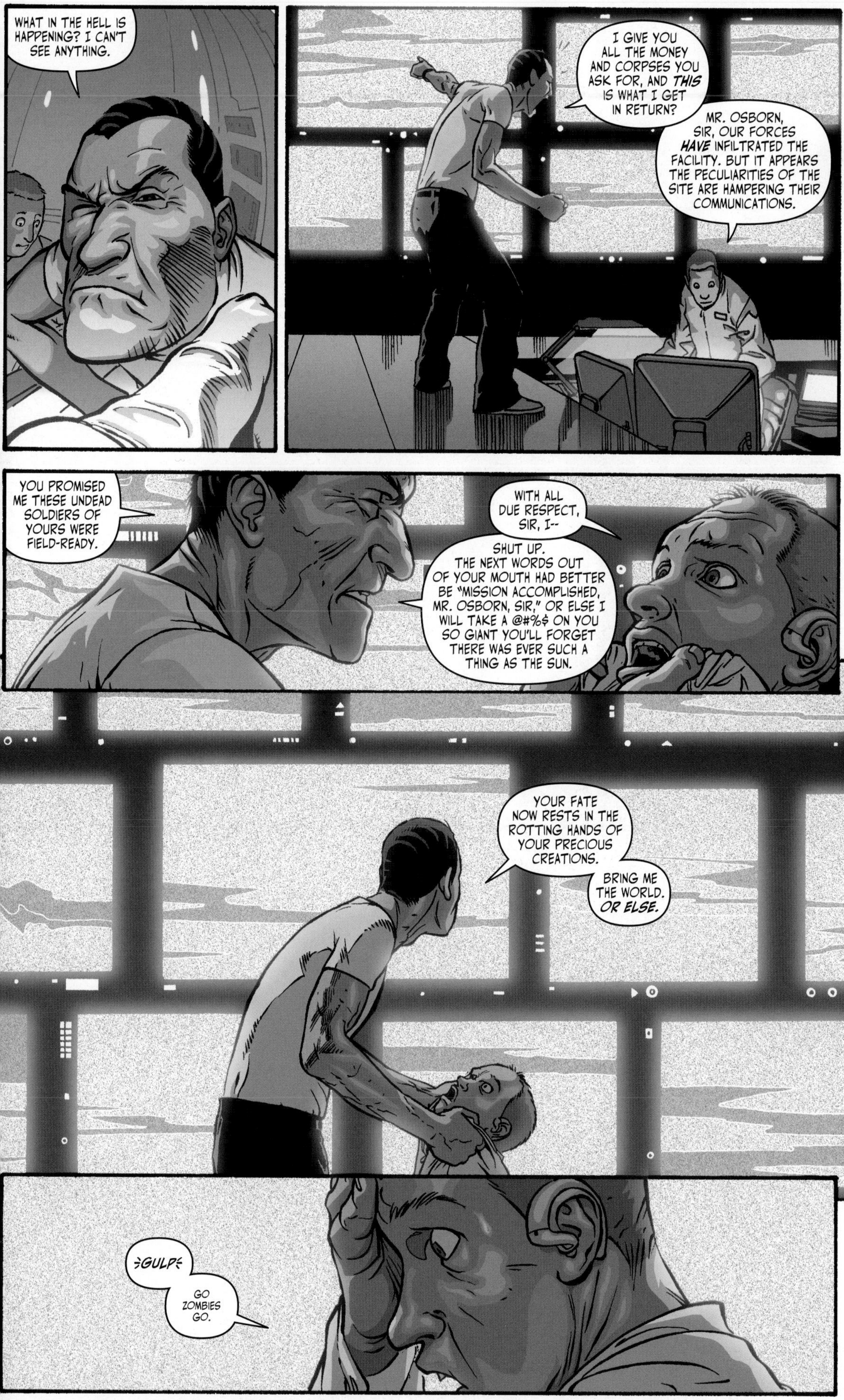
WHAT IN THE HELL IS HAPPENING? I CAN'T SEE ANYTHING.
I GIVE YOU ALL THE MONEY AND CORPSES YOU ASK FOR, AND THIS IS WHAT I GET IN RETURN?
MR. OSBORN, SIR, OUR FORCES HAVE INFILTRATED THE FACILITY. BUT IT APPEARS THE PECULIARITIES OF THE SITE ARE HAMPERING THEIR COMMUNICATIONS.
YOU PROMISED ME THESE UNDEAD SOLDIERS OF YOURS WERE FIELD-READY.
WITH ALL DUE RESPECT, SIR, I--
SHUT UP. THE NEXT WORDS OUT OF YOUR MOUTH HAD BETTER BE "MISSION ACCOMPLISHED, MR. OSBORN, SIR," OR ELSE I WILL TAKE A @#%$ ON YOU SO GIANT YOU'LL FORGET THERE WAS EVER SUCH A THING AS THE SUN.
YOUR FATE NOW RESTS IN THE ROTTING HANDS OF YOUR PRECIOUS CREATIONS.
BRING ME THE WORLD. OR ELSE.
GULP
GO ZOMBIES GO.

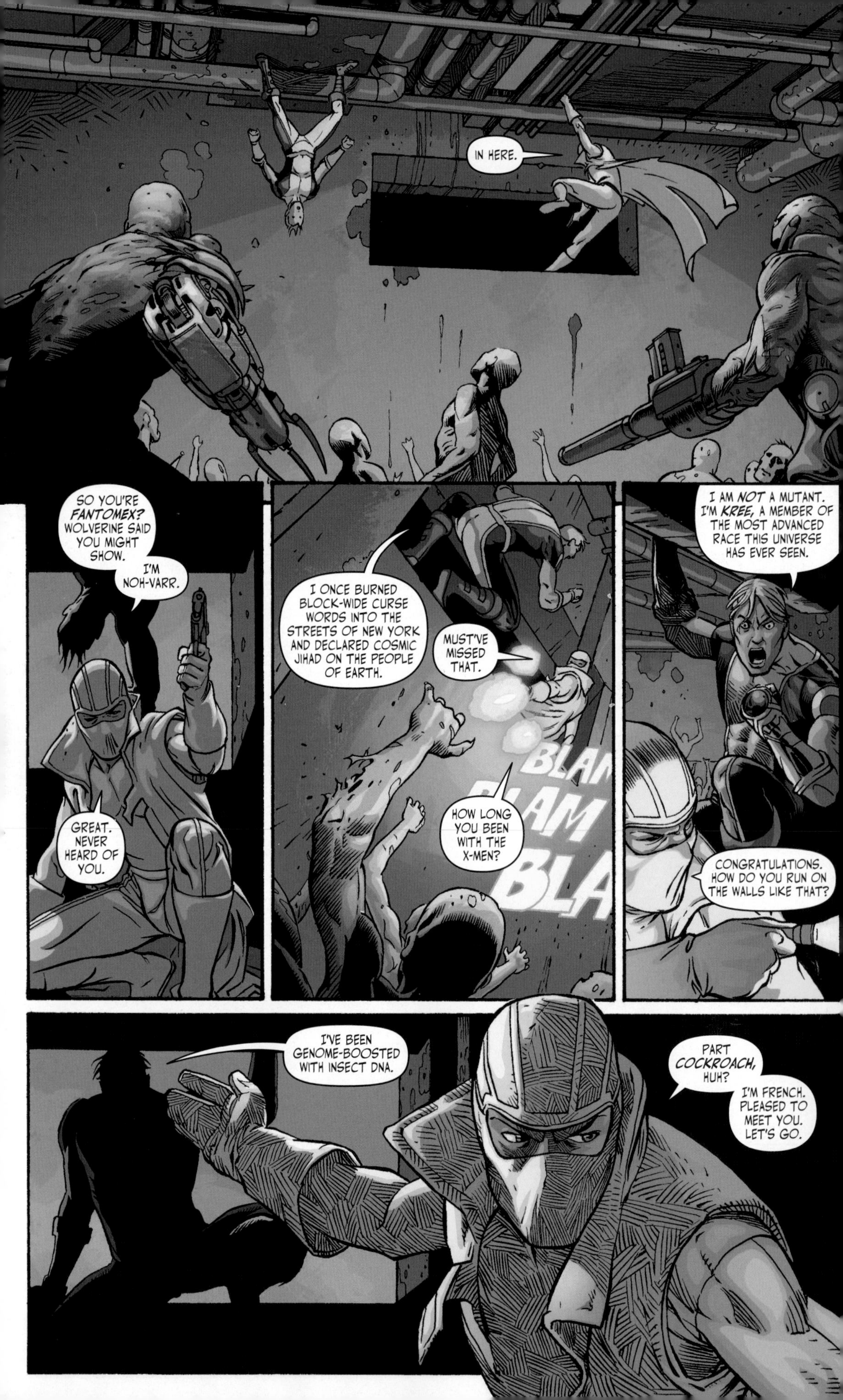
IN HERE.
SO YOU'RE FANTOMEX? WOLVERINE SAID YOU MIGHT SHOW.
I'M NOH-VARR.
GREAT. NEVER HEARD OF YOU.
I ONCE BURNED BLOCK-WIDE CURSE WORDS INTO THE STREETS OF NEW YORK AND DECLARED COSMIC JIHAD ON THE PEOPLE OF EARTH.
MUST'VE MISSED THAT.
BLAM BLAM BLA
HOW LONG YOU BEEN WITH THE X-MEN?
I AM NOT A MUTANT. I'M KREE, A MEMBER OF THE MOST ADVANCED RACE THIS UNIVERSE HAS EVER SEEN.
CONGRATULATIONS. HOW DO YOU RUN ON THE WALLS LIKE THAT?
I'VE BEEN GENOME-BOOSTED WITH INSECT DNA.
PART COCKROACH, HUH?
I'M FRENCH. PLEASED TO MEET YOU. LET'S GO.

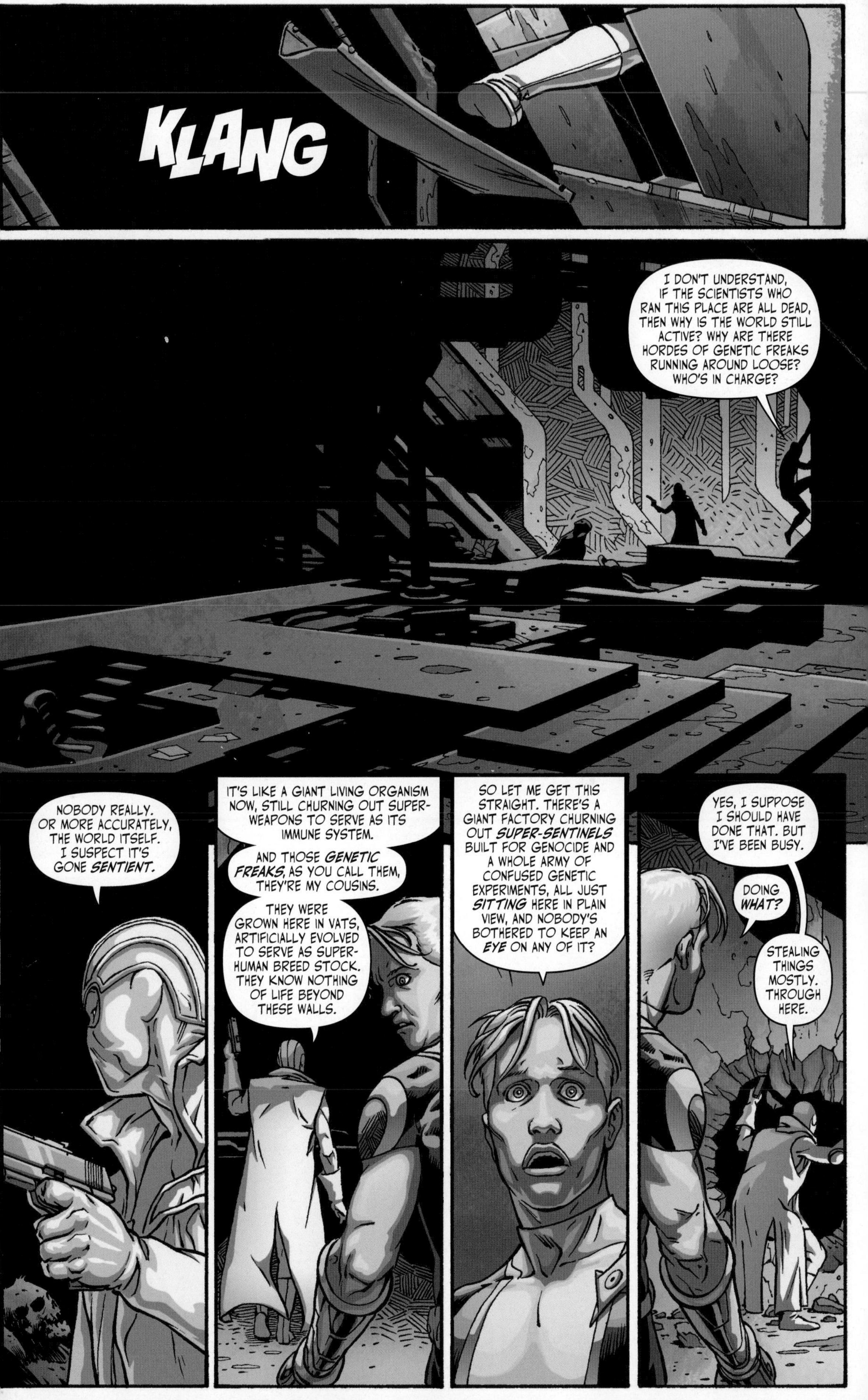
KLANG
I DON'T UNDERSTAND, IF THE SCIENTISTS WHO RAN THIS PLACE ARE ALL DEAD, THEN WHY IS THE WORLD STILL ACTIVE? WHY ARE THERE HORDES OF GENETIC FREAKS RUNNING AROUND LOOSE? WHO'S IN CHARGE?
NOBODY REALLY. OR MORE ACCURATELY, THE WORLD ITSELF. I SUSPECT IT'S GONE SENTIENT.
IT'S LIKE A GIANT LIVING ORGANISM NOW, STILL CHURNING OUT SUPER-WEAPONS TO SERVE AS ITS IMMUNE SYSTEM.
AND THOSE GENETIC FREAKS, AS YOU CALL THEM, THEY'RE MY COUSINS.
THEY WERE GROWN HERE IN VATS, ARTIFICIALLY EVOLVED TO SERVE AS SUPER-HUMAN BREED STOCK. THEY KNOW NOTHING OF LIFE BEYOND THESE WALLS.
SO LET ME GET THIS STRAIGHT. THERE'S A GIANT FACTORY CHURNING OUT SUPER-SENTINELS BUILT FOR GENOCIDE AND A WHOLE ARMY OF CONFUSED GENETIC EXPERIMENTS, ALL JUST SITTING HERE IN PLAIN VIEW, AND NOBODY'S BOTHERED TO KEEP AN EYE ON ANY OF IT?
YES, I SUPPOSE I SHOULD HAVE DONE THAT. BUT I'VE BEEN BUSY.
DOING WHAT?
STEALING THINGS MOSTLY. THROUGH HERE.

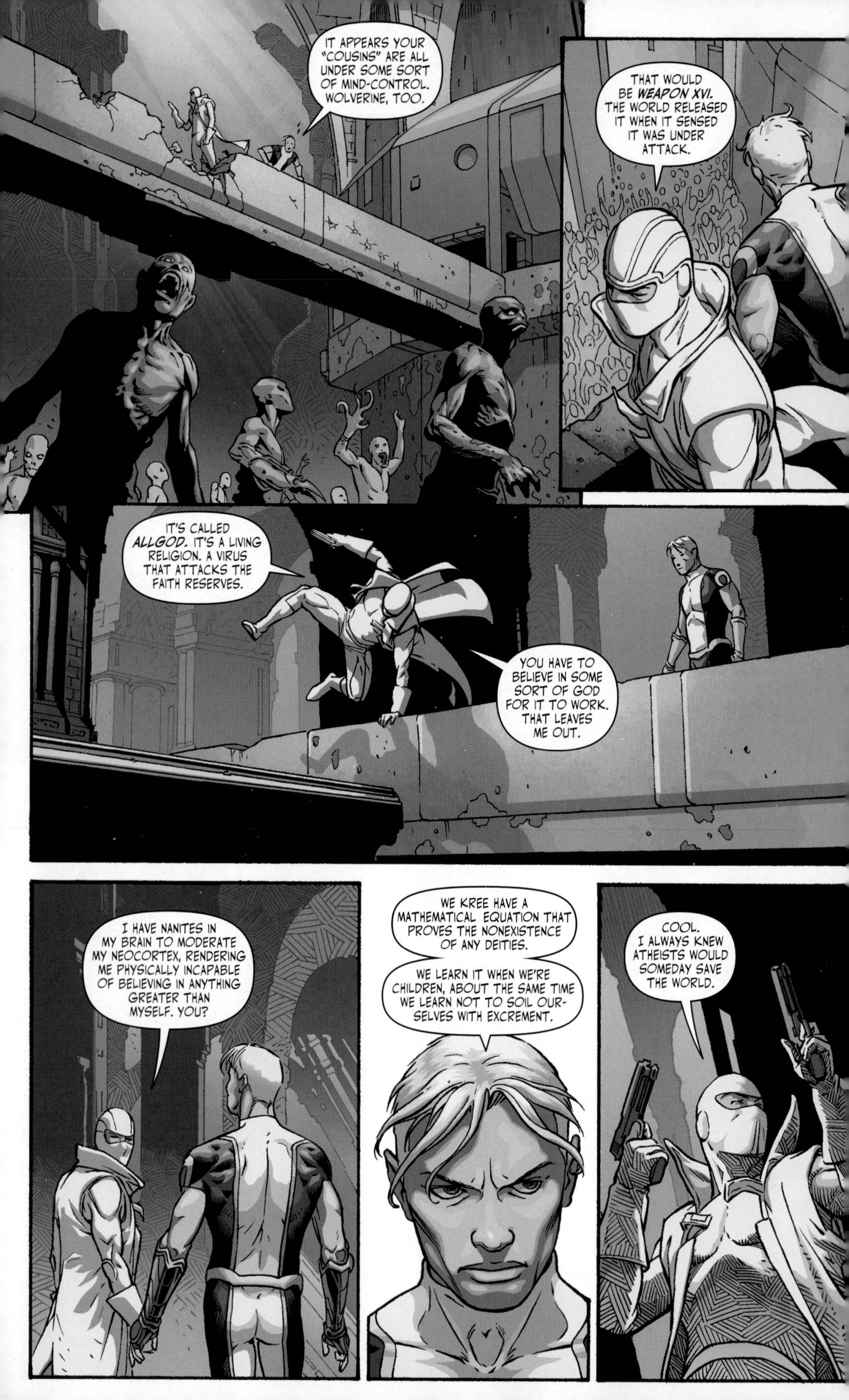
IT APPEARS YOUR "COUSINS" ARE ALL UNDER SOME SORT OF MIND-CONTROL. WOLVERINE, TOO.
THAT WOULD BE WEAPON XVI. THE WORLD RELEASED IT WHEN IT SENSED IT WAS UNDER ATTACK.
IT'S CALLED ALLGOD. IT'S A LIVING RELIGION. A VIRUS THAT ATTACKS THE FAITH RESERVES.
YOU HAVE TO BELIEVE IN SOME SORT OF GOD FOR IT TO WORK. THAT LEAVES ME OUT.
I HAVE NANITES IN MY BRAIN TO MODERATE MY NEOCORTEX, RENDERING ME PHYSICALLY INCAPABLE OF BELIEVING IN ANYTHING GREATER THAN MYSELF. YOU?
WE KREE HAVE A MATHEMATICAL EQUATION THAT PROVES THE NONEXISTENCE OF ANY DEITIES.
WE LEARN IT WHEN WE'RE CHILDREN, ABOUT THE SAME TIME WE LEARN NOT TO SOIL OURSELVES WITH EXCREMENT.
COOL. I ALWAYS KNEW ATHEISTS WOULD SOMEDAY SAVE THE WORLD.

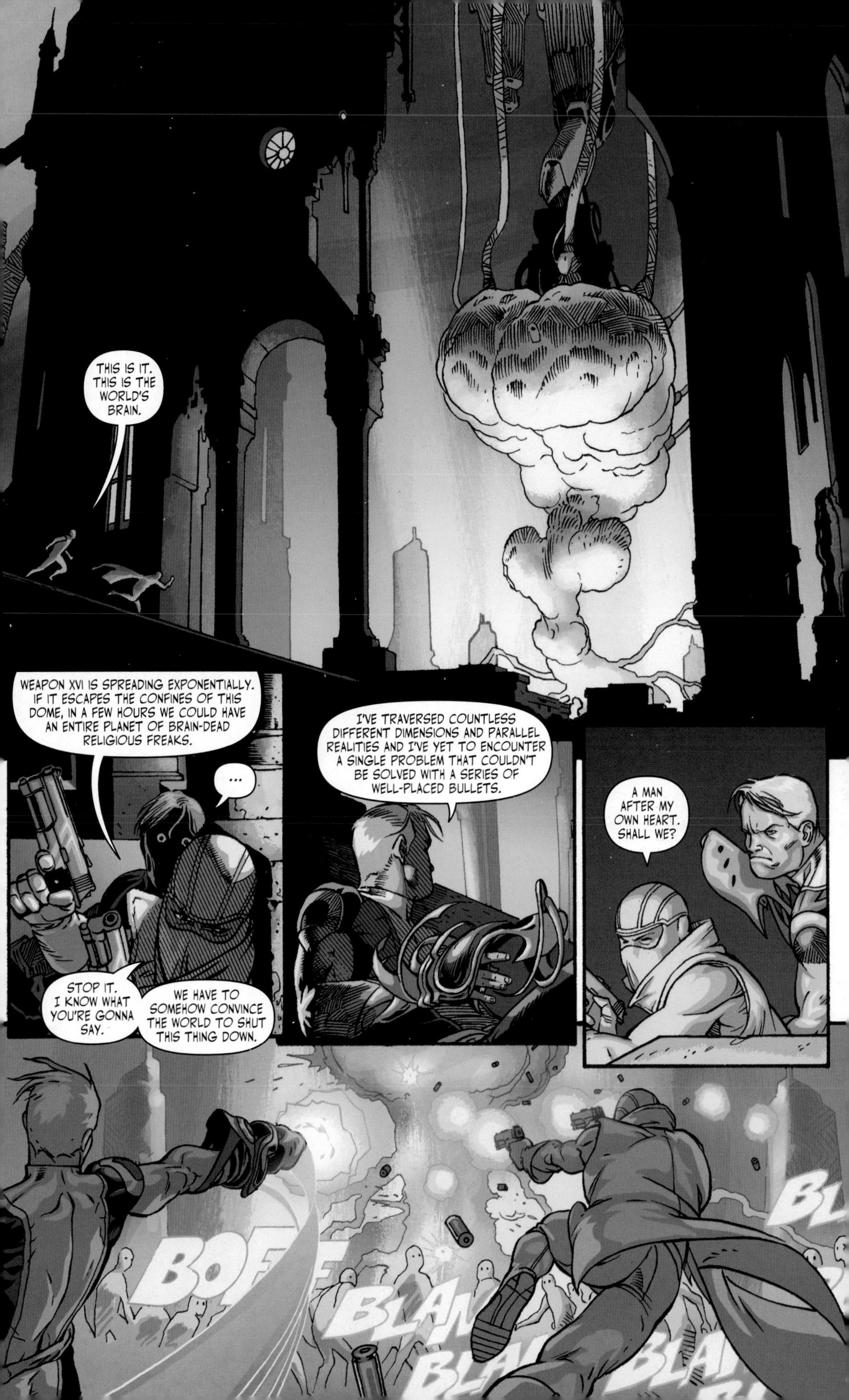

THIS IS IT. THIS IS THE WORLD'S BRAIN.
WEAPON XVI IS SPREADING EXPONENTIALLY. IF IT ESCAPES THE CONFINES OF THIS DOME, IN A FEW HOURS WE COULD HAVE AN ENTIRE PLANET OF BRAIN-DEAD RELIGIOUS FREAKS.
...
STOP IT. I KNOW WHAT YOU'RE GONNA SAY.
WE HAVE TO SOMEHOW CONVINCE THE WORLD TO SHUT THIS THING DOWN.
I'VE TRAVERSED COUNTLESS DIFFERENT DIMENSIONS AND PARALLEL REALITIES AND I'VE YET TO ENCOUNTER A SINGLE PROBLEM THAT COULDN'T BE SOLVED WITH A SERIES OF WELL-PLACED BULLETS.
A MAN AFTER MY OWN HEART. SHALL WE?

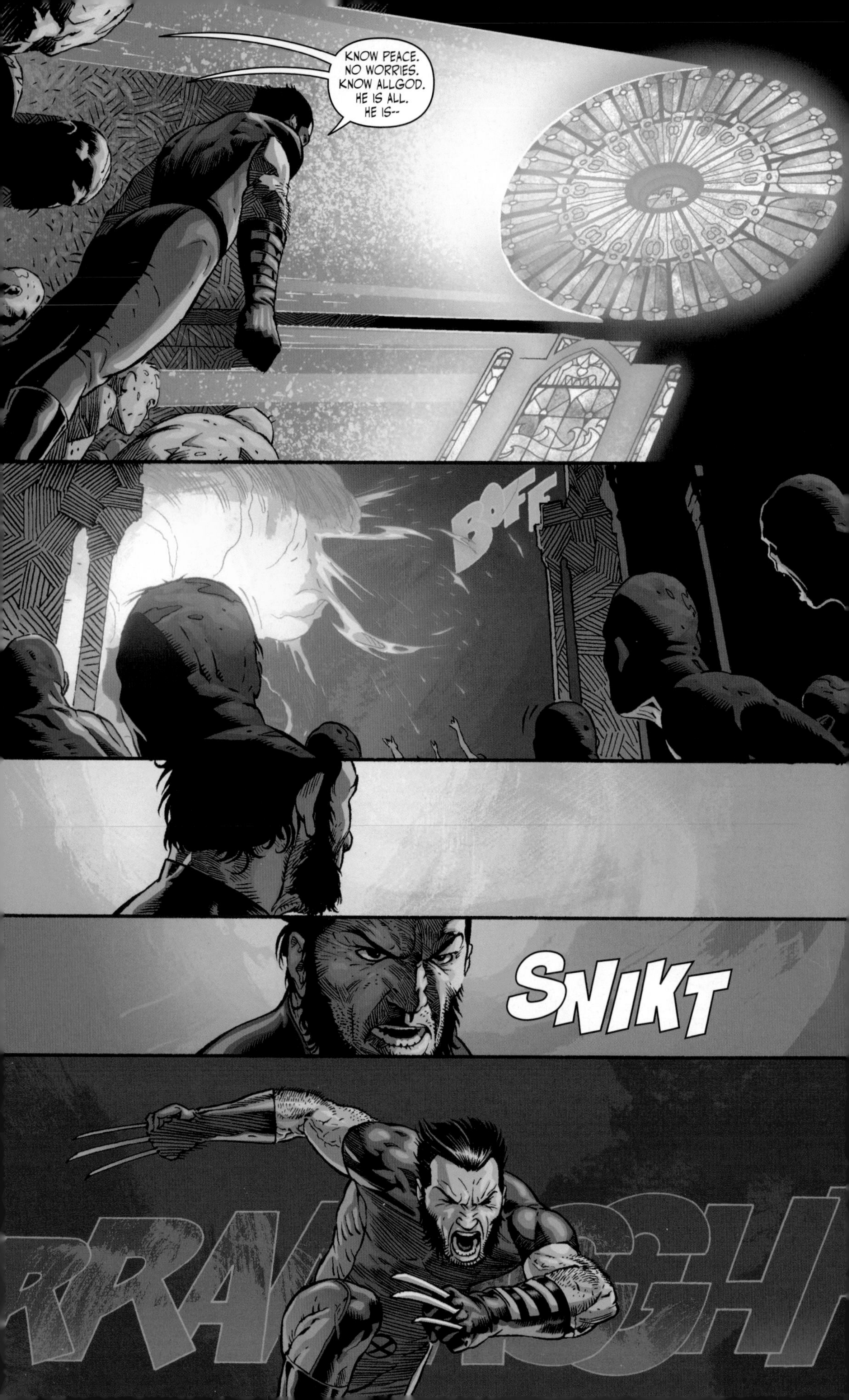
KNOW PEACE. NO WORRIES. KNOW ALLGOD. HE IS ALL. HE IS--
BOFF
SNIKT

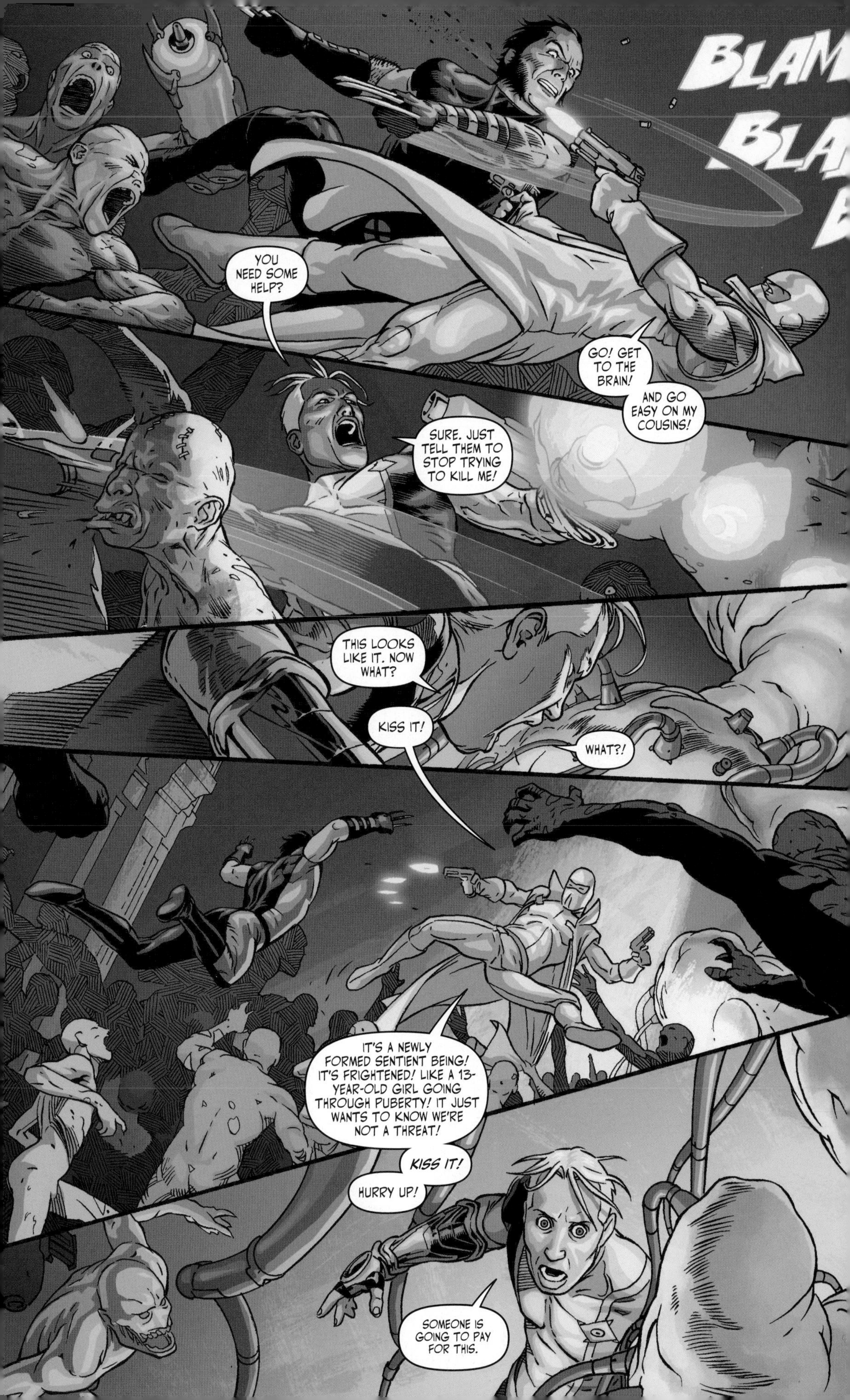
BLAM BLA B
YOU NEED SOME HELP?
GO! GET TO THE BRAIN!
AND GO EASY ON MY COUSINS!
SURE. JUST TELL THEM TO STOP TRYING TO KILL ME!
THIS LOOKS LIKE IT. NOW WHAT?
KISS IT!
WHAT?!
IT'S A NEWLY FORMED SENTIENT BEING! IT'S FRIGHTENED! LIKE A 13-YEAR-OLD GIRL GOING THROUGH PUBERTY! IT JUST WANTS TO KNOW WE'RE NOT A THREAT!
KISS IT!
HURRY UP!
SOMEONE IS GOING TO PAY FOR THIS.

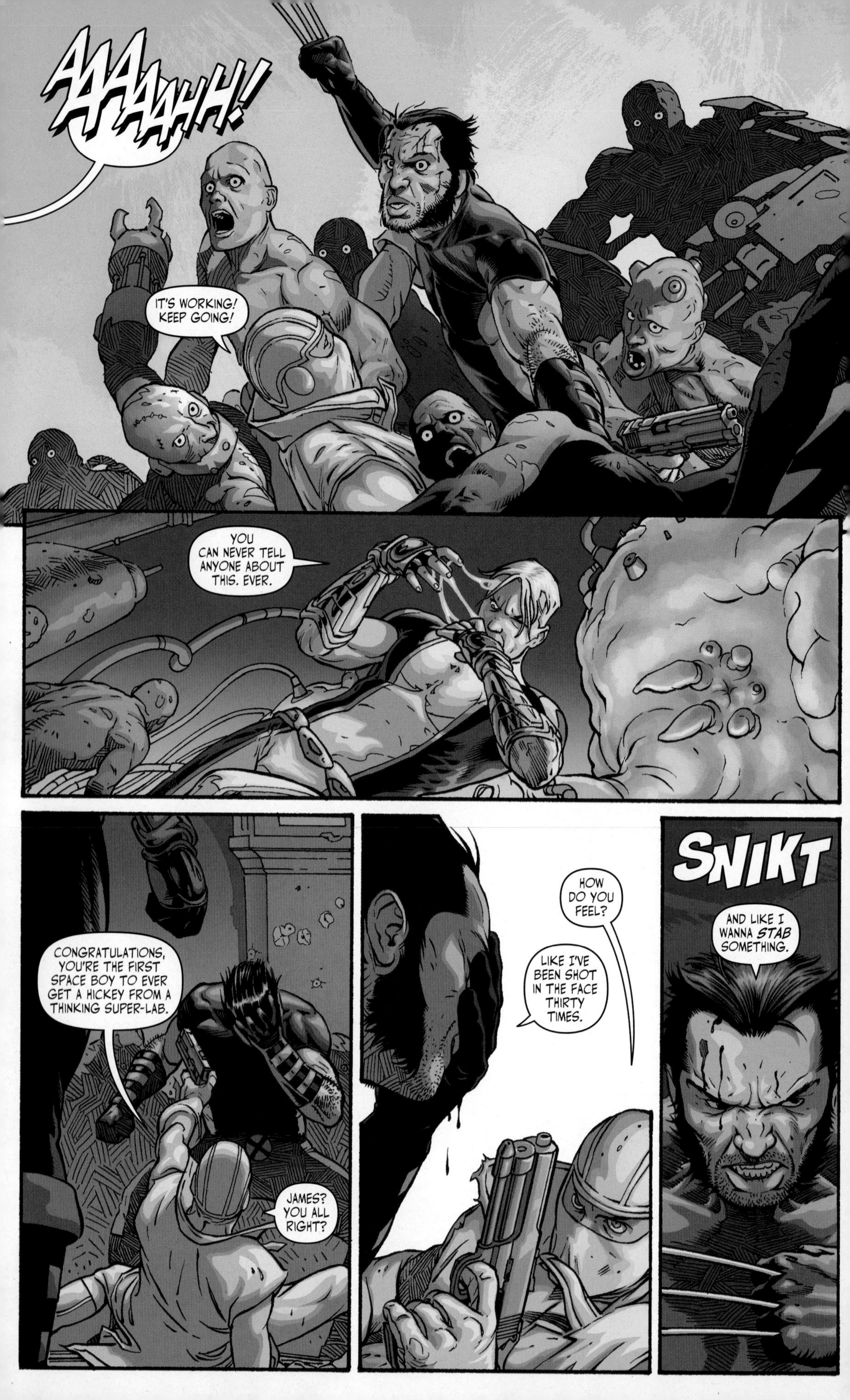
AAAAAHH!
IT'S WORKING! KEEP GOING!
YOU CAN NEVER TELL ANYONE ABOUT THIS. EVER.
CONGRATULATIONS, YOU'RE THE FIRST SPACE BOY TO EVER GET A HICKEY FROM A THINKING SUPER-LAB.
JAMES? YOU ALL RIGHT?
HOW DO YOU FEEL?
LIKE I'VE BEEN SHOT IN THE FACE THIRTY TIMES.
SNIKT
AND LIKE I WANNA STAB SOMETHING.

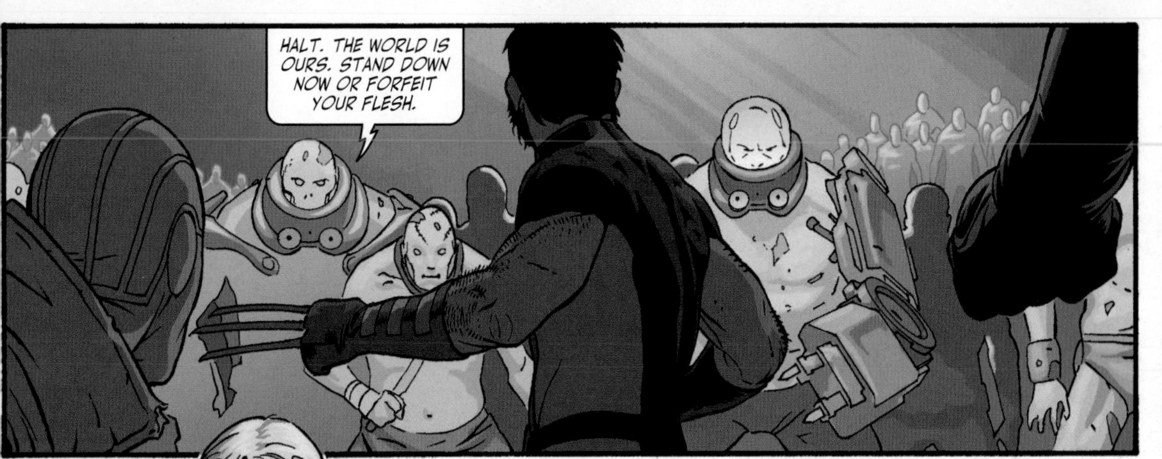
HALT. THE WORLD IS OURS. STAND DOWN NOW OR FORFEIT YOUR FLESH.

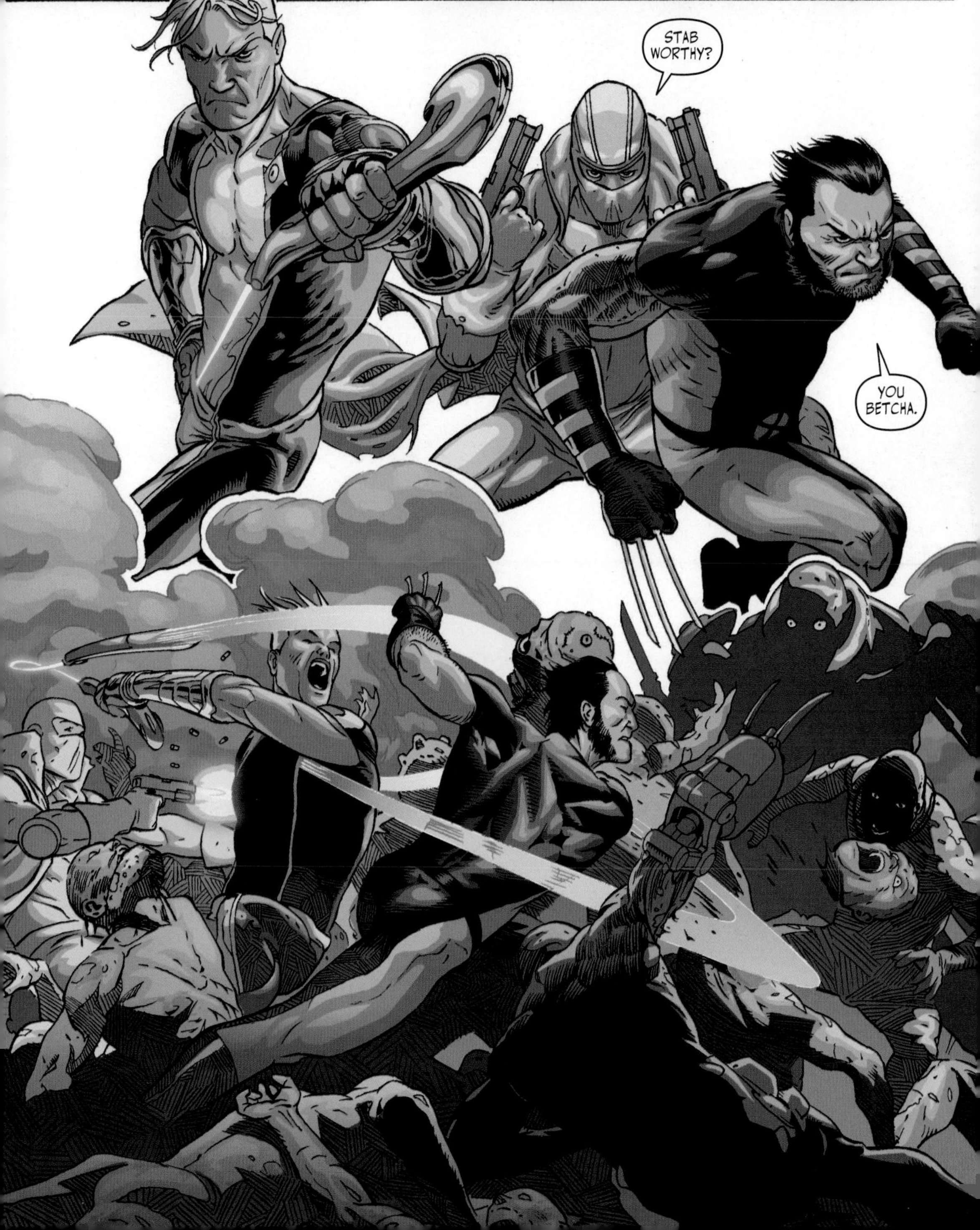
STAB WORTHY?
YOU BETCHA.

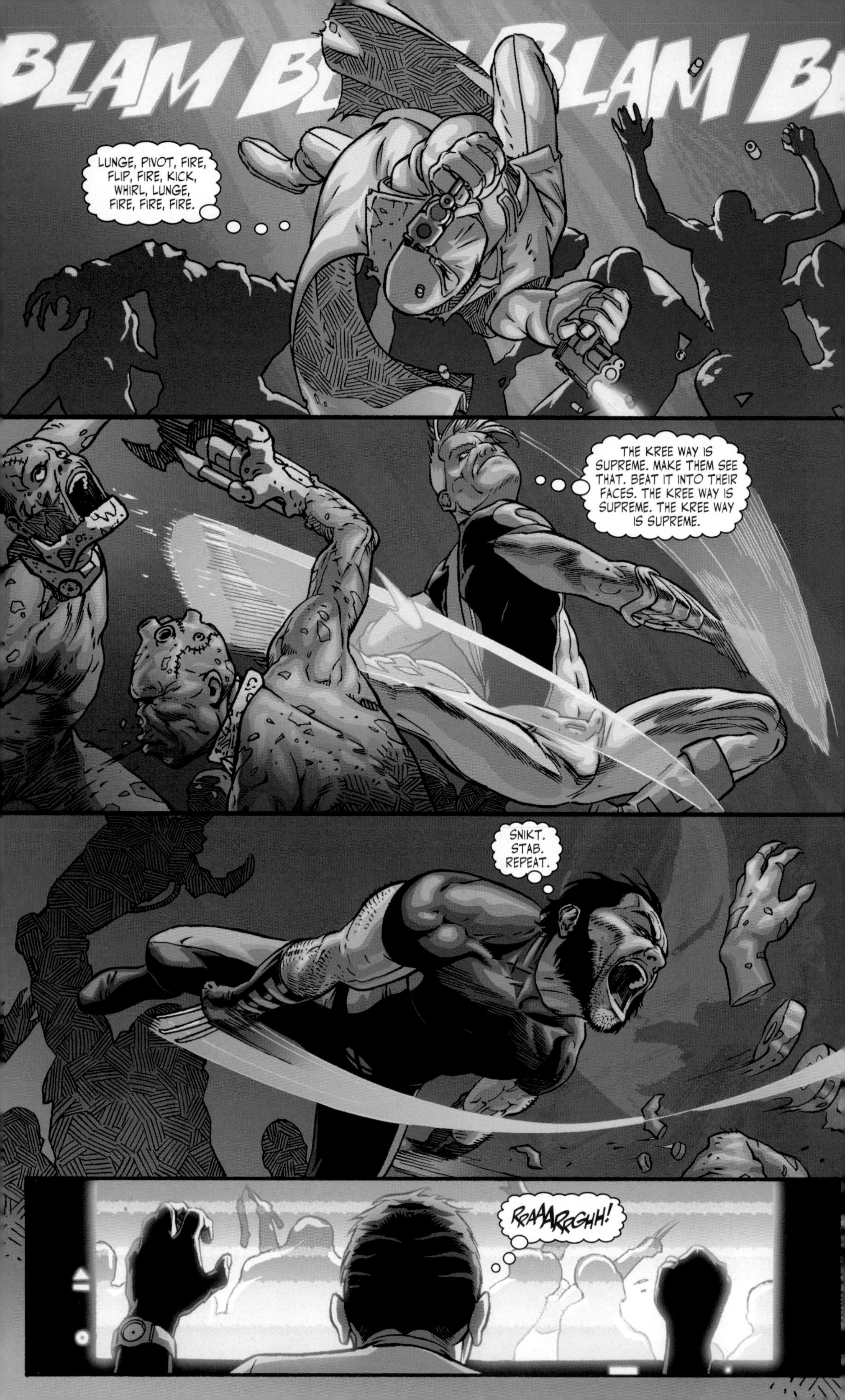
BLAM BL BLAM B
LUNGE, PIVOT, FIRE, FLIP, FIRE, KICK, WHIRL, LUNGE, FIRE, FIRE, FIRE.
THE KREE WAY IS SUPREME. MAKE THEM SEE THAT. BEAT IT INTO THEIR FACES. THE KREE WAY IS SUPREME. THE KREE WAY IS SUPREME.
SNIKT. STAB. REPEAT.
RRAAAARRGHH!

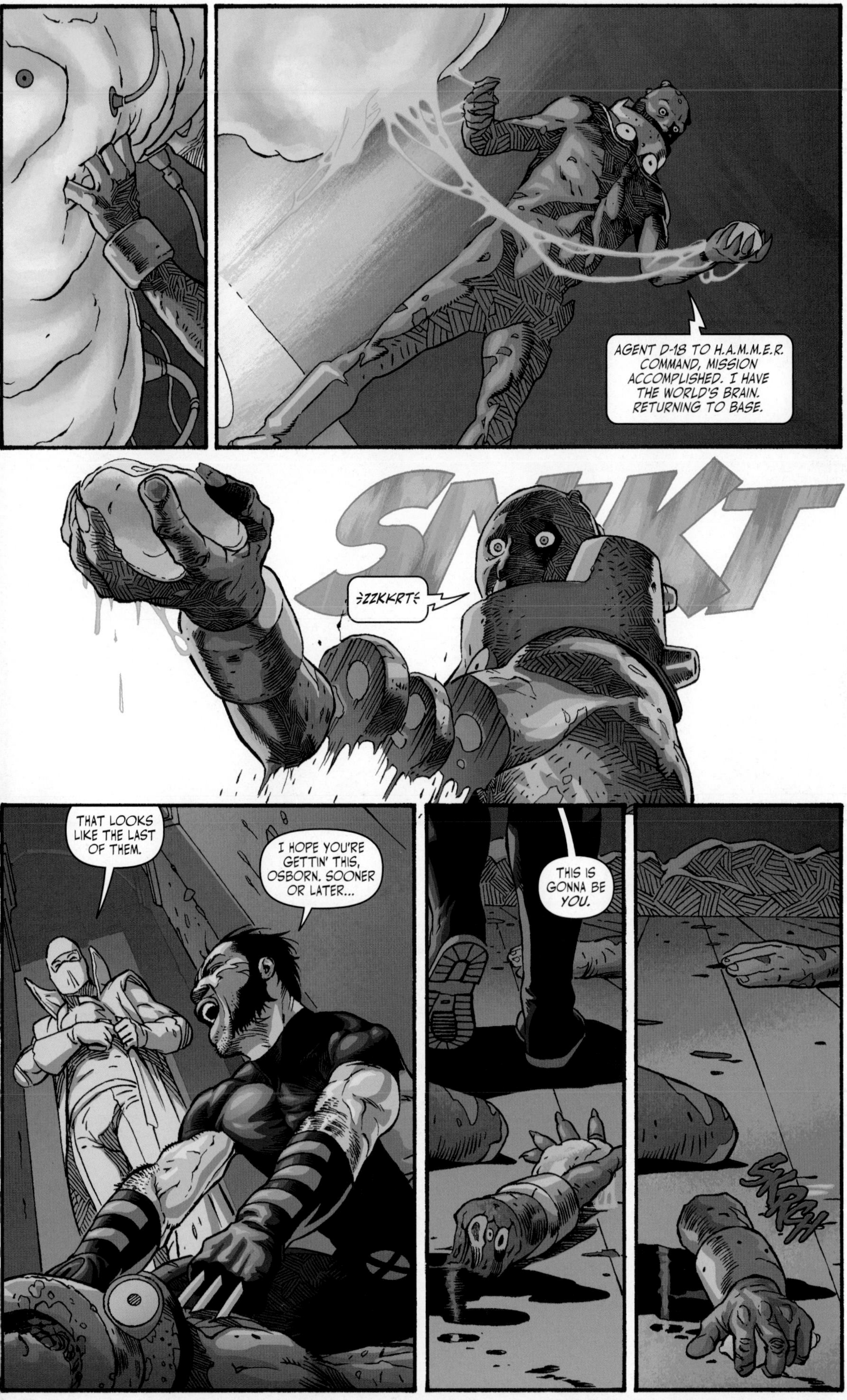
AGENT D-18 TO H.A.M.M.E.R. COMMAND, MISSION ACCOMPLISHED. I HAVE THE WORLD'S BRAIN. RETURNING TO BASE.
SNIKT
ZZKKRT
THAT LOOKS LIKE THE LAST OF THEM.
I HOPE YOU'RE GETTIN' THIS, OSBORN. SOONER OR LATER...
THIS IS GONNA BE YOU.
SKRCH

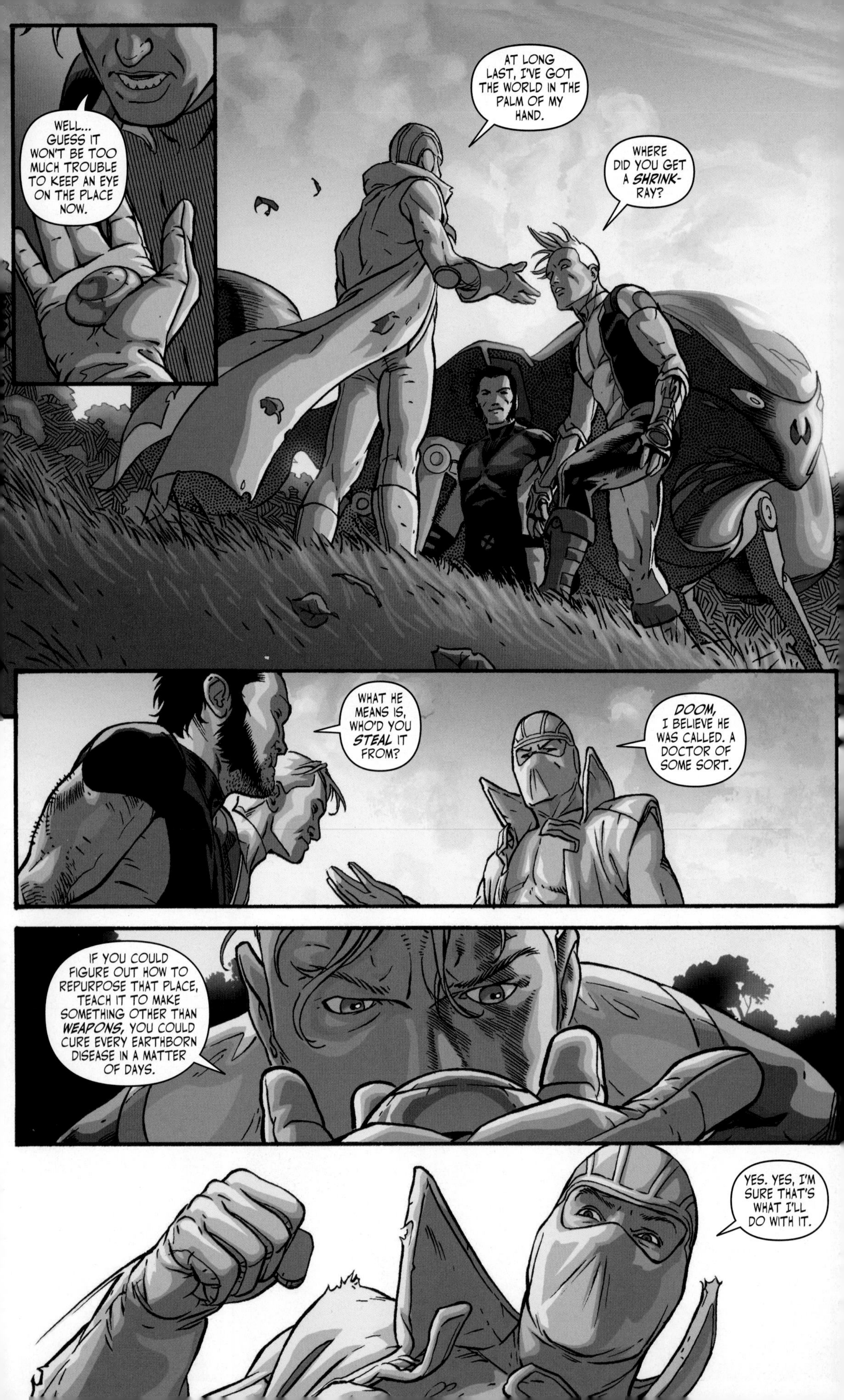

WELL... GUESS IT WON'T BE TOO MUCH TROUBLE TO KEEP AN EYE ON THE PLACE NOW.
AT LONG LAST, I'VE GOT THE WORLD IN THE PALM OF MY HAND.
WHERE DID YOU GET A SHRINK-RAY?
WHAT HE MEANS IS, WHO'D YOU STEAL IT FROM?
DOOM, I BELIEVE HE WAS CALLED. A DOCTOR OF SOME SORT.
IF YOU COULD FIGURE OUT HOW TO REPURPOSE THAT PLACE, TEACH IT TO MAKE SOMETHING OTHER THAN WEAPONS, YOU COULD CURE EVERY EARTHBORN DISEASE IN A MATTER OF DAYS.
YES. YES, I'M SURE THAT'S WHAT I'LL DO WITH IT.

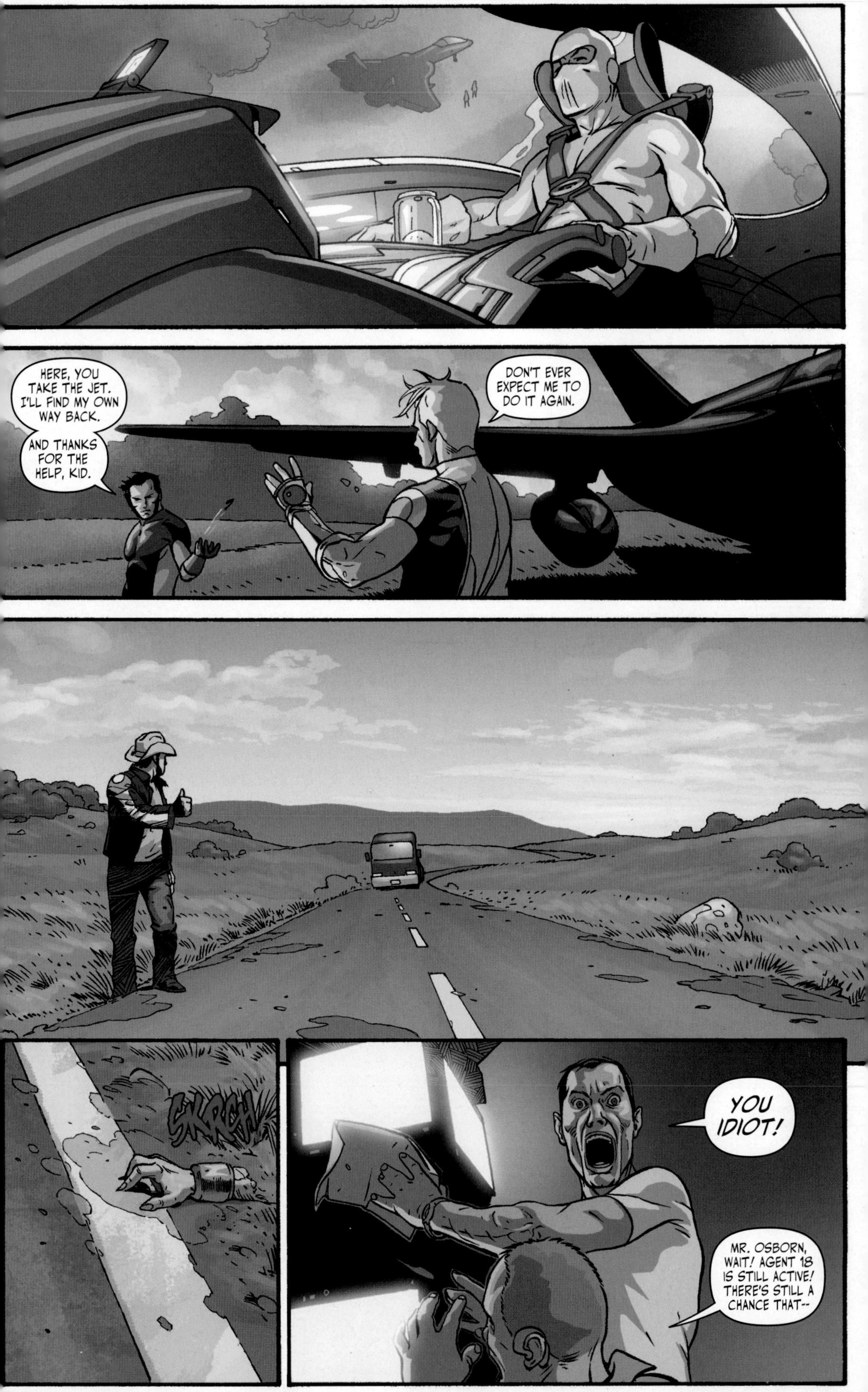
HERE, YOU TAKE THE JET. I'LL FIND MY OWN WAY BACK.
AND THANKS FOR THE HELP, KID.
DON'T EVER EXPECT ME TO DO IT AGAIN.
SKRCH
YOU IDIOT!
MR. OSBORN, WAIT! AGENT 18 IS STILL ACTIVE! THERE'S STILL A CHANCE THAT--

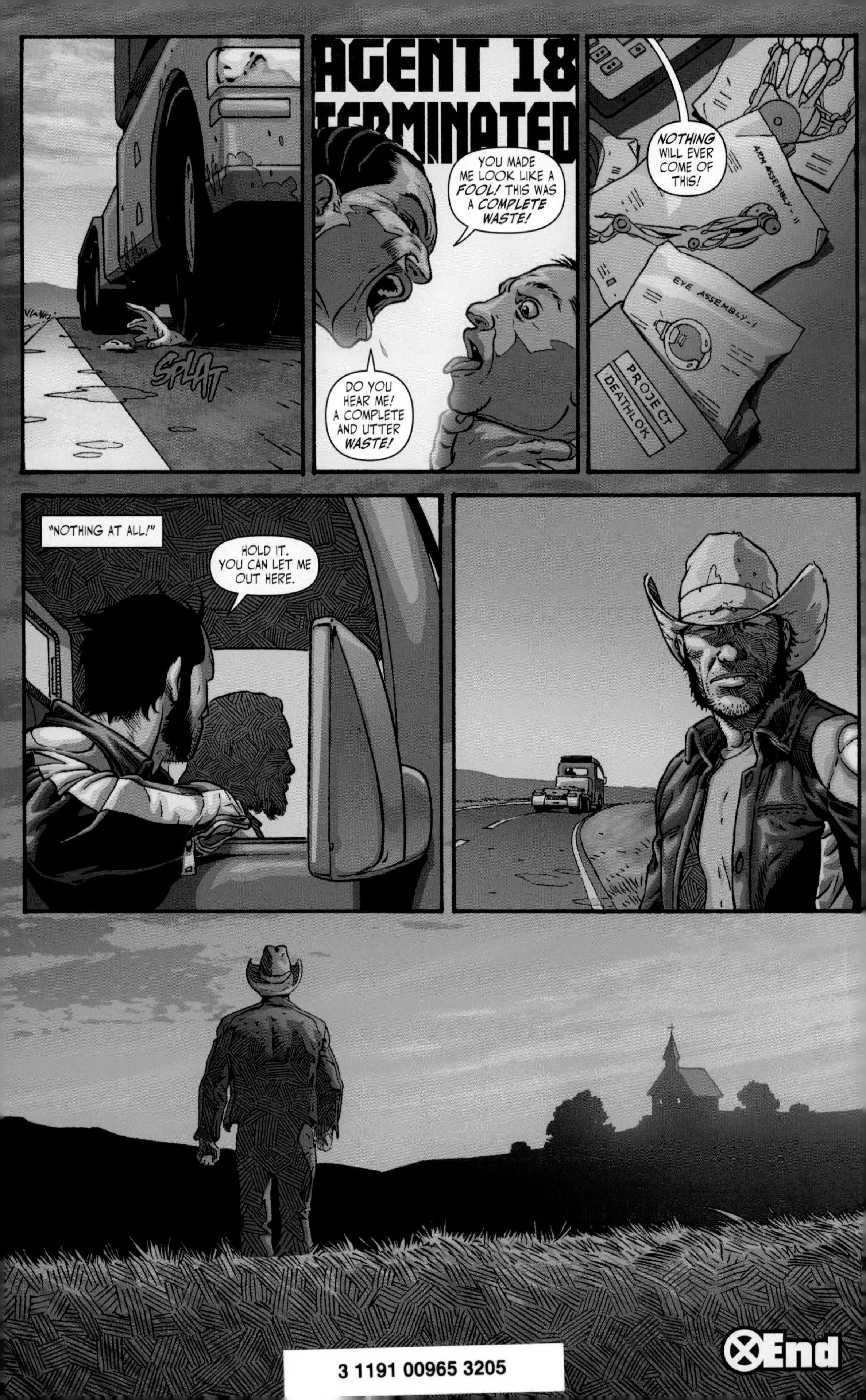
SPLAT
AGENT 18
ERMINATED
YOU MADE ME LOOK LIKE A FOOL! THIS WAS A COMPLETE WASTE!
DO YOU HEAR ME! A COMPLETE AND UTTER WASTE!
NOTHING WILL EVER COME OF THIS!
ARM ASSEMBLY – II
EYE ASSEMBLY – I
PROJECT DEATHLOK
"NOTHING AT ALL!"
HOLD IT. YOU CAN LET ME OUT HERE.
End

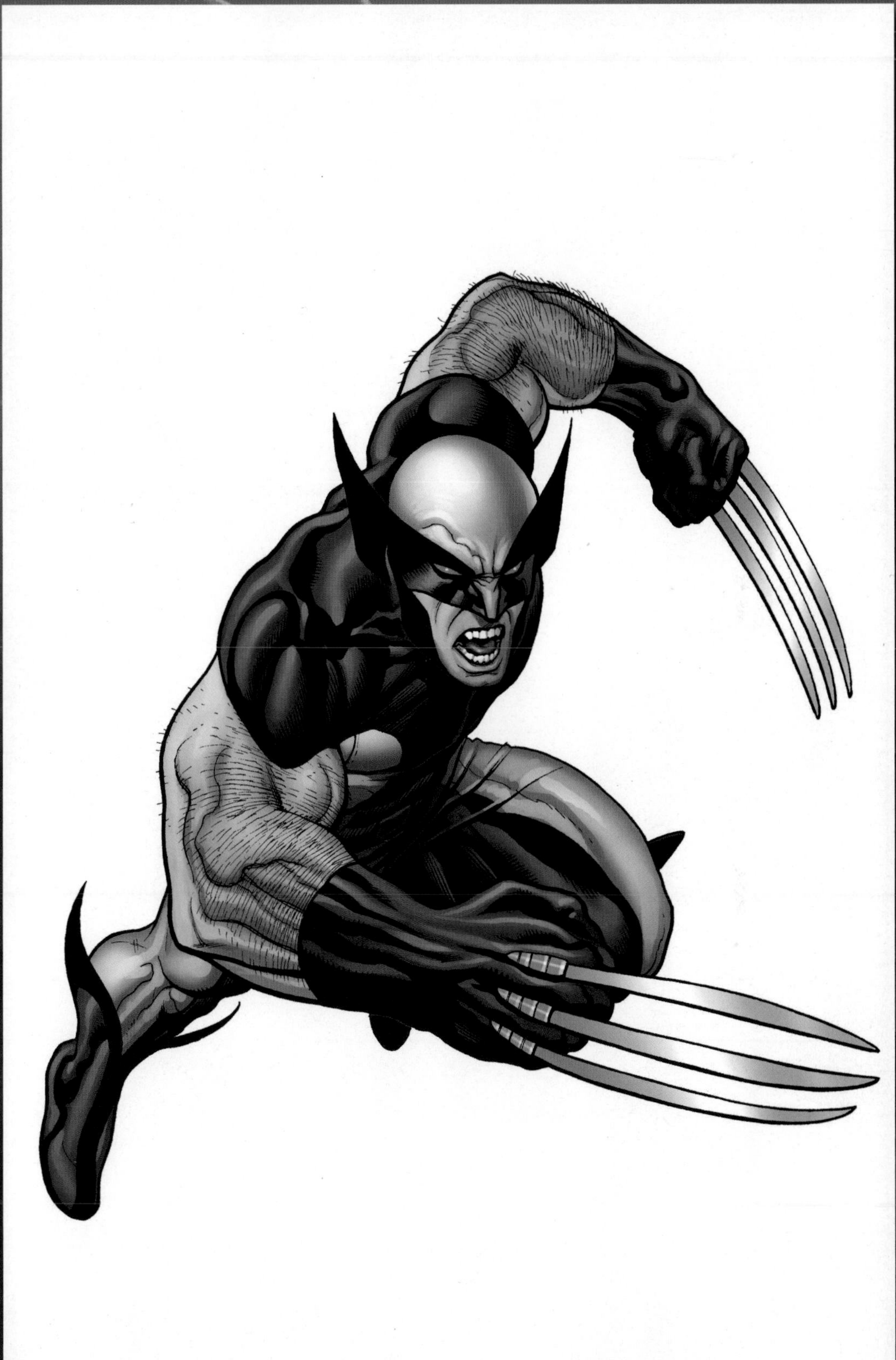

DARK REIGN: THE LIST — WOLVERINE HERO VARIANT
BY FRANK CHO

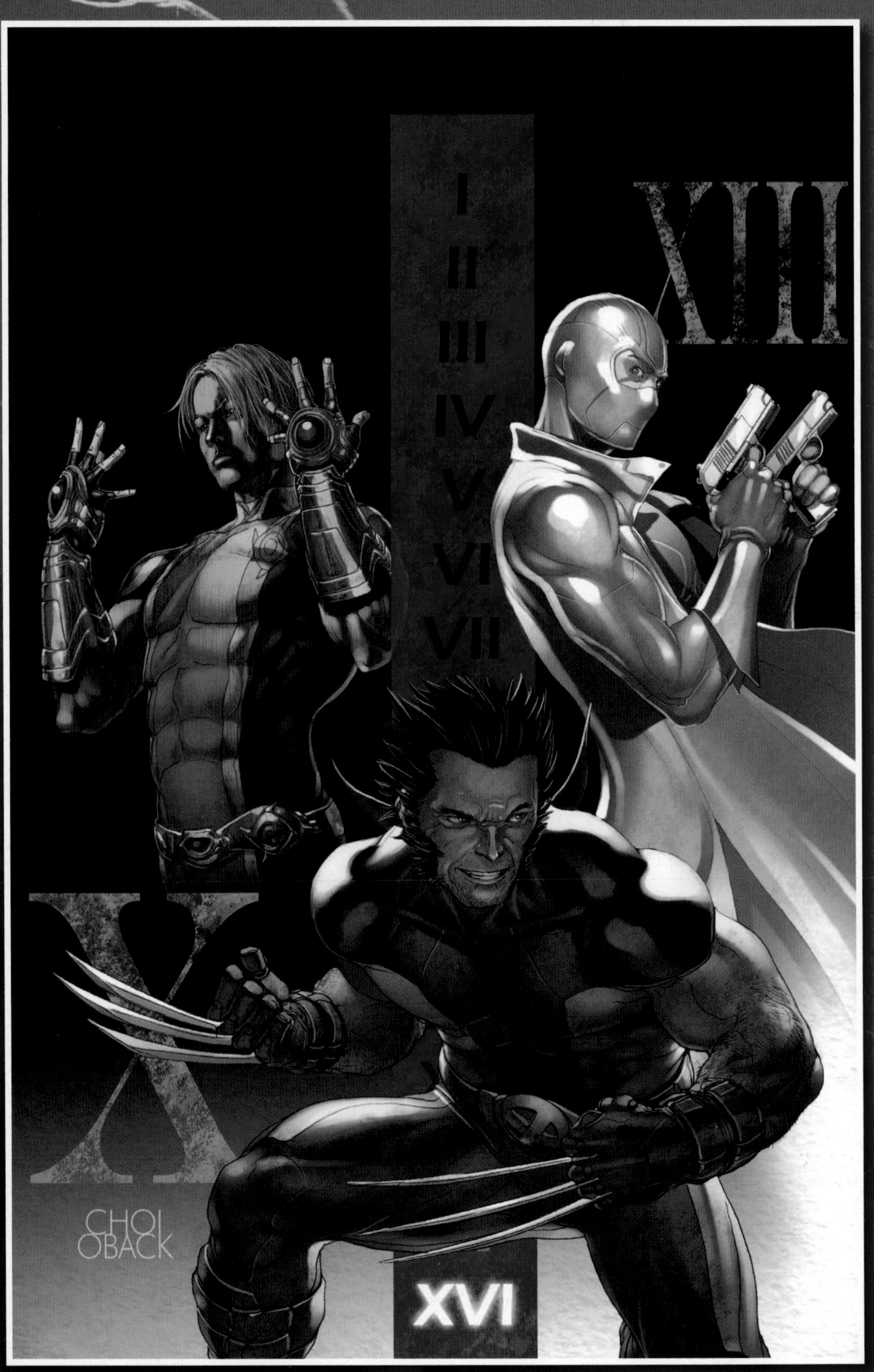
XIII
I
II
III
IV
V
VI
VII
X
CHOI
OBACK
XVI

DARK REIGN: THE LIST — WOLVERINE 2ND PRINTING VARIANT
BY MIKE CHOI AND SONIA OBACK